THE
FREE SEA

THE
FREE SEA

The American Fight for Freedom of Navigation

JAMES KRASKA AND RAUL PEDROZO

Naval Institute Press
Annapolis, Maryland

Naval Institute Press
291 Wood Road
Annapolis, MD 21402

Library of Congress Cataloging-in-Publication Data
Names: Kraska, James, author. | Pedrozo, Raul A., author.
Title: The free sea : the American fight for freedom of navigation / James Kraska, Raul Pedrozo.
Description: Annapolis, Maryland : Naval Institute Press, 2018. | Includes bibliographical references and index.
Identifiers: LCCN 2017061364 (print) | LCCN 2018017306 (ebook) | ISBN 9781682471173 (ePDF) | ISBN 9781682471173 (ePub) | ISBN 9781682471166 (hardback) | ISBN 9781682471173 (ebook)
Subjects: LCSH: Law of the sea—United States—History. | Freedom of the seas—United States—History. | Contiguous zones (Law of the sea)—United States—History. | Mare clausum. | Navigation. | Maritime boundaries. | Freedom of the seas. | BISAC: HISTORY / Military / Naval. | LAW / Maritime.
Classification: LCC KZA1146.U6 (ebook) | LCC KZA1146.U6 K73 2018 (print) | DDC 341.4/50973—dc23
LC record available at https://lccn.loc.gov/2017061364

♾ Print editions meet the requirements of ANSI/NISO z39.48-1992 (Permanence of Paper).
Printed in the United States of America.

26 25 24 23 22 21 20 19 18   9 8 7 6 5 4 3 2 1
First printing

Maps created by Chris Robinson.

To
John Norton Moore

CONTENTS

ILLUSTRATIONS

Maps

Tables

PREFACE

This book springs from the need for leaders in the United States and elsewhere to understand the centrality of freedom of the seas to U.S. economic prosperity and strategic security. It is easy to become absorbed in the cacophony of fast-moving economic and security news cycles. The case studies in this volume demonstrate instead one of the few core foundations of America's place in the world—the ability to use the oceans freely.

Each chapter stands on its own, but we hope that combined they present the arc of policy-related and strategic thinking inside the United States on how to contend with interference to American rights and freedom at sea. We have traced the lineage of freedom of navigation from its earliest roots in Rome to its most recent persistent challenger in China. We have relied on our more than fifty years combined experience in working on these issues, advising practitioners ranging from commanding officers of individual warships to the most senior military officers and civilian leaders in the Department of Defense, Department of State, and the White House.

We are indebted to our many friends and colleagues who helped to form these ideas and encouraged us to capture the history of U.S. experience with freedom of navigation. Foremost among these, and to whom we are especially grateful, is our mentor and tireless champion of freedom of navigation for fifty years, Ambassador John Norton Moore. Moore served as chair of the National Security Council (NSC) Interagency Task Force on Law of the Sea (which coordinated eighteen U.S. government agencies in developing American oceans policy), deputy special representative of the president for the Law of the Sea, United States ambassador for the Law of the Sea, and director of the NSC and State Department office for the Law of the Sea (D/LOS). He also was a U.S. representative and deputy head of the U.S. delegation for the Law of the Sea, and he chaired the U.S. delegation to the 1972 New York session of the Seabeds Committee. As a professor at the University of Virginia School of Law and Georgetown

University Law Center, Professor Moore teaches the most comprehensive courses offered on the international law of the sea. He is the intellectual inspiration for this study.

We thank Professor Moore also for providing, in his capacities as director of the Center for Oceans Law and Policy and director of the Center for National Security Law at the University of Virginia School of Law, the means for us to work with Pelham G. Boyer, former managing editor of the Naval War College Press. Pelham provided exacting editing of the text and greatly improved our work. Additionally, we value our relationship with Professor Robert F. Turner, distinguished fellow and associate director at the Center for National Security Law, and we deeply appreciate the support provided by the Center.

We are grateful to the Judge Advocate General's Corps (JAGC) of the U.S. Navy, in which we served for decades, for fostering a sense of inquiry and policy acumen that combines the practice of law with the profession of arms and service to the nation. The ideas expressed in this volume first took shape while we served as JAGC officers. We also thank the library staff at the U.S. Naval War College, in Newport, Rhode Island. In particular, the ever-cheerful Julie Zecher was astute at locating historical references. Finally, we are deeply appreciative of our partners, Chizu and Stacy, who over the years have supported our scholarly work. This book would not have been possible without their love and encouragement.

ABBREVIATIONS

AGER	Auxiliary General Environmental Research
AGI	Auxiliary General Intelligence
AGTR	Auxiliary General Technical Research
AWACS	Airborne Warning and Control System
CAP	combat air patrol
CIA	Central Intelligence Agency
CIC	Combat Information Center
CINCPAC	Commander in Chief, Pacific Command
CINCPACFLT	Commander in Chief, U.S. Pacific Fleet
CIWS	close-in weapon system
CJCS	chairman of the Joint Chiefs of Staff
CMS	China Maritime Surveillance
CNFJ	Commander, U.S. Naval Forces Japan
CO	commanding officer
COLREGS	International Regulations for Preventing Collisions at Sea
COMINT	communications intelligence
COMSEC	communications security
COMSEVENTHFLT	Commander, U.S. Seventh Fleet
CPA	closest point of approach
CSG	Carrier Strike Group
CTF	Commander, Task Force
CTG	Commander, Task Group
CTU	Commander, Task Unit
DCI	Director of Central Intelligence
DEPSECDEF	Deputy Secretary of Defense
DIA	Defense Intelligence Agency
D/LOS	Law of the Sea (Department of State)
DMA	Dangerous Military Activities Agreement

DMAHC	Defense Mapping Agency and Hydrographic Center
DMZ	demilitarized zone
DoD	Department of Defense
DoS	Department of State
DOS/OMA	Department of State Office of Maritime Affairs
DPRK	Democratic People's Republic of Korea
DRV	Democratic Republic of Vietnam
EEZ	exclusive economic zone
ELINT	electronic intelligence
EMCON	emissions control
EOD	explosive ordnance demolition
FANK	Forces Armées Nationale Khmer
FAO	Food and Agricultural Organization
FDR	Franklin Delano Roosevelt
FIR	Flight Information Region
FLEC	Fisheries Law Enforcement Command (China)
FON	freedom of navigation, Freedom of Navigation program (U.S.)
FONOP	freedom of navigation operation
FRUS	*Foreign Relations of the United States*
GAO	Government Accounting [later, Accountability] Office
GCC	Gulf Cooperation Council
GPO	Government Printing Office
HARM	high-speed antiradiation missile
HASC	House Armed Services Committee
ICAO	International Civil Aviation Organization
ICJ	International Court of Justice
ICS	International Code of Signals
IFF	identification, friend or foe
ILM	*International Legal Materials*

IMO	International Maritime Organization
INCSEA	Incidents at Sea Agreement
IRGC	Islamic Revolutionary Guard Corps (Iran)
ISR	intelligence, surveillance, and reconnaissance (operations)
IUU	illegal, unregulated, unreported (fishing)
JAGC	Judge Advocate General's Corps
JCS	Joint Chiefs of Staff
JRC	Joint Reconnaissance Center
KCNA	Korean Central News Agency
KGB	Komitet Gosudarstvennoy Bezopasnosti
LNG	liquefied natural gas
LRCC	Libyan Revolutionary Command Council
LTE	low-tide elevation
MAC	Military Armistice Commission
MAGTF	Marine Air-Ground Task Force
MARAD	Maritime Administration
MCM	mine countermeasures
MCRM	*Maritime Claims Reference Manual*
MEU	Marine expeditionary unit
MFA	Ministry of Foreign Affairs (Soviet)
MMCA	Military Maritime Consultative Agreement
MSB	mobile sea base
MSC	Military Sealift Command
MSO	ocean minesweepers
MSR	marine scientific research
M/V	motor vessel
NAVSECGRU	Naval Security Group
NATO	North Atlantic Treaty Organization
NDBP	*Naval Documents Related to the United States Wars with the Barbary Powers*
nm	nautical mile

NNSC	Neutral Nations Supervisory Committee
NOTAM	notice to airmen
NOTMAR	notice to mariners
NSA	National Security Agency
NSC	National Security Council
NSG	Naval Security Group
OL	"Oscar Lima" ("Heave to or I will open fire")
OOD	officer of the deck
OOME	open-ocean missile exercise
OPAREA	operational area
OPINTEL	operation intelligence
OPORD	Operational Order
PACFLT	U.S. Pacific Fleet
PACOM	U.S. Pacific Command
PCIJ	Permanent Court of International Justice
PLA	People's Liberation Army (China)
PLAAF	PLA Air Force
PRC	People's Republic of China
PT	patrol torpedo boat
PTF	patrol torpedo boat, fast
RAM	Rolling Airframe Missile (System)
RIMPAC	Rim of the Pacific
RIO	radar intercept officer
ROE	rules of engagement
RPG	rocket-propelled grenade
SAG	surface action group
SBU	Navy Special Boat Unit
SecDef	Secretary of Defense
SECNAV	Secretary of the Navy
SIG	Senior Interagency Group
SIGINT	signals intelligence
SMS	special mission ship

SOAR	Special Operations Aviation Regiment
SOF	Special Operations Forces
SRBOC	Super Rapid Blooming Off Board Chaff
SRO	sensitive reconnaissance operations
SROE	standing rules of engagement
SRUF	standing rules for the use of force
Stat.	*U.S. Statutes at Large*
T-AF	Technical-Auxiliary General
TIAF	*Treaties and Other International Acts Series*
UNCLOS	UN Convention on the Law of the Sea
UNCMAC	United Nations Command Military Armistice Commission
UNSCR	United Nations Security Council Resolution
UNTS	*United Nations Treaty Series*
USSR	Union of Soviet Socialist Republics
UST	*Treaties and Other International Acts of the United States of America*
UUV	unmanned underwater vehicle
WBLC	waterborne logistic craft

INTRODUCTION

T his book chronicles the major episodes in American history that challenged U.S. freedom of navigation and overflight in the oceans. From its earliest days to the present, the United States has enjoyed a peculiar and enviable geographic security, situated as it is between quiescent Canada and Mexico. That neither neighbor has posed an existential threat to the United States has provided a sense of security as rare for states as it is underappreciated by Americans. Virtually all U.S. contacts with the outside world, and the connection to the centers of power in Asia and Europe in particular, occur through the oceans. The United States exchanges goods and culture by sea and relies on the oceans as a barrier to stop foreign aggression. The United States also uses the oceans to project power. Today the United States is practically the only nation able to launch and sustain an intercontinental war, which it has done twice in Europe (World Wars I and II), twice in East Asia (the Korean Peninsula and the conflict in Indochina), and three times in Central Asia (Afghanistan once and Iraq twice). Thus, freedom of navigation has been and remains essential to American economic prosperity and strategic security.

— — — • — — —

The oceans are the world's largest domain of maneuver, constituting a continuous, global body of water covering 71 percent of the surface of the Earth.[1] The unified world ocean has an area of more than 139 million square miles (361 million square kilometers) and a total volume of 322,280,000 cubic miles (1,347,000,000 cubic kilometers)—97 percent of the water on the planet. Frozen seawater trapped at the poles accounts for another 2.2 percent of the world's water. The relatively free interchange of water and aquatic life among the oceans means that we should think of the seas as a single body of water. This interconnected quality has made the oceans an essential route for regional cabotage (transport within a region by an external carrier), shipping, and transcontinental voyages, as well as cultural diffusion, commercial trade, military transportation, strategic mobility, immigration, and (less fortunately) the transmission of disease. The oceans constitute a domain principally useful for mobility—shipping is the most efficient method of transporting large quantities of heavy cargo and material long distances—and sea power exploits the physical fact of the global ocean's unity.

Throughout the ancient world and extending into the modern period, the political order largely has been an outgrowth of the sea as a vector for transit. Greek civilization, the Roman Empire, the Ottoman expansion, the Columbian Exchange, the rise of the Dutch Provinces, and British hegemony were made possible by international sea transportation. The United States has stepped into this line of succession to rely on unimpeded use of the oceans for economic prosperity and strategic security.

For most of the past century, the United States made ensuring access to the global commons an enduring security interest. Freedom of the seas and unimpeded access to the associated aerospace have been prerequisites to freedom of action. The doctrine, force structure, and capabilities of the U.S. Navy and Air Force exploit the global commons as maneuver space for power projection. Indeed, the U.S. military's role as the steward of the global commons—and the oceans in particular—has facilitated an international system in which peace and prosperity can flourish.

Strategic access to the oceans is most critical in the near-shore, inland, and coastal-sea regions. Politically, it is the littoral seas that matter most, and the Pentagon is more concerned with the littoral regions than it is with anywhere else on the planet. The coastlines of Asia, Africa, and Latin America teem with idle adolescents growing up amidst rapid political and economic change. Nontraditional security threats are proliferating. The littoral regions represent a relatively small portion of the world's surface, but 70 percent of the world's population lives in them; more than 80 percent of the world's capital cities are located there. Nearly all of the major global marketplaces for international trade can be found on the coastline. Because of the concentration of numerous ethnic groups, the shorelines are also dynamic political centers, susceptible to ethnic instability and armed conflict.

In the late fifteenth century, the Portuguese and Spanish empires asserted control over the vast and unexplored American and Asian oceans. Christopher Columbus' voyages ignited a controversy over ownership of the newly encountered continents. The division of the world ocean into two spheres—one controlled by Castile (Spain), the other by Portugal—was memorialized by Pope Alexander VI in the bull *Inter Caetera* in 1493, adjusted slightly the next year in favor of Portugal in the Treaty of Tordesillas. Using a meridian located 370 leagues west of the Cape Verde Islands, which were already owned by Portugal, the two powers between them laid claim to all of the New World. The agreement was extended to the east with the Treaty of Saragossa, 1529, which recognized Portuguese ownership of the Moluccan Islands (modern-day Indonesia).

Spain and Portugal proved unable to obtain international acceptance for their claims over the sea. As the Iberian powers extracted vast hordes of gold and silver from the New World and began founding agricultural colonies, French, Dutch, and British sea raiders disregarded the papal bull and began targeting "treasure fleets," carrying specie to Europe. Flouting the Treaty of Tordesillas, seamen from France, the nascent Dutch Republic, and eventually England began to enter "Spanish" and "Portuguese" waters, disrupt the carrying trade, and develop colonies in the New World. Excluded from the original and restrictive Iberian maritime bargains, the emerging maritime states adhered to a liberal view of the oceans based on freedom of the seas.

The devastation of the Thirty Years' War—the Bourbon and Hapsburg rivalry that engulfed central Europe—inspired Italian theologian Alberico Gentili and Dutch jurist Hugo Grotius to collect and publish the laws of war and peace. These early masters produced treatises that reflected the accepted rules applicable in the global commons. This book arises from the legacy of Grotius' classic 1609 work, *The Free Sea*. Grotius repudiated Portugal's claim to the waters of Southeast Asia. Writing during the Dutch war of independence, or Eighty Years' War (1568–1648), Grotius championed access to the oceans for the United Provinces; his work marks the rise of the first maritime power outside of Latin Europe. The concept of freedom of the seas had been inherited from Rome and already was part of the legal lexicon, but Grotius and Gentili added a veneer of natural-law theology, arguing that the sea had been created by God and by nature was open to all men, its use common to all.[2]

The Dutch, British, and eventually the Americans were concerned with what today we would call "global governance," or the maintenance of the world system, rather than the narrow pursuit of simple national interest. The commitment to protecting freedom of the seas was made a priority for diplomacy, backed by overwhelming sea power. The liberal order of the oceans assumed iconic status, and over the modern era all maritime powers championed the concept. During the Cold War, for example, a Soviet-American condominium recognized the oceans as a global commons, open to all nations. The two superpowers worked in tandem at the Third United Nations Conference on the Law of the Sea, from 1973 to 1982, to enshrine broadly unrestrictive rules for freedom of navigation and overflight. The liberal order of the oceans prevails today as the law of the maritime commons, a globally accepted norm that provides stability and predictability in international affairs and a basis for at least a minimum public order of the oceans. Ambassador John Norton Moore has called freedom of navigation in the oceans the original "common heritage" of all mankind.[3]

The United States, which arose as an independent state within the context of Pax Britannica, was early confronted with infringements of its maritime rights. In chapters 1 through 3 we chronicle the earliest challenges to U.S. freedom of navigation. First, France conducted an eighteen-month campaign against American merchant ships, in the Quasi-War of 1798–1800. As that conflict abated, the Barbary States afflicted American shipping, seizing vessels and seafarers with impunity. The United States fought two wars against the Barbary principalities—first in 1803–4 and then in 1815—that finally ended the infernal tributary system and won free transit in the Mediterranean Sea. During the War of 1812, the United States faced British interference. This time, the threats to American freedom of navigation arose from attacks on commercial shipping, which was emerging as a competitor of established carriers in Europe. The idea of "freedom of navigation" now coalesced around the right of merchant ships to trade freely within the imperial systems constructed by France and Britain.

Chapters 4–9 focus on the next major challenges to freedom of navigation, emerging during the world wars and persisting throughout the early Cold War. During World War I, German U-boat attacks on neutral U.S. shipping brought the United States into the war. Americans themselves accepted a rather elastic view of their obligations as neutrals, while insisting on the full range of protections to merchant ships afforded by the "cruiser rules" then in force. Germany, unable to resist the temptation to employ its powerful submarine force to control the North Atlantic, circumvented the rules. The world wars produced broad agreement, initiated by the United States, that ships of all nations had unfettered freedom of navigation in peacetime, as did neutral states in time of war. These liberal values were incorporated into the United Nations Charter and formed the basis for the postwar order of the oceans.

Since the inception of the present international system in 1945, the UN Charter has served as the essential treaty underlying world order. The charter governs affairs of war and peace among all states and embodies the norms of the international community. The postwar challenges to freedom of navigation arose within the charter regime and in the context of the Cold War. The 1964 Gulf of Tonkin, 1968 *Pueblo*, and 1975 *Mayaguez* incidents were emblematic, episodes in which communist governments unilaterally attempted to control U.S. warships and commercial vessels in international waters. The first and last of these three challenges were met with strong American responses. Because of its close connection with security on the Korean Peninsula, the *Pueblo* incident ended in a negotiated settlement—one, in fact, that humiliated the United States. The final two case studies of the Cold War era occurred during the 1980s: Libya's pronouncement of the "Line of Death" in the Gulf of Sidra and Iran's wholesale "Tanker War" in the Persian Gulf.

Chapters 10 and 11 explore challenges to U.S. freedom of navigation in the contemporary era, a multipolar world. These incidents have arisen against a backdrop of the norms reflected in, and strengthened by, entry into force of the 1982 UN Convention on the Law of the Sea (UNCLOS) in 1994. After the UN Charter, UNCLOS is the most comprehensive agreement in existence, and it manifestly captures the historical rules of customary law and legal doctrine concerning freedom of navigation and overflight at sea.

The case studies in chapters 10 and 11 involve the United States and another nuclear-armed, autocratic major power—respectively, the Soviet Union and the People's Republic of China. The Soviet Union's claimed restrictions on innocent passage in the Black Sea and China's ongoing interference with American warships and naval auxiliaries in the East and South China Seas underscore the risk posed by illegal coastal state interference on freedom of navigation. Chapter 12 considers how the United States can more effectively push back against China's unlawful claims. These measures include strengthening the U.S. Freedom of Navigation program and implementing legal countermeasures to induce compliance on the part of China.

If the past is prologue, the United States will continue to be challenged in its exercise of navigational rights and freedoms. From its origins to the present, the United States has learned that standing on principle and upholding the rule of law in the oceans requires a powerful navy. As the nation now reconsiders its place in the world and reexamines its military force structure, we believe it must strengthen its naval forces or risk loss of the freedom to act freely in large areas of the oceans. We hope the case studies in this volume both convey the rich story of the struggle to maintain freedom of the seas and illuminate the costs of failure to assert, in a tangible way, American rights and freedoms beyond the territorial seas.

James Kraska
Newport, Rhode Island

Raul "Pete" Pedrozo
Honolulu, Hawaii

"MILLIONS FOR DEFENSE— NOT A CENT FOR TRIBUTE"

The Quasi-War (1798–1800)

France was the first genuine ally of the United States, and French forces were instrumental in the American victory in the Revolutionary War.[1] Ironically, the United States fought its first war as an independent country against France. Just two decades after the American Revolution, the United States, a weak upstart and a newly independent colony, was embroiled with France, one of the two most powerful nations in the world, in a "quasi-war" over the right to freedom of navigation on the high seas. The United States was motivated by principles fashioned from a strong sense of egalitarianism and liberty, a sense that colored the governing philosophy of American leaders in domestic politics and international affairs. Then, as now, the United States government was divided on how forcefully it should assert its right to freedom of the seas.

The Federalists favored closer relations with Great Britain, and at points throughout the 1790s they called for a declaration of war against France. These were business-oriented men; their ranks included Alexander Hamilton, George Washington, John Jay, John Adams, and Charles Cotesworth Pinckney. The Republican Democrats, led by Thomas Jefferson and James Madison (and later, Henry Clay and Andrew Jackson) saw in Revolutionary France a natural ally to be cultivated. They viewed Great Britain as the greater threat to freedom of the seas—a sentiment that would lead Madison and the Republican Democrats to declare war in 1812. They viewed France, on the other hand, as a catalyst for the demise of absolute monarchies in Europe and the spread of universal liberalism.[2] For Republican Democrats, negotiations were the key to defending navigational rights against French encroachment. Both the Federalists and Republican Democrats valued freedom of the seas for commercial and ideological reasons, disagreeing mainly over whether France or Great Britain posed the greatest threat to American sovereignty and freedom to use the oceans.

Even Thomas Jefferson, who devalued international banking and commercial links with Europe, realized that his ideal agrarian society based on liberty would have to rely on maritime trade to sell agricultural products abroad.[3] Hence the Jeffersonian vision of the United States as an "Empire of Liberty" and a beacon of hope for the world would be invoked by later presidents in the Spanish-American War, the world wars, the Cold War, and the war on terrorism. In each case, freedom of navigation in the oceans would be the principal means of spreading American values. Distinguished American historian Samuel Flagg Bemis called the doctrine of freedom of the seas the "ancient birthright" of the American republic.[4] The Quasi-War was the first conflict in which the United States vindicated its birthright.

—— ——— —— — ◆ — ——— —— —

During the American Revolution, French support for the United States was linked with France's geopolitical relationships in the New World and in Europe. The Battle of Saratoga immediately reset the board; after the American victory, Spain and France went all-in to help the United States. Serving in Paris at the time, Benjamin Franklin and his fellow commissioners saw their difficulties with the French government disappear. France rushed to offer the United States a military alliance to prevent the colonies from being enticed by England with an accommodation, such as some form of limited self-government, like that enjoyed by Canada. The United States, however, was emboldened by its own success. The colonies had declared their independence on July 4, 1776. The Articles of Confederation followed, on

July 9, 1778, only after the Battle of Saratoga and the conclusion of two treaties with France on February 6, 1778—a treaty of amity and commerce and one of alliance.[5] Both agreements recognized the independent United States of America. To sweeten the deal further, France renounced any claim on territories held by Britain or the United States in mainland North America. (At the time, Louisiana was held by Spain.) For its part, Spain sought to weaken British power in order to retake Gibraltar, and it had invaded and occupied West Florida, lost to Great Britain after the Seven Years' War.

On March 6, 1778, France formally announced the two agreements with the United States. Nearly simultaneously, France and Britain recalled their ambassadors from London and Paris; a state of undeclared war now existed between them. The following week, King Louis XVI received the American representatives. Meanwhile in Britain, Prime Minister Frederick Lord North, attempted to convince Parliament to wean the Americans away from France, but King George III still refused to concede independence to the colonialists. The American Revolution dragged on.

The Royal Navy outgunned all other naval powers combined, and the British used this power with impunity to control trade flows. British warships conducted unlimited searches and arrests of neutral ships and cargoes, under the pretense that the affected trade only strengthened its adversaries. In order to counter the supremacy of the Royal Navy, the American colonies and a handful of European states asserted the long-standing legal doctrine "free ships make free goods" as a tangible expression of freedom of the seas.

Even as a colony, the United States operated a large commercial fleet but next to no navy, the functions of which it outsourced to privateers. The Americans promoted a liberal wartime trading system, one that protected freedom of the seas for all states during time of peace and for neutral states during periods of conflict. During the American War of Independence, American leaders adopted a maximalist view of the doctrine of "free ships make free goods," using law as a weapon in lieu of naval power. Even before they established their independence, the American colonies opened all their ports to foreign commerce, except British ships, on April 6, 1776. This act was the first irrevocable step toward independence, as it directly repudiated the American Prohibitory Act, passed by the British parliament in December 1775.[6] The principle of "free ships make free goods" was codified in the American alliance treaty with France and in U.S. treaties with Holland, Sweden, Prussia, and Morocco.

A more open and competitive trading system benefited the United States, which pushed to protect and even broaden its neutral rights amidst conflicts that engulfed its trading partners in Europe. Toward this end, the Continental Congress proposed and developed a "Plan of Treaties," which also became known as the "American Plan," or the "Model Treaty." The "Model Treaty" was a draft agreement comprising some thirty articles designed to liberalize trade between the United States and France.[7] The draft served as the basis for all but one U.S. trade treaty before 1800.[8]

On September 17, 1776, the Continental Congress adopted the "Model Treaty" as a framework for reciprocal commercial terms with France and Spain. As these powers were frequently engaged in wars on the Continent, the "American Plan" called for the right of neutral states to trade at any belligerent port not under blockade.[9] Neutral ships would be entitled to carry any goods except contraband—and contraband was defined narrowly, as armaments and ammunition. The Americans did not regard food, naval stores, or other goods owned by a belligerent government as contraband if they were carried in neutral hulls. France accepted these principles in 1778, and they were memorialized in the Treaty of Amity and Commerce, although the text was adjusted to "most-favored-nation" trading privileges.[10] The two nations concurrently signed the Treaty of Alliance.[11] The "Model Treaty," successful as a point of departure for trade negotiations, also formed the basis for the U.S.-France Convention of 1800 that ultimately ended the Quasi-War.

– – – – • – – – –

For the Americans, the Anglo-French War was the third in recent memory: the two antagonists had clashed at sea during the Seven Years' War and the American Revolutionary War, 1778–83. In both cases, the Americans had been adherents of Adam Smith, believers in free trade. They regarded monopolizing the trade of one's colonies in time of peace and infringing neutral rights in time of war as inimical to prosperity for all. Benjamin Franklin captured the American ideal: "Commerce, consisting in a mutual Exchange of the Necessaries and Conveniences of Life, the more free and unrestrained it is, the more it flourishes; and the happier are all the Nations concerned in it."[12]

The U.S. Constitution was signed on September 17, 1787, replacing the 1778 Articles of Confederation. The first session of Congress convened on March 4, 1789, sitting until September 29, as the United States began operating under the Constitution. That same year France was cast into the cataclysmic social and political upheaval of the French Revolution. The revolution overthrew the monarchy and spawned a host of conflicts that morphed into the Napoleonic Wars and lasted until 1815. From 1793 to 1815, France was engaged in almost continuous war with Great Britain and other states, on a battlefield that extended from western and central Europe and the Italian Peninsula to the Caribbean colonies and the Middle East.

Because of France's aid during the Revolutionary War, Americans were still largely pro-French, although most wanted to stay out of European politics. The British continued to aggravate the nascent republic, however, by not carrying out all of their commitments under the Treaty of Paris. George Washington transmitted that agreement to the Senate on June 11, 1789. The Senate rendered unanimous advice and consent, passing a statute to implement the treaty on April 14, 1792. Despite treaty provisions that required England to relinquish forts it controlled in U.S. territory "with all convenient speed," British garrisons lingered for a decade at Detroit, Lernoult, Michilimackinac (present-day Mackinac), Niagara, Ontario, Oswegatchie, and Presque Isle.[13] On June 8, 1794, John Jay arrived in London to lead U.S. negotiations to resolve these disputes, but some of the British frontier outposts would resurface as scenes of fighting in the Northwest during the War of 1812.

Neutrality was the first foundation of American foreign policy, backed up by the doctrine of freedom of the seas. The Continental Congress had resolved that the true interest of the United States "requires that they should be as little as possible entangled in the politics and controversies of European nations."[14] This approach diverged from the quest of European states for control of the oceans.[15]

In peace, as it had in war, the United States found its ideal of free commerce on the seas at the mercy of the Royal Navy. Jay's only leverage with respect to Great Britain was the implicit threat that the United States would once again join Russia, Sweden, and Denmark to defend neutral rights. Russia had proposed the first League of Armed Neutrality in 1780. Denmark joined the effort, declaring the Baltic Sea to be a neutral area on May 8, supported by a Russo-Danish convention for armed neutrality on July 9.[16]

No longer a cobelligerent with the United States, France now posed challenges to American neutrality. France and Britain ramped up their war at sea, and the United States was caught in the middle. As 1790 drew to a close, the United States was engaged with France in a dispute over maritime commerce, a dispute that would culminate eight years later in the undeclared Quasi-War. Despite the assistance provided by France in bringing the American Revolution to an end, and royal decrees granting waivers of duties in 1787–88, American trade began to revert to its former channels: trade with England increased, while commerce with France languished.[17] France complained that U.S. restrictions on trade violated article V of the Treaty of Amity and Commerce of 1778. In retaliation, the National Assembly of France imposed measures against American trade. In 1792, President Jefferson directed Gouverneur Morris, American minister plenipotentiary to France, to negotiate a new treaty of commerce. Morris duly proposed it on July 9, 1792.[18] The French Revolution intervened, however.

The First Republic, an outgrowth of the French Revolution, fought a series of wars on the Continent against European monarchies. On August 27, 1791, the Holy Roman Emperor, Leopold II, and King Frederick William II of Prussia, in collaboration with emigrant French nobles, issued the Declaration of Pillnitz, proclaiming support for King Louis XVI against the revolutionaries. They threatened intervention if the monarch were deposed. Revolutionary leaders regarded the Pillnitz Declaration as an affront and an interference in the internal affairs of France.[19]

The European powers, disturbed at the radicalization emerging in France, considered intervention to prevent the spread of revolutionary fervor. Austria positioned troops along the border; France demanded their withdrawal.[20] The Austrian reply was evasive, and the National Assembly declared war on April 20, 1792. The following month, King Louis XVI was overthrown and the First French Republic was proclaimed. The king was tried and beheaded by guillotine on January 21, 1793, ending a thousand years of French monarchy.

As France slid into war in the fall of 1792, its government appointed M. Edmond C. Genêt as ambassador to the United States. Genêt arrived carrying some 250 to 300 blank commissions authorizing U.S. ships to serve as privateers and prey on British commerce.[21] He landed on April 8, 1793, in Charleston, South Carolina, rather than Philadelphia, the capital, and set about issuing the commissions to ships outfitted and manned by mixed crews of American and French sailors.[22] Genêt traveled by land to Philadelphia, greeted along the route by cheers from pro-French Americans. Genêt's privateers began seizing British prizes and bringing them into U.S. ports for condemnation, some taken while inside the territorial waters of the United States. The British ship *Embuscade* was captured in Delaware Bay (though it was surrendered after the British minister protested). President Washington was alarmed that Genêt was violating American territorial sovereignty and acting in ways counter to the obligations of neutral states.

Genêt was received as French ambassador, and two weeks later President Washington issued a U.S. proclamation of neutrality.[23] American seafarers, however, continued to accept offers to serve as privateers against the shipping of France's enemies, undermining Washington's position. French consuls in the United States sat as admiralty courts in prize cases, a practice Genêt defended as consistent with the U.S.-French treaties. Article XVII of the Treaty of Amity and Commerce, Genêt claimed, precluded the United States from interference with French adjudication of prize cases brought into U.S. ports. The United States objected that its commitment to observe neutrality toward France did not oblige it to violate the duty of neutrality toward third states.[24] Furthermore, it held, the conduct of prize cases by French officials in American ports was a violation of American sovereignty, and the right of consular officials to try prize cases had not been ceded by the United States in the consular treaty. To maintain its neutrality, the United States halted the fitting-out and arming of privateers and forbade those already operating from reentering the United States. The announcement created an impasse. The United States requested France to recall Genêt; in retaliation, France requested and obtained Gouverneur Morris' recall from Paris.

Washington's declaration of neutrality stated that "it appears that a state of war exists between Austria, Prussia, Sardinia, Great Britain, and the United Netherlands, on the one part, and France on the other." The United States would act with "sincerity and good faith" to "pursue a conduct friendly and impartial toward the belligerent powers."[25] His proclamation also announced that Americans who participated in the conflict would be liable to punishment and forfeiture. France and the pro-French Democratic-Republicans criticized the proclamation as a repudiation of U.S. treaty commitments with France; Thomas Jefferson and James Madison were deeply concerned, holding that the president, who had no authority to declare war, lacked also the power to declare neutrality.

– – – – • – – – –

Meanwhile, concern over not French privateers but Barbary corsairs was spurring Congress to create a naval force. On March 27, 1794, Congress authorized $688,888 for the construction of four ships of forty-four guns and two ships of thirty-six guns.[26] These original six frigates of the U.S. Navy were the *Constitution, President, United States, Congress, Constellation,* and *Chesapeake*. Built to a hybrid design, American frigates had enough firepower to engage most enemies yet were fast enough to outpace the massive English and French ships of the line. Congress authorized the completion of the six frigates and their outfitting; the actual funds came in two tranches. Keels for all six ships were laid, but just three—the *United States, Constellation,* and *Constitution*—were finished before the agreement with Tripoli in 1796 undercut their justification. Only after the start of the

Quasi-War were the remaining vessels completed and outfitted: the *Congress* and the *Chesapeake* were launched in late 1799, the *President* in April 1800.

As the wars between Britain and France raged on the Continent, American ships were subjected to British as well as French aggression. The two European powers sought to cut each other off from trade with the United States. Britain issued orders in council that made the rights of neutral trade secondary to those of belligerents. France disavowed the principle of "free ships make free goods," which had been codified in article XXIII of the Treaty of Amity and Commerce, under the rationale that the United States was unwilling to compel England to observe the same rule. When the United States began to resist the seizure of American vessels by Britain, France relented, for a time. The ruling French Committee of Public Safety adopted a decree on January 4, 1795, that permitted American vessels to transport enemy merchandise, reestablishing "free ships, free goods."[27]

During this period the Royal Navy began the impressment (forcible recruitment) of American sailors from the decks of U.S. ships, and this provocation would become one of the bases for the War of 1812. Britain also seized American ships in the West Indies that were trading with France. The United States protested these violations of its neutrality. The continued British occupation of frontier forts in the Ohio Valley also rankled the Americans. The Jay Treaty of November 1794 stipulated that the British Army would withdraw from these last remaining redoubts on American territory—garrisons in western Pennsylvania and north of the Ohio River, and along the shores of the Great Lakes. The U.S.-Canadian boundary was submitted to arbitration, and American ships were officially granted the right to trade with British colonies in India and the Caribbean. The treaty also protected neutral American shipping trading with French colonies in the West Indies from capture as prizes. The Jay Treaty benefited the United States, which wanted to normalize relations with England and eject British troops from the United States. The main benefit for Britain was to draw the United States away from France.

The treaty compromised on the principle of "free ships make free goods," which meant that the nationality of the ship determined the neutral or belligerent legal status of the cargo. That principle had been a major element of the 1779 Treaty of Amity and Commerce with France, as well as U.S. bilateral treaties with the Netherlands (1782), Sweden (1783), Prussia (1785), Morocco (1787), Tripoli (1796), and Tunis (1797). The Jay Treaty departed from the principle of "free ships, free goods": it provided that Britain could seize goods on neutral American ships bound for enemy ports in Europe, angering France. These terms undermined American aspirations and the prevalent law of nations, which held, under the rubric of "free ships make free goods," that neutral ships always were exempt from capture unless carrying contraband to a belligerent. If the Jay Treaty thus accommodated both British and American interests, then, it spurred France to take even more extreme measures against American shipping.[28]

American leaders were divided on the Jay Treaty. Thomas Jefferson and James Madison opposed the agreement, favoring a foreign policy tilt toward France. Even after the excesses of the French Revolution became apparent—the Reign of Terror (1793–94), the Thermidorian Reaction (1794), the ascendancy of the five-man Directory (1795–99), and the rise of Napoleon Bonaparte—Jefferson's faction still believed in the original values of the French Revolution as an antidote to the monarchies in Europe.

The Federalists, including George Washington and Hamilton, supported the treaty and leaned toward Britain. The Jay Treaty passed the Senate by a vote of twenty to ten—exactly two-thirds—and entered into force on February 29, 1796. The agreement immediately caused problems between the United States and France. France bitterly complained that the treaty violated international law, as well as the 1778 Treaty of Amity and Commerce, and betrayed the special French-American relationship. Just days later, on March 2, 1796, the executive Directory of France contravened parts of the 1778 agreement, putting the two states on a collision course.

— — — ● — — —

From October 1796 to June 1797, French raiders captured 316 American ships.[29] This number amounted to 6 percent of the nation's merchant ships. The Federalist Northeast was especially hard hit. In the period 1797 to

1799, for example, Newburyport, Massachusetts, lost seventy-seven ships.[30] Philadelphia merchants claimed to have lost 2 million dollars to French raiders.[31] Between December 1796 and February 1797, marine insurance rates skyrocketed from 6 to 30 percent of the value of the cargo. Insurance to cover ships on voyages to Europe doubled, and for ships bound for the West Indies insurance premiums rose 200 to 600 percent.[32]

France objected to the "insidious" 1793 neutrality proclamation by President Washington.[33] The Americans argued that their balanced, impartial neutrality was necessary and even in France's interest. France, however, bristled at U.S. government efforts to punish American privateers aiding the French.[34] France also asserted that British warships were being admitted into American ports after having taken French prize vessels, in violation of article XVII of the Treaty of Amity and Commerce. The United States countered that the article did not forbid enemy warships that had ever taken a French prize from entering U.S. ports, or even enemy warships with prizes in tow to enter American ports, but only required such warships to "depart as soon as possible." Yet by the terms of the Jay Treaty, France was no longer permitted to sell captured British prizes in U.S. ports as it formerly had done. The United States said that practice had been a temporary privilege, not a right under the Treaty of Amity and Commerce.

The United States was in a dilemma—permitting French privateers and warships to use American ports as part of their war effort was a violation of neutrality, while the 1778 Treaty of Alliance required that American ports be open to French (as well as English) ships. The United States could not close its ports to French warships, but it hoped its closing down of French consular prize courts and preventing the licensing and arming of American merchant vessels as privateers would placate Britain without alienating France.

Nevertheless, France felt abandoned and issued a series of decrees aimed at coercing greater cooperation from Washington. The first decree, of January 4, 1795, reiterated the terms of the 1778 Treaty of Commerce respecting contraband and the carriage of enemy goods. Disappointed that Jefferson was not elected president, the Directory issued a second decree on March 2, 1797, that clarified the authority of French warships under the first decree:[35]

all enemy property and all property "not sufficiently ascertained to be neutral" conveyed under an American flag could be confiscated. American privateers operating on behalf of England were to be regarded as pirates. Two days later, on March 4, 1797, President John Adams, a Federalist, took the oath of office.

The greatest impact of these decrees related to documentation of vessels. The sea letters, or passports, required under the Treaty of Amity and Commerce during time of war had certified the name of the ship, the names of the crew, and the type and origin of the cargo. Merchant ships visited by naval personnel of the other party were to offer such passports for inspection, after which they could continue safely on their voyages.[36] France deemed documentation under U.S. law to be insufficient, and vessels had been seized as prizes for minor irregularities in bills of lading, crew lists, or other papers.[37] The new decree changed these rules: it was tantamount to a "general and summary confiscation" of American vessels.[38] Captured American merchant ships were now taken to prize courts in the French West Indies, where they often were condemned without trial or opportunity for their owners to offer a defense.[39]

The second decree modified the terms of the 1778 treaty to make U.S. vessels and their cargoes subject to capture for any cause that was lawful in Jay's treaty. Americans found serving on board British warships were treated as pirates if captured, and hanged, even if they had been impressed against their will. President Adams turned to diplomacy to lower the temperature in relations with Paris. He hoped that private claims by shipowners against France for capture of U.S. merchant ships might address the problem without antagonizing France.

The United States sought regular communications with France and in November 1796 sent Federalist stalwart Charles Cotesworth Pinckney to Paris as ambassador. Pinckney's credentials were refused. The Directory insisted that the issues raised by the Jay Treaty had first to be resolved. After weeks of discourteous treatment, Pinckney was forced to retire to the Netherlands. After this insult, President Adams delivered, on May 16, 1797, a special message to Congress in which he pledged to continue to treat with France. At the same time, however, he asked Congress to "adopt such measures . . . as exigencies shall be found to require."[40] "We shall convince France and the world," the president declared, "that we are not a degraded people, humiliated under a colonial spirit of fear and a sense of inferiority, fitted to be the miserable instruments of foreign influence, regardless of national honor, character, and interest."

The Senate on May 23 issued a reply to the president that offered support and urged fortitude, arguing that the rights of the U.S. government were "inseparably connected with the dignity, interest, and independence" of the country.[41] Thomas Jefferson, as vice president and president of the Senate, signed the message, despite his French sympathies. Jefferson was uneasy that talk of war while negotiations were being opened would send a mixed message, or even be viewed as provocative. Just days later the U.S. House of Representatives too offered its support to President Adams.[42]

The United States enacted laws to ensure neutrality in the war between England and France. On June 14, 1797, the Fifth Congress passed a law that made acts of privateering against nations at peace with the United States a crime subject to a fine of $10,000 and imprisonment for ten years.[43] An Act Providing a Naval Armament was signed into law on July 1, 1797, authorizing the president to "man and employ" the frigates *United States*, *Constellation*, and *Constitution*.[44] The *Constitution* and *United States* were rated at forty-four guns and the *Constellation* at thirty-six, but all three ships often sailed with even more.

– – – • – – –

Despite the Pinckney rebuff, on May 31, 1797, President Adams nominated to the Senate three envoys extraordinary and ministers plenipotentiary to the French Republic.[45] In mid-July the three emissaries—Elbridge Gerry, Pinckney, and John Marshall—were approved, and soon after they left for France. Marshall and Gerry sailed to the Netherlands, where they joined Pinckney, and the three men arrived in Paris on October 4. The Americans carried diplomatic credentials to negotiate with the French foreign minister, the Marquis de Talleyrand, and the Directory to try to resolve the growing differences between the two states.

During a succession of visits, four professed representatives of Talleyrand informally welcomed the American delegation, but the Directory refused them official recognition. In their correspondence back to the United States the envoys code-named Talleyrand's representatives: Nicholas Hubbard (later "W"), Jean Hottinguer ("X"), Pierre Bellamy ("Y"), and Lucien Hauteval ("Z"). Messrs. X, Y, and Z pressed the American envoys for payment of a *douceur*, or conciliatory bribe, of £50,000 as a precondition to meeting Talleyrand. The French government insisted on a low-interest loan of 32 million florins and that the United States pay off claims filed by American shipowners against France. The terms of the ultimatum were reduced to writing and delivered to the Americans, who objected that the demand was degrading. The American negotiators firmly walked away from requests for payment of a bribe, stating in correspondence home that they had replied, "No, no, no; not a six-pence."[46] In any case, the American intermediaries were skeptical that French policy would change even if the conditions were met.

On January 17, 1798, the Directory issued yet another decree, this one declaring that every vessel at sea loaded in whole or in part with goods from Britain or from English territories would be seized as a prize, regardless of its flag.[47] Any merchant ship with English goods on board was considered fair game. The decree also forbade entry into French ports of any ship that had on any previous voyage entered a British port or any English possession. The Directory was casting a wider net to raise funds sorely needed for its wars in Europe.

In a message to Congress on February 5, 1798, President Adams recounted a letter of October 22 from Pinckney, now governor of South Carolina, that described French attacks against English shipping within U.S. territorial waters. For example, in October 1797 the *Oracabissa*, carrying sugar and rum loaded in Jamaica, was damaged in a storm and approached Charleston, South Carolina.[48] On the sixteenth the ship had taken on a pilot when it encountered a French privateer, the *Veritude*, under a Captain Jourdain. The crew of the *Veritude* boarded and set fire to the *Oracabissa*, in retaliation for a British frigate's having burned a privateer previously commanded by Jourdain.

Three weeks later, Thomas Pickering, the third American secretary of state, set forth a detailed list of France's violations of international law. The offenses included a campaign of "spoliation and maltreatment" of U.S. vessels by French warships and privateers; an eleven-year embargo on U.S. ships entering the port of Bordeaux; the failure by French colonial administrations in the West Indies to pay bills and debts lawfully due to American citizens; seizure of private cargoes and their appropriation to public use; and the capture, detention, and condemnation of American ships as prizes in violation of bilateral treaties.[49]

By March 2, the three American diplomats in Paris had still not been accredited. President Adams, receiving dispatches from Paris on March 4, was outraged at the insulting French behavior. On March 19, the president delivered a report to Congress declaring that the United States had to prepare for the worst.[50]

Seeing no ground for compromise and not authorized to pay bribes or extend loans, the American representatives in Paris broke off negotiations on April 3, 1798. Upon the arrival in the United States of the latest dispatches from Pinckney, Marshall, and Gerry, along with Pinckney and Marshall themselves, President Adams declared, "I will never send another minister to France without assurances that he will be received, respected, and honored as the representative of a great, free, powerful, and independent nation."[51] President Adams and the Federalists were in favor of war, but the pro-French Democratic-Republicans were suspicious of the president's motives. The House Republicans, in fact, suggested that Adams was manufacturing a crisis with France—a country that should be a natural ally.

This failure of the American emissaries to resolve differences with France ushered in a crisis. The United States had viewed French attacks on U.S. merchant ships with growing alarm and was now dismayed by France's refusal to negotiate amicably. Between 1796 and 1798 France captured more than three hundred American merchant ships, and the indignity of the attacks and their collective economic impact were becoming unbearable. The X, Y, Z affair was the last straw.

The rumors of the mistreatment of American envoys in Paris slowly leaked to Congress and newspapers over the spring of 1798. On June 2, 1798, the House voted to request the president to release decoded transcripts of the diplomatic mission to Paris; President Adams transmitted a complete set the following day, changing only the names of the three French interlocutors to "X," "Y," and "Z." The contents were already widely known, but the revelations awed even the Jeffersonian Republicans, who nonetheless feared the Federalist program would lead to conflict.[52]

Between April and June 1798, in fact, the Federalists and the president enacted a package of legislation to prepare the country for war. The United States had no navy, but the three frigates still under construction would be ready for action, and the Department of Treasury had some fifteen revenue cutters available. Construction of twelve ships with twenty-two guns each was authorized on April 27, 1798, at a cost of $950,000.[53] On April 30, President Adams signed a law that established the Navy Department. The close vote (forty-seven to forty-one) in favor of creating the Department of the Navy underscored a lingering ambivalence in Congress about expenditures for national defense. Adams appointed Georgetown, Maryland, merchant Benjamin Stoddert as the first Secretary of the Navy;[54] he was sworn into office on June 19. Another $250,000 was appropriated to strengthen the defenses of ports and harbors.[55] Eighty thousand dollars was spent to acquire ten galleys for coastal defense (these ships would prove woefully few and in any event inadequate).[56] The president also signed into law, on May 28, 1798, an act to authorize U.S. warships to seize any armed vessel hovering off the coast of the United States that had committed "depredations" on American commerce.[57]

A host of additional laws were adopted in June 1798. On June 13, President Adams signed an act suspending commercial trade with France and its dependencies.[58] The act forbade American ships from entering any port of France or its dependencies. Ships undertaking voyages to foreign ports were required to post bonds equal to the value of the ship and its cargo, to be forfeited if the vessel entered into French jurisdiction for the purpose of trade. Likewise, French vessels were barred from American ports.

Secretary Stoddert quickly began to acquire merchant ships and convert them into warships, while working furiously to complete the authorized frigates. By the end of 1798, the U.S. Navy had twenty-one warships in service, one year later thirty-three, and by the end of 1800, fifty-four. Revenue cutters were authorized to carry up to seventy Marines.[59] The masters and crews of American merchant ships were authorized to defend their vessels against attempts at search or seizure by French warships and privateers and to retake their ships if captured.[60] At a banquet reception for John Marshall on June 18, 1798, Robert Goodloe Harper, a South Carolina Federalist and chair of the House Ways and Means Committee, captured the mood of the country. He proclaimed a toast that became a famous refrain: "Millions for defense—not a cent for tribute!"[61] The call would become a national rallying cry; Jeffersonian opposition to a stronger approach toward France evaporated.

On June 22, Congress passed statutes to increase the size of the Navy and to raise an army.[62] George Washington was appointed as commanding general of the Army on July 13, 1798; he would serve in that position until his death on December 14, 1799. A statute was passed on June 25 to permit the arrest and expulsion of aliens and to authorize the defense of merchant ships against attacks by French warships and privateers.[63] Captured French privateers could be brought into U.S. admiralty courts and condemned as prizes; American vessels being used as French privateers and captured were to be restored to their rightful owners upon payment of salvage.[64] In order to deter American ships from sailing under French letters of marque, armed merchantmen had to post bonds equal to double the value of the ship at sailing.[65] The president was authorized to issue rules for the use of force by armed merchant vessels, to "prevent any outrage, cruelty or injury which they may be disposed to commit" in actions against French privateers or in recovery of U.S. ships. Should French warships begin to comply with the laws of war and respect American neutral rights, however, U.S. ships would submit to France's belligerent right of visit and search to confirm the neutral character of their cargoes.

On July 7, 1798, President Adams signed an act that annulled the treaty of alliance with France.[66] Two days later, Congress authorized the president to deploy U.S. warships on the high seas with orders to "subdue, seize or take" any armed French vessel as prize.[67] The law also authorized the president to award commissions to license armed merchant ships as privateers to capture any armed French vessel. Captured vessels were to be brought into American ports and adjudicated by admiralty courts; prisoners were to be delivered to a U.S. marshal. Condemned prizes and their cargoes would be forfeited and the sums realized from them distributed to the captors (except, as noted, for recaptured American vessels).

Congress established the U.S. Marine Corps on July 11, 1798;[68] five days later, funds were appropriated for the three long-deferred thirty-two-gun frigates—the *Chesapeake*, *Congress*, and *President*—that had been authorized on March 27, 1794.[69] On August 21, 1798, the attorney general, Charles Lee, advised the secretary of state that a legally authorized "state of maritime war" existed between the two nations.[70] "France is our enemy," Lee said, "and any American citizen that renders aid or assistance to her commits treason."

Congress also passed legislation to ensure that pro-French citizens did not interfere with U.S. foreign relations by freelance negotiations with Paris. Aside from Gerry, still in France without credentials or authority, there was an enterprising state legislator and pacifist Quaker from Pennsylvania, Dr. George Logan, who made his own attempt at resolving differences with France. Armed with a certificate of private citizenship signed by Vice President Thomas Jefferson, Logan did not officially represent the United States. Convinced he could negotiate a settlement, however, he left for France on June 12, 1798, where he was hailed as an envoy of peace. The Directory, smarting from the backlash of the X, Y, Z affair, realized it had pushed the Americans too far. The embargo on American merchant ships was lifted, and detained American ships and sailors were freed.[71]

The Federalists did not welcome Logan's trip to Paris, however. President Adams recommended to the Senate on December 12, 1798, legislation to control unaccountable citizen-diplomats such as Logan, to prevent "officious interference" by individuals with the "temerity and impertinence . . . to interfere in public affairs between France and the United States."[72] The resulting Logan Act of January 30, 1799, forbade unauthorized American citizens from negotiating with foreign governments.[73] One week later, Congress passed a law further restricting trade with France.[74] The statute provided that no ship owned by a resident of the United States was allowed to "proceed directly, or from any intermediate port or place, to any port or place within the territory of the French Republic." Vessels in violation of the law could be forfeited, along with their cargoes. The statute was tested in the Supreme Court case of the *Flying Fish*.

— — — — • — — — —

The Danish-flagged brigantine *Flying Fish*, which had left the French port of Jérémie, Haiti, bound for Saint Thomas, was captured by the frigate *Boston*, under Capt. George Little, on December 2, 1799, near the island of Hispaniola.[75] The *Flying Fish* was carrying Danish neutral cargo owned by Samuel Goodman, an inhabitant of Saint Thomas, a Danish territory. It was seized pursuant to an act of Congress of February 9, 1799, that authorized seizure of vessels sailing to French ports. The merchant ship was taken as a prize into Boston, where its case went to trial. The court directed a restoration of the vessel to its owner because the ship was neutral property, but declined to award damages, as the Navy had had probable cause to seize it. The Circuit Court of Massachusetts reversed the decision. Because the *Flying Fish* had been on a voyage from, not to, a French port, and had carried neutral (free) cargo, accordingly, the ship had been immune. The Supreme Court affirmed the appellate decision.

In another Supreme Court case, *Bas v. Tingy*, the Court held that France was "the enemy" and that therefore payment of salvage was due to Captain Tingy, who had recovered an American ship taken by a French privateer.[76] The decision turned on the distinction between two statutes: the first dealt with ships recaptured from "any nation in amity with the United States," whereas the second law addressed ships recaptured from "the enemy." The question was whether France was "in amity" with the United States or "the enemy," a belligerent with which the United States was at war. The Supreme Court concluded that a state of war existed between France and the United States, albeit a "legally imperfect" one.[77]

— — — — • — — — —

During the Quasi-War the U.S. Navy fought the French in the Caribbean Sea and offered to support the revolution for Haitian independence led by Toussaint L'Ouverture.[78] By the summer of 1798, French privateers and warships were struggling, worn down by the Royal Navy. The large U.S. frigates *Constitution*, *United States*, and *Constellation* put to sea that summer and performed admirably. Few French warships escaped the British blockade, so even the relatively small U.S. Navy outmatched them. The Navy quickly swept the eastern seaboard of French warships and privateers.

The Americans lost only a single warship during the conflict—the fourteen-gun schooner *Retaliation*. The *Retaliation* had been the French vessel *La Croyable*, taken as prize by the *Delaware* under Capt. Stephen Decatur. *La Croyable*, the first American capture of the Quasi-War, had been condemned in a U.S. court, purchased by the U.S. Navy, and pressed into service as the *Retaliation*. Sailing in the West Indies under Lt. William Bainbridge, the *Retaliation* was accompanied by the twenty-gun converted merchant ship *Montezuma* and the eighteen-gun *Norfolk*. On November 20, 1798, the *Montezuma* and *Norfolk* peeled off on a chase, leaving the *Retaliation* isolated. The thirty-two-gun frigate *L'Insurgente* and the forty-gun frigate *Volontaire* overtook it, and, badly outgunned, the U.S. warship struck its colors. The following June, however, the twenty-eight-gun *Merrimack* recaptured the *Retaliation*.

Another U.S. warship, the *Enterprise*, captured eight French privateers and warships and liberated eleven American merchant vessels. The twelve-gun schooner *Experiment* was also successful, capturing French prizes on several cruises to the Caribbean Sea. In the most storied engagement of the Quasi-War, and the first American naval battle since the Revolutionary War, the *Constellation* encountered the French frigate *L'Insurgente* northeast of the island of Nevis on February 9, 1799. Under the command of Thomas Truxtun, the *Constellation* maneuvered so as to rake the French warship with the fire of its thirty-eight guns with relative impunity for more than an hour. Captain Barreaut surrendered the *L'Insurgente* to the *Constellation*. The two warships put into St. Kitts for repairs, to the applause of the British onlookers who greeted them. Not quite one year later, the *Constellation* hammered the fifty-two-gun frigate *La Vengeance* in a nighttime battle. The French warship was heavily damaged but escaped in the dark.

Truxtun's two engagements were the only major naval battles of the war, but they exhibited American naval skill that presaged the strong showing that would be made in the Barbary Wars and the War of 1812. For most of the Quasi-War, France had only two or three frigates operating in the West Indies, and Truxtun defeated two of them. By the end of 1798, nearly the entire American fleet was preying on French ships in the West Indies.

On November 9, 1799, the young Napoleon Bonaparte overthrew the Directory, and on December 14, George Washington died—events that marked the passing of an era. The campaign for the presidential election of 1800 between John Adams and Thomas Jefferson unfolded simultaneously with negotiations with France to end the war. On September 30, 1800, American and French envoys signed a peace agreement known as the Treaty of Mortefontaine.[79] The treaty terminated the 1778 Treaty of Alliance. The decision to cancel it reflected George Washington's 1796 admonition to avoid entangling alliances, except as temporary measures in case of emergency, and also the preference of John Adams to maintain an independent foreign policy. Washington had stated: "Our detached and distant situation invites and enables us to pursue a different course.... Why forego the advantages of so peculiar a situation? Why quit our own to stand upon foreign ground? Why, by interweaving our destiny with that of any part of Europe, entangle our peace and prosperity in the toils of European ambition, rivalship, interest, humor or caprice?"[80] The United States would not enter into an alliance with another country until it joined with the "Big Four" during World War II and signed the 1942 Declaration by United Nations at the First Washington Conference.

The Treaty of Mortefontaine also normalized bilateral trade, conferring "most favored nation" status on each party, and required the return of captured prizes. Word of the breakthrough did not reach Washington, D.C., until the first week of November 1800, however, which was too late to help

John Adams in his bid for reelection. The treaty called for the restoration of warships and private vessels that had been taken and created a new form of passport that rendered safe conduct and passage to commercial ships. The Senate, to deal with questions of order arising during its consideration of the treaty, adopted its first set of rules of procedure for treaties transmitted to it by the president. The Senate gave the president the authority to exchange or repatriate French citizens captured during conflict.[81]

The president ratified the treaty on February 18, 1801, with the advice and consent of the Senate, excepting provisions on no indemnities or compensation for captured prizes in article II. The parties exchanged instruments of ratification on July 31, 1801, with a reservation as to the stipulation in article II. The president returned the treaty and reservation for further advice and consent; it was returned once again and fully ratified. The president promulgated the treaty by proclamation on December 21, 1801.

The United States filed at least 6,479 claims involving more than 2,300 vessels lost to enemy action during the war—most of them taken as prizes.[82] Tactically, however, the Quasi-War was an American victory. The United States captured some eighty-five French privateers, losing only the *Retaliation*. The U.S. Navy also trained a generation of officers who later would fight in the wars against Tripoli: Stephen Decatur, Oliver Hazard Perry, William Bainbridge, Charles Stewart, and David Porter.[83] Strategically, the war also redounded to the benefit of the United States, as France, absorbed in the Napoleonic Wars, would later relinquish the Louisiana Territory.

"OUR COUNTRY RIGHT OR WRONG"

The Barbary Wars (1801–16)

The United States was a relative latecomer to Barbary piracy, which predates the discovery of the New World. Attacks by North African principalities on U.S. shipping were just one element of a three-hundred-year clash between East and West that played out in the Mediterranean Sea. In 1620, just after the Pilgrims landed at Plymouth, the Barbary pirates reached the height of their power. The hapless men they captured often were chained to oars in war galleys or were put to hard labor constructing harbor fortifications in North Africa. Others were ransomed for extravagant sums or sold at auction. Women and children were conscripted into harems or sold into slavery.[1] In 1625, a Moroccan corsair captured the first American colonial ship sailing from Plymouth colony with a cargo of beaver pelts, bound for England. The Pilgrims on board were taken to Morocco and enslaved.

Attacks against Christian shipping were launched from Salé and Rabat in northwest Morocco on the Atlantic Ocean and from the fortresses of Algiers, Tunis, and Tripoli on the Mediterranean Sea. The Barbary pirates also sailed as far north as Iceland, pillaging shoreline settlements. Over a period of three hundred years, Barbary corsairs seized between 1 million and 1.25 million Europeans and Christians.[2] The capture of European and

American slaves left an indelible impression on Western culture and was reflected in literature from Cervantes to Molière to Voltaire, as well as on the popular stage.[3]

The life awaiting captured seafarers was particularly cruel and reprehensible. Chained to their oars, they sat, ate, slept, and defecated on a one-foot-wide bench; often they were not unchained for months at a time or until they collapsed from exhaustion and died—at which point they were thrown overboard.

The Barbary States absorbed Western seafaring expertise and naval weapons technology through captured European prisoners and mercenaries. Europeans were especially instrumental in helping the Barbary pirates gravitate from oar to sail, which increased the endurance of ships and enabled longer patrols at sea. As galleys gave way to wind-powered ships, slaves were removed from benches and sold in slave markets.

Each European state was on its own in contending with the Barbary States. The strongest nations were able to negotiate and enforce favorable treaties to protect their shipping. In turn, the Barbary States paid tribute to the grand seigneur in Constantinople. England, for example, signed in 1682 its first treaty of commerce and peace with Algiers, permitting English ships to "freely pass the Seas and Traffic without any Search."[4] Massive British ships of the line patrolled to ensure compliance. This carrot-and-stick approach protected British shipping. Britain was also able to rely on supplies from North African coastal towns to provision its Mediterranean fleet and garrison at Gibraltar and thereby avoid Spanish and French naval squadrons menacing routes back to Plymouth and Portsmouth. Colonial American ships too were under the protection of the Royal Navy.

On September 3, 1783, the United States and Britain signed the Treaty of Paris, which ended the American war for independence.[5] Given the acrimony between Christian and Muslim states throughout the Mediterranean Sea and the relentless Islamic advance into Eastern Europe and the Balkans, as well as the Barbary raids along the coast of southern Europe, there is no doubt that for Europeans the conflicts with the Barbary States were inescapably part of a broader religious and political clash. Not so for the United States. For the Americans, whose territory lay well beyond the reach of Barbary attack, the conflicts with the Barbary States were merely about the principle of freedom of the seas and the right to trade. After the Treaty of Paris, the vulnerability of American shipping, no longer under the protection of the Royal Navy, soon became painfully evident to the new republic. By this act of peace with its former colonial overlord, the United States found itself virtually alone and unprotected from Barbary piracy. The door was opened for war.

— — — — • — — — —

In May 1784, the U.S. Congress commissioned John Adams, Benjamin Franklin, and Thomas Jefferson as special ministers plenipotentiary in Paris, to negotiate treaties with all of the Barbary States and the Ottoman Empire. The commissions directed these men to negotiate treaties with some twenty-three European nations, beginning with Great Britain.[6] Furthermore, treaties of friendship, or "amity and commerce," were to be pursued with the Barbary States of Morocco, Tunis, Algiers, and Tripoli as well.[7]

The commissions and the envoys' instructions were virtually identical. The United States sought trade deals of "perfect reciprocity"—that is, in which parties had guaranteed access to each other's ports. When he left Boston for France on July 5, 1784, Thomas Jefferson carried the commissions with him. But the commissions gave no authority to send agents to North Africa or to pay the tribute that was certain to be a condition for negotiations; accordingly, they were impossible to implement. As U.S. minister in France, Jefferson was implacable in his view that if these practical barriers remained the United States had no choice but to fight.

On October 11, 1784, a Moroccan warship out of Salé seized the U.S. brigantine *Betsey*, which had sailed from Boston to Tenerife in the Canary Islands, with a stop in Cádiz. The crew of the *Betsey* was treated relatively well; Sidi Mohammed III had taken the ship as a way to induce the United States to enter into a treaty of peace and friendship.[8] The sultan had sent letters eagerly seeking such a treaty but had not received a reply from the Americans, who were preoccupied with negotiations to end the war of independence. Having grown impatient, Sultan Mohammed took the *Betsey* to impress on the United States the urgency of a deal. Mohammed was considered unique among the Barbary rulers as a "man of liberality and spirit."[9] In 1777, Morocco had been the first country to recognize American independence and therefore the most approachable of the Barbary States.[10] But even the most cordial of them had a rather remarkable way of demonstrating friendly intentions.

The captain and crew of the *Betsey* were released to the Spanish minister, who sent them on to Cádiz, where they arrived safely and in good shape on July 19, 1785.[11] Ultimately, American commissioners appointed Thomas Barclay to negotiate with Morocco, and the two states signed a treaty on June 28, 1786, with the helpful intercession of Spain, which was in negotiations with the United States over the Mississippi region.[12] Moroccan agents had been attempting to sign a treaty with the United States since 1782. The treaty with Morocco provided for trade between the two states on equal terms, or a "most favored nation" basis. The treaty also stipulated the rights of the two states as neutrals during naval conflict. During time of war, neither party would join a belligerent against the other. If either party were at war with another nation and seized a prize that contained persons or effects from the other party, the captured seafarers and cargo would be released. The two states also agreed that commercial ships in convoy led by a warship of one party were exempt from the belligerent right of visit and search by the other. The two states pledged to replenish each other's ships in port, extend such courtesies as gun salutes, and respect the sovereign immunity of each other's warships. Ships of neither party would be detained in port "on any pretense whatever," and the American consul was recognized as the authority to adjudicate disputes among American citizens in Morocco.

Signed in Marrakesh, the Moroccan-American Treaty of Friendship is the oldest unbroken treaty of friendship between the United States and another country.[13] The treaty was a favorable and dignified agreement, one that did not require the usual payment of tribute. It established friendly commercial relations and provided that any captives taken during a future conflict were to be treated as prisoners of war rather than enslaved. Relations between Morocco and the United States continued amicably until Morocco was incorporated as a protectorate under French sovereignty in 1912.

— — — — • — — — —

The regency of Algiers, the most powerful of the Barbary States and the most recalcitrant, proved more difficult to placate than Morocco. Less than one year after the *Betsey* was taken, Algiers struck American shipping. On July 25, 1785, Algerine corsairs on board a fourteen-gun xebec, a three-masted vessel, captured the U.S. schooner *Maria* off the coast of St. Vincent, in the Caribbean. The six-man crew of the American ship, which was owned by a Bostonian, was taken hostage. Five days later and less than two hundred miles from Lisbon, Algerine pirates seized the *Dauphin*, which belonged to an American citizen in Philadelphia.[14] The ships and their combined crews of twenty-one persons were held for ransom. The dey of Algiers demanded payment of $59,496 for their safe return.[15]

In a letter to John Jay the following month, Thomas Jefferson insisted the United States had to "preserve an equality of right" to the oceans, including shipping and fishing and "other uses of the sea."[16] While the United States lacked the naval force to send against Algiers, Jefferson was keenly aware of the role of deterrence to prevent aggression at sea, stating that it was in the interest of the United States to punish the first insult, because "an insult unpunished is the parent of many others."

After nearly a year in captivity, the prisoners wrote to Jefferson, who was in Paris, to outline the ransom demanded by Algiers.[17] The letter pleaded persuasively for payment of a sizable ransom and advised against a naval war. Algiers sought to convince the Americans that war would be costly and unsuccessful, that the easiest way to resolve the crisis was tribute. The prisoners underscored that, declaring that "money is the God of Algiers & Mahomet their prophet." Kidnapping for ransom was, in any case, a successful business model. The prevailing price for the return of a hostage was between $1,200 and $2,920 and more than $4,000 for the captain of a ship.[18] In 1786, there were 2,200 American captives in Algiers; three years later, through the attrition of death and release upon payment of ransom, there were only 655.

The United States dithered, unable to come up with such huge sums. The new country still owed large war debts to France. Under the Articles of Confederation, ratified in March 1781, Congress had no means to extract taxes from the constituent states. Several attempts to negotiate the release of the hostages were unsuccessful; because the United States could not meet the price of extortion, the dey declined to sign a peace agreement to forestall future seizures of American vessels.

Writing to John Adams on July 11, 1786, Jefferson "very clearly thought it would be best to effect a peace through the medium of war."[19] Both justice and American honor, Jefferson averred, demanded military action. Only force would "procure respect in Europe." Adams, in London as the U.S. minister to Britain, believed, however, that the United States could not fight Algiers, because a war could prove open-ended, and the American people would not tolerate a long conflict. "To fight them at the expense of millions," he argued, "seems not to be economical." Although Adams generally supported the creation of a navy, he thought that naval force would "make bad worse with the Algerines."[20]

- - - - • - - - -

The Moroccan seizure of the *Betsey* and the capture of the *Maria* and *Dauphin* by Algiers opened a thirty-year American struggle against the Barbary States to protect freedom of navigation in the Mediterranean Sea. Nevertheless, nearly a decade passed before Barbary piracy became a front-page issue again in the United States. The U.S. Constitution, written in 1787–88, replaced the Articles of Confederation on March 4, 1789. John Adams and Thomas Jefferson left London and Paris and returned to the United States, Adams as vice president and Jefferson as secretary of state. The new nation was consumed with growing pains. The greatest debates of the day arose from Secretary of the Treasury Alexander Hamilton's fiscal and debt proposals and from events in Europe, which hampered American shipping.

The independent United States had to develop trading relationships on its own for the first time. Seeking to diversify their trading partners, American merchants sought to expand trade into Europe, especially France.

American leaders promoted a radical notion of unfettered trade, a view that upset the established order of closed mercantilist systems. The United States sought free and liberal trade with all nations.[21] However, the French Revolutionary Wars from 1792 to 1802 and the overlapping Napoleonic Wars from 1799 to 1815 disrupted these hopes.

Despite President Washington's proclamation of U.S. neutrality, French and British warships and privateers found the vast American merchant fleet a tempting target.[22] Neutral ships were legally immune from attack by belligerent states and protected from the effects of war—at least in theory. Operating under the neutral flag of the United States, the American merchant fleet, which handled the carrying trade, was unique in its ability to earn windfall profits during the conflicts. Shipping revenue soared as goods became scarcer in Europe. With numerous states at war, relatively safe carriage on neutral ships was harder to obtain. The burgeoning commercial shipping industry of the United States stepped into the breach and generated huge returns. One 250-ton merchant ship cost $15,000 to $20,000 and had a capacity of about six modern international shipping containers. During the war years, the owners could pay for that ship with the profit from a single voyage. At the same time, however, absent a navy, U.S. ships were at risk of seizure by belligerents in Europe and unprotected from the depredations of North Africa.

— — — — • — — — —

Algerine seizures prompted Congress to approve the Navy Act on March 20, 1794, authorizing funds for the construction of six frigates, which would be ready in two years.[23] The legislation contained a clause that would halt warship construction if the United States reached a peace deal with Algiers. Congress also approved a million dollars "to defray any expenses which may be incurred, in relation to the intercourse between the United States and foreign nations" (i.e., tribute)—nearly half the federal budget for that year.

Meanwhile, negotiations dragged on, and the dey of Algiers raised his ransom to $2 million. Finally, the talks culminated in a humiliating agreement reached on September 5, 1795, requiring the United States to pay about $600,000 in exchange for the return of the American citizens and a treaty of peace.[24] At the eleventh hour, however, the dey raised the stakes once again, insisting on delivery to him personally of presents valued at $200,000 in exchange for the release of the prisoners. The amount included substantial naval stores, such as powder, shot, oak timber, masts, and three completed vessels—a brig and two schooners. These additional demands increased the deal to nearly a million dollars, about 16 percent of the nation's revenue. Although unable to meet the new demands, Congress ratified the treaty on March 6, 1796. At the same time, the Navy Act was revised downward to three ships: the forty-four-gun *United States* and *Constitution* and the thirty-six-gun *Constellation*.

Under the new administration of John Adams, in February 1798 the United States delivered, in partial fulfillment of its treaty obligations with Algiers, the $150,000 frigate *Crescent* and $180,000 schooner *Hamdullah*.[25] The *Crescent* carried thirty-six guns—a mixture of six- and nine-pounders. The nearly $40,000 schooner *Skojoldibrand* and the $4,200 brig *Pasha* were still under construction in the United States.[26] The provision of armaments, cash, and most galling of all, warships was humiliating. Sending completed warships to the Barbary States was not only painful but woefully counter-productive, as they were used to prey on new victims.

Other countries too paid grotesque ransoms. Spain furnished $20,000 and a warship and France provided two warships and $10,000. The United States, having no navy, paid the most.[27] The lavish terms Algiers imposed on the United States provided incentive for the other Barbary States to extort similar arrangements.

Tripoli struck against the United States in August 1796, seizing the *Betsy* (not to be confused with the *Betsey*, taken in 1784) and the *Sophia*. The *Sophia* was released because it carried treaty money owed to the dey of Algiers, but the *Betsy* was converted to war and its crew enslaved. After haggling over ransom, on November 4, 1796, the United States and Tripoli signed a treaty of peace and friendship that was witnessed in Algiers the following year.[28]

In July 1797, a new consul, William Eaton, was appointed to Tunis. Shortly thereafter, the United States and Tunis signed a truce for a period of six months.[29] Tunis extracted $180,000 for this temporary peace. The bey of

Tunis, Hamouda Pasha, signed the agreement as commander of the "frontier post of the Holy War."[30] Even then U.S. problems were not over. The terms of bilateral treaties between the United States and various Barbary powers expired in due course or were otherwise constantly in flux, as the United States generally was unable to meet its payment obligations. The angry Barbary rulers would seek greater concessions as punishment, appreciating that the United States was making enormous profits in the carrying trade.

The demands escalated. In December 1799, the United States agreed to pay Tripoli $18,000 per year to secure the safety of American trade in the Mediterranean Sea. In September 1800, Capt. William Bainbridge arrived at Algiers on board the twenty-four-gun frigate *George Washington* bearing tribute in arrears for Dey Bobba Mustapha. The dey ordered Bainbridge, under threat of war, to deliver the loot to the sultan in Constantinople, which he reluctantly did.[31] On October 19, 1800, the *George Washington*, laden with gifts and a contingent of Algerine officials ("20 gentlemen, 100 negro Turks, 60 Turkish women, two lions, two tygers, four horses, 200 sheep, besides jewels and money"), arrived in Constantinople.[32] Bainbridge was beside himself, writing "none can express but those who feels [*sic*] it," at having to deliver, in a U.S. frigate, extortion money in fealty to the sultan.[33]

Running for president in the election of 1800 against the Federalist incumbent John Adams, Vice President Thomas Jefferson bemoaned the indignity at the hands of the Barbary States and the dishonor of American ships "subjected to the spoliations of foreign cruisers."[34] In spite of its respectable, if modest, frigate navy, the United States was still compelled to pay huge sums to the "petty tyrant" of Algiers.

— — — ● — — —

Jefferson won the election of 1800 and was sworn into office on February 17, 1801. The change of administration presaged a new approach to contending with the Barbary States: Jefferson pledged to use force to put an end to the extortion. Less than two weeks after taking power, Jefferson was faced with his first opportunity to change course. The new president had argued for years that payment of tribute was not only an insufferable disgrace but in the long run bound to be costlier than fighting. "I am an enemy to all these douceurs, tributes and humiliations," he declared to James Madison, "I know that nothing will stop the eternal increase from these pirates but the presence of an armed force."[35]

During the previous summer, the eighteen-gun Tripolitan warship *Tripolino* had captured the U.S. brig *Catherine*, which was bound for the coast of Tuscany. The pasha released the crew in October 1800 but then became incensed when he learned that he was receiving less in annual tribute from the Americans than was Algiers. Tripoli threatened to declare war on the United States if it did not increase its annual payments. On February 26, 1801, the United States refused the new demand, and on March 14 Tripoli declared war, chopping down the flagstaff at the American consulate.[36]

Jefferson inherited a nascent navy, one that was becoming a force to be reckoned with. Although it could not hope to match the massive seventy-four-gun ships of the line of the major European powers, its smaller, faster frigates could flee if necessary. They were heavily armed compared to European frigates and plainly outgunned the Barbary fleets. The original U.S. Navy was a constabulary force, ideally suited to this kind of war.

On May 20, 1801, as commander in chief, Jefferson ordered a squadron to patrol the Mediterranean Sea and become "acquainted with the coasts & Harbors . . . where their services in all probability will frequently be required."[37] Upon arrival in the Mediterranean, should one or more of the Barbary powers be found to have declared war on the United States, the American commander was to distribute his forces "so as best to protect our commerce & chastise their insolence." On the other hand, the rules of engagement were entirely defensive, requiring "rigorous moderation" in all interactions at sea. The U.S. squadron was instructed to maintain the "suppression of all passions which might lead to the commitment of our peace or our honor."

The squadron got under way in early June 1801, under the command of Commo. Richard Dale. The group consisted of the forty-four-gun frigate *President*, the thirty-six-gun *Philadelphia*, commanded by Capt. Samuel Barron, the thirty-two-gun *Essex*, under Captain Bainbridge, and the twelve-gun schooner *Enterprise*, commanded by Lt. Andrew Sterett. Upon arrival at Gibraltar on June 30, 1801, Commodore Dale learned that the pasha of Tripoli had declared war on the United States.[38] Tripoli had seized five U.S. merchant ships, and the American consul fled to Tunis.[39] Dale ordered the *Philadelphia* to approach Tripoli and search for enemy vessels, keeping far enough away from the harbor so as not to constitute a blockade, which would be an act of war.[40] The remainder of the squadron split to convoy the numerous U.S. vessels sprinkled throughout the region. The *Enterprise* was ordered to the British territory of Malta to take on fresh water.[41]

On the return voyage from Valletta on August 1, 1801, the *Enterprise* lured a Tripolitan ship, the *Tripoli*, by deceptively flying the Union Jack. The *Tripoli* hailed the *Enterprise* thinking it was a British ship and said it was searching for American merchant vessels, upon which the *Enterprise* closed in and engaged. The glaring contrast in skill between the American and Tripolitan crews was palpable. The *Enterprise* prevailed in America's first victory at sea.

During those three hours the *Tripoli* had stricken its colors three times to feign surrender and draw the Americans above deck where they could be cut down by sharpshooters, but finally the ship was vanquished.[42] The ship's guns were thrown overboard, and it was stripped and left as a floating wreck; the *Enterprise*'s orders did not permit the taking of prizes, since there had been no congressional declaration of war.

The *Enterprise*'s victory helped bolster support for Jefferson's actions. On February 6, 1802, Congress adopted legislation authorizing the president "fully to equip, officer, man, and employ such of the armed vessels of the United States as may be judged requisite . . . for protecting effectually the commerce and seamen thereof on the Atlantic Ocean, the Mediterranean and adjoining seas."[43] The act also empowered the president to initiate "acts of precaution or hostility as the state of war will justify, and may, in his opinion, require."

Commodore Dale sailed back to Norfolk, Virginia, in April 1802, leaving behind the other ships in the squadron to maintain pressure on Tripoli. Command in the Mediterranean transferred to the politically connected

Richard Valentine Morris. Morris departed from Hampton Roads on April 27, 1802, on board the thirty-eight-gun frigate *Chesapeake*. His voyage was to be ignominious, and a frustrated Jefferson would recall Morris eighteen months later. This second squadron was more powerful than Dale's—mounting 180 guns instead of 126—but Morris was less successful than his predecessor. He exercised poor judgment from the start and never operated with the sense of mission or urgency appropriate to a war footing. Morris spent a lackadaisical summer, first in Gibraltar, socializing with Royal Navy officers, and then touring Italian, French, and Spanish ports. The lack of vigor with which Morris prosecuted the war against Tripoli led William Eaton, the long-serving American consul, to write to Secretary of State James Madison in September 1802 that American warships had "totally abandoned" the coast of Tripoli. "Thus ends the expedition of 1802!"[44]

Finally making his way to Porto Farina (present-day Ghar al Milh), Tunis, in the spring of 1803, Morris went ashore to consult with Eaton. Attempting to return to the *Chesapeake*, however, Morris and his companion Capt. John Rodgers were taken hostage for affronting the dey by failing to offer a customary farewell salutation and gift. Morris was released only upon payment to compensate for the slight; the required $34,000 was cobbled together from Morris' personal funds and by issuance of a public bond.[45]

From Tunis, Morris headed to Tripoli, where he arrived on May 22, 1803—more than one year after he began his deployment.[46] The U.S. squadron had been maintaining the loose blockade against Tripoli. In early June, U.S. warships set upon a flotilla of ten small craft carrying some twenty-five tons of wheat in a bay thirty-five miles northwest of Tripoli. Trapped along the shore, the entire group was wiped out.[47] Except for this interception, however, neither the blockade nor Morris' efforts to negotiate a treaty with the Tripolitans bore success.

Morris withdrew to Gibraltar, only to learn that President Jefferson had replaced him with William Eaton. Later, a board of inquiry would charge that Morris "did not conduct himself, in his command of the Mediterranean squadron, with the diligence or activity necessary to execute the important duties of his station; but that he is censurable for his inactive and dilatory conduct of the squadron under his command."[48] The tribunal concluded that Morris "might have acquitted himself well in the command of a single ship . . . but he was not competent to the command of a squadron."

— — — — • — — — —

Jefferson was eager to recover the initiative in the Tripoli war, lost by Morris' "two years' sleep."[49] A third squadron was ordered to the Mediterranean Sea, this time under the leadership of Commo. Edward Preble. The squadron comprised seven ships, including the forty-four-gun *Constitution*, the thirty-six-gun *Philadelphia* (under command of Captain Bainbridge), the sixteen-gun brigs *Argus* (commanded by Lt. Isaac Hull) and *Siren* (under Lt. Charles Stewart), and three twelve-gun schooners (the *Enterprise*, *Nautilus*, and *Vixen*). The ships reached Gibraltar on September 12, 1803.[50]

The American squadron took up a position outside Tripoli harbor to blockade the port. The *Philadelphia* arrived on October 7, 1803.[51] Early in the morning of October 31, the ship approached the shore in chase of a corsair vessel attempting to break the blockade and, about 11:30 a.m., ran aground on an uncharted reef.[52] The *Philadelphia* held fast in twelve feet of water about one and a half miles from land. In an attempt to reduce the ship's weight and draft, anchors were cut away, the hold was pumped, and heavy articles thrown over the side, but it did not refloat. The tide heeled over the *Philadelphia* so badly that its guns could not be brought to bear on the Tripolitan gunboats that, attracted by the spectacle, began a steady fire.[53]

Orders were then given to destroy everything of value, and the gunner was instructed to turn the seacock that flooded the magazine and to secure the key.[54] Captain Bainbridge struck the colors, "as no hopes remained of saving the ship and no possible means of defending her."[55] Bainbridge later explained that the decision to yield was unanimous among the officers, given the futility of exposing men to a situation "where neither perseverance nor fortitude would be of any benefit to our Country or ourselves."[56] The crew drilled holes in the bottom to flood the ship, dampened the gunpowder, and threw the guns over the side. At sundown, the Tripolitans took possession of the ship and stopped the water pouring into the hull. The entire complement of officers and crew was taken from the ship and enslaved. Bainbridge wrote a letter, the "most distressing of my life," to inform the Secretary of the Navy with "deepest regret" that the ship had been lost.[57] Tripolitan harbor boats swarmed around the grounded vessel, stripping it of anything of value. Thanks to strong winds and a storm surge on the following day, as well as the carpentry of fifty of the enslaved crew who had been brought back under guard, the *Philadelphia* was refloated. Eventually, Tripoli even raised the cannon that had been thrown overboard.

Less than four months later, the *Philadelphia* was a raging inferno. Lt. Stephen Decatur was ordered to enter the harbor at night and destroy the ship.[58] On February 16, 1804, he placed a force on the *Intrepid*, a seventy-ton Tripolitan ketch originally named *Mastico* that had been captured as prize by the *Enterprise* and towed to Malta. For this mission the *Intrepid* had been rigged in Mediterranean style to deceive the Tripolitans, and an Arabic-speaking Sicilian pilot, Salvador Catalano, was on deck and dressed in Turkish fashion. Under cover of darkness, the boarding party hidden below deck, the *Intrepid* sneaked into Tripoli Harbor and approached the *Philadelphia*, which lay at anchor. The pilot of the *Intrepid* hailed the warship for permission to tie up for the night.

As soon as the *Intrepid* drew alongside, however, Decatur's men leaped from hiding, stormed the *Philadelphia*, and recaptured it. Unable to sail the recaptured ship because it had lost its foremast, the Americans set charges and set it ablaze. Soon the frigate was an inferno, burning to the waterline and drifting aimlessly in front of the pasha's seaside castle. As a poetic parting shot, the *Philadelphia*'s guns, still loaded and heated by the fire, went off in a broadside, striking the fort.

The operation was an immense success. Lieutenant Decatur reported to Capt. Edward Preble: "I boarded her with sixty men and officers leaving a guard onboard the ketch for her defense; and it is with the greatest pleasure that I inform you that I had not a man killed in this affair, and but one only slightly wounded . . . and as each of their conduct was so highly meritorious."[59] When he heard about the feat, British admiral Horatio Lord Nelson remarked that, if true, it was the most "bold and daring act of the age."[60]

Congress promoted Decatur to the rank of captain—the youngest officer in the U.S. Navy ever to hold that rank. In Tunis, the American chargé d'affaires wrote to Tobias Lear, U.S. consul in Algiers, that the destruction of the *Philadelphia* had "made much noise in Tunis, and is the only occasion on which I have heard our Countrymen spoken of with due respect."[61] Yusuf Karamanli, the pasha of Tripoli, began to bargain for a truce. Preble kept up the pressure.

— — — — • — — — —

On August 3, 1804, the U.S. squadron launched a fierce attack against the walls of Tripoli and the ships in the harbor.[62] Captain Decatur led six gunboats into the harbor and engaged nineteen Tripolitan gunboats, a brig, two schooners, and a galley.[63] The enemy fleet was defeated, three of their best craft taken by force and one sunk. During the rout of Tripoli's forces, James Decatur, Stephen's brother, was killed, shot in the head while leaping on board an enemy boat to accept its surrender. Stephen Decatur was enraged at the perfidy and immediately went after the Tripolitan gunboat. He and his men boarded the ship and a melee ensued, and Decatur narrowly missed death when a blow at his head was taken instead by a wounded sailor, Reuben James. James had lost the use of both of his arms from battle injuries yet stepped in front of the descending sword and blocked it with his head, saving Decatur by unsurpassed heroism and self-sacrifice.[64] Decatur struggled on the ground with his opponent. Finally, the American officer pulled a pistol from his sash and shot the Tripolitan dead.

The squadron attacked again on August 7. The next day, the pasha made overtures through the French consul. He suggested the release of American prisoners, mostly taken from the *Philadelphia*, and reduced his demand to $150,000 from $500,000.[65] Instead, Commodore Preble offered the pasha a "gift" of $20,000, which was rejected. Attacks resumed on the nights of August 24–25, the twenty-eighth, and on September 3.[66] On the latter night, the ketch *Intrepid* was packed with explosives—a hundred barrels of powder and 150 shells—and sent into the harbor as a fireship.[67] The vessel attracted fire from the shore, however, and was apparently met by Tripolitan gunboats. The fireship blew up prematurely, killing the sailors on board—who had probably detonated it when they were discovered.[68] A crewman on the *Nautilus*, which had followed the *Intrepid* to pick up its crew after they had positioned it, recounted that the fireball was an "awful explosion."[69] Against the black sky, "for a moment, the flash illuminated the whole heavens around, while the terrific concussion shook everything far and near. Then all was hushed again and every object veiled in a darkness of double gloom." The gun batteries of Tripoli fell silent, and shrieking was heard in the town. In the morning, it became evident that the fireship had destroyed a number of Tripolitan boats and caused damage on the shore.[70]

At this point the Americans believed that Tripoli had been reduced to its "last extremity," but the besieged city-state continued to resist, and the U.S. squadron awaited reinforcements.[71] Preble had spent the summer blockading and bombarding Tripoli, while awaiting a more powerful force with which to achieve a decisive victory. The perseverance of the Americans impressed European officials, who initially had discounted their effort.

A fourth squadron, led by Commo. Samuel Barron, now arrived to continue the naval operations begun under Preble. Here were the new forces needed to prosecute the war to conclusion, but Barron assumed theater command, as he was senior to Preble. The combined force was the most powerful American squadron ever assembled to that date and was well positioned to achieve victory. Barron, however, was unwell, and would remain so throughout his time in the Mediterranean. He would bring the war to an end, but less conclusively than Preble had envisioned. The squadron now spent much of its time in Malta, leaving four or five vessels on station off Tripoli, or showing the flag in other Barbary ports to dissuade their rulers from joining the fray against the Americans. Barron's illness likely caused him to negotiate a less satisfying peace than might have been achieved.[72] The commodore did, however, support one of the most intriguing operations in the annals of U.S. military history. William Eaton, a former Army captain who was still consul in Tunis, now styled an agent for the Barbary Regencies, accompanied Barron. President Jefferson had authorized Eaton to conduct an auspicious special operation aimed at regime change in Tripoli.

– – – – •– – – –

Yusuf Pasha, the third son of Ali Karamanli, had murdered his eldest brother, Hassan, and seized the throne. Hamet Karamanli, the middle brother, was, as the older, the lawful heir to Ali under the laws of primogeniture, but Yusuf deposed him in 1793. Two years later, Yusuf cast Hamet out of the kingdom and kept his wife and children as prisoners. Hamet wrote to President Jefferson, offering to make a deal: American military assistance in gaining power in Tripoli in exchange for peaceful relations. William Eaton made his way to Egypt on board the brig *Argus* to meet Hamet, who was involved in a Mameluke insurrection against Ottoman Turkish rule. Eaton traveled with his party down the Nile Delta in Lower Egypt in two forty-ton river schooners, searching for Hamet near Cairo.

The *Argus*, under command of Isaac Hull, now promoted to the rank of master commandant, waited for Eaton in the Bay of Abu Qir, between the town of Abu Qir and the Rosetta mouth of the Nile. Hamet was holed up in Minyeh in Upper Egypt with three thousand Mameluke soldiers, surrounded by eight thousand Albanian mercenaries and Levantine Turks.[73] On February 23, 1805, Eaton and Hamet signed a contract, which was forwarded to Secretary of State Madison.[74] The agreement stipulated that Eaton was the commander of the expedition to aid Hamet Pasha, ostensibly to overthrow Yusuf and install Hamet on the throne in Tripoli. The Senate never ratified the treaty, however, and it is unclear whether Eaton was acting beyond his authority. The agreement also specified that the United States would provide money, ammunition, and provisions, which Eaton estimated would be $20,000. The agreement launched one of the most amazing military expeditions in U.S. military history. Gathering in Alexandria on March 8, 1805, the total force, about five hundred men, included Hamet's Egyptian mercenaries, a handful of loyalists, eight U.S. Marines, and two Navy midshipmen. There were also forty Greeks, about 160 Turks, and two to three hundred Arab or Berber mercenaries, and others. This motley host set off across five hundred miles of North African desert to conquer Derna.

Along the way, the expedition contended with starvation and mutinous Arab factions. On April 15, at the Gulf of Bomba, some forty miles from

Derna, the army was met and provisioned by the *Argus*. After the resupply, fire from the *Argus*, *Nautilus*, and *Hornet* supported the advance on Derna. Eaton's forces attacked and took the city on April 27, 1805. U.S. Marine Corps 1st Lt. Presley O'Bannon led the Marines and a landing force from the ships, while Hamet's men attacked from the land. Derna was captured with few casualties. Eaton and two Marines were wounded, and one Marine died in the fighting.

When Derna fell before the combined amphibious and ground attack on April 27, 1805, O'Bannon raised the American flag over its walls—the first time the U.S. flag had flown over a conquered foreign city. After the battle, Eaton and his forces quickly made ready to head for Benghazi, some two hundred miles farther westward along the coast. Six hundred miles beyond Benghazi lay Tripoli and the pasha. By this time, the pasha had become alarmed that the U.S. force—a Navy squadron offshore and the ground invasion closing in—might actually threaten his rule. Eaton offered peace terms through the Spanish consul at Tripoli.

Meanwhile, on May 22, 1805, Commodore Barron had resigned due to ill health, and command of the squadron had passed to Capt. John Rodgers. Consul General Tobias Lear, dispatched from Malta to Tripoli to negotiate terms of peace, signed an agreement with Pasha Yusuf on June 3, 1805. The United States agreed to supplement an exchange of prisoners with a $60,000 payment—$140,000 less than demanded by the pasha.[75] The treaty required the pasha to "deliver up to the American squadron now off Tripoli, all the Americans in his possession." About three hundred American prisoners were exchanged for Tripolitan subjects held by American forces. Article III committed the United States to evacuate Derna and "persuade Hamet to withdraw" from Tripolitan territory in exchange for freedom for his wife and children.

Eaton and the Federalists were dismayed that Jefferson stopped short of overthrowing Yusuf, suggesting that Lear had negotiated prematurely. The president explained, however, that he had never authorized an actual land attack on Tripoli, with either American troops or Hamet's proxy forces.[76] In response to Eaton's claim that Barron had rendered "verbal instructions" to commit the United States to installing Hamet, Jefferson said such action would have been "entirely unauthorized, so far beyond our views, & so onerous, and could not be sanctioned by our government."[77] The importance of the treaty, however, lay not in the internecine disputes of the ruling house of a North African principality but the right of free navigation it secured for American ships. The United States, for the first time, had conducted a ground war on foreign soil and threatened to overthrow a standing government, all in order to vindicate maritime rights.

The Napoleonic Wars still raged on the Continent, and Britain remained dominant at sea. U.S. naval power had been decisive against individual Barbary powers, but it was dwarfed by British sea power. Commodore Preble had a squadron mounting 150 guns to blockade Tripoli. In contrast, Lord Nelson commanded a fleet with some 900 guns when he engaged the French fleet at the Battle of the Nile in 1798.[78] In the Battle of Trafalgar fought in 1805 off Cádiz, Spain, Nelson defeated a Franco-Spanish fleet that boasted 2,640 guns.[79] The British blockade of France markedly hampered maritime traffic in the Mediterranean.

— — — — • — — —

The aggravation of Barbary attacks on American shipping was to come to a stop only after the United States fought a second Barbary War, which began at the end of the War of 1812. Tobias Lear first arrived in Algiers as American consul in November 1805. Haji Ali ben Khrelil expelled him on July 25, 1812. By then, Dey Ali was looking to renege on the 1795 treaty with the Americans.[80] At the same time, he rejected the annual American tribute as too low, especially given the passage of years. Ali demanded an immediate cash payment. On the day Lear was expelled, Algerine corsairs captured the unarmed U.S.-flagged brig *Edwin*.

In the final two years of the Jefferson administration, Algiers had captured the *Eagle* of New York, the *Violet*, which was a brig out of Boston, and the *Mary Ann*, a schooner from New York. The *Mary Ann* incident was particularly interesting: after Algiers fighters subdued the ship and installed a prize crew on board, the American crew overpowered the captors and escaped. The dey was outraged and compelled Lear to pay $16,000 in reparations for the *Mary Ann*'s prize crew or be imprisoned.

James Madison, who had been sworn into office on March 5, 1809, was absorbed in the War of 1812 and could do little to confront Algiers. The dey collaborated with the British to time his severance of diplomatic relations with the United States with the start of the War of 1812. Whitehall assured Dey Ali that as the "two strongest naval powers in the Mediterranean," Algiers and Britain would act in concert against the Americans.[81] The Royal Navy maintained an effective blockade of the Atlantic seaboard of the United States, greatly reducing U.S. Mediterranean commerce and keeping American warships in port. The war with Britain ended with the Treaty of Ghent, signed on December 24, 1814—and just months later the United States was at war again with Algiers.[82] On February 23, 1815, President Madison sent a message to Congress requesting a declaration of war on Algiers. Congress complied on March 3.

Commodore Bainbridge and Commodore Decatur each outfitted a squadron to prosecute the war. The squadron led by Decatur was ready first, and it got under way from New York in May. Decatur sailed on board the forty-four-gun frigate *Guerriere*, accompanied by the thirty-eight-gun *Macedonian* and the thirty-six-gun *Constellation*, the sloops *Epervier* (eighteen guns) and *Ontario* (sixteen), three fourteen-gun brigs, and two twelve-gun schooners. (The *Guerriere* was a new ship, launched the year before and named after the HMS *Guerrière*, a thirty-eight-gun frigate defeated by the *Constitution* during an engagement about four hundred miles off the coast of Nova Scotia on August 19, 1812.)

Passing Gibraltar on June 15, Decatur's squadron entered the Mediterranean Sea. On the morning of June 17, 1815, the *Constellation* sighted the forty-six-gun Algerine warship *Mashouda* off the coast of Cape Gata, Spain, and began to fire on it. The *Guerriere* closed alongside the *Mashouda* and fired a broadside.[83] Forty-two-pound shot from the *Guerriere*'s carronades swept the deck and killed the Algerine captain, Raïs Hamidou. The *Epervier* joined the fray, firing broadsides into the *Mashouda*. The Algerine ship turned into the wind and surrendered. The *Guerriere* had lost one sailor killed and three wounded to sharpshooters in the *Mashouda*'s rigging, and three others had died and seven were wounded when a gun burst. The Americans took 406 prisoners and the Algerine warship as a prize. Two days later, Decatur's squadron pursued the Algerine twenty-two-gun *Estedio* off Cape Palos and ran it aground. Only one small boatload of the *Estedio*'s crew escaped to shore; the remaining eighty members of the crew surrendered.

William Shaler, who had been appointed consul general for the Barbary States and was eventually to reside in Algiers, was with Decatur on board the *Guerriere*. The U.S. squadron arrived off Algiers on June 28 and set a blockade. Speaking through the Swedish consul, Decatur offered to negotiate a settlement. Decatur, who had already taken two Algerine warships and captured hundreds of prisoners of war, pressed his advantage. Hoisting a white flag and Swedish colors, the *Guerriere* approached the city. A letter from President Madison dated April 12 was delivered to Dey Omar Agha. (On April 7, Dey Omar had succeeded Mohamed Kharnadji, who was in office for only seventeen days after succeeding Dey Ali.) In it Madison stated that the United States had declared war on Algiers but that a negotiated peace could be "founded on stipulations equally beneficial to both parties." Another letter, this one from Decatur and Shaler and signed on June 29, warned Dey Omar that they would "treat upon no other principle than that of perfect equality."[84] The United States would accept terms only on the basis of "most favored nation," and it would not agree to pay tribute "under any form whatever." Decatur also insisted that discussions for peace, which began on June 30, be conducted on board the *Guerriere*, where he would have the psychological edge.

The American terms were reluctantly accepted on July 3, 1815.[85] First, all ten American captives held by Algiers would be released. Second, the United States would, in turn, release the hundreds of prisoners of war it held. Third, the dey would compensate the United States $10,000 for the ship *Edwin* and other property seized by Algiers. Fourth, the dey agreed that in the event of future hostilities, all American captives would be treated humanely as prisoners of war and not forced into slavery.

Decatur reported on July 5, 1815, to the Secretary of the Navy that peace "has been dictated at the mouths of our cannon."[86] Remarkably, the treaty had been "concluded less than six weeks after the departure of the squadron from New York."[87] The U.S. Navy had had surprising success in frigate engagements against the Royal Navy during the War of 1812, and the new victory against Algiers heightened its growing reputation. The Senate ratified Decatur's treaty with Algiers on December 5, 1815. At the time, the treaty was the most favorable agreement ever reached between a Western nation and a Barbary State, and it set the stage for the demise of Barbary piracy.

Having defeated the most powerful of the Barbary States, Decatur sailed to Tunis and Tripoli and obtained similar agreements. In Tunis, Decatur demanded, and was paid, $46,000 for two British vessels originally taken as prizes by an American privateer but later seized by Mahmud, dey. From Tunis Decatur sailed to Tripoli, arriving on August 5, 1815. Pasha Yusuf had just learned of the American victory at Algiers. Decatur demanded $30,000 in compensation for two prizes given up to the British. The American consul suggested that their combined value was actually only $25,000; Decatur accepted the lower figure, on condition of the release of ten Westerners, Danes and a Sicilian family, held prisoner by Pasha Yusuf. The *Guerriere* set sail from Tripoli on August 9, 1815. Decatur steered for home, reaching the Strait of Gibraltar on October 6, in time to pass Commodore Bainbridge's squadron entering the Mediterranean. Bainbridge had left Boston on July 3, and his squadron included the seventy-four-gun *Independence*, the first American ship of the line. The appearance in Algiers, Tripoli, and Tunis of a second, even more powerful squadron soon after the *Guerriere* had a salutary effect on the Barbary powers.

One year after having signed the agreement with the United States, Dey Omar Agha of Algiers repudiated the peace and once again began enslaving Christians. After British and Dutch naval forces briefly bombarded Algiers on August 27, 1816, Omar relented. U.S. commissioner William Shaler concluded negotiations on a second treaty of peace with Algiers on December 23, 1816. The dey, forced to yield, begged Shaler for a certificate stipulating that the treaty had been imposed on him under duress.[88] This statement may have prolonged the ruler's life by a few months, but like his predecessors he was assassinated. In September 1817, after another humiliating defeat—this time by the Royal Navy—Dey Omar was killed in a power struggle with his janissaries.

— — — ● — — —

As would be the case in future conflicts over freedom of navigation, the United States was reluctant to wage the Barbary Wars. The liberal concept of freedom of the seas infused the philosophy and sense of justice of early American leaders. But these men, no matter what political inclination or factional stripe, also possessed what today would be considered an uncanny patriotism, "America First," best captured by the famous toast of Stephen Decatur in 1816: "Our Country! In her intercourse with foreign nations may she always be in the right; but right or wrong, our country!"[89]

"FREE TRADE AND SAILOR'S RIGHTS"

The War of 1812 (1812–14)

The War of 1812 was a direct consequence of the U.S. position within the Anglo-French rivalry in Europe, and the ensuing wars on the Continent were fought against the backdrop of the mercantilist system. Under the imperial mercantilist economic system prevalent from the fifteenth to the twentieth century, the mother country oversaw access to trade with its dependent colonies. These monopolies kept the colony dependent on the mother country, while protecting home industry against unregulated competition. After the American Revolutionary War, the United States was thrust outside the English colonial system and therefore had the freedom to trade with other states, but at the same time it lost preferential access to the British market and the protection of the Royal Navy. The Founding Fathers were products of the Enlightenment and Anglo-Saxon liberalism; now they fashioned a new republican ideology based on unfettered trade. These new ideas challenged the existing order, setting up a clash of American peacetime values and Old World wartime strategy.

The hub-and-spoke system of mercantilism was particularly damaging to the American economy, since it prevented Americans from trading lawfully with British or French possessions in the West Indies, even though they were close to American ports and markets. Even in time of peace, mother countries often looked the other way, permitting U.S. carrying trade directly with their colonies, as well as smuggling. Once war erupted in Europe, a closed economic system was less beneficial to the mother country—particularly France, which was continually under British blockade. During wartime, merchant shipping between France and its colonies was at risk of capture by the Royal Navy and condemnation in British ports, so France formally opened its carrying trade to neutral ships.

Trade by neutral states was protected by the law of nations. Under long-standing law of naval warfare, ships from neutral states could claim immunity from capture as prizes so long as they were not carrying contraband to a belligerent state. The United States was the greatest beneficiary, as it had a large and sophisticated shipping fleet and maritime industry, and it lay along the routes from the West Indies to Europe. By inserting itself into the carrying trade, however, American shipping faced unique challenges that tested the strategic, political, and legal dimensions of neutrality in the Napoleonic Wars. Yet in the decades leading up to the War of 1812, the United States had neither a navy nor a coherent naval policy by which to navigate the new seascape.[1]

Since the Revolutionary War period, the United States had hoped to ride the crest of a movement toward reawakened neutral rights, but its plans were undermined by European power politics. The devastating conflicts of the French Revolutionary Wars from 1792 to 1802 and the Napoleonic Wars from 1803 to 1815 pitted France against a shifting coalition of powerful adversaries, especially Britain. Both European powers routinely encroached on American neutral rights and hampered American commercial trade, leaving the two American political parties grappling with how to respond.

As the world's dominant maritime power and a key member of the coalitions, in both conflicts Britain blockaded France and its allies on the Continent. Cut off from its colonies, France opened the carrying trade to American shipping. Markets in continental Europe were especially attractive to American merchant shipping because wartime scarcity of goods there had brought high inflation and meant windfall profits. As the leading neutral maritime state, the United States gained handsomely from the carrying trade. Leveraging its status as a neutral state and bolstering its commercial fleet by high import duties on goods delivered in foreign hulls, the United States saw its merchant fleet capacity expand rapidly from 1789 to 1810 (see table 1). The British believed that U.S. merchant ships supported the commerce of its enemy and thereby acquired enemy character.

U.S. aspirations toward a liberal maritime regime were to run headlong into the British "Rule of 1756."[2] The two decades of the French Revolutionary Wars and Napoleonic Wars were marked by contending proclamations by which Britain and France sought to disrupt the commerce of each other. These competing wartime policies concerned blockade, contraband, freedom of navigation for neutral shipping, and the fate of a vessel captured as a prize. Britain having the more powerful navy, its orders and actions had a greater impact than France's on neutral shipping, particularly that of the United States. On June 8, 1793, Britain issued a retaliatory Order in Council that permitted seizure of all cargoes bound for France or blockaded ports allied with France. On November 6, Britain refined the order to authorize the seizure of any vessel involved in the French carrying trade. Six months after the original order, on January 8,

TABLE 1. EXPANSION OF U.S. MERCHANT FLEET, 1789–1810

Year	U.S. Fleet Tonnage	Percentage of U.S. Overseas Trade Carried on U.S. Ships
1789	123,893	23
1790	346,254	40
1791	363,110	55
1800	667,107	89
1810	981,019	91

Source: Winthrop L. Marvin, "The American Merchant Marine," *American Monthly Review of Reviews* 21 (January–June 1900): 320.

1794, the policy was modified to apply only to direct colonial trade with Europe, thereby permitting trade between French colonies in the West Indies and the United States.

This provision directly interfered with neutral rights and in effect resurrected the Rule of 1756. The Rule of 1756, a vestige of the Seven Years' War (1756–63), stipulated that Britain would neither trade with any neutral nation that also traded with its enemy nor open any new trading routes during wartime. That is, neutral states prohibited from colonial carrying trade during peacetime would also be prohibited during wartime. Thus, by the rule, France could not break voyages with stops in American ports to maintain trade links with its colonies. When France and Britain clashed again during the French Revolutionary and Napoleonic Wars, the United States was added to the equation. France invited neutral American ships to carry trade to and from its Caribbean colonies, reaping the benefits of participating in France's exclusive market. To do so, the United States rejected the legality of the Rule of 1756 generally, arguing that the principle had never entered into accepted customary law and that even if it had it was now obsolete.[3]

Like France during the Seven Years' War, the Americans now tried to circumvent the Rule of 1756 through broken voyages. The Americans had a system of "drawbacks" to evade U.S. customs duties on broken voyages. American merchants would carry goods from France or its Spanish allies to a port in the United States, where they would be off-loaded, inspected by U.S. customs, and then reloaded, often onto the same ship, which would continue on to a Spanish or French colony in the West Indies, such as Cuba. Often the vessel would then make the same trip in reverse, with another intermediate stop in the United States.

The ship's master would pay the U.S. import duty, but much of it would be refunded, in a "drawback," on the grounds that the goods did not actually enter the stream of American commerce. The theory was that the circular route (from France to the United States to the French West Indies and back to the United States and on to France again), carriage in free American hulls, and off-loading (and reloading) in neutral American ports cleansed

French goods of their belligerent character. The United States and France viewed each leg of the voyage as a separate transaction, by which reasoning the goods were protected under American neutrality and inviolable by the Royal Navy.

The doctrine of "continuous voyage" countered broken voyages. In Britain's view, regardless of how the cargo was transferred or routed, its passage constituted a single continuous voyage. The theory was that by assisting the belligerent during wartime, the neutral state was abandoning neutrality and subjecting its ships to capture and condemnation as prizes of war. In other words, the Rule of 1756 made a distinction between trading *with* the enemy, which neutrals could lawfully do, and trading *for* the enemy, which they could not. British orders were refined again on January 25, 1798, to allow neutral ships to carry goods from French, Spanish, or Dutch colonies to England or to neutral ports in the United States or Europe.

– – – – • – – – –

The High Court of Admiralty dismantled the doctrine of broken voyage in the *Essex* case, which was decided on appeal.[4] The case involved the American brig *Essex*, which in 1799 had sailed with a full load of wine from Barcelona for the Spanish colony of Cuba. Along the way the brig called at Salem, Massachusetts, where the goods were off-loaded and immediately reloaded for Havana. That is, the ship was conducting a broken voyage between Barcelona and Havana, with a stop in Salem to circumvent the Rule of 1756.

The *Essex* was intercepted by the British privateer *Favourite* and taken to the British prize court in the Bahamas. The court held that the *Essex* had been in fact on a single "continuous voyage" from Spain to Cuba, despite the layover, and therefore subject to capture and condemnation as a prize. The stop in Salem had been made "solely to color the true purpose" of the voyage to Spain; the asserted destination was "falsified by the evidence." After the *Essex* decision, the British began to crack down. The United States felt stung by what it perceived as violations of its neutral rights and sovereignty at sea. The real object of British policy, however, was France.

The Royal Navy smashed French and Spanish naval forces at Trafalgar on October 21, 1805, and made Britain the unchallenged global sea power. Less than six weeks later, Napoleon destroyed Austrian and Russian armies at Austerlitz and made France the dominant land power. To bring its sea power more effectively to bear to strangle Napoleon's continental fortress, on April 8, 1806, Britain blockaded shipping from the rivers Ems, Weser, and Elbe, flowing into the North Sea, and the Trave, flowing into the Baltic Sea. The blockade was expanded on May 16, 1806, to extend 1,500 kilometers from the Elbe, west of Hamburg on the North Sea, to Brest, France. On November 21, Napoleon responded by issuing the Berlin Decree, which declared England to be under blockade by France and established the "Continental System."[5] Even neutral ships carrying British goods were barred from European ports. Ships that attempted to break the decree were subject to capture. Any vessel coming from England or the English colonies was subject to seizure. Every vessel that was found to have violated the decree was subject to condemnation. France lacked the means to enforce the decree completely, but Napoleon could close the ports of continental Europe to British shipping.

In November 1807, another Order in Council required all shipping to the Continent to pass first through a British port. Britain was still dependent on trade with Europe. Accordingly, the Orders in Council permitted neutral vessels to trade with the Continent if they first stopped at British ports, paid customs duties, and were issued licenses. By this scheme, Britain would be the entrepôt, or point of deposit, through which all ocean commerce must pass. Furthermore, some British merchants were granted exemptions from the restrictions that applied to neutral ships. James Madison complained that the Orders in Council were motivated by pure mercantilism, converting a war measure to enforce belligerent rights into an unlawful monopoly privilege.[6] For his part, one month later, on December 17, 1807, Napoleon issued the Milan Decree to strengthen the Continental System. The Milan Decree stated flatly that no European state could trade with Britain.

These dueling orders severely undercut American neutral rights and the advantages enjoyed by the largest neutral-flagged carrier. From 1803 until the issuance of the Orders in Council in 1807, Britain captured some 528 U.S.-flagged ships, and France seized 206 from 1803 until the Berlin Decree of 1806.[7] The United States was caught in the middle, but it was the impressment of sailors from American ships that most incensed American public opinion.

— — — — • — — — —

The deplorable reputation of roaming press gangs searching for crews to fill the ranks of the Royal Navy is well deserved. In 1770, the lord mayor of London complained to the Board of Admiralty that the city's economy was being disrupted, that tradesmen and servants were being whisked off to naval service in large numbers.[8] The issue was especially inflammatory in the United States because it coupled insult to national identity with the trampling of the plebeian rights, of the agency and autonomy, of individual sailors. American colonialists had once rioted over impressment by the Royal Navy, and the practice continued to galvanize and radicalize the waterfront.[9]

In 1810, the Royal Navy operated more than 900 warships, including 152 ships of the line, a force that required 130,000–140,000 sailors.[10] Britain's small population and the dreadful conditions of service at sea meant that voluntary enlistments were insufficient, so the Royal Navy resorted to offering rewards to volunteers, conscription, and impressment to fill its ranks. The Board of Admiralty operated an Impressment Service for the express purpose of seeking volunteers but also to cajole, trick, and sometimes coerce men into the navy.

Conditions in the service of the Royal Navy were often appalling, causing as many sailors as came in the front door to disappear out the back—mostly through desertion, followed, far behind, by accidents, illness, and death in combat.[11] The grim plight of the sailors and the presence of thousands of pressed men only exacerbated structural shortages. The story of Robert Fosper, a gunner's mate on the HMS *Resolution*, was just one of many testimonials laid before the House of Commons in a debate over how to attract more men to the Royal Navy. Fosper's life on board the British man-of-war was all too typical of what was driving men in large numbers to risk flogging by deserting. He had been forcibly held in the king's service for seventeen years; he had "twice endeavored to hang himself, was cut down, and cruelly restored to the same endless bondage."[12]

The British accused the Americans of enticing or seducing sailors to abandon the Royal Navy. The American shipping industry was a haven for Royal Navy deserters, as it offered better pay and working conditions. The attraction of relatively high merchant pay was seen as the main cause of manning shortfalls in the Royal Navy. The more men that were impressed into the Royal Navy, the higher the wages rose for merchant seaman generally—typically double or triple the navy pay. The problem was compounded by a system of "back pay," withholding Royal Navy pay to prevent desertion, under the theory that sailors who were owed money were less likely to go over the side. Seamen were often cheated, however, especially if they were turned over to new ships and found their pay ledgers wiped clean. That practice was so entrenched during the Napoleonic Wars and so damaging that Horatio Nelson referred to it as the "infernal system."

In the United States, Secretary of the Treasury Albert Gallatin estimated that some nine thousand British-born sailors were in the U.S. merchant marine.[13] Britain did not recognize the liberal American naturalization laws, which accepted British subjects and made them American citizens. British subjects, accordingly, could not escape their duty by becoming American citizens, and there was no statute of limitations on desertion from the Royal Navy. British officers boarded American merchant ships in British ports and on the high seas and forcibly removed sailors—Royal Navy deserters, British subjects, naturalized citizens, and occasionally natural-born Americans. (One investigation of naval seamen in New York City found that only 42 percent were American born, 49 percent were recent emigrants, and 9 percent naturalized citizens.[14] In an 1808 investigation on the origins of 150 sailors, 134 came from Britain, with 80 of those from Ireland.) The practice of impressment of sailors from American ships was so galling that Senator (and future president) John

Quincy Adams, son of President John Adams, called it an "authorized system of kidnapping on the oceans."[15]

By 1812, the State Department believed, 6,257 Americans had been forcibly removed from U.S. ships; other estimates range from 6,500 to 10,000.[16] The chronic lack of official verifiable documentation of the legal status of sailors entering the American merchant marine and U.S. Navy gave rise to continuous disputes. Sailors often had no way to demonstrate citizenship, and the United Kingdom found the view that the American flag protected every individual sailing under it "too extravagant as to require any serious refutation."[17] Jefferson and Madison nevertheless refused to issue any official documentation for naturalized citizens, arguing that their presence on board American ships was sufficient proof of nationality.

The only issue more important than impressment of American sailors was the principle of freedom of the seas itself. Rufus King, the American minister in London, reported that he could not make progress on impressment unless he conceded Britain's concept of *mare clausum*, or special dominion over the "narrow seas," or waters around the British Isles—specifically the Irish, Scottish, and North Seas.[18] During negotiations in 1802, Admiral John Jervis (Lord St. Vincent), First Lord of the Admiralty, had consented to a two-part agreement that would have resolved the issue of impressment for five years. First, no seaman would be demanded or taken from a public or private ship belonging to, or in the service of, a citizen (or subject) of one of the parties. Second, each party would prohibit its citizens or subjects from concealing or carrying away from the territories or possessions of one nation a seaman belonging to the other. The Americans embraced these provisions.

When these terms were reduced to writing, however, Charles Jenkinson, the Earl of Liverpool (previously Lord Hawkesbury), now the president of the Board of Trade, demanded a third provision expressly distinguishing the high seas from "the Narrow Seas . . . immemorially considered to be within the Dominions of Great Britain." This correction was in the draft sent to the British king, and it made the price too steep for the Americans. The U.S. envoy was "not a little disappointed" and "concluded to abandon the Negotiation" rather than accept Britain's *mare clausum*. Rufus King believed that, although resolving the issue of impressment was critically important for the United States, sanctioning the principle of *mare clausum* "might be productive of more extensive evils" than impressment itself.

– – – – • – – – –

The former colony and the imperial superpower were headed for conflict, and it finally came in 1807, when four deserters from a British warship enlisted on the thirty-six-gun frigate *Chesapeake*. On June 22, the U.S. ship, under the command of Capt. James Barron, set sail from Norfolk to join a squadron deploying to the Barbary Coast. The *Chesapeake* was shadowed off Norfolk by the fifty-gun HMS *Leopard*, under Captain Salusbury Pryce Humphreys.[19] Humphreys was under orders to search American ships for Royal Navy deserters. The *Leopard* approached the *Chesapeake* and demanded that it heave to and allow a party to come on board to search for deserters—Captain Barron declined.

In response and without warning, the *Leopard* fired three broadsides into the unprepared U.S. warship, which got off but a single shot. Three American sailors were killed and eighteen wounded. The *Chesapeake* struck its colors, and a British boarding party carried away four deserters. The sole British citizen among them was tried and hanged from the yardarm of a Royal Navy warship in Halifax Harbor on August 31, 1807. The other three men were awarded a punishment of five hundred lashes. The sentence was commuted, and these "lucky" souls spent five years in jail before making their way back to the United States.

The *Chesapeake* affair angered both Democratic-Republicans and Federalists, and it fueled passions that eventually led to war. President Jefferson could have obtained a declaration of war, but he desperately sought to avoid armed conflict. Jefferson demanded an apology, but the nation was too weak to go to war to vindicate its rights. Instead, the president turned to economic coercion—unilaterally restricting trade. This approach was to prove deeply unpopular and woefully ineffective.

– – – – • – – – –

In desperation, on December 22, 1807, Jefferson signed into law the Embargo Act.[20] The act prohibited American ships from trading in any foreign port.[21] Although he anticipated that this extreme approach would harm the American economy, Jefferson believed that France and Britain would feel such pain that they would be compelled to respect the rights of U.S.-flagged shipping. After all, American ships handled much of the carrying trade of the West Indies, and both Britain and France were dependent upon American agriculture.

The Embargo Act did not have a detrimental impact on British markets, however, as the loss of American shipping was offset by an increase in commerce from South America. But the consequences for the United States were dire. Without foreign export markets, agricultural prices fell and earnings collapsed. Unemployment increased, and smuggling spread as traders tried to circumvent the law. Foreign vessels could off-load cargo at U.S. ports; however, they had to leave empty of American exports. The Embargo Act was in effect a self-imposed blockade, one that devastated the American economy. Foreign trade plunged despite widespread violation of the law, especially in New England.

The deeply unpopular Embargo Act was repealed on March 1, 1809, just three days before the end of President Jefferson's second term, and was replaced by the Non-Intercourse Act.[22] The new legislation lifted the embargo on American merchant ships except those bound for British or French ports. But this law too was ineffective. The statute did not bring France and Britain to heel, and it proved just as damaging to the American economy as the Embargo Act, since Britain and France were the greatest potential markets for American products and agriculture.

President James Madison, like Jefferson a Democratic-Republican, was sworn into office on March 4, 1809, and inherited the problems of blockade and impressment. Madison signed Macon's Bill Number 2 on May 1, 1810, the third American attempt at commercial warfare. This law fared no better than the first two.[23] The statute canceled the embargoes against Britain and France for three months and offered an incentive to them to stop attacks on

American shipping. That is, if during the three-month period either country recognized U.S. neutral rights and ceased attacks upon American shipping, the United States would end trade with the other—unless that other state agreed to respect U.S. neutral rights as well.

Napoleon Bonaparte accepted the American incentive as a way to advance what he called the "Continental Plan" to cut off Britain from Europe. Although suspecting that Napoleon never actually intended to stop attacks on American ships, Madison accepted his assurances anyway in the hope that Britain might reciprocate. This incorporation of American trade within the Continental System, however, exacerbated U.S. relations with Britain and now led to war. The British continued their blockade and impressment, and Napoleon indeed reneged on his commitment to respect American neutral rights.

But just as the Embargo Act and Non-Intercourse Act failed to stem British impressment, so too did Macon's Bill No. 2. On May 1, 1811, the thirty-eight-gun HMS *Guerrière* stopped and boarded the American merchant brig *Spitfire* and seized an apprentice sailing master, John Diggio, an unmistakably American citizen, born in Cape Elizabeth, Maine. Americans were outraged at this slight to national honor. Tensions ran high, and Secretary of the Navy Paul Hamilton sortied the forty-four-gun *President*, under Capt. John Rodgers, to search for the *Guerrière* and recover the detained American. The *President* set sail from Annapolis on the sixteenth.

The *President* missed the *Guerrière* but did encounter another British warship two weeks after leaving port. Sailing off the coast of North Carolina in darkness and fog, the *President* encountered a ship and chased it for seven hours. The *President* was the faster vessel and eventually closed on the mysterious ship. The two foes challenged one another in the dark. Shrouded in fog, the mystery vessel claimed to be a Royal Navy ship of the line but proved to be the twenty-two-gun *Little Belt*. The *President* and *Little Belt* traded barrages, but the smaller ship was no match for the American frigate. Within fifteen minutes the *Little Belt* was defeated, badly damaged and with thirteen killed and nineteen wounded. Back home, the British were furious, as were the Americans, since both sides alleged the other had fired first. For their part, the Americans swelled with pride at this justified retribution for the attack on the *Chesapeake*.

At the outbreak of the war, the United States had just thirteen "blue water" warships: the three famous "superfrigates" (the *United States*, *Constitution*, and *President*), three regular frigates, five sloops, and two brigs. Britain's Halifax squadron alone numbered 111 ships, including seven ships of the line and thirty-one frigates.

Overall, in 1807 the Royal Navy operated 113 ships of the line (though the number declined to ninety-eight by 1814 as fighting with France took its toll). In comparison, France had thirty-four ships of the line in 1807, which increased to eighty by 1813, with thirty-five more under construction. The United States would not acquire a ship of the line until the massive ninety-gun *Independence* was launched in 1814. The ship put to sea too late to see action in the War of 1812, and although it made an appearance in the second Barbary War in 1815, it did so only after peace had been secured there.

– – – • – – –

Relations between Britain and the United States continued to worsen. Believing war to be only days away, President Madison on April 1, 1812, sent to Congress a secret message seeking a sixty-day embargo of American shipping in order to keep the merchant fleet in port and protect it from capture by the Royal Navy.[24] Led by Speaker Henry Clay of Kentucky and Representative John Calhoun of South Carolina, the House of Representatives passed the war measure on June 4, 1812, by a vote of seventy-nine to forty-nine. Congressional delegations from the South and West supported the decision for war, while those from the Northeast were largely opposed. This division of sentiment would continue during the war itself.

Meanwhile, the economic embargo against Britain continued to play out. Macon's Bill No. 2 immediately began to face the resistance that its predecessors had. On June 1, 1812, Madison had sent a message to Congress that set forth American grievances against Britain. There were three main issues: first, unlawful impressment of American sailors from American ships; second, the Orders in Council that impeded American trade and violated American neutral rights; and third, British support for Indian uprisings in the Northwest Territory.[25] The first two issues were the gravamen of U.S. injuries and the central causes of the war, and they had percolated for two decades. "Had not Great Britain persevered so obstinately in the violation of these important rights," President Madison later recalled, "the war would not have been declared."[26] Further, the attack by the HMS *Leopard*, which was a plausible basis for war, had occurred five years before. Britain had not relented since then, and infringements on American rights continued unanswered. Indeed, in Madison's view, the United States now had no choice but to respond to a war that had been imposed upon it. His message to Congress concluded:

> British cruisers have been in the practice also of violating the rights and the peace of our coasts. They hover over and harass our entering and departing commerce. To the most insulting pretensions they have added the most lawless proceedings in our very harbors, and have wantonly spilt American blood within the sanctuary of our territorial jurisdiction. . . .
>
> Whether the United States shall continue passive under these progressive usurpations, and these accumulating wrongs; or, opposing force to force in defense of their national rights, shall commit a just cause into the hands of the Almighty disposer of events . . . is a solemn question, which the Constitution wisely confides to the Legislative Department of the Government. In recommending it to their early deliberations, I am happy in the assurance that the decision will be worthy the enlightened and patriotic councils of a virtuous, a free, and a powerful Nation.[27]

The declaration passed the House overwhelmingly; it cleared the Senate on June 15 by a vote of nineteen to thirteen. The vote marked the first time Congress declared war pursuant to the Constitution. Madison signed the measure into law three days later.

The Federalists uniformly opposed war, as did a member of Congress from Virginia, John Randolph, who led a wing of archconservatives who had separated from Jefferson and Madison. Not one of the thirty-nine Federalists in Congress supported the call to arms;[28] critics began to refer to the conflict as "Madison's War." But in fact, no proponent of the war advocated invasion of Canada, though the temptation hung in the background. The legislation authorizing war was entitled merely, "An act declaring war between Great Britain and her dependencies, and the United States and their territories." It conferred upon the president the authority only to instruct U.S. Navy commanders to "recapture any vessel . . . previously captured by the British" and to interdict Royal Navy warships "hovering on the coasts of the United States for the purpose of interrupting their lawful commerce."[29]

The British were not keen to fight. The day following Madison's declaration, by chance, Britain repealed the Orders in Council, conceding this issue to the United States and lending new hope that conflict could be avoided. Word of the British concession, however, did not cross the Atlantic until weeks later. Trapped by the tyranny of distance and the slowness of communication, the two sides slid into war.

The conflict that came to be known as the "War of 1812" actually lasted thirty-two months—longer than the American involvement in the Mexican-American War, Spanish-American War, or World War I. For the British, the war was a mere sideshow to the epic conflagration in Europe against Napoleon.[30] The Napoleonic Wars ended with the surrender of French forces to the Sixth Coalition at the Battle of Paris on March 30–31, 1814. Only after the defeat of Napoleon and his abdication of the throne could Britain turn its full attention toward its American war. At the same time, however, London's principal motivation for war evaporated, and peace with the United States was quick in coming.

— — — — ● — — — —

The British ruled the waves, but their control over the vast territory of North America was much more tenuous. Although the causes of the war for the most part arose at sea, the decisive battles occurred on land. First, the United

States attempted to capture Canada and drive Britain from North America. The war hawks in Congress were especially confident that British subjects living below the forty-ninth parallel north, marked by the modern border of Ontario, would embrace the opportunity to join the United States. The American invasion of Canada did not prove easy, however; three attempts were turned back. In July 1812, Gen. William Hull entered Canada from Detroit, only to retreat back to the United States and surrender to General Isaac Brock at Fort Detroit on August 17. Later, Hull was convicted of cowardice and neglect of duty. In October 1812, Gen. Stephen van Rensselaer crossed the Niagara River into Canada but was defeated at the Battle of Queenston Heights. Gen. Henry Dearborn led another expedition toward Montreal, but his force was insufficient and the advance bogged down.

— — — — ● — — — —

The Americans fared better at sea. In early June 1812, Secretary of the Navy Paul Hamilton dispatched two U.S. naval squadrons, under Commo. John Rodgers and Capt. Stephen Decatur. Three days after the declaration of war, Rodgers got the frigate *President* under way, accompanied by the thirty-six-gun *Congress* and the sloops *Hornet* and *Argus*, of eighteen and sixteen guns, respectively. This was the largest U.S. squadron to take to sea since the first Barbary War. The first blood was shed in the naval war just two days out from New York, when Rodgers, stalking a British Jamaica convoy, encountered the British frigate HMS *Belvidera*, (thirty-two guns).

On June 23, 1812—just five days after the war started—the *Belvidera* encountered the *President*, flagship of Commodore Rodgers, the *Congress*, and the *United States*, under Captain Decatur. The *Belvidera* fled, and the three American frigates pursued. Rodgers caught and engaged the *Belvidera*, firing bow guns and making contact with the stern of the enemy ship. Several British sailors were killed and wounded. The British responded, and a lucky hit or an exploding gun on board the *President* set off secondary explosions that killed two and wounded nineteen American sailors. The *Belvidera* escaped to Halifax. For three weeks, Commodore Rodgers searched unsuccessfully for the elusive British convoy, approaching within three hundred miles of the British coast. "We have lost the *Belvidera*," Decatur later lamented, "she ought to have been ours."[31] The inconclusive engagement was the first shot in the naval war of 1812.

Later that summer, on August 19, 1812, on board the *Constitution*, Capt. Isaac Hull encountered the HMS *Guerrière* about seven hundred miles east of Boston. The *Guerrière* twice crossed the bow of the *Constitution*, firing both times. The *Guerrière* had painted a message across the fore-topsail: "NOT THE LITTLE BELT." The two ships closed, the *Constitution* approaching from the *Guerrière*'s port quarter. The ships exchanged broadsides, and the two frigates pounded each other for twenty minutes. Then the *Guerrière*'s mizzenmast collapsed, hampering its ability to maneuver and allowing Hull to steer across his adversary's bow and rake it with cannon fire. The *Guerrière* capitulated, and the action ceased. The next morning, Captain Hull evacuated the Royal Navy sailors from their ship and tended to the wounded. The *Guerrière* was so badly damaged that Hull burned it at sea.

The United States made a good showing in naval action, prevailing, on balance, in one-on-one encounters. On October 18, 1812, the sloop of war *Wasp*, for example, captured the brig HMS *Frolic*. The two were evenly matched eighteen-gun warships. But just hours later, the *Wasp* and the prize crew it had sent on board the *Frolic* surrendered to the seventy-four-gun ship of the line HMS *Poictiers*, which arrived soon after the initial battle. The intervention of the *Poictiers* may be seen as a metaphor for the battle between the U.S. Navy and the Royal Navy. Although American seamanship and bravery equaled those of the British, the best in the world, the sheer might of the Royal Navy was bound to win if its full force were brought to bear.

Captain Bainbridge set sail on the *Constitution* on October 27, 1812, with the twenty-gun sloop of war *Hornet*, planning to link up with the *Chesapeake*, the thirty-six-gun *Constellation*, and the thirty-two-gun *Essex* near the Cape Verde Islands. He failed, however, to rendezvous with his squadron and instead made for Rio de Janeiro to resupply. On December 29, the *Constitution* spotted the thirty-eight-gun HMS *Java*. Bainbridge closed on the ship and fired two broadsides from his port side, damaging the British frigate's rigging and sails. The *Java* crossed astern of the *Constitution* and delivered a broadside that destroyed the ship's wheel, killed several American sailors, and wounded Bainbridge. The *Constitution*, using the tiller to steer, maneuvered into the windward position. The American frigate pounded the *Java*, damaging its bowsprit, which considerably slowed the British frigate. The *Java*'s foremast was cut by another broadside; the *Constitution* continued to pound the *Java*, shooting into its stern and bow, raking it lengthwise. The *Constitution* emerged victorious from the bloody, three-hour encounter. The British had suffered 124 casualties, the United States thirty-six.

Six weeks after the victory by the *Constitution*, Captain Decatur got under way from Boston on board the forty-four-gun *United States*. At sunrise on October 25, 1812, his ship came into contact with the thirty-eight-gun HMS *Macedonian*. The *United States* seized the windward advantage and brought to bear its long-range twenty-four-pounder cannon, which cut into the *Macedonian* and toppled its mizzenmast. His ship immobilized, Captain John Carden of the *Macedonian* struck his colors and surrendered. The ship was landed as a prize at New York, to public fanfare.

During the first year of the war in the Atlantic Ocean, U.S. and Royal Navy forces were more evenly matched than they would be later in the war, after the Royal Navy rotated forces into the theater to gain control. Meanwhile, however, the relatively balanced order of battle had produced three remarkable victories by American frigates. The *Constitution* bested the Royal Navy twice, capturing the HMS *Guerrière* on August 19, 1812, and dispatching the HMS *Java* on December 29, 1812. The engagement with the *Guerrière* earned the *Constitution* the nickname "Old Ironsides," which it bears even today, as the world's oldest commissioned warship still afloat. The frigate *United States* defeated the *Macedonian* on October 25, 1812. These successes would impel American public opinion to continue to support the war. By the end of 1812, the Royal Navy had lost six engagements with the U.S. Navy, which surprised and exasperated British citizens, political leaders, and naval commanders. More battles followed, U.S. frigates holding their own in one-on-one engagements. But the U.S. Navy could not hope to hold off the overwhelming weight of the Royal Navy, and as the war dragged on the British fleet began to establish sea control.

– – – – • – – – –

Britain maintained a blockade of the American coast and steadily tightened the noose throughout the war by increasing the number of vessels on station (see table 2). The American warships were eager to leave harbor and search for prizes on the high seas, avoiding engagements with ships of the line or larger flotillas. Soon after the declaration of war in 1812, for example, the *Essex* under Capt. David Porter evaded the blockade and slipped out of Delaware Bay to try to unite with Bainbridge's squadron. The rendezvous failed, and the *Essex* headed south. Soon, the American warship rounded Cape Horn, the rocky headland of Hornos Island in southern Chile's Tierra del Fuego archipelago. Once in the Pacific Ocean, the *Essex* made a brief stop in Peru and then sailed toward the whaling grounds near the Galapagos Islands in search of British prizes. The *Essex* prominently flew a banner that read, "Free Trade and Sailor's Rights." On August 13, 1812, the *Essex*, with her gunports closed and disguised as a merchantman, lured and then captured the twenty-gun British sloop of war HMS *Alert*. The *Alert* was the first British warship to surrender in the War of 1812. In the spring of 1813, the *Essex* captured thirteen British whalers, the largest of which, armed with twenty guns, the Americans renamed *Essex Junior*.

TABLE 2. ROYAL NAVY VESSELS ON BLOCKADE DUTY, 1812–15

Date	Number of Vessels	Geographic Scope
July 1812	19	New York to Savannah blockade declared December 1812, extended to Narragansett Bay in November 1813
July 1813	57	
Dec 1813	72	New Orleans blockaded May 1814
Nov 1814	121	
Jan 1815	136	New England blockaded 1814

Source: Gene Allen Smith, "The Naval War of 1812 and the Confirmation of Independence, 1807–1815," in *America, Sea Power, and the World*, ed. James C. Bradford (Hoboken, N.J.: Wiley-Blackwell, 2016), 49.

On February 24, 1813, the sloop of war *Hornet* under James Lawrence sank the brig-sloop HMS *Peacock* at the mouth of the Demerara River in eastern Guyana. The two warships exchanged broadsides, but the *Hornet* prevailed and forced the *Peacock* to strike. The British ship sank shortly afterward, and its officers and crew were loaded onto the *Hornet*, which set sail for Martha's Vineyard, Massachusetts. Lawrence was promoted to captain and assumed command of the *Chesapeake*.

Nonetheless, the British blockade was choking American commerce and preventing the nation's warships from getting to sea. The frustration among U.S. Navy captains was palpable, as they were confident that they could best the Royal Navy in even matches. Indeed, usually they did, but not every time. Captain Lawrence, now in the *Chesapeake*, allowed himself to be goaded out of Boston on June 1, 1813, to engage the HMS *Shannon*. Both ships were armed with thirty-eight guns. Captain Philip Broke of the *Shannon* had been on blockade duty off the coast for fifty-six days. The ships met at the Boston Light, between Cape Ann and Cape Cod, and engaged in an intense melee. The American ship suffered a devastating defeat in just fifteen minutes.

A British sniper shot and killed Lawrence, who gasped these dying words: "Don't give up the ship!" But his men could not prevent it: a British boarding party overwhelmed them and seized the vessel. His final command was published weeks later in a Baltimore newspaper and became an iconic rallying cry for the U.S. Navy.[32] The Battle of Boston Harbor, as the engagement became known, cost nearly fifty sailors killed, a hundred wounded, and the capture of the entire crew and the frigate *Chesapeake*. The British took the damaged ship and its crew to Halifax, Nova Scotia, where the sailors were imprisoned and the ship was repaired and taken into Royal Navy service.

On August 14, 1813, the *Argus*, raiding British merchant shipping, was captured by the more heavily armed HMS *Pelican*. The *Pelican* brought the U.S. ship into Plymouth, England. Three weeks later, the twenty-gun U.S. Navy brig *Enterprise* defeated the fourteen-gun Royal Navy brig *Boxer*.

Meanwhile, the *Essex* reprovisioned in the Marquesas Islands in French Polynesia. Captain Porter set sail for Valparaiso, Chile, arriving on January 12, 1814. On February 3, two British frigates, the thirty-six-gun HMS

Phoebe and the twenty-eight-gun *Cherub*, entered the harbor. Being in a neutral port, the warships warily eyed each other for almost two months. The *Essex* got under way on March 28 when a storm ripped away its anchor. Captain Porter made a run for the open ocean but failed to lose his pursuers. Retreating back toward Chile, hugging the territorial waters, the *Essex* entered a small, shallow harbor. Undeterred by Chile's neutrality, the HMS *Phoebe* hammered the American ship, which suffered heavy casualties and struck its flag.

On April 14, the sloop of war USS *Peacock* captured the brig sloop HMS *Epervier* after a brief engagement off Cape Canaveral, Florida. The *Peacock* and its prize evaded other Royal Navy units and put in at Savannah, Georgia. That June, a new *Wasp* sank the HMS *Reindeer*. Isolated single-ship actions, however, could not weaken the British blockade, let alone turn the tide of war.

With the end of the Napoleonic Wars in the spring of 1815 the Admiralty and War Office devised a four-prong strategy to defeat the Americans, an outcome that they hoped would lead to the dissolution of the young republic. The Royal Navy reinforced the blockade, which the previous spring had been extended to include New York and New England (from Rhode Island to Maine); at the beginning of the war, New York and New England had been spared because public sentiment there was against the war. Second, a Royal Navy presence in Chesapeake Bay would pin down U.S. troops, preventing their deployment northward. Third, a ground invasion southward through Plattsburgh (New York), Burlington (Vermont), and Albany (New York) along the Lake Champlain corridor would sever New England from the remainder of the Union. Fourth, the conquest of New Orleans would close the Mississippi River to American exports. As one British column cut south along Lake Champlain, it was planned, the other was to land in the Gulf of Mexico, capture New Orleans, and proceed northward. Raids along the Eastern Seaboard of the United States destroyed U.S. ships at anchor. On August 22, 1814, Royal Marines struck the U.S. gunboat station on the Patuxent River. The Americans lost a privateer, seventeen gunboats, and thirteen merchant schooners, either captured by the British or destroyed by retreating U.S. forces.[33]

On August 24, four thousand British troops routed a larger, polyglot U.S. force at Bladensburg, Maryland, and then entered Washington, D.C., unopposed. They burned the Treasury Department, the War Office, the Capitol, and other government buildings—including the President's House, which later would be rebuilt as the White House. Retreating U.S. troops destroyed stores and vessels at the Washington Navy Yard, including a nearly complete frigate. The British set the fires in retaliation for the U.S. arson of government buildings during its invasion of York (Toronto), the capital of the province of Upper Canada (present-day Ontario) the previous April. As quickly as they had come, the British forces withdrew in the aftermath of a heavy storm that quenched the fires and damaged some of the British landing ships.

British columns next moved on Baltimore, Maryland, by land and from the sea in a combined-arms pincer campaign to take the fourth-largest city in the United States. The amphibious assault against Baltimore proceeded from September 12 to 15; an initial engagement at North Point was inconclusive but bought the Americans more time to strengthen the city's fortifications. During a twenty-five-hour siege on September 13 to 14, the Royal Navy bombarded Fort McHenry, which guarded the harbor. The British fleet included rocket-firing ships with such evocative names as *Volcano*, *Aetna*, *Meteor*, and *Devastation*. As a squadron of American gunboats threatened the British rear, however, the Royal Navy commander, Vice Admiral Sir Alexander Cochrane, called off the assault and withdrew. The attack on Fort McHenry inspired thirty-five-year-old lawyer Francis Scott Key to spy the "star spangled banner" through the haze of the "dawn's early light," observations that he wrote down in a poem that was set to music, became an instant hit, and eventually the national anthem.

— — — — ● — — — —

Talks to end the war had already begun in Ghent on August 8, 1814, and a treaty was signed on December 24.[34] During these negotiations the fight continued. The war on land was marked by a British advance in the mid-Atlantic, notably the razing of Washington and the Battle of Baltimore. At sea there were unrelenting engagements as well, with the *Wasp* (II) sinking the *Avon* on September 1. The sticking point for the talks was what had started the conflict to begin with—impressment of American sailors. Secretary of State James Monroe passed on to the American delegation in Ghent President Madison's unequivocal directions: "This degrading practice must cease; our flag must protect our crews or the United States cannot consider themselves an independent nation."[35] Ironically, though, the treaty that ended the conflict did not even mention either that or the other major cause of war for the Americans—the British blockade.

On January 13, 1815, some three weeks after the Treaty of Ghent was signed, the *President* ran aground in New York Harbor while trying to run the British blockade. News of the peace agreement still had not reached North America. The *President*'s copper-sheathed bottom was damaged, but gale winds prevented the ship from reentering the harbor, and it made for sea. After two days, during which it was pursued by four ships of the Royal Navy's blockading squadron led by the exceptionally quick forty-gun HMS *Endymion*, the American ship was caught. The British squadron closed in, and the *President* eventually surrendered. The HMS *Endymion* sailed the captured U.S. warship to Bermuda where it was placed in Royal Navy service.

The far more consequential Battle of New Orleans, January 8 to 15, 1815, was also fought, unbeknownst to the participants, after the signing of the Treaty of Ghent.[36] The southern half of the British pincer movement took the form of a force of sixty warships and eight thousand troops sent to capture New Orleans and then advance up the Louisiana Territory. The January 8 attack on the city faltered, however; the British advance crumbled before Gen. Andrew Jackson's line of defense. In less than an hour, the British lost 251 killed, 1,259 wounded, and 484 missing, most of whom were taken prisoner. Thus, about one-quarter of the British force was destroyed in just minutes. American casualties were miraculously light—only seven killed and six wounded.[37]

The American victory was one of the most lopsided in the history of arms—a rout on the order of Agincourt, with Americans in the role of the English archers and the British cast as the luckless French knights.[38] The repulse led to an eventual withdrawal to Mobile Bay, Alabama. As the British prepared to attack Mobile, word of the end of the war reached the combatants. With the Senate ratification of the Treaty of Ghent on February 18, 1815, the war officially ended.

News of the war's end still had not reached many units at sea, including the *Hornet*. The ship had successfully navigated through the British blockade and headed for a secret U.S. squadron rendezvous near the remote island of Tristan da Cunha in the South Atlantic. In the final naval action of the war, the *Hornet* captured the nineteen-gun brig-sloop HMS *Penguin* off Tristan da Cunha on March 23. The prize was so badly damaged that it was set ablaze after being emptied of stores.

The Treaty of Ghent recognized that the war had been fought to a draw. Neither side lost territory; the treaty codified the state of affairs before the conflict began—the *status quo ante bellum*. The issue of impressment of American sailors was made moot by the defeat of Napoleon, after which the Royal Navy was no longer as desperate for able seamen.

The war-fighting record of the United States was mixed, but it had been able to hold the line against Britain, especially at sea. During the war the United States seized 165 British vessels and a few troop transports, and American privateers captured 1,344 British merchant ships.[39] Of the latter, however, some 750 were later recaptured by the British, returned to neutral-flag states, or lost at sea—often burned by the captors once their valuable cargoes were off-loaded because it was impossible to bring them into port through the British blockade.

The Royal Navy captured 1,400 American merchant ships and privateers. Britain, always viewing the conflict through the prism of the French wars, was never as emotionally invested in the conflict as the United States. London could walk away without a sense of clear-cut victory. On the other hand, the British continually believed the upstart Americans should be taught a lesson and that the new country might actually collapse with just the right nudge. In the end, both sides proved intractable, and the dominant American presence on land would only grow stronger. The British could defeat the U.S. forces in pitched battles, but the United States was remarkably durable. The Americans emerged from the war with a renewed sense of national pride, sovereignty, and self-confidence.[40]

The war also underscored the deep commitment of the United States to the egalitarian principles of freedom of navigation. Having established a democracy on the bedrock of individual liberty and equality, as imperfect as it was, American leaders began to insist that those principles were equally valid in their foreign relations. This penchant for equal treatment as a sovereign state, including sovereign neutral rights, was deeply embedded in the American political psyche. While leaders differed on whether it was the British or French empire that posed the greatest threat to these ideals, Americans of all stripes were strongly nationalist and willing to send the nation to war to vindicate its cause.

"ALL FREEDOM . . . DEPENDS ON FREEDOM OF THE SEAS"

The World Wars (1914–45)

There were no major maritime conflicts from the end of the Napoleonic Wars in 1815 until the sinking of the *Lusitania* one hundred years later. The 1915 attack on the passenger liner was a harbinger of a thirty-year struggle with Germany for recognition of unfettered freedom of the seas. During this period there was a massive shift in thinking about navigational rights. At the dawn of the twentieth century, freedom of the seas mostly still meant the rights of neutral states to enjoy undiminished use of the oceans. The prescribed "cruiser rules" dated to the seventeenth century and were vestiges of the era of war as a lawful, albeit regulated, human enterprise. By the close of World War II, freedom of the seas was to acquire a peacetime context that presaged efforts by coastal states to restrict navigation and overflight in the oceans and airspace in close proximity to their territories.

– – – – • – – – –

There is scarcely a subject in history more written about than the start of World War I. The most prominent histories of the war focus on the run-up to the "guns of August": the assassination of Archduke Ferdinand on June 28, 1914, in Sarajevo; Germany's "blank check" to Austria-Hungary in the first week of July; German mobilization and declaration of war on Serbia during the last week of July; Russia's order of mobilization on July 30, despite a warning from Germany; and German mobilization and declarations of war against Russia, on August 1, and France, on August 3. Germany invaded Belgium on August 4 in order to knock France quickly out of the war. Britain's ultimatum to Germany to respect Belgian neutrality expired, and the following day Great Britain declared war on Germany.[1] However, the origins of the entry of the United States into the war lie not in Luxembourg and Belgium but in the North Atlantic. The United States joined the conflict to protect its right to freedom of the seas, not to settle scores on the continent of Europe. Germany had failed to take account of the effect of unrestricted submarine warfare on neutral states—principally the United States—and this miscalculation would lead to its defeat.[2]

The concept of "freedom of the seas" continued to mean freedom of neutral states to use the seas during time of war. The term became synonymous with the British naval effort against the German campaign of unrestricted submarine warfare, and it would be adopted once again by the Americans to vindicate their cause. The idea of "freedom of the seas" was to undergo, over the period of the two world wars and the peace agreements that followed them, a shift from a wartime right of neutral states to a peacetime right of all states. President Woodrow Wilson was the first American champion of this change. He began the war with talk of the American right to navigate freely as a justification of neutral rights. By the end of the war he was speaking about freedom of navigation more broadly, to include peacetime access to the oceans for all states.

On August 19, 1914, just as Europe erupted in war, Wilson delivered to Congress an address in which he cautioned that the United States "will act and speak in the true spirit of neutrality."[3] But deep cultural, economic, and political ties with France and Britain pulled the United States toward these democracies. With its large merchant fleet and leanings toward the Allies, the United States slid into a morass of maritime law. Shippers' goods were intercepted by the Allies, and the United States dickered with all belligerents on the rights of its neutral ships, neutral goods, and neutral citizens.

— — — — • — — — —

On October 20, 1914, the SS *Glitra* became the first British casualty of German submarine warfare. The ship was bound for Stavanger, Norway, with a load of coal, iron plate, and oil when it was stopped and searched by the U-boat, or submarine, *U-17* just fourteen nautical miles (nm) west-southwest of the present-day municipalities of Bokn and Karmøy, Norway. The sinking was carried out in accordance with prize rules: the Germans placed the crew in lifeboats before scuttling the ship. Britain declared the entire North Sea a war zone on November 4, 1914, announcing that enemy ships as well as neutral vessels risked striking mines or encountering other dangers of war.[4]

On January 22, 1915, the *U-21* sank the British steamship *Durward* off the coast of Belgium as it was on its way from Leith to Rotterdam. The submarine placed the crew in lifeboats and towed them to within five hundred yards of Maas Lightship before vanishing below the surface.[5] The same submarine struck again one week later, attacking four merchant ships less than forty nautical miles from Liverpool and sending three to the bottom. This pattern would begin to unravel when British merchant ships began to fight back. British liners were told to maneuver evasively and, if possible, ram submarines.

Germany declared its own war zone on February 4, 1915, in the waters near Great Britain and Ireland and "the whole English Channel," within which it would destroy all enemy merchant shipping.[6] Neutral states were warned that their crews, passengers, and cargoes in the war zone were in imminent danger of being mistaken for belligerents. Secretary of State William Jennings Bryan responded in a diplomatic note on February 10, 1915, that stated that the United States had "grave concern" about the creation of the German war zone.[7] The "sole right" and indeed the duty of a belligerent on the high seas, Bryan stated, was to visit and search neutral ships to determine if the cargo was contraband. To attack in a designated war zone without ensuring the belligerent nationality of the ship and the contraband character of the cargo was "unprecedented in naval warfare" and infringed on the right to use the seas freely.

On February 15, 1915, Germany notified the United States that Britain was arming its merchant ships to confront submarines and had offered a high bounty for the first rammed submarine. Because submarines on the surface were vulnerable to naval guns, Berlin warned, U-boats might have to strike first, in defiance of the cruiser rules. Accordingly, Germany could offer "no further assurance" of the safety of neutral ships in the war zone.[8] Neutral vessels were "most earnestly warned" against entering the area.

Britain and France retaliated by tightening their blockade. On March 1, 1915, the Allies asserted a full blockade of Germany, to be enforced by the interception and detention of any ship with contraband cargo believed to be bound for Germany: "The British and French Governments will therefore hold themselves free to detain and take into port ships carrying goods of presumed enemy destination, ownership, or origin. It is not intended to confiscate such vessels or cargoes, unless they would otherwise be liable to condemnation."[9]

The Allies criticized Germany for failure to conduct visit and search of merchant ships or to adhere to the laws of war that required ships captured as prizes to be adjudicated before prize courts. In practice, Germany's outright sinking of vessels was permissible only in extraordinary circumstances, and only after crews were put safely into lifeboats. Submarines, however, were at a distinct disadvantage in that it was difficult for them to put prize crews on board captured ships and take them into port. Submarines that surfaced to warn merchant ships were vulnerable to attack or ramming. At a minimum, the merchant vessel might radio naval forces for assistance, which is what happened in the case of the British steamship *Falaba*.

— — — • — — —

The German submarine *U-28* torpedoed and sank the 4,086-ton passenger ship RMS *Falaba* on March 28, 1915, off the coast of Africa. The ship was on a run from Liverpool to Sierra Leone when it encountered a submarine flying the British flag. As the two vessels closed, however, the ensign was replaced with the German naval flag. The submarine signaled the *Falaba* to stop and abandon ship. Instead, the *Falaba* maneuvered to keep the submarine astern, whereupon the U-boat signaled that it would fire if the ship did not stop immediately.[10] About ten minutes later, the submarine torpedoed the *Falaba*.[11] Thus, only about twenty minutes transpired between the initial order to stop and the attack. Britain deemed this window of time "grossly insufficient" for the safe abandonment of passengers from the ship and held that it appeared to be designed to maximize casualties.[12] One surviving passenger reported, "Had the submarine given us ten or fifteen minutes more before firing a torpedo, all might have been saved as there were plenty of boats, no excitement, perfect order."[13] Reports also suggested that Germans on board the U-boat had jeered as the victims struggled to escape.

One hundred and four people were killed, including an American passenger named Leon Chester Thrasher.[14] Thrasher, a young mining engineer from Massachusetts, was the first American casualty of the war. In a telegram after the incident, Germany explained that the crew of the *U-28* had been unable to rescue the passengers of the *Falaba* out of consideration for its own safety.[15] Furthermore, Germany charged the liner with violations of the cruiser rules that made the tragedy all but inevitable. Fearful of remaining vulnerable on the surface, the *U-28* had been compelled to strike and dive. The attack on the *Falaba* was followed by that on the *Lusitania*, which galvanized Americans against Germany.

– – – – • – – – –

One week before the *Lusitania* went down, a German submarine struck a lesser-known American ship. On May 1, 1915, a German submarine attacked the tanker *Gulflight*.[16] The American ship was under escort by the Royal Navy at the time, and the German submarine later reported that it did not see the American flag until after the torpedo was in the water.[17] The *Gulflight* was damaged but survived. Germany apologized for the attack and offered reparations, but the incident fed ill will in the United States toward Germany.[18]

The sinking of the RMS *Lusitania* on May 7, 1915, was a game changer. The luxury liner, built in part with government money, was obliged to serve the British nation in time of war. In addition to passengers, the *Lusitania* was carrying small-arms munitions when it got under way from New York on May 1, 1915—the same day the *Gulflight* was attacked. When the *Lusitania* approached British waters, a German submarine sank it; 1,198 people perished, including 128 Americans.[19] The American and British publics were outraged; Walther Schwieger, the captain of the *U-20*, was vilified as a mass murderer. The *New York Times* reported that London was filled with "horror and utter amazement."[20]

While Germany expressed "deep regret" over the loss of life, it forcefully argued that Americans had knowingly placed themselves in harm's way by traveling on enemy shipping. American passengers on enemy ships assumed the risks of their own irresponsible behavior.[21] This line of argument ignored, however, the differences between war on land and warfare at sea. Beyond three miles from shore the oceans were regarded as a global commons. Belligerents had a right, exercised through the procedures of visit and search, to seize contraband and condemn prizes but not to target neutral merchant ships unless they aided the enemy. Germans, on the other hand, called American passengers on board enemy ships *Schutzengel*, or "guardian angels" that served to protect the ship as "human shields."

The United States sent a long and detailed démarche to Germany on May 13, 1915, that discussed the attacks on the *Lusitania*, *Falaba*, *Gulflight*, and *Cushing*. (The U.S.-flagged *Cushing* had been attacked by a German aircraft off the Dutch coast on April 28; Germany had offered an apology and reparations.) The note pleaded with Germany to observe "rules of fairness, reason, justice, and humanity" by respecting the rights of neutral ships and neutral seafarers on board belligerent ships.[22] In effect, the United States insisted upon strict German compliance with the cruiser rules, which were impossible for submarines to implement.

— — — — • — — — —

Later that summer, on August 19, 1915, the submarine *U-24* sank the *Arabic*, a British steamer bound for New York.[23] The ship went down fifty miles south of Kinsale, Ireland. Of the 433 passengers on board, forty-four were killed, including two Americans. In response to criticism from the United States and other neutral states, Germany issued more restrictive rules to its U-boat captains on September 1, 1915. Henceforth, liners would not be sunk without warning or heed to the lives of noncombatants so long as the ships did not try to escape or offer resistance.[24] The policy was known as the Arabic Pledge, but it was not clear whether it was actually a new approach or not. However, no more vessels were sunk throughout the winter of 1915–16.

At the same time, President Wilson was also angry at British interference with American commerce. First, the Royal Navy blockaded the North Sea and the Atlantic Ocean in order to stem the flow of war matériel to the Central Powers. Anglo-American relations were strained when Britain began to seize U.S. merchant ships suspected of carrying contraband. Throughout the fall of 1915, the United States, Germany, and the Allies exchanged numerous diplomatic notes defining contraband, which now included such seemingly benign goods as cotton.[25] Other dual-use items, such as resins and turpentine, were also targeted by the Allied blockade, to an extent that hampered American commerce.[26] Britain even listed tobacco as contraband.

On November 9, 1915, the General Board of the Department of the Navy declared the U.S. fleet insufficient "to give due weight to the diplomatic remonstrances of the United States in peace [or] to enforce its policies in war."[27] The Navy, unable to protect the nation's neutral rights and woefully unprepared for war, should be expanded, the General Board asserted, to make it equal to that of any other nation. The Naval Appropriations Act of 1916 provided for a force of 156 ships—the largest peacetime buildup in American history up to that point.[28] On December 7, 1915, President Wilson declared in his State of the Union address that the shipbuilding program would produce a fleet "fitted to our needs and worthy of our traditions": 27 battleships of the first line, 6 battle cruisers, 25 battleships of the second line, 10 armored cruisers, 13 scout cruisers, 5 first-class cruisers, 3 second-class cruisers, 10 third-class cruisers, 108 destroyers, 18 fleet submarines, 157 coastal submarines, and sundry other ships. The fleet was slowly taking shape when the United States entered the war, and it became immediately apparent that this new, top-heavy force structure, designed to fight other great surface naval powers, was unsuited to the cat-and-mouse game of antisubmarine warfare.

——— —— — —— ● —— —— — ——

On March 24, 1916, the *U-29* torpedoed the SS *Sussex*, an unarmed French passenger steamer that made cross-channel runs between Folkestone and Dieppe. The ship did not sink, yet the entire bow, as far aft as the bridge, was blown away in a massive secondary explosion, which suggested she had been carrying ammunition. Some 80 of the 325 passengers were killed, and many people were injured, including two Americans. The single smokestack and gray superstructure of the vessel had convinced the commander of the *U-29* that it was a warship, possibly a minelayer.[29]

On April 18, a U.S. démarche to Germany noted that the *Sussex* attack was just one among numerous attacks against civilian ships in violation of the cruiser rules and that the "roll of Americans who have lost their lives" in them had "grown month by month until the ominous toll has mounted into the hundreds."[30] The "Sussex Note" threatened to sever diplomatic relations with Germany unless submarine attacks against unarmed passenger and freight ships ceased.

Two weeks later—on May 4, 1916—Germany caved in to Wilson's demands and issued the "Sussex Pledge." The German Empire promised it would henceforth act "in accordance with the general principles of visit and search and destruction of merchant vessels recognized by international law." Merchant ships "both within and without the area declared as a naval war zone" would not be attacked "without warning and without saving human lives, unless these ships attempt to escape or offer resistance."[31] This agreement to ease Germany's campaign of unrestricted submarine warfare was designed to avert a break with the United States. Other than a recommitment to the Arabic Pledge, however, it was unclear whether there was anything new in the pronouncement. The Allied merchant ships continued to fight back when attacked, making German adherence to the cruiser rules nearly impossible. Still, the United States reiterated on May 8, 1916, that its neutral rights were not "in any way or in the slightest degree" contingent upon the conduct of other belligerents at sea. The rights of neutral ships, that is, were "single, not joint, and absolute, not relative."[32]

The Sussex Pledge persisted for nearly eight months until it was withdrawn in early 1917. In the meantime, the United States continued to brandish the rights of neutral ships. The American view was steadfastly maximalist, insisting on neutral rights for American ships as well as for American citizens and property on belligerent ships. The only way to ensure such protection would be a strict adherence to the cruiser rules, the capturing of prizes and the adjudication of them in port. Submarines, of course, were unable to do these things.

On January 22, 1917, President Wilson delivered his "peace without victory" speech, calling freedom of the seas the "*sine qua non* of peace, equality, and cooperation."[33] He insisted that the "paths of the sea must alike in law and in fact be free." The president understood that his proposal for free seas was "no doubt a somewhat radical reconsideration" of past practice, although he thought that the "motive for such changes is convincing and compelling." He declared, "There can be no trust or intimacy between the peoples of the world without [it]. The free, constant, unthreatened intercourse of nations is an essential part of the process of peace and of development. It need not be difficult either to define or to secure the freedom of the seas if the governments of the world sincerely desire to come to an agreement concerning it."

In this declaration, peacetime freedom of the seas and wartime neutral rights were, for the first time, intermixed. The concept acquired an importance beyond the mere safe transit of ships or even the protection of neutral passengers on board belligerent merchant vessels. Freedom of the seas merged into Wilson's overall aspiration for a liberal world order. It also entered into the pantheon of American strategic thought. A liberal maritime order was an essential element of an international system of governance based on the rule of law and equality among states.

– – – – • – – –– –

On January 31, 1917, Germany resumed unrestricted U-boat warfare.[34] Germany's change in course initiated the heaviest shipping losses since the beginning of the war. So many vessels were sunk that it was difficult for leaders in the United States and Britain to keep track of them, a problem exacerbated by continuous flag-hopping to U.S. or other neutral flags.[35] From February to July 1917, between thirty and forty American ships were lost to German submarines.

On February 3, 1917, the United States severed diplomatic relations with Germany.[36] Hours later the American liner *Housatonic* was scuttled by a German submarine and sent to the bottom. The *U-53*, under command of the mercurial Lt. Hans Rose, surfaced near the *Housatonic* about sixty miles off the Isles of Scilly, southwest of Britain, and at 10:30 a.m. fired two warning shots. The vessel's master, Thomas A. Ensor, took a small boat to the *U-53* and presented his ship's papers. Upon finding the vessel was carrying a cargo of wheat bound for London, Lieutenant Rose announced that he was obliged to sink the ship. While the thirty-seven crew members of the *Housatonic* boarded lifeboats, scuttling charges were set. The charges were fired, and the submarine towed the lifeboat for several hours before encountering a British trawler, the *Salvator*. The submarine fired a round from its 88-mm deck gun, attracting the attention of the *Salvator*. Then the U-boat submerged, whereupon the *Housatonic*'s crew was rescued.

The *U-53* was well known in the United States. Lieutenant Rose was a notorious U-boat "ace," credited with 210,000 tons of shipping sunk.[37] His humane treatment of the crew of the *Housatonic* earned accolades; the *New York Times* noted that the *Housatonic* had been warned before being sunk and considered the placing of the crew in a "place of safety" on board lifeboats laudable.[38] This principled approach prevented the *Housatonic* from becoming a casus belli, a cause for war. If Germany had continued in this vein, it is unlikely Wilson would have found sufficient pretext to enter the war.

The schooner *Lyman M. Law* was the next U.S. merchant ship sunk. The ship went down in the Mediterranean Sea off the coast of Sardinia on February 12. As in the *Housatonic* incident, the crew of the *Lyman M. Law* was put into lifeboats, and they landed safely at Cagliari. The *U-35*, under command of the dashing Lothar von Arnauld de la Perière, had conducted a visit-and-search of the schooner.[39] After some apparent debate among the

German officers, von Arnauld decided the ship was carrying contraband and ordered the vessel scuttled.[40] The submarine put the crew of the *Lyman M. Law* in a boat and provided them with food, water, and gasoline.[41] Still, the incident cast Germany in a bad light, as the crew later complained that the submarine boarding party seized ship's stores by force and wanted to "ransack" their galley for food, a case of high seas robbery.[42]

Soon after the *Lyman M. Law* incident, the RMS *Laconia* was sunk. The submarine *U-50* put two torpedoes into the British-flagged Cunard liner, which was on a voyage from New York to Britain.[43] The attack violated the Sussex Pledge, and three Americans died—leading many to suggest that this was the "overt act" that would bring the United States into the war. Wilson, however, considered neither the *Lyman M. Law* nor the *Laconia* attack a sufficient trigger to justify war. Adding fuel to the fire: two weeks after the *Law* was sunk, a diplomatic scandal incensed Americans and accelerated the popular tilt against Germany.

On February 24, British intelligence officials passed to Walter Hines Page, the American ambassador to Britain, a decoded note from the German foreign secretary, Arthur Zimmermann, to Count Johann von Bernstorff, the German ambassador to Mexico. The "Zimmermann Telegram" proposed that if the United States did not remain neutral in the war, Germany and Mexico could join forces. Germany would help Mexico recover Texas, New Mexico, and Arizona, thereby opening a new front along the U.S. southern border. The State Department released the telegram to the newspapers on March 1, 1917.[44] Two days later, Zimmermann admitted that the telegram was authentic. The Germans had hoped to capitalize on poor relations between the United States and Mexico and the chaos of the ongoing Mexican revolution, but the telegram turned American public sentiment squarely against Germany. Even this revelation, however, was an insufficiently "overt act" to trigger entry into the war.

The problem from Germany's perspective was that Allied shipping had begun to fight back, alerting Royal Navy warships nearby, firing concealed guns at the submarines, attempting to ram, or taking evasive action and fleeing. Germany thought of itself as the victim of continual Allied violations of the cruiser rules. If Allied ships would simply follow submarines' instructions, all lives would be saved. Passengers and crew would alight to lifeboats, and the vessels would be sunk.

— — — — • — — — —

Four more U.S.-registered ships went down in March 1917, just as President Wilson issued an executive order to arm merchant vessels. On March 12, the *U-62* sank the steamship *Algonquin*. The submarine gave no notice but waited until the ship's crew had evacuated on lifeboats before destroying it with gunfire. At the time the *Algonquin* was an American-flagged ship; the vessel had been transferred from the British to the American flag two years after the war had begun—a change that Germany did not recognize. Article 56 of the 1909 Declaration of London concerning the Laws of Naval War held that such flag transfers after the initiation of hostilities were evasions and void. Furthermore, the vessel held a cargo of foodstuffs, which were considered contraband of war.

On March 16, the 4,115-ton steamship *Vigilancia* was sunk, with a loss of fifteen men who drowned when two of the four lifeboats were swamped as the ship went down. The following day, the 5,252-ton *City of Memphis* was torpedoed, as was the *Illinois* the day after that. Unlike the *Falaba*, *Lusitania*, *Arabic*, *Sussex*, and *Laconia*, the tranche of ships sunk in March were U.S.-flagged. Those earlier cases, like others involving Allied-flagged ships, had cost American lives but had not been attacks on American sovereignty.[45] The *Algonquin* was at least nominally U.S.-flagged, and its sinking raised the stakes higher, yet it was not until the *Vigilancia* that war appeared imminent. The ship was American-owned, American-flagged, and American-operated, and it was flying the American flag.

The *Vigilancia* was the first American ship whose intentional sinking by Germany resulted in casualties, and that made its loss a defining moment. In the event, the sinking of the *Vigilancia* was one of three incidents that ultimately led to the call for war in Washington. The *U-70*, under the command of Otto Wünsche, had torpedoed the *Vigilancia* 150 miles west of Britain. It had not been transferred from another registry, like the *Algonquin*, or unintentionally targeted, like the *Gulflight*. In contrast to such cases as the *Housatonic* and *Lyman M. Law*, the *Vigilancia*'s papers had never been examined to determine whether contraband was on board. Throughout 1915 and 1916, Germany had stressed compliance with the Declaration of London, particularly its article 50, by which merchant mariners would be evacuated to a "place of safety" before a ship was sunk. The departure from this practice by Wünsche epitomized unrestricted submarine warfare and precipitated American entry into the war.

The day the *Vigilancia* went down, the passenger steamer *City of Memphis* got under way from Cardiff for New York. The vessel was stopped, boarded, and released with a stern warning on January 30, 1917, one day before the resumption of unrestricted U-boat warfare was announced. The ship had been carrying contraband—a cargo of cotton bound for Le Havre, France. It was strongly warned that if it were caught again, it would be sunk. The ship met its fate six weeks later. On March 17, 1917, the *UC-66* interdicted it thirty-five miles south of Fastnet, Ireland. The submarine was under Herbert Pustkuchen, who had commanded the *UB-29* in its attack on the *Sussex* on March 24, 1916. In accordance with the cruiser rules, the *UC-66* warned the ship and permitted evacuation to lifeboats. Once the crew was off the ship, the submarine sank it with surface naval gunfire. The *City of Memphis*, however, flew a neutral flag and did not carry contraband and therefore was legally immune from attack. The vessel was in fact empty, but Pustkuchen never bothered to check. Furthermore, although the crew survived, that was confirmed only four days later; they became scattered at sea and drifted into different ports.

The next day, the U.S.-flagged 5,225-ton tanker *Illinois* spotted a German submarine in the English Channel. The submarine closed, and the crew of the *Illinois* fled, under fire, in the lifeboats. Once the ship was evacuated, German sailors placed timed explosives along its hull. The *Illinois* too had no cargo on board, and the sinking was an unlawful encroachment on neutral rights. The insult was somewhat ameliorated, however, by the German submarine's towing the *Illinois*' lifeboats toward Alderney to ensure the safety of the crew.

Secretary of State Robert Lansing's private notes at this time reveal that President Wilson still opposed war.[46] Lansing himself, however, considered that the attacks on the *Vigilancia*, *City of Memphis*, and *Illinois* "manifestly constituted overt acts" justifying a declaration of war against Germany. The cabinet convened in an atmosphere of crisis on March 20, with even the most committed neutralists finally in agreement that a state of war existed between the United States and Germany. The following day, the U.S. tanker *Healdton* was torpedoed by a German submarine twenty-five miles north of Terschelling, Holland. One of the lifeboats capsized, and twenty crew members drowned. Wilson had not revealed his views during the meeting, but the next day he asked to address a joint session of Congress at the earliest practical date, which was April 2. In the interim, Wilson did not confide in anyone, which heightened the drama of his address. The United States stood on the brink of war.

— — — — •— — — —

On March 30, Secretary Lansing collected into a single memorandum a list of offenses by Germany that justified war. The violations coalesced in four broad categories. First, there had been twenty-two cases of improper activities by German officials in the United States. Second were the violations of American diplomatic rights, including the Zimmermann Telegram; Lansing presented a list. Third was a list of 225 American lives lost during attacks on twenty-two ships. These had been mostly British vessels, although three were American: the *Gulflight*, *Vigilancia*, and *Healdton*. Fourth, the memorandum identified seventeen American ships damaged or sunk by German submarines, and the list also included the *Gulflight*, *Vigilancia*, and *Healdton*. The memorandum recounted that since February 1, the *Housatonic*, *Lyman M. Law*, *Vigilancia*, *City of Memphis*, *Illinois*, and *Healdton* had been sunk. The attacks on the *Housatonic* and *Lyman M. Law*, however, had already been deemed by the administration not to rise to the level of an "overt act," and it was still unclear whether the *Healdton* had been sunk by a torpedo or had hit a British mine. That left the three attacks on March 16, 17, and 18—on the *Vigilancia*, *City of Memphis*, and *Illinois*—as the collective casus belli.

Citing Germany's resumption of unrestricted U-boat warfare, President Wilson asked the joint session of Congress on April 2 for a declaration of war. Germany's policy, he stated, had swept aside every restriction, sinking liners and merchantmen without mercy. These violations of international law constituted a "war against all nations," presaging the American inclination for global order.[47] As Austria-Hungary had not actually attacked U.S. shipping, the president declined to declare war on that German ally.[48] As Congress debated the call to war, members received word that the *Aztec* had been sunk on April 1, with 28 lives lost. The *Aztec* was the first American armed merchant vessel sunk by a U-boat.[49] Just as Congress was closing debate on April 4, members heard that the 7,924-ton steamship *Missourian* had been torpedoed and shelled without warning by a German submarine.[50] That same day, the Senate voted 82 to 6 in favor of a declaration of war. On April 6, the House voted 373 to 50 in support of the declaration, casting the United States into the war.

The U.S. Navy now adopted a defensive posture designed to protect vulnerable shipping lanes. It operated almost exclusively in convoy-escort and antisubmarine roles, rather than power projection. The main mission of the Navy was to ferry an American expeditionary army of some two million men and its supplies to Europe and thereafter provision it indefinitely.[51] In this task the Navy was to be remarkably successful—of the 1,720,360 soldiers transported in ships to fight on the Continent, not one was lost at sea to enemy attack or mishap while under U.S. Navy escort.[52]

One year after the resumption of unrestricted U-boat warfare, Wilson delivered a speech on peace terms to end World War I. They were reduced to "Fourteen Points." Point II called for "freedom of navigation upon the seas, alike in peace and in war, except as the seas may be closed in whole or in part by international action."[53] This provision reflected the importance of the concept of freedom of the seas to what Wilson hoped would be a new world order, complete with rules and institutions—a society of nations. On October 6, 1918, the German government requested an immediate armistice and notified the U.S. government that it accepted the Fourteen Points as a basis for peace negotiations. Wilson's quixotic adviser Edward Mandell House, known as "Colonel House," was dispatched as special envoy to the Paris Peace Conference. On October 29, 1918, House telegrammed Wilson requesting approval to make a more expansive and detailed exposition of the Fourteen Points. Point II, for instance, concerning "absolute freedom of navigation," needed to be read in connection with Point XIV, which proposed the estab-lishment of a League of Nations.[54] Free navigation would be secured under three conditions:

1. General peace, under which no serious dispute exists. In general peace, there would be "implied freedom to come and go" outside the territorial sea.
2. General war entered into by the League of Nations to enforce "international covenants," in which case the League would be expected to cut off all trade with the outlaw nation.
3. A limited war not involving a breach of "international covenants" and therefore not involving the League of Nations. This presented the greatest challenge. During such a limited war, neutral ships and neutral property were to be protected by the belligerents.[55]

President Wilson replied that this framework was satisfactory but that "details of application mentioned should be regarded as merely illustrative suggestions and reserved for the peace conference."[56] British prime minis-ter Lloyd George objected that Great Britain could not accept such terms without qualification.[57] If freedom of the seas were to be a condition of peace with Germany, George would be unwilling to discuss it, although, he supposed, it might be feasible as part of an overall package that included the creation of the League of Nations. But later that same day, George declared flatly that Britain could not accept Point II "under any circumstances," as it took away from Britain the power of blockade. Colonel House reported that Georges Clémenceau, the French prime minister, had immediately accepted Point II but that Lloyd George had stated, "It is impossible for any British Prime Minister to do this."[58] The next day, House relayed to the president a cable from the Allies containing acceptance of the terms set forth by Wilson in his January 8, 1918, speech and subsequent addresses.[59] They reserved for the negotiations at the conference any position on freedom of the seas, since there were varying interpretations of the concept. The United States forwarded to Germany the Allied memorandum on November 5 without comment.[60] The armistice was signed on November 11, 1918.

The plenary session of the Paris Peace Conference did not consider the issue of freedom of the seas. In September 1919, nevertheless, President Wilson called freedom of the seas one of his driving concerns at the peace conference in order to ensure that neutral states could use the seas even if other states were at war. However, Wilson believed that with the establishment of the League of Nations, there were no neutral states any longer and that therefore it was unnecessary to define the concept with greater fidelity.

— — — — • — — — —

Whereas wartime rights to freedom of the seas had focused on neutral rights and belligerent obligations under the cruiser rules, the aftermath of the war brought to the surface disagreements over peacetime rights to use the oceans. The international law of the sea was one element of the shift from wartime to a peacetime order based on the rule of law. In 1927, the Permanent Court of International Justice decided in the case of the SS *Lotus* that freedom of the high seas meant the absence of territorial sovereignty upon the high seas or of any authority of coastal states to exercise jurisdiction over foreign vessels.[61]

In April 1930, naval armament talks began in London. Delegates drafted rules for the use of force by submarines in a time of war—that is, whether submarines had to comply with the cruiser rules. The United Kingdom, Japan, France, Italy, and the United States agreed on April 22, 1930, that they must conform "to the rules of international law to which surface vessels are subject."[62] Submarines were not permitted to attack or sink merchant ships except "in the case of persistent refusal to stop on being duly summoned, or of active resistance to visit or search, [by] a warship." Furthermore, the passengers, crew, and ship's papers had first to be removed to "a place of safety." Lifeboats in themselves were not regarded as places of safety unless the safety of the passengers and crew was ensured with respect to sea and weather conditions, proximity to land, or the "presence of another vessel which is in a position to take them onboard." In short, both submarines and surface ships had to comply with the same rules. The agreement among the major maritime powers did not, however, address the complaints that had been raised by Germany all along—that the cruiser rules placed submarines at a distinct disadvantage in naval warfare.

— — — — ● — — — —

The challenges to freedom of the seas resurfaced during World War II. The technological advances in submarines and the introduction of naval aviation made the threat to Atlantic communications in 1941 even more worrisome than it had been during World War I. Still, President Franklin Delano Roosevelt (FDR) declined to settle for a strategy of coastal defense and insisted on unimpeded use of the oceans.[63] Like Wilson, FDR viewed freedom of the seas as the cornerstone of American strategy in peacetime and in war. On August 14, 1941, FDR and Prime Minister Winston Churchill of the United Kingdom met for a conference at Argentia, Newfoundland, in a secluded bay. There the leaders of the free world crafted the Atlantic Charter. The president and prime minister agreed that all freedom depends on freedom of the seas. The principles of freedom of the seas were incorporated into the document, which Roosevelt and Churchill released as a charter of the war aims of the Allied powers. The seventh of eight principles stated that all nations enjoy the right to traverse the high seas and oceans without hindrance.

The threat of Nazi Germany and submarine warfare had become acute, and the United States, although a neutral in the conflict, would not sit idle. "We could not wait until bombs fell on the United States," FDR later remarked, "[o]ur Bunker Hill might be thousands of miles away." The Department of State suggested that security was indivisible, arguing against "regional cliques" of states and in favor of united nations focused on maintaining the international system.

The following month, the destroyer USS *Greer* (DD 145) was involved in an incident with the German submarine *U-652*. On September 4, 1941, the *Greer* was tracking a German submarine in support of a British aircraft that was attacking it with depth charges. The submarine fired several torpedoes at the American warship, which all missed. Germany claimed that the ship had fired first, but President Roosevelt countered that the "blunt fact" was that the submarine had "fired first upon this American destroyer without warning."[64] The following day, German aircraft bombed and sank the American merchant ship SS *Steel Seafarer* in the Red Sea, about 220 miles from Suez.[65] The day after the *Steel Seafarer* went down, surviving crew members from the Panamanian-flagged SS *Sessa* were rescued at sea. The ship had been torpedoed on August 17, 1941.[66] The sole American crew member had perished in the attack. The ship had been carrying foodstuffs, cereals, and lumber for the government of Iceland.

Just days later—on September 11, 1941—FDR told the nation in a radio "fireside chat" that he had ordered U.S. naval and air forces to strike German submarines and surface raiders in waters vital to American interests. He called the attack on the *Greer* "piracy—morally and legally." The *Greer* incident, along with others, was part of a "Nazi design to abolish the freedom of the seas," to "acquire absolute control and domination" of the oceans.[67] He viewed Germany's policy as part of a broader strategy to "dominate the United States and the Western Hemisphere by force." German submarines and raiders were the "rattlesnakes" of the Atlantic Ocean; Roosevelt announced that U.S. forces would take preemptive action when they were found in American "defensive waters."

> When you see a rattlesnake poised to strike, you do not wait until he has struck before you crush him. . . . Upon our naval and air patrol . . . falls the duty of maintaining the American policy of freedom of the seas—now. That means, very simply and clearly, that our patrolling vessels and planes will protect all merchant ships—not only American ships but ships of any flag—engaged in commerce in our defensive waters. They will protect them from submarines; they will protect them from surface raiders.[68]

Additional incidents during the fall of 1941 stoked the fire. A German submarine torpedoed the USS *Kearney* (DD 432) off the coast of Iceland on October 17. The U.S. destroyer had dropped depth charges on German submarines in a "wolf pack" that had been stalking a British convoy and its Canadian escorts. A torpedo from the *U-568* struck the *Kearney* on the starboard side, killing eleven men and injuring twenty-two.

On October 27, President Roosevelt discussed the attack on the *Kearney* in a radio address. He once again firmly set forth American policy: "Freedom of the seas is now, as it has always been, a fundamental policy of your Government and mine."[69] American resolve, he continued, was "expressed in the orders to the American Navy to shoot on sight. Those orders stand." This was the first time the president used the term "shoot on sight." Samuel Elliot Morison later remarked that from this point on the United States was in a "de facto naval war with Germany on the Atlantic Ocean."[70]

The president also pledged that U.S. merchant ships would be armed, reiterating a message he had sent to Congress on the issue on October 9, 1941.[71] Congress had revoked Section VI of the Neutrality Act of 1939 on October 17, giving the president legislative power to make good on this commitment. By the end of November 1941, the United States had put in place elements of a comprehensive plan for national defense, including a massive expansion of the armed forces; increased military aid to Britain, China, and Russia; lease of eight strategic bases from Britain to create a "protective girdle of steel along the Atlantic seaboard of the American Continent"; landing fields in Greenland; and responsibility for the defense of Iceland.[72]

Nazi Germany, of course, saw things very differently. Its eventual declaration of war on the United States on December 11, 1941, cited the attacks against German submarines by the *Greer* and *Kearney*, and even the German sinking of the destroyer *Reuben James* (a unit of the Neutrality Patrol, on October 31) as justification.[73] These neutral American warships, Germany reasoned, had placed themselves in the midst of combat between belligerents and had therefore lost their neutral status. The United States, Germany argued, could not call itself a neutral and then insert itself into the conflict, even into individual tactical engagements.

— — — — ● — — — —

Meanwhile, the principles in the Atlantic Charter were gaining currency. Churchill and Harry Hopkins, an aide to President Roosevelt, completed the "Declaration of the United Nations" on December 29, 1941. With Churchill's edits the finished manuscript reads in part, "Peace should enable all men to traverse the high seas and oceans without hindrance." Continuing the pattern of organic interrelationship among the elements of international peace and security contained in Woodrow Wilson's Fourteen Points, the 1941 declaration attached freedom of the seas to "freedom from want" and to the idea of economic liberalism and nondiscrimination.[74] These principles were to be widely accepted; the declaration was formally issued on January 1, 1942, with twelve states signing the text. By 1945, twenty-six states had signed the principles that would govern the new world order.[75]

The doctrine of freedom of the seas, explicitly endorsed in the Declaration of the United Nations, was subsequently incorporated into article 3 of the Charter of the United Nations. All the major powers, including the permanent five members on the United Nations Security Council, endorsed the declaration and the charter. Freedom of the seas had evolved from a matter of neutral rights during armed conflict to a generalized peacetime right enjoyed by all states.

"BLANK CHECK"

The Gulf of Tonkin Incident (1964)

The American involvement in Vietnam sprang from the Manila Pact. President Dwight D. Eisenhower had signed the treaty in 1954, and the Senate approved it in February 1955. Nearly a decade later, President Lyndon B. Johnson summarized American regional interests in Southeast Asia in four simple propositions. First, America keeps its word; the United States would honor its commitments to regional states. Second, the entire Southeast Asian region was at risk; a threat to any nation in that region was a threat to all of them, as well as to the United States (this captured the "domino theory"). Third, the United States had peaceful intentions; Washington did not have military, political, or territorial ambitions in the area. Fourth, the Indochina War involved a greater struggle for freedom in South Vietnam and Laos.[1]

In order to aid South Vietnam, the United States ramped up pressure against the Democratic Republic of Vietnam (DRV, or North Vietnam) during the early 1960s. The government of President Ngo Dinh Diem fell in 1963, adding to the sense of disquiet and urgency in Washington, D.C. By 1964, the United States had embarked on a concerted campaign to degrade DRV capabilities and induce leaders in Hanoi to the bargaining table.[2] One element of this strategy involved intelligence collection against the DRV by U.S. warships in international waters under the DeSoto patrol program. The Gulf of Tonkin incident arose from these DeSoto naval patrols.

"DeSoto"was the code name for a classified signal intelligence (SIGINT) program and warship "presence" campaign along Asian coastlines to collect shore-based radio and radar transmissions. DeSoto operations also were designed to demonstrate the right of U.S. warships to operate in international waters.[3] Proposed by Commander, U.S. Seventh Fleet (COMSEVENTH-FLT) in March 1962, the DeSoto patrols had been designed to "collect intelligence concerning [Chinese communist] electronic and naval activity[,] . . . establish and maintain Seventh Fleet presence" in the region, and serve as a "minor cold war irritant" to China.[4] China protested the patrols but did not tangibly react to the American presence. In October and November 1962, the USS *Hollister* (DD 788) and USS *Shelton* (DD 790) conducted the first DeSoto patrols near North Korea. North Vietnam was added in December, when the USS *Agerholm* (DD 826) sailed around Hainan Island and entered the Gulf of Tonkin. Six patrols were conducted in 1963 along the coastlines of China, the Soviet Union, North Vietnam, and Indonesia. The earliest DeSoto patrol units were ordered to stay at least twenty miles from the coast, but this limit was calibrated for each mission and over time crept closer to shore, although always remaining in international waters.

The Seventh Fleet commander revised the DeSoto program in 1964 to encompass all-source intelligence gathering. Ships were to collect intelligence on foreign surface-warfare and air-defense postures along the coastline and on merchant shipping; collect by SIGINT, photography, and visual observation; and record hydrographic and meteorological data.[5] The USS *Craig* (DD 885) conducted the first 1964 mission, from February to March. The warship followed a course from near Hainan Island toward Macao and Taiwan.[6] SIGINT equipment on board provided tactical intelligence and intercepted communications in reaction to the vessel's presence. Intelligence was collected within a small temporary van manned by a complement of Navy cryptologists, a Naval Security Group (NSG) element. DeSoto ships also received support from communications-intelligence sites in the Philippines and probably elsewhere in the region. There were indications that North Vietnam was aware of the presence of the *Craig* offshore, but the ship had been unmolested.

The United States was quite cautious in approaching foreign coastlines during DeSoto patrols. The early *Craig* patrol was authorized to operate no closer than four nautical miles from the coast of Vietnam, as the United States recognized a three-nautical-mile territorial sea.[7] France claimed the three-nautical-mile limit when it had controlled Vietnam.[8] Since China claimed a twelve-nautical-mile territorial sea, similar patrols approached no closer than fifteen nautical miles from its coast. The United States did not recognize China's claim beyond three nautical miles, but the greater political sensitivity of China cautioned a greater standoff distance.[9]

Four DeSoto patrols were conducted from December 1962 until July 1964.[10] In late July, the USS *Maddox* (DD 731) followed the *Craig*. The *Maddox* was equipped for high-frequency and very-high-frequency voice intercept and collection of electronic intelligence (ELINT).[11] The ship belonged to the task group led by the carrier *Ticonderoga* (CV 14).

During the *Maddox* operation the closest permitted approach to Vietnam was eight miles from the mainland or four miles from islands.[12] The ship was directed to remain at least 15 nm from China.[13] The *Maddox* was under the command of Capt. John Herrick, who held explicit orders from Commander in Chief, Pacific (CINCPAC) to locate and identify all coastal radar transmitters and navigational aids. The ship also was ordered to spot Vietnamese fleet junk movements along the coast that might be connected to Vietcong maritime supply and infiltration routes.[14]

– – – – • – – – –

During this period, South Vietnamese forces were conducting what were known as OPLAN 34A missions, constituting a hit-and-run campaign that potentially overlapped with DeSoto patrols. Under OPLAN 34A, South Vietnamese Special Forces launched commando raids and seaborne attacks along the coast of North Vietnam. These operations were not terribly effective, however. There was something of a symbiotic relationship between the two missions, because DeSoto patrols were interested in detecting North Vietnamese reactions to OPLAN 34A strikes and harassment. The OPLAN 34A attacks were part of the American strategy of graduated response, meant to slowly tighten the noose around North Vietnam and convince it to relent in the struggle. Although no American participated in actual 34A raids, American planners, trainers, and logisticians supported them.

On the night of July 30–31, South Vietnamese commandos hit Hon Me Island off the coast of North Vietnam, while commando boats bombarded enemy positions on Hon Ngu Island.[15] On board the *Maddox*, Captain Herrick observed afterward the retreating commando boats and intercepted DRV communications indicating that North Vietnam could not catch them. The U.S. warship withdrew from the scene, well out to sea.[16] Apparently, the *Maddox* was unaware of the action against Hon Me.

The following afternoon, a U.S. naval intercept site in the Philippines reported a transmission stating that the originator, possibly a patrol boat, intended to "fight the enemy tonight."[17] The intelligence was passed to the *Maddox*. Upon receipt of the message and corroborating intelligence from the NSG detachment on board his own ship, Captain Herrick terminated the DeSoto mission and headed east from the patrol area at ten knots. No attack came that night, however, so the next day the *Maddox* turned back west and reentered the patrol area. The showdown occurred on August 2.

North Vietnam now began to concentrate P-4 and Swatow-class patrol torpedo boats (PTs) at Hon Me Island. The objective may have been to prepare to repel further OPLAN 34A attacks, but U.S. Navy cryptologists regarded it as prelude to an attack. At 1144, a Marine SIGINT group at Phu Bai intercepted communications from a Swatow-class patrol boat directing two units, the *T-142* and *T-146*, to vector for a planned attack. These two boats were to be joined by the *T-166* and *T-135* in following an "enemy" that was, the analysts assessed, probably the current DeSoto mission. Five Vietnamese patrol boats were now concentrated at Hon Me, and the *Maddox* had seen them as it headed northeast away from the island. The Americans intercepted contradictory Vietnamese orders, one of them from Haiphong cautioning the patrol boats not to attack the U.S. warship during the daytime. Around 1400, however, three P-4 patrol boats—the *T-333*, *T-226*, and *T-339*—were ten miles north of Hon Me.

They accelerated and began to bear down on the *Maddox*. The P-4s were Chinese-built, Soviet-designed craft, each armed with machine guns and two torpedoes.

The U.S. ship changed course and accelerated to twenty-five knots to avoid them. The *Maddox* turned away to the southeast; the PTs headed northeast to the point it had just left.[18] The PT boats found themselves well west of their target and were obliged to pursue it toward the southeast, rather than closing on a collision course *from* the southeast, as they would have wished. This geometry meant that instead of closing rapidly on the *Maddox* and suddenly launching torpedoes, the PT boats had to chase it, all the while in range of its 5-inch guns. The American interception of a second Vietnamese message to attack the *Maddox* had given the destroyer a decisive tactical advantage.

With the boats in pursuit, the *Maddox* sent by "flash" precedence (i.e., fastest possible handling) a message to commands in the Pacific region warning that it was being chased by high-speed craft that plainly intended to attack with torpedoes, and that the *Maddox* would fire in self-defense if necessary.[19] At 1507 the *Maddox* reported that it was being attacked by three DRV P-4 patrol torpedo craft and that it was "opening up with five-inch battery" (the ship had three twin five-inch turrets, two forward and one aft).[20] Captain Herrick fired three or four warning shots at 9,800 yards at 1507 and engaged with rapid fire moments later. Three torpedoes were seen in the water, but all missed their mark.[21] The PTs completed their attack at 1529, and COMSEVENTHFLT directed the U.S. warship to retire from the area, firing in self-defense if necessary.[22] Only a single machine-gun round had struck the *Maddox*, and there were no casualties.[23]

During the attack Captain Herrick had requested air cover from the *Ticonderoga*, some 280 miles away. The destroyer USS *Turner Joy* (DD 951), which was on station as a "watchdog" picket for the aircraft carrier at the mouth to the Gulf of Tonkin, began to prepare for a rendezvous, expected at 1900. Four F8-E Crusaders converged on the *Maddox*. The F-8s assembled overhead, observed the ship firing, turned in pursuit of the three retreating PT boats, and engaged them with Zuni rockets and

20-mm cannon.[24] No Zunis made direct hits, but all three boats were struck by 20-mm gunfire. One of them was left dead in the water; the other two, damaged, headed for the beach. The Vietnamese had offered only minimal antiaircraft gunfire but believed they had struck at least one jet, as one trailed black smoke after the strafing run. In fact, the smoke was normal for J-57 engines at 100 percent military power.[25] Likewise, the aircraft thought they had inflicted greater damage on the PT boats than they actually had, due to a large amount of smoke from them. The boats in fact were not fatally damaged; the smoke came from smoke generators and was meant to screen their retreat.

A second flight of F-8s arrived later but was directed to orbit and hold fire unless the enemy PTs resumed the engagement.[26] The order to cease fire likely was the result of a misunderstanding, whereby the restriction not to enter within three nautical miles of the coast was misinterpreted as an order to cease fire.[27] All three of the patrol boats eventually made their way back to port, the unit that initially was dead in the water having finally restarted its engines.[28] That craft, the *T-339*, had four sailors killed and six wounded.[29]

There was to be considerable confusion and debate on the American side as to whether any of the PTs had been sunk. When the four U.S. aircraft departed the area they reported one PT dead in the water, apparently sinking.[30] The mystery was conclusively solved in 1966, when three boats were sunk by U.S. aircraft and survivors were picked up. The boats were the *T-333*, *T-336*, and *T-339*—the same three involved in the August 2, 1964, incident.[31]

Captain Herrick—who was not only commanding officer of the USS *Maddox* but a destroyer-division commander and Commander, Task Group 72.1—assessed that the United States was already at war with North Vietnam: "It is apparent that DRV has cut down [*sic*] the gauntlet and now considers itself at war with the U.S. It is felt that they will attack U.S. forces on sight and with no regard for cost. U.S. ships in the Gulf of Tonkin can no longer assume that they will be considered neutrals exercising the right of free transit. They will be treated as belligerents from first detection and must consider themselves as such."[32] As soon as the first engagement came to an end, Commander in Chief, U.S. Pacific Fleet (CINCPACFLT) sent a message to Washington stating that in view of the attack on the *Maddox*, it was "in our interest that we assert right [to] freedom of the seas" and resume the patrols at the earliest possibility.[33]

--- --- --- ● --- --- ---

The following day the United States issued a demarche to North Vietnam protesting the "unprovoked attack" on U.S. naval forces operating on the high seas.[34] The note was the first diplomatic correspondence sent by the United States to North Vietnam. In it the United States claimed its warships had been operating "freely on the high seas, in accordance with the rights guaranteed by international law to vessels of all nations. They will continue to do so and will take whatever measures are appropriate for their defense."[35] President Johnson stated that the United States would not "run away," although it also would not "be provocative." If North Vietnam should persist in attacks, it "will be under no misapprehension as to the grave consequences" that would result.[36] This reflected the U.S. realization that the DeSoto operations were "rattling" Hanoi, and the United States did not intend to stop them.[37]

COMSEVENTHFLT ordered the *Turner Joy* to continue the DeSoto patrol, joining the *Maddox* on August 3. The chairman of the Joint Chiefs of Staff (JCS) issued new rules of engagement to CINCPAC for the mission. Rather than permitting American ships to operate outside of eight nautical miles of the mainland of Vietnam and at least four from the islands, the *Maddox* and the *Turner Joy* were now told to approach no closer than 11 nm from the shore of Vietnam.[38] There was some suspicion that Vietnam actually claimed a twelve-mile limit. The legal rationale for authorizing warships to go as close as 11 nm was that by penetrating one mile into the claimed territorial sea, the United States demonstrated that it did not acquiesce to that excessive claim. The chairman of the JCS also ordered the ships to engage and destroy any Swatow-class vessels or PT boats in the area.[39] The ships were authorized to fire their 5-inch batteries landward of the 11-nm distance;[40] however, they were not authorized to pursue North Vietnamese forces into the nation's territorial waters or airspace.[41]

To put North Vietnam on notice and inform the American people, President Johnson made public his instructions to the *Maddox* and the *Turner Joy*. The president also pledged that the patrols would continue. If U.S. forces were attacked, he promised, the United States would not merely reply to the opposing force but destroy it.[42] The administration still thought the August 2 attack had been an isolated incident. With a measure of tough talk and continued operations, albeit farther from shore to avoid being unnecessarily provocative, the government hoped the incident would not be repeated. Communications interceptions suggested that a local North Vietnamese commander might have acted impulsively. In his memoirs, President Johnson later wrote that he did not order a retaliatory strike because it was unclear whether Hanoi or a rogue commander had ordered the attack on the *Maddox*.[43] Furthermore, it was also unclear whether Hanoi had lost control of its forces. The United States was not taking any chances. Air Force combat aircraft were deployed to the Philippines, and a second aircraft carrier—the *Constellation* (CV 64)—was dispatched to link up with the *Maddox* and the *Turner Joy*.

North Vietnam was indignant yet elated that it had "beaten" the American fleet. Leveraging a patriotic David-and-Goliath narrative, North Vietnam reveled in how its small, low-technology torpedo boats had "damaged" a U.S. warship, inflicted "casualties" on its officers and men, and shot down one of the jets that had attacked them.[44] These claims were exaggerated, yet North Vietnam did cause the United States to pull back farther from the coastline. Although the United States steadfastly maintained that it was not driven from the gulf, U.S. warships did not make any similar close approaches to the coastline for six months.[45]

— — — ● — — —

A second incident occurred two days later, evidently caused by confusion of U.S. units in the area. The "fog of war" produced conflicting narratives and interpretations of a second attack. The scheduled OPLAN 34A mission for the night of August 3–4 went as planned. A South Vietnamese task group of four PTFs (patrol torpedo boat, fast) shelled a radar station at Vinh Son for twenty-five minutes, as well as a security outpost on the riverbank at Cua Ron.[46] Each of the boats carried an eighteen-man South Vietnamese crew, a 57-mm recoilless rifle, and other weapons.[47] One of the DRV vessels, probably a Swatow, chased the PTF 6 for forty minutes but failed to catch it.[48] Military Assistance Command Vietnam (MACV) asked the *Maddox* to stay north of 19°20', to avoid mutual interference between the OPLAN 34A operation and the DeSoto patrol.[49] Captain Herrick did not receive the transmission in time, however, and the two destroyers wandered closer to the OPLAN 34A targets, although still some fifty miles away.[50]

Conspiracy theorists were quick to suspect that the *Maddox* was set up, placed in harm's way to attract a second DRV attack and thus provide justification for greater American involvement in the Indochina War. Rumors arose on the *Maddox* itself that a fleet tugboat was waiting with the American task force over the horizon to retrieve the damaged ship once it had been attacked by the North Vietnamese. Someone on board the illusory tug was supposed to have told a crew member of the *Maddox* that the destroyer was expected to be sunk or suffer heavy casualties. Further, George Ball, undersecretary of state at the time, stated there was "no question" that some in the administration were "looking for any excuse to initiate bombing."[51] The idea quickly gained traction that the second incident was, or even both were, fabricated as a pretext to drag the United States into the war.[52] In response to this criticism, Secretary of Defense Robert McNamara would declare, "I find it inconceivable that anyone remotely familiar with our society and our system of government could expect the existence of a conspiracy, which would include almost all, if not all, of the chain of command in the Pacific, the chairman of the joint chiefs of staff, the secretary of defense and his chief civilian assistants, the secretary of state and the President of the United States."[53]

In any case, if the United States had staged a provocation in order to retaliate, it could have done a better job of positioning its forces. The OPLAN 34A attacks appear to have been rather distant from the DeSoto patrols, although there may have been some relationship between the two; another PTF raid set for the night of August 4–5 was recalled when the

Maddox and *Turner Joy* reported contact with the enemy. In the most thorough academic study of the Tonkin Gulf attacks, Edwin E. Moïse concludes that there was a genuine effort to keep the OPLAN 34A operations separate from the DeSoto patrols; however, North Vietnam may not have viewed them the same way.[54] On August 6, Secretary McNamara learned of the OPLAN 34A raids of August 3–4. In testimony before the Senate Foreign Relations Committee three years later, he noted that on August 4, the night of the second incident, the *Maddox* and *Turner Joy* were some seventy miles from the South Vietnamese action against coastal targets in North Vietnam.[55] The action at sea thought to have occurred, moreover, took place only twenty-two hours later. He maintained it was "difficult to believe," in the face of the president's announcement following the first attack on August 2, that U.S. patrols off the coast of North Vietnam that were meant to assert the right to freedom of the sea would be connected to actions by South Vietnam some seventy miles south.

In any case, a series of incidents reported as North Vietnamese attacks occurred on August 4, although it is not clear what actually transpired. The *Maddox* and the *Turner Joy* spent August 4 transiting from north to south about sixteen miles from the coastline of North Vietnam.[56] A small U.S. Marine Corps intelligence detachment issued a flash-precedence warning on the night of August 4 of a North Vietnamese naval operation planned against the DeSoto patrol.[57] This message reached the *Maddox* at 1816. The night was dark, with rain and a thick overcast. At 1940, another flash-precedence message, based on communications intelligence, advised U.S. forces that there were "imminent plans of DRV Naval Action possibly against [the] DeSoto Mission."[58] The *Maddox* and the *Turner Joy* had also been warned of "military action" against "enemy forces," so they prepared for battle. The *Maddox* acknowledged the warning of "imminent" attack an hour later and reported that it was heading south at "best speed."[59]

In retrospect, however, the intercepted North Vietnamese message likely referred to a planned engagement against South Vietnamese forces conducting that night's OPLAN 34A attack;[60] in either event, Hanoi protested the OPLAN 34A attack and believed that the two destroyers were part of

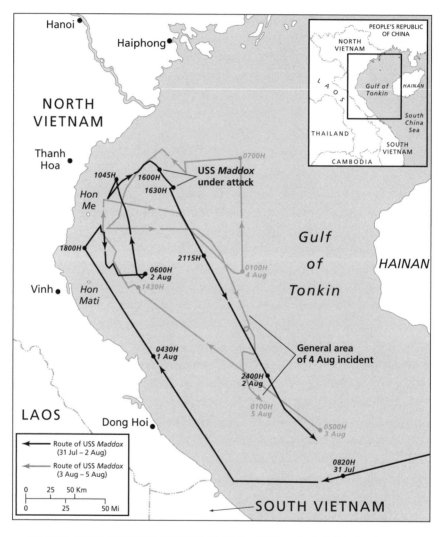

MAP 1. THE NORTH VIETNAMESE ATTACK ON U.S. NAVAL FORCES IN THE GULF OF TONKIN, AUGUST 2–4, 1964

it. This inference, though incorrect, was reasonable based upon the proximity—70 nm—of the destroyers to the OPLAN 34A action that night.[61] Although North Vietnam did not accuse the *Maddox* of any involvement in the July 30–31 OPLAN 34A attack, it confidently maintained that the two destroyers participated on August 3–4.

The *Turner Joy* arrived on the scene and concurred with the *Maddox*'s observations of surface contacts ("skunks") and air contacts ("bogies") on its radars.[62] The *Maddox* went to General Quarters at 1958 and the *Turner Joy* six minutes later. Radar indicated at least three skunks running parallel to the *Maddox* and possibly two more.[63] The *Ticonderoga*, loitering twenty-seven miles from the destroyers, launched six aircraft to overfly the destroyers. They were orbiting the destroyers by about 2100, when the *Maddox* detected a new skunk at fifteen miles with a speed of thirty knots.[64] The carrier aircraft were overhead the *Maddox* and the *Turner Joy* but could not see anything; just then the *Maddox* identified three more radar contacts only fifteen miles away, closing at thirty knots. Over the next several hours, although the U.S. aircraft could clearly spot the wakes of the destroyers, they were unable to find any signs of skunks. One radar contact was determined to be several vessels, but the carrier aircraft vectored to the area could not find anything there—even though the radar "blip" closed to 11.5 miles. Half an hour later, one of the contacts suddenly veered, as if launching a torpedo, and a new skunk lit up on the *Turner Joy*'s radar.

Just after 2100, the *Maddox* opened fire against a PT boat making an attacking run from the west.[65] Aircraft from the *Ticonderoga* and the *Constellation* launched to strike at the attacking craft. As the original presumed PT boats opened the distance to forty miles and disappeared from radar, the *Turner Joy* reported three new skunks at thirteen miles, closing at forty knots.[66] The *Maddox* opened fire on one of them.[67] Thus continued the first of many mysterious contacts that appeared throughout the night, as the *Maddox* and then the *Turner Joy* found themselves in the midst of an engagement.

At 2134 the *Maddox*'s surface search radar detected another skunk at 4.8 miles. The ship's fire-control radar briefly locked on to the target.[68] By about 2140, both U.S. destroyers were firing at surface radar contacts, but they had a difficult time keeping their fire control locked on to any target. More contacts were detected, closing from west to east; they would appear and then disappear from radar. The *Turner Joy* believed it was being swarmed, as its radar showed solid "blips" of "contact after contact." The ship fired some three hundred rounds and dropped depth charges (against incoming torpedoes) as it "dodged" several dozen torpedoes reported by the *Maddox*.[69] Similarly, at 2152, the *Maddox* reported it was under continuous torpedo attack.[70] Between 2140 and 2215, both the *Maddox* and the *Turner Joy* acquired multiple objects on radar and took evasive action against targets that were moving quickly, while others were moving slowly.[71] Three objects were thought to be PTs lying in wait to ambush the destroyers. Dozens of illumination shells were fired, but no boats were sighted.

The "fight" continued for two hours, with no period of more than five minutes without a contact on radar.[72] The sonar on board the *Maddox* detected twenty-six torpedoes in the water; the radar on the *Turner Joy* acquired numerous surface contacts. The incident was over before midnight; Captain Herrick reported one or two North Vietnamese boats sunk and another damaged. But soon he began to have doubts about the entire action, "except for [the] apparent ambush at the beginning."[73]

As Captain Herrick reported his review of the night's action, he raised questions about the many reported contacts and torpedoes fired. "Overeager sonarmen may have accounted for many reports. No actual visual sightings by the *Maddox*."[74] Herrick had reported that the *Maddox* and *Turner Joy* were in the clear, and that the *Turner Joy* had been fired upon by small caliber guns and illuminated by a spotlight. The *Turner Joy* tracked two sets of contacts and fired on thirteen individual vessels. The U.S. warship believed it had three positive hits, with one vessel sunk, and probable hits on three more. Still, the *Turner Joy* could not confirm visual sightings or wakes. In conclusion, the ship had reported that it held "many doubts" about the entire action, although it was convinced of the initial ambush.[75]

The "torpedoes" in the water had been most likely wakes caused by the high-speed maneuvers of the U.S. warships. The U.S. ships probably were chasing radar anomalies caused by weather patterns, such as high humidity and temperature inversion, or flocks of birds, or even the nearby carrier aircraft.[76] Some operators theorize that schools of fish are capable, by disturbing the water's surface, of reflecting radar waves. Radar contacts were eventually believed to be surface swells produced by the storms, and perhaps even the blades of the ships' propellers protruding above the surface during turns.[77] The Gulf of Tonkin is in fact prone to these anomalies, called "Tonkin ghosts" or "Tonkin spooks." False and spurious radar contacts in the region are widely noted, and they can be nerve-racking because they are indistinguishable from real ships. The confusion caused by the radar and sonar irregularities and the inability of the carrier-based aircraft to find any attackers was amplified by "bedlam" over the American radio circuits: "'Torpedo bearing . . . ,' 'Turning hard to port,' 'Sonar bearing . . . ,' 'Radar contact! Radar contact!'"[78]

Cdr. James B. Stockdale, who was that night flying an F-8 from the *Ticonderoga*, later provided a "bird's eye" view of the action in a collection of interviews of U.S. Navy pilots who had served during the Vietnam War:

> I had the best seat in the house from which to detect boats—if there were any. I didn't have to look through the surface haze and spray like the destroyers did, and I could see the destroyers' every move vividly. . . . When the destroyers were convinced they had some battle action going, I zigged and zagged and fired when they fired. . . . The edges of the black hole I was flying in were still periodically lit by flashes of lightning—but no wakes or dark shapes other than those of the destroyers were visible to me.[79]

In several instances, the U.S. aircraft overhead narrowly avoided targeting the *Maddox* and *Turner Joy*, in cases of mistaken identity. The most harrowing is narrated by Lt. Cdr. John Nicholson, who led a flight of three A-4 Skyhawks on the night of August 4. He recalls that when he arrived on the carrier's flight deck, "rain was coming down like hell, with lightning and thunder." His aircraft was the first one off the catapult that night, as confusion permeated the operations area:

We began searching for ships, and I saw two high-speed wakes heading 180 degrees, heading south. The guy in CIC [a warship's Combat Information Center] said, "That's not us, we're heading 000," and I recall him calling that heading because 000 is 360. Aviators use 360 and black shoes [surface warfare officers] use 000. Boch was with me, and he said, "Roger, I've got two wakes; they're heading 180." The voice in the CIC said, "Those must be the PT boats, take them under attack." We armed, and I said, "One in," as we went into our run, and all of a sudden I heard, "hold fire, hold fire"—it was the two destroyers heading 180—and the attack was broken off.

Talk about history being made; we were within split seconds of dumping on those two tin cans—I mean split seconds. From that point on, I lost total faith in who the hell was controlling down there.[80]

Radio messages were transmitted to the National Military Command Center in the Pentagon, which was twelve hours behind local time in the Gulf of Tonkin. These messages reached the secretary of defense and the chairman of the Joint Chiefs of Staff, Gen. Earle Wheeler, about 0900 local in Washington, D.C. As they were reading the message, A1H Skyraiders from the *Ticonderoga* were in the air; the aircraft carrier was holding at a position one hundred nautical miles east-northeast of Da Nang.

The secretary of defense called the president to inform him of the attack and then met with Deputy Secretary of Defense Cyrus Vance and Adm. Henry Mustin of the Joint Staff to develop options. They produced four possible courses of action that would deliver a sharp but limited blow: air strikes against patrol torpedo boats and their bases, air strikes against petroleum installations, air strikes against bridges in North Vietnam, and air strikes against prestige targets, such as a steel plant. They also offered one option that would exert slow and continuous pressure at the strategic level—mining ports in North Vietnam.[81]

About the same time, the Joint Chiefs of Staff directed that all PTFs engaged in OPLAN 34A were to discontinue operations and return to Da

Nang.[82] CINCPAC ordered the destruction of all DRV patrol boats and Swatows in the general area of the Gulf of Tonkin. U.S. aircraft were not to enter Vietnam's three-mile limit, while U.S. warships could not approach closer than eleven miles from the coast.[83] CINCPAC issued rules of engagement on August 4 that granted authority to the fleet commander to declare hostile and engage any North Vietnamese aircraft "whose actions and behavior indicate with reasonable certainty" that they intend to attack U.S. forces.[84] CINCPAC also ordered the immediate airlift of naval mines to either the *Ticonderoga* or *Constellation* for possible use against five Swatow bases in North Vietnam.[85]

The retaliatory strikes were code-named Pierce Arrow. In the late morning of August 5, strike aircraft from the *Ticonderoga* were launched against several targets in North Vietnam, including almost half of the country's naval installations.[86] The sixty-four sorties resulted in widespread damage to North Vietnamese shore installations and patrol craft.[87] The primary target was the Vinh oil storage area; eight tanks were destroyed, and the petroleum storage area was set ablaze.[88] Carrier aircraft also hit PT and Swatow boats at Quang Khee, Ben Thuy, Hon Me Island, the Song Ma estuary, Hon Bay, and Port Walnut.[89] In midafternoon, two more waves of aircraft—this time from the *Constellation*—struck targets in North Vietnam.

The oil storage facility was 90 percent destroyed, and twenty-nine DRV naval vessels were totally destroyed or damaged.[90] Two American aircraft from the *Constellation* were lost in the raids, and one was seriously damaged. One pilot was killed and another captured.[91] The August 5 airstrikes were significant as the first U.S. bombings of North Vietnam.[92] Within a month, the United States had sent ninety-three U.S. warplanes to South Vietnam and Thailand to pre-position for additional operations.[93]

— — — — ● — — — —

The shadowy nature of the August 4 incident immediately called into question whether the warships had been attacked at all. The secretary of defense and Joint Chiefs of Staff met and determined, on the basis of five critical factors, that the August 4 attacks had in fact occurred. First, the

Turner Joy apparently had been illuminated by a searchlight and had been fired on by automatic weapons.[94] The *Turner Joy* had reported tracking two sets of contacts, firing on thirteen contacts, positively hitting three, sinking one (based on the disappearance of the radar "blip"), and probably hitting others.[95] Second, crew members on one of the U.S. ships thought they had seen bridge lights of an enemy patrol craft. Third, U.S. aircraft apparently had been shot at. Fourth, the North Vietnamese had announced (in a message intercepted by the Americans) that two of its boats had been "sacrificed." Fifth, the leaders relied on the assurances of CINCPAC, Adm. Ulysses S. Grant Sharp, that there really had been an attack, of which he was thoroughly convinced.[96]

The supposed illumination from the bridge of an attacking PT and evidence of a searchlight could be explained by any number of theories, such as lightning, reflections of the muzzle flashes of the destroyers' own guns, aircraft tracers, flares from the ships and aircraft, or star shells reflecting off the clouds.[97] Further, the visual evidence of the searchlight on the *Turner Joy* and bridge lights of a Vietnamese patrol boat proved sketchy. But SIGINT was considered by American leaders as the "smoking gun" that proved North Vietnam had conducted the August 4 attack. Even that evidence, however, would prove elusive. In retrospect, the "sacrifice" referred to had probably occurred on August 2, as had indications that U.S. aircraft received fire.

It was unclear exactly where the U.S. ships were operating and how close to the coastline the incident had occurred. The president was briefed that the attack took place some thirty miles offshore. Secretary of Defense Robert McNamara later would say American ships never approached closer than five nautical miles to any Vietnamese island in August 1964.[98] The more likely figure is probably nine or ten miles, by the USS *Maddox* on August 3 and 4. After the Gulf of Tonkin incident, the closest permissible approach for the DeSoto patrols was changed to 12 nm.[99]

The secretary of defense was also incorrect in reporting that North Vietnamese patrol torpedo boats had fired first during the August 2 attack.[100] Much would be made of this issue later, although the *Maddox*'s first rounds were said to be warning shots that "went down range" (i.e., for effect) only after the Vietnamese boats displayed an attack profile by closing at constant bearing. In any event, the question of "who fired first" was always somewhat immaterial, since American understanding of the law of self-defense permits the use of force against adversaries that demonstrate hostile intent. U.S. ships never have to "take the first hit."[101] Furthermore, it would become evident in subsequent years that the attacks on U.S. forces likely had been at least influenced by, if not triggered by, the South Vietnamese OPLAN 34A raids. The North Vietnamese had seen the DeSoto patrols and OPLAN 34A as connected, while American leaders had not.

The after-action interviews of the participants, and the investigation and analysis by COMSEVENTHFLT, CINCPAC, and Department of Defense (DoD) concluded that a second attack had occurred on August 4.[102] Although the crew on the *Maddox* had been alarmed, and perhaps confused, by repeated sonar reports of torpedoes in the water, the *Turner Joy*'s crew had missed most of these reports and remained professional, calm, and "very well organized."[103] The authenticity of the attacks on August 2 made the August 4 incident seem more credible, and so the fog of war and a sense of wounded honor drove the Johnson administration to retaliate. This second attack was all that was needed to justify air strikes against North Vietnam.[104]

— — — ● — — —

The U.S. Navy's mission in the war was made more difficult by the comingling of DRV warships with civilian craft, which were collectively a force multiplier for North Vietnam. Hanoi made extensive use of civilian fishing vessels in its war effort. North Vietnam also employed coastal shipping to send supplies and forces into South Vietnam. These vessels, which ranged in size from small junks and sampans to large, self-propelled barges, were dubbed "waterborne logistic craft" by the Americans—shortened to WBLCs and pronounced "WEE-bliks."[105]

In response, in 1966 the United States initiated Operation Sea Dragon to interdict WBLCs on their north-to-south voyage. Destroyers were assigned to stations, disabling, boarding, and destroying logistics craft and hitting targets on the beach with naval gunfire. Of course, using civilian fishing vessels as intelligence platforms and military transports violated the law of naval warfare and made them subject to attack by U.S. forces. In its first year, Sea Dragon destroyed 382 WBLCs, damaged another 325, and struck shore batteries and radar sites along the coast. These operations hampered the movement of forces and supplies into the South and forced logistics movements back into the congested land routes and inland waterways, where they were exposed to attack from the air.

American officials knew North Vietnam used its fishing vessels to report the positions of U.S. warships in the Gulf of Tonkin. In the action of August 2, fishing vessels tracked U.S. naval contacts and relayed their positions so that patrol boats could attack. A declassified National Security Agency report notes that a message was sent from "an unidentified vessel to an unidentified shore based shipping net control station" at the same time that the *Maddox* passed two fishing vessels at a distance of two thousand yards.[106] Soon thereafter, the *Maddox* engaged in the naval battle with three North Vietnamese gunboats. Captain Herrick reported during the incident that North Vietnamese PTs enjoy an advantage, "especially at night" because they could hide among concentrations of junk sailing vessels throughout the region.[107]

— — — — • — — — —

A third incident, as mysterious as the second, occurred on September 18, 1964, when the destroyers USS *Morton* (DD 948) and USS *Richard S. Edwards* (DD 950) were conducting a DeSoto mission.[108] In a replay of the August 4 events, the two destroyers reported elusive radar contacts with the "enemy" and thought they were under attack. The North Vietnamese had in fact tracked the U.S. ships but were ordered to "avoid provocation" and to "disperse to camouflage."[109]

By then, North Vietnam had called the August 4 attack a "fabrication."[110] From the beginning, competing narratives and contradictory evidence prevented a clear understanding of what had transpired. The American SIGINT community began to analyze and decipher the puzzle, and a picture that placed in question the purported attacks of August 4 began to emerge. Perhaps the greatest indication was the "dog that did not bark"—the complete lack of North Vietnamese naval communications normally associated with a naval engagement. "Nothing as much as a single 'bark' was intercepted."[111]

Even the August 2 attack had occurred against the backdrop of North Vietnamese attacks on U.S. aircraft overflying Laos. At the time, however, once everyone in the U.S. government was convinced that the attack of August 4 had occurred, the first attack appeared not an isolated incident created by a local commander but the beginning of a concerted campaign to challenge the U.S. Navy's right to traverse international waters. As time passed, some of the major participants clung to the idea; McNamara, for example, would write that the overall evidence for a second attack was convincing.[112] Similarly, the U.S. Navy's history of the Vietnam War resolutely declares the evidence for a second attack was "conclusive."[113]

Nevertheless, a top-secret analysis of National Security Agency SIGINT during the August 4 incident establishes that no attack happened that night.[114] Instead, it suggests, some of the mysterious radar contacts may have been North Vietnamese units trying to salvage the two boats damaged on August 2. It is also possible that Chinese vessels were observing the American warships and were mistaken for attacking Vietnamese. In any event, it is fairly certain U.S. forces were fighting a phantom foe. Several days later, President Johnson remarked to Under Secretary of State George Ball, "Hell, those dumb, stupid sailors were shooting at flying fish!"[115]

Moïse's exhaustive study concludes that the second attack on August 4 did not occur but that the administration acted in good faith in holding that it had.[116] The question has for years captured the attention of reporters and scholars, but it is sufficient for our purposes to understand that CINCPAC, the U.S. Navy, and the administration *thought* the second attack occurred and that freedom of the seas was threatened. The DoD acted accordingly.[117] The president took his message to the American people and a joint session of Congress. On August 5, President Johnson met with legislators from both parties and delivered to them an urgent message that placed the Gulf of Tonkin incident within the context of "supporting freedom and peace" in Southeast Asia.[118] The president described the Southeast Asia Collective Defense Treaty (Manila Pact) as the basis for American defense commitments in the region.

Johnson recommended that Congress pass a resolution expressing support for "all necessary action" to protect U.S. armed forces and to assist other nations. Secretary of State Dean Rusk and Secretary of Defense Robert McNamara testified before a joint session of the Senate Foreign Relations Committee and the Armed Services Committee in support of a congressional resolution.[119] The resulting Gulf of Tonkin Resolution was to be criticized later as the "blank check" that opened the door to a decade of U.S. combat operations in Indochina.[120]

In December 1971, as political support for the Vietnam War was at its nadir, Senator William J. Fulbright sent a letter to Secretary of Defense Melvin R. Laird requesting that one of Fulbright's staff members be permitted to visit the National Security Agency to review the original message traffic and form an independent judgment as to whether there was a basis for the belief that a second attack actually occurred.[121] The Fulbright staff report concluded that the Johnson administration "honestly thought" that SIGINT proved there was an attack on the *Maddox* and the *Turner Joy* on August 4, but that the belief was erroneous, that the key intercepted radio traffic from North Vietnam likely referred to the attacks on August 2.

— — — — • — — — —

On August 5, 1964, the Johnson administration took the matter to the UN Security Council. Ambassador Adlai Stevenson delivered a statement approved by the secretary of state. The American narrative styled its strikes against North Vietnam as a lawful action in self-defense against an armed attack in international waters.[122] The United States briefed both the August 2 and August 4 incidents to the Security Council. The air strikes on the torpedo-boat facilities on the mainland were presented as a lawful measure in self-defense: "I want to emphasize that the action we have taken is a limited and measured response, fitted precisely to the attack that produced it, and that the deployments of additional U.S. forces to Southeast Asia are designed solely to deter further aggression. . . . Let me repeat that freedom of the seas is guaranteed under long-accepted international law applying to all nations alike."[123]

The United States had taken no action until its ships were fired on and only then resorted to the use of force in self-defense, which is another tenet of international law. Stevenson also declared that the attacks by North Vietnam fit within a larger pattern of terrorism and chaos sowed by Hanoi and Beijing in Indochina since 1950. These "wanton acts of violence" were designed to sabotage the "international machinery" established by the 1954 Geneva agreements to stabilize the region. "The attempt to sink United States destroyers in international waters is more spectacular than the attempt to murder the mayor of a village in his bed at night. But they are both part of the pattern . . . to subjugate the people of Southeast Asia to an empire ruled by means of force."[124]

The United States recommended a "very easy way" to restore stability to the region. First, all states in the region needed to make and abide by a "simple decision to leave their neighbors alone."

> Stop the secret subversion of other people's independence. Stop the clandestine and illegal transit of national frontiers. Stop the export of revolution and the doctrine of violence. Stop the violations of the political agreements reached at Geneva for the future of Southeast Asia.
> The people of Laos want to be left alone.
> The people of Vietnam want to be left alone.
> The people of Cambodia want to be left alone.[125]

That same day, the Soviet premier, Nikita Khrushchev, sent a letter to President Johnson asserting that while "we do not know exactly now just what has happened," the problems in the region were being exacerbated by U.S. warships operating in the Gulf of Tonkin, which "cuts deeply into the territories" of North Vietnam and China.[126] Given the proximity of Vietnam and China to the Gulf of Tonkin, Khrushchev argued, the introduction of American warships "cannot be viewed in any other way" than as an effort at gunboat diplomacy and intimidation. Johnson replied that the United States did not seek a permanent military presence in Vietnam. He also asked the Soviet Union to intervene with either North Vietnam or China to persuade it against further "reckless action."[127]

The Tonkin Gulf incident generated effects both short term and long term. In the short term, it cemented ties between American and South Vietnamese armed forces. Within one week of the Gulf of Tonkin incident the United States was engaged in combined war planning with the Republic of South Vietnam. On, apparently, August 7, Gen. William Westmoreland, who led U.S. forces in Vietnam from 1964 to 1968, met with Gen. Nguyen Khanh, the military leader and putative head of state after a coup in South Vietnam.[128] The United States and South Vietnam had been planning their campaigns unilaterally. General Westmoreland now called for greater synchronization. While Westmoreland pushed the Vietnamese to plan for defense in the case of "overt aggression" from the North, Khanh interjected that North Vietnam already had committed aggression against the South. Westmoreland emphasized pacification in the South and interdiction of forces from the North, which led Khanh once again to ask how the United States defined "overt aggression." Khanh was convinced that the Vietcong, or even the People's Army of Vietnam, would not invade with "ID cards and in uniform" but rather as guerilla insurgents.

– – – – – • – – – – –

As the U.S. administration planned a long-term response to the incident, it sought to answer why North Vietnam had initiated the engagement in the first place. In early 1964, North Vietnam's position and prospects in the South had substantially improved. North Vietnam had become more confident. When American bombing became routine the following year, North Vietnam was openly contemplating a full-scale war against the United States.[129] The United States assessed that North Vietnam was motivated by a desire to decouple the United States from South Vietnam. The actual Gulf of Tonkin attack may have anticipated a passive U.S. response, which would have helped persuade the Khanh government that the United States was unreliable.[130] North Vietnam hoped to entice the United States to the negotiating table to obtain more favorable terms, to make a show of force against the United States, and to weaken American political support in Saigon.

The Gulf of Tonkin incident instead steeled American resolve not to "rush in" to negotiate with North Vietnam, lest it appear overeager and a "paper tiger."[131] The United States slowly began to realize that the incident in the Gulf of Tonkin was not an isolated, separate attack but rather part of the larger and more complex problem of North Vietnamese subversion of Indochina. Khanh, whom the U.S. embassy described as in a "euphoric" state over the Gulf of Tonkin incident, hoped the United States would parlay its reaction into meaningful force to compel the North to comply with the 1954 and 1962 peace accords. Indeed, the brief and inconclusive battle in the Gulf of Tonkin colored the early American view of the conflict as largely a conventional assault by the armed forces of North Vietnam against the South.[132] Although a ground invasion from the North ultimately proved central to the fall of South Vietnam, it was just one dimension of the complex conflict, which included elements of a civil war and indigenous support for the Vietcong in South Vietnam.[133]

In short, the Gulf of Tonkin incident was a major milestone on the road to American involvement in the Vietnam War. Henry Kissinger later disagreed with this view, arguing in his revisionist account that the incident was not a "major factor" in the U.S. commitment of ground forces to Vietnam.[134] He suggests that the incident was simply a "small step on a long road" toward deepening American involvement in the conflict. His assessment, offered with regard to whether President Johnson was entirely candid about the incident, is unconvincing when viewed in the context of the times. In fact, the attack on the USS *Maddox* was decisive in building political support for the decade-long American intervention. The Department of State, for example, renewed its attention to the communist violations of the 1954 and 1962 peace accords. The United States shifted from being a marginal player, a defender and supporter of South Vietnam, into a protagonist, in direct confrontation with Asian communist regimes.[135] The events of early August could not have been more significant to the United States and Vietnam; they led to a widening, even dispositive, American role in the war.

The Gulf of Tonkin Resolution, championed by President Lyndon Johnson, was driven by a sense of urgency. Congress enacted the joint resolution on August 10 by a vote of 88 to 2 in the Senate and 416 to none in the House.[136] The resolution was not just popular in Congress—Johnson had the overwhelming support of the American public. In a Harris poll released on August 10, 85 percent supported the president's August 5 strike on North Vietnam in retaliation for the Gulf of Tonkin attacks; just 3 percent opposed.[137] Before the Gulf of Tonkin incidents, 58 percent had been critical of how Johnson was handling Vietnam. Thus, in a flash, the Gulf of Tonkin incidents converted the president's greatest foreign-policy vulnerability into an unalloyed asset.[138] Polling figures strongly indicate a long-standing trend in American foreign policy, one that dates to the earliest days of the Republic: the American public generally is complacent about overseas threats or even resistant to accepting they exist, but once U.S. ships are attacked, righteous indignation overtakes the underlying cause of tensions that led to the incident.

The Gulf of Tonkin Resolution charged the communist regime in North Vietnam with "deliberately and repeatedly" attacking U.S. naval forces "lawfully present in international waters." The attack was launched "in violation of the Charter of the United Nations and international law." The first clause gives the sense of the Congress in that it approved and supported the "determination of the President, as commander in chief, to take all necessary measures to repel any armed attack against the forces of the United States and to prevent further aggression." This language was defensive in nature and clearly within the existing ambit of the constitutional power of the commander in chief to defend U.S. armed forces anywhere. The second clause states that the United States was "prepared, as the President determines, to take all necessary steps, including the use of armed force, to assist any member or protocol state of the Southeast Asia Collective Defense Treaty requesting assistance in defense of its freedom." The Johnson administration viewed this remit as equivalent to a declaration of war.[139] This language came to be known as the "blank check," and it presaged the slide into a war in Indochina.

"FALSE SENSE OF SECURITY"

The USS *Pueblo* Incident (1968)

On January 23, 1968, North Korean naval and air forces attacked the USS *Pueblo* (AGER 2) as it steamed more than fifteen nautical miles (nm) off the coast of Ung-Do Island. The ship was collecting military intelligence in international waters. After a brief engagement, North Korean forces boarded the ship, seized the crew, and sailed the intelligence vessel back to Wonsan, in the Democratic People's Republic of Korea (DPRK). The crew members were taken to Pyongyang where they were repeatedly interrogated, brutally beaten, and threatened with execution for the next eleven months. The crew was finally repatriated to U.S. control at the Panmunjom de facto border on December 23, 1968. The ship, however, was never returned; it is currently berthed on the Botong River in Pyongyang as a floating tourist attraction, next to the Fatherland War of Liberation Museum.

At the time of the incident, the United States claimed a 3-nm territorial sea, but North Korea claimed a 12-nm territorial sea.[1] Hence, by either American or DPRK standards, the *Pueblo* was operating on the high seas at the time of the attack. A fundamental tenet of international law is that all ships, including warships, enjoy high seas freedoms of navigation and overflight beyond the territorial seas of other nations.[2] Another long-standing principle is that warships (and other government-owned or -operated noncommercial vessels) on the high seas have complete immunity from the jurisdiction of any state other than the states whose flags they fly.

The DPRK's action was a direct affront to the time-honored principles of freedom of the high seas and the sovereign inviolability of warships under the international law of the sea.

At the time, American mission planners, intelligence analysts, and military leaders believed, incorrectly, that the DPRK would honor these customary legal norms. This error was dangerous and reflects a uniquely American trait: that of assuming other countries will comply with international standards, even after they have publicly renounced them. Since the *Pueblo* was to remain outside of the DPRK territorial sea at all times, Americans assumed that DPRK forces might harass the ship but would not aggressively interfere with its mission. Although a military response was considered to counter the DPRK attack, the Johnson administration ultimately elected to focus on diplomatic efforts to resolve the crisis and try to recover safely the ship and its crew.[3]

The *Pueblo* incident, coupled with the attack on another intelligence-collection ship, the USS *Liberty* (AGTR 5), the previous year by Israeli air and naval forces, resulted in a wholesale reevaluation of the U.S. intelligence-collection program. The use of maritime platforms equipped with passive electronic intelligence (ELINT) capabilities to gather intelligence was suspended and ultimately stopped.[4] By the end of 1970, all of the Navy's maritime collection platforms of the *Liberty*-type Auxiliary General Technical Research (AGTR), *Victory*-type Technical-Auxiliary General (T-AF), and Auxiliary General Environmental Research (AGER) categories had been decommissioned, and the AGER signal intelligence (SIGINT) program had come to an end.

— — — — • — — — —

Starting in the 1950s, both the United States and the Soviet Union (USSR) increasingly used surface ships to collect communications intelligence (COMINT) and ELINT against their adversaries. Lacking sufficient global land-based SIGINT facilities, the Soviet Union took the lead in this endeavor, using converted oceangoing fishing trawlers (AGIs) as its preferred intelligence-gathering platforms. At the height of the Cold

War, nearly sixty Soviet AGIs were deployed around the world to monitor U.S. and North Atlantic Treaty Organization (NATO) naval activities and exercises. AGIs also maintained a permanent presence off the U.S. coasts in the vicinity of Puget Sound, Washington; San Diego, California; San Francisco, California; Norfolk, Virginia; Groton, Connecticut; Kings Bay, Georgia; and Jacksonville, Florida—all U.S. fleet concentration areas. The AGIs normally operated just outside the 3-nm American territorial sea, "cueing" Soviet submarines to U.S. ships and submarines departing their home ports for patrols on the open sea.

American SIGINT collection against communist countries initially relied on surveillance aircraft, submarines, and low-earth-orbit satellites. Space and weight constraints and the inability of these platforms to remain on station for any length of time, however, limited their utility.[5] Seaborne platforms, on the other hand, could carry a variety of sensors (including photographic, hydrographic, and acoustic) and bring them to bear on a target simultaneously, greatly enhancing coverage. Moreover, surface ships had substantial endurance and were better "suited [than aircraft and submarines] for target acquisition and sustained collection."[6] As a result of these advantages the National Security Agency (NSA) and the U.S. Navy developed a program that focused on surface ships as dedicated SIGINT collection platforms. The initial phase of the program used converted World War II *Liberty*-type cargo vessels (Auxiliary General Technical Research, or AGTRs) and *Victory*-type cargo ships (Technical-Auxiliary General, or T-AF). As the program matured, the decision was made to convert smaller ships to conduct the SIGINT collection mission, as a cost-saving measure and a counterbalance to the Soviet AGI threat.[7] Accordingly, three World War II–era light cargo ships were converted and designated by the Navy as Auxiliary General Environmental Research intelligence collection platforms—the USS *Banner* (AGER 1), USS *Pueblo* (AGER 2), and USS *Palm Beach* (AGER 3).

By the late 1960s, it had become clear to the U.S. Intelligence Board that there were inadequate SIGINT resources devoted to the Korean peninsula. Tensions were high in the region, and the DPRK was increasing the number of Armistice Agreement violations. There were significant intelligence shortcomings, especially in "indications and warning" information, as well as in comprehensive data on North Korean military and naval targets.[8] American officials believed this information could be obtained by stationing ships off the North Korean coast for extended periods of time to focus on short-range (low power) communications, which could not be collected from fixed or shore-based installations.

The USS *Banner* was the first of the AGERs to deploy and collect SIGINT against Russian, Chinese, and North Korean targets. The ship's collection operations in the Sea of Japan and the Yellow and East China Seas in 1967 and 1968 were successful, although they had been risky. When near the Russian or Chinese coasts, the *Banner* was routinely harassed by Soviet or Chinese warships. A number of vessels would surround *Banner*, making it difficult to maneuver without a collision.[9] On two occasions, Soviet or Chinese ships ordered the *Banner* to heave to or be fired upon, but both times the threat did not materialize. North Korean reaction to the *Banner* deployments, in contrast, was passive, even when a U.S. surveillance ship loitered off Wonsan for a day and a half in early 1967. This pattern created a false sense of security in the mind of American planners that communist Korean forces would observe the long-established principles of freedom of the seas and the immunities enjoyed by warships. One year later the USS *Pueblo* (AGER 2) would conduct a similar operation off Wonsan but would not be so fortunate.

– – – – • – – – –

In November 1967, the *Pueblo* departed San Diego en route to its new home port in Yokosuka, Japan, via Hawaii. The ship was under the command of Cdr. Lloyd Bucher. Upon its arrival in Hawaii, the U.S. Pacific Fleet (PACFLT) staff told Commander Bucher that the *Pueblo*'s initial patrol would be off the North Korean coast in the Sea of Japan.

Rear Adm. Frank Johnson—Commander, U.S. Naval Forces Japan (CNFJ), and Commander, Task Force 96 (CTF 96)—assessed the mission's risk as "minimal." Three factors drove this determination: first, the *Pueblo* would be operating in international waters. Second, North Korean naval activity in January and February was historically low. Third, past operations suggested that North Korea would not become aggressive, as it did not react to previous deployments of the USS *Banner*.[10] In December 1967, Rear Admiral Johnson passed his assessment to Adm. John Hyland, Commander in Chief, U.S. Pacific Fleet (CINCPACFLT), along with a detailed mission proposal. Admiral Hyland immediately forwarded the message to Adm. U. S. Grant Sharp Jr., Commander in Chief, Pacific Command (CINCPAC), who passed it on to the Joint Chiefs of Staff (JCS) on December 23. Admiral Sharp calculated that the *Pueblo* faced minimal risk because it would be operating in international waters.[11]

At the time all military reconnaissance operations had to be approved by the JCS. Approval was contingent on a number of factors, including the political climate and sensitivity of the region, the likelihood of a hostile response, and a balancing test that weighed the importance of the operation against the risks involved.[12] Before making a decision, the proposal had to be vetted with the Joint Reconnaissance Center (JRC) staff.[13] The vetting process included a risk assessment by the Defense Intelligence Agency (DIA). Lacking information to contradict these judgments, the JRC concurred that the operation posed minimal risk and added it to the monthly schedule. Deputy Secretary of Defense Paul Nitze approved the schedule on December 27.

The reconnaissance schedule, including the *Pueblo* mission, was sent to the covert-action oversight group in the National Security Council called the "303 Committee" on December 29 to go through a final policy review and executive-branch approval. The committee accepted the schedule but warned that the experience of the *Banner* and the belligerent North Korean posture generally suggested that the *Pueblo* operation was a "risk mission." The committee never believed, however, that the *Pueblo* would be seized in international waters; the committee expected the ship to be "shadowed, bullied, and bumped" but saw "no reason to expect seizure on the high seas."[14]

NSA analysts too expressed concern that it was highly possible that the *Pueblo* would incite a hostile reaction. These analysts believed the DPRK leadership was too unpredictable and might attack a U.S. spy ship at any time. Senior leaders at the agency, however, believed the NSA would overstep its responsibility and leave itself open to criticism if it tried to insert itself into Navy operations. Accordingly, the NSA leadership watered down a strongly worded message to the secretary of defense that had been drafted by the analysts to make it less obtrusive. Consequently, when the JRC returned the issue to CINCPAC, the risk assessment had not been changed. CINCPAC thus failed to direct the U.S. Seventh Fleet or the Fifth Air Force to place a protective force on standby to support the *Pueblo* should the need arise.[15]

CINCPAC's inaction is understandable, given prior North Korean, Soviet, and Chinese reactions to American intelligence-collection platforms. In early 1967, the NSA had sent a similar message to the JRC and JCS advising on the possibility of DPRK hostile action against the *Banner's* impending mission off the peninsula, yet North Korea had not reacted. Moreover, historically, the intensity of coastal-state reaction to the presence of an intelligence collector had depended on the nature of the platform. Hostile reaction by DPRK, Soviet, or Chinese forces had normally been reserved for U.S. airborne, not surface or subsurface, intelligence collection. Surface units had typically been subjected only to nonlethal harassment, such as passing close aboard, bumping, or endangering navigation. None of these responses involved the use of weapons. In the case of the *Pueblo*, Navy officials incorrectly assumed that the DPRK would continue to observe this distinction. In retrospect, given the 303 Committee's assessment that the *Pueblo* might be seriously harassed by DPRK forces, it would have been prudent for CINCPACFLT and CTF 96 to request a protective hovering force just over the horizon.

American planners appear to have disregarded other warning signals since fall 1966 signifying a more aggressive DPRK policy toward South Korea and the United States. This tougher policy included deliberately increasing tension along the demilitarized zone (DMZ), landing infiltrators from the sea inside South Korea, and shooting at South Korean fishing and patrol boats.[16] As it turned out, when Commander Bucher asked the PACFLT assistant chief of staff for operations what would happen if his ship was attacked during the patrol, he was informed that "there's absolutely nothing we can do about it at the time," because all regional air and naval assets were otherwise committed.[17]

The *Pueblo*'s ill-fated mission had three priorities. The first was to collect SIGINT in the Sea of Japan to determine the nature and extent of naval activity in the vicinity of the DPRK ports of Ch'ongjin, So'ngjin, Mayang Do, and Wonsan; second, sample the electronic environment of the east coast of the DPRK, with emphasis on intercepting and fixing the positions of coastal radars; and third, intercept and conduct surveillance of Soviet naval units in the Tsushima Strait in an effort to determine the purpose of their presence there.[18] The *Pueblo* was specifically instructed not to approach within 13 nm of the DPRK or Soviet coast or offshore islands.[19] The secondary purposes of the mission were to observe the DPRK and Soviet reaction to an overt intelligence collector operating near its coast and actively surveilling Soviet naval units; evaluate the *Pueblo*'s capabilities as an intelligence collector and tactical surveillance ship; and report any deployment of DPRK or Soviet ships or aircraft that might indicate imminent attack against U.S. forces.[20]

The *Pueblo* was ordered to depart Sasebo, Japan, on January 8, 1968, and proceed via the Tsushima Strait to its operational area (OPAREA). The ship was to conduct collection operations in OPAREAs Mars, Venus, and Pluto until January 27 and then proceed south along the Korean Peninsula to the Tsushima Strait and conduct surveillance of Soviet forces there until February 4. In order to avoid drawing unwanted attention, Commander Bucher was ordered to stow or cover all defensive weapons (ten Browning semiautomatic rifles and two .50-caliber machine guns) and to maintain strict radio silence until he made contact with Soviet forces in the Tsushima Strait. Bucher was additionally instructed to employ his weapons "only in cases where threat to survival is obvious." Accordingly, the two .50-caliber machine guns were wrapped in tarps and were useless during the subsequent armed encounter.[21]

On January 16, 1968, confident that he had not been detected, Commander Bucher reached the northernmost limit of the *Pueblo*'s operating area, just south of Vladivostok. The ship remained on station off Ch'ongjin for two days (OPAREA Pluto), with a closest point of approach (CPA) to the DPRK coast of 15 nm. The *Pueblo* encountered several merchant vessels going in and out of port, but they did not appear interested in the U.S. surveillance ship.[22] On the evening of January 17, the *Pueblo* moved southward along the DPRK coast, arriving in OPAREA Venus off So'ngjin the following morning. The ship's CPA to the DPRK landmass was 16 nm. Two days later, the *Pueblo* continued south toward OPAREA Mars, the southernmost limit of its deployment, where it was to take station off Mayang-Do and remain some 14 to 15 nm offshore.

In the early evening hours of January 20, a DPRK subchaser of a modified SO-1 type passed within four thousand yards of the *Pueblo*. The *Pueblo*'s crew did not detect any electronic signals emitted by the SO-1, however, and the subchaser did not appear to have any interest in the U.S. ship. Commander Bucher therefore determined that his mission had not been compromised and carried on toward Wonsan and to OPAREA Mars, maintaining radio silence en route. Because the ship had maintained strict emissions control (EMCON)—in effect, radio silence—to avoid detection, even American officials were unaware of the *Pueblo*'s exact location.

— — — — • — — —

The *Pueblo* arrived on station as planned on January 22 and took a position 15 nm east of Wonsan. Around noon that day, two North Korean fishing trawlers (similar to Soviet *Lentra*-class AGIs) spotted it. One of these ships passed within a hundred yards of the *Pueblo*'s starboard beam. Whether or not the SO-1 had reported the *Pueblo* on the evening of January 20, it was now clear that the mission had been compromised. Several hours later, the two trawlers returned, this time coming within thirty yards. At the time, the *Pueblo* was 18.2 nm from Ung-Do and displaying the international signal flag for hydrographic operations.[23] Commander Bucher immediately broke EMCON and reported that his ship had been detected. The message, however, was not transmitted until the following morning because the ship was not in communication with headquarters in Japan.

As night approached, the *Pueblo* moved farther out to sea to avoid inadvertently drifting into DPRK territorial waters. Throughout the night, the *Pueblo*'s crew detected eighteen vessels and one large orange flare, but there was no further harassment. Accordingly, Commander Bucher sent a second message advising that he no longer considered the vessel to be "under surveillance," that he was reverting to strict EMCON and intended to remain near Wonsan. Unbeknownst to Bucher, earlier in the day thirty-one North Korean infiltrators dressed in South Korean army uniforms had been killed in a botched raid on the South Korean presidential residence (the Blue House).[24]

Shortly before noon on January 23, the *Pueblo*'s officer of the deck (OOD) reported that an SO-1 subchaser, hull number SC-35, was closing in. Commander Bucher ordered the ship's oceanographers to collect water samples and a signalman to hoist the "flag signals indicating hydrographic work in progress."[25] The SO-1 circled the American reconnaissance ship; the second time around, it queried the *Pueblo* as to its nationality. Commander Bucher responded by hoisting the American flag.[26]

According to subsequently declassified SIGINT, the North Koreans now knew the *Pueblo*'s nationality and hull number and that it was an electronic reconnaissance ship. On the third pass, the SO-1 hoisted the flag signal "Heave to or I will open fire." Commander Bucher responded via flashing light that the DPRK unit was interfering with the *Pueblo*'s free passage in international waters. At the time, the two warships were between 15.5 and 15.8 nm from the nearest DPRK land, Ung-Do Island.[27] Bucher reported his present situation via flash-precedence message (in a format known as a "Pinnacle I/CRITIC") to headquarters, as well as his "intention to remain in the area if at all possible."[28] Based on the earlier bluff against the USS *Banner* by Soviet forces during its mission in early 1967, the CNFJ duty officer misinterpreted the DPRK actions as merely harassment and intimidation.[29]

The SO-1 was soon joined by three fast torpedo patrol (PT) boats, which surrounded the *Pueblo*, and two MiG fighter jets, which overflew the U.S. ship at an altitude of about four thousand feet. When one of the PT boats positioned itself in an apparent attempt to board the *Pueblo*, Commander Bucher changed course and made for the open sea at full speed, signaling the North Koreans via flashing light that he was leaving the area. The SO-1 responded by signaling the *Pueblo* to "follow in my wake; I have a pilot on board." Bucher immediately advised higher headquarters of this situation, reporting his intention to depart the area.

Despite Bucher's efforts to remain in international waters, the North Korean boats' superior speed and maneuverability forced his ship farther south toward the coast. The SO-1 once again raised the flag signal "OL," or "Oscar Lima"—"Heave to or I will open fire." Bucher did not comply, and the four North Korean vessels opened fire with their 57-mm batteries and machine guns. At this point Commander Bucher set General Quarters and ordered the crew to begin destruction of the ship's classified holdings and equipment. The crew's ability to do so was strikingly inadequate. The crew had never practiced or drilled procedures for emergency destruction; in any case, the ship's incinerator could not handle the large volume of material that had to be burned. Commander Bucher had forbidden the crew from going topside, even to General Quarters stations, which prevented the dumping of material over the side. For destroying classified equipment there were three fire axes, three sledgehammers, and some chipping hammers. The ship's two electric shredders were worthless for a mass destruction evolution. Accordingly, very little of the classified material on board the ship was actually destroyed.

Realizing that the *Pueblo*'s crew was destroying its classified material, the North Koreans intensified their attack until the ship came to "all stop." The SO-1 then again directed Bucher, "Follow me, I have a pilot on board." Commander Bucher complied and turned the *Pueblo* toward the Korean coast, while simultaneously transmitting another CRITIC message (a Pinnacle II). He reported his position, broadcasting a number of SOSs. He also indicated that the "*Pueblo* was holding emergency destruction procedures.

Commander Bucher then went below to determine the status of the emergency destruction. He discovered that there was still a large amount of

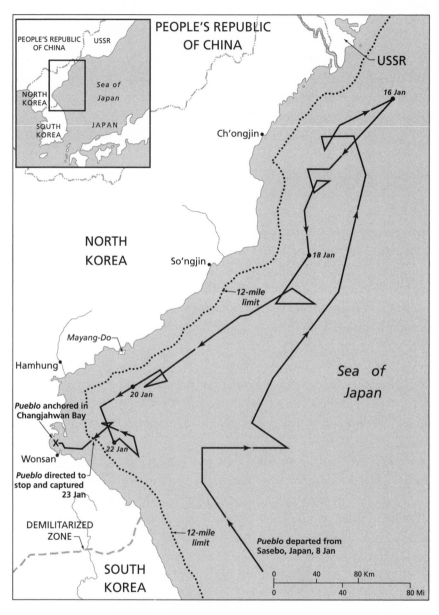

MAP 2. THE CAPTURE OF THE USS *PUEBLO* (AGER-2) BY NORTH KOREA ON JANUARY 23, 1968

classified material to be destroyed. He therefore ordered the ship stopped to allow the crew more time to destroy material. Seeing the crew throwing articles overboard and burning material, the SO-1 resumed its attack.[30] It was during this brief engagement that four crew members were seriously wounded; one, Fireman Duane Hodges, was wounded critically and would die soon after.

Unwilling to endanger further the safety of his crew, Commander Bucher ordered "all ahead one-third" and informed headquarters that he would surrender the ship. Once the *Pueblo* was within 12 nm of the North Korean coast, Bucher was directed to stop. Shortly thereafter, ten North Korean soldiers boarded; an hour later, a second DPRK boarding party, including a pilot, was received on board; and around 7 p.m., the *Pueblo* arrived in Wonsan Harbor. As later confirmed by reconnaissance photos taken by an SR-71 aircraft on January 26, the *Pueblo* anchored in Chang-jahwan Bay, a few miles from the Munch'on Naval Base.

CNFJ had immediately requested air support from the Fifth Air Force to assist the *Pueblo*, but there were no aircraft on strip alert (ready for imme-diate takeoff) in Japan. The mission's "execute order" had not requested air cover in the event of a contingency. The Fifth Air Force staff determined it would take two or three hours to prepare and launch aircraft to support the captured U.S. ship.[31]

The speed with which the North Koreans reacted to the *Pueblo*'s presence suggests that Pyongyang had advance knowledge of the ship's mission and had planned a set of responses to counter its intelligence collection. For example, all of the North Korean gunfire was directed at the *Pueblo*'s superstructure, evidence that the DPRK intended to seize the vessel rather than sink it. The fact that the SO-1 had a pilot on board supports this conclusion as well. SIGINT analysis by the NSA after the incident confirmed it. It is also interesting that the DPRK boarding did not occur until the *Pueblo* had been escorted into the claimed 12-nm ter-ritorial sea. By delaying the boarding, the DPRK bolstered its assertion that the *Pueblo*'s seizure was justified because the U.S. intelligence ship had violated DPRK sovereignty.

Immediately following the seizure of the ship, American commanders in the Pacific began planning a military response. These efforts came to a grinding halt, however, when Gen. Earle Wheeler, the chairman of the Joint Chiefs of Staff (CJCS), directed there would be no show of force in the area of the incident. Subsequent orders from the JCS instructed U.S. naval and air forces to remain at least 80 nm from the DPRK coast when north of a line extending east of the DMZ. Additionally, the USS *Enterprise* (CVN 65) task group had to stay south of latitude 38° N in the Sea of Japan. The aircraft carrier was directed not to take overt action without new orders. Orders were also issued to restrict augmentation of U.S. forces in Korea, except upon JCS approval. The Pentagon developed military options: deployment of the USS *Banner* with an escort to the incident area, mining of DPRK ports, major strikes against North Korean targets, and interdiction of DPRK shipping. President Lyndon Johnson rejected them in favor of diplomacy.[32]

The following day, the Korean Central News Agency (KCNA) broadcast a "confession" by Commander Bucher. It stated that the *Pueblo* had violated DPRK territorial waters and had been executing missions for the Central Intelligence Agency (CIA). Bucher had in fact signed the confession, but only after being kicked unconscious, "threatened with being shot, and being told that unless he signed, his crew would be executed one-by-one right before his eyes."[33] Later that afternoon, the United States issued a press release rebutting the DPRK allegations: "The *Pueblo* was under orders . . . to stay at least thirteen miles from North Korean territory. There is no evidence to suggest that these orders were disobeyed. There is much . . . evidence . . . from the *Pueblo*'s own radio transmissions and from the information broadcast from North Koreans . . . in their own internal reports, that the orders were obeyed."

Simultaneously, on January 24, representatives of the two states met at a previously scheduled meeting of the Military Armistice Commission in Panmunjom. Rear Adm. John Smith, the senior American negotiator, informed his North Korean counterpart, Major General Pak Chung Kuk, that the *Pueblo* had been seized in international waters in violation of international law. Smith insisted that the DPRK return the ship and its crew and apologize for the incident. He also warned that the United States could demand compensation. Major General Pak summarily rejected the American ultimatum. A request by the State Department to the Soviet Union to intercede on behalf of the United States and seek the *Pueblo*'s release was likewise rejected outright.[34]

Two days later, the American ambassador to the United Nations, Arthur Goldberg, addressed the UN Security Council. Ambassador Goldberg presented the council with the intercepted SIGINT confirming that the DPRK knew that the *Pueblo* was virtually unarmed, and that a U.S. ship was attacked in international waters.[35] The *Pueblo*'s lack of preparedness to repel the boarding and destroy its classified material reinforced the U.S. position that the vessel had not been inside the DPRK's territorial waters. American officials had been convinced that the Soviet Union would advise the DPRK to resolve the incident if tensions were to rise sharply on the peninsula as a result of the seizure.[36] Instead, the Soviet representative at the meeting, Platon D. Morosov, refuted the American presentation, citing Commander Bucher's confession, in which he admitted the *Pueblo* had come within 7.6 nm of Nodo Island. The Soviet minister of foreign affairs, Andrei Gromyko, had a similar reaction.[37]

President Johnson sent a personal note to Chairman Alexei Kosygin expressing his disappointment. The president emphasized that a similar attack on a Soviet AGI would be unacceptable to the Kremlin and repeated the request for Soviet intercession with Pyongyang.[38] Kosygin's response, two days later, was less than adequate, questioning the American assertion that the *Pueblo* had been attacked and seized in international waters. The Soviet Union had, Kosygin indicated, information that confirmed the *Pueblo* had been legally detained in DPRK territorial waters, that it had acted against generally accepted norms of international law protecting the inviolability of territorial waters.[39] The United States was therefore completely responsible for the incident. Kosygin cautioned the president not to do anything that could "add fuel to the fire" by pressuring the DPRK and urged the United States to resolve the incident diplomatically. Finally, Kosygin complained about the concentration of U.S. naval forces off the

Korean Peninsula.[40] (It was subsequently learned that Moscow had sent two messages to Pyongyang urging it to settle the incident quickly.)[41]

On January 26, the KCNA released the text of a supposed media interview in which Commander Bucher stated that the *Pueblo*'s mission had been a preparation for a war of aggression. The text also had Bucher saying that he had opened fire on the patrol ships as they approached. Bucher had concluded the interview with a plea for leniency. The next day, the DPRK delivered an official message to the senior member of the United Nations Command Military Armistice Commission (UNCMAC), via the two communist members (Poland and Czechoslovakia) of the Neutral Nations Supervisory Committee (NNSC), warning the United States not to use force to free the *Pueblo* and its crew. If it did, the message warned, the Americans would not free the crew but "only get bodies."[42] An unofficial message delivered at the same time advised that the crew was in good physical condition. The body of the deceased crew member was being preserved, and the wounded were being provided medical care. The next day, Washington responded by acknowledging the status of the crew and declaring that they were entitled to the protection of the Geneva Conventions of 1949.[43] The United States also requested an immediate public or private meeting of the senior members of the UNCMAC.

— — — — • — — —

Official negotiations to secure the release of the *Pueblo* and its crew commenced at Panmunjom on February 2, 1968. Initial discussions with DPRK officials, as well as experience with the DPRK in similar situations, made clear that the expeditious release of the ship and its crew was unlikely. In May 1963, for example, North Korea had shot down a U.S. Army OH-23 helicopter that had strayed over the DMZ. The two-man crew was held captive for a year before being returned to U.S. control.[44] As expected, the *Pueblo* talks dragged on for the better part of a year. A final agreement on the release of the crew (but not the ship) was signed only on December 23, 1968.[45] At 11:30 a.m., the eighty-two surviving members of the crew of the *Pueblo* walked across the "Bridge of No Return" at Panmunjom to freedom.

The United States argued that the *Pueblo* had been illegally seized in international waters, more than 15 nm from the nearest land—a fact confirmed by the *Pueblo*'s messages transmitted during the attack, as well as intercepted DPRK transmissions.[46] The *Pueblo* had been more than 15 nm from Ung-Do Island when it was hailed by the DPRK submarine chaser and subsequently boarded.[47] This evidence demonstrated that the U.S. warship was lawfully operating in international waters. Although the United States recognized that it was common for surveillance ships to be harassed, the DPRK seizure of a sovereign immune vessel on the high seas was unprecedented and against all principles of international law and state practice. Under international law, warships have complete immunity from the jurisdiction of any state except the flag state.[48] Furthermore, intelligence collection beyond the territorial sea was a standard practice by the navies of the world. The *Pueblo*'s surveillance on the high seas conformed to state practice and could not be characterized as an illegal act of aggression.

Moreover, the United States emphasized that even if the *Pueblo* had inadvertently strayed within 12 nm of land, warships are not subject to seizure in the territorial sea unless they engage in hostility.[49] In this case, the *Pueblo* had not even returned fire when it was attacked by DPRK vessels, and it had offered no resistance to the boarding.[50] Normal procedure would have been for the DPRK vessels to request the *Pueblo* to depart the territorial sea or escort it back to international waters. To support its position, the United States offered three examples of Soviet intrusions into American territorial waters. On April 7, 1965, the Soviet ship *Barometer* had come within 2.8 miles of Puerto Rico as it maneuvered near U.S. naval forces. On October 23, 1965, the Soviet ship *Arban* had entered U.S. territorial waters off San Pedro, California. Finally, on December 6, 1966, the Soviet ship *Teodolit* had violated U.S. territorial waters on three separate occasions.[51] In each of these cases the United States had observed the plain rules of international law and simply requested the ship to depart and had not attempted to assert any jurisdiction over it. The seizure of the *Pueblo* and its crew and the killing of an American sailor were also in violation of the law governing the use of force. American officials further insisted the

American crew had not committed any crimes, and any attempt to try the crew under North Korean law would be contrary to the protections afforded by the 1949 Geneva Conventions.[52]

The DPRK accused the United States of espionage and aggression, as confirmed by the crew's purported confessions and the ship's documents.[53] Based on this evidence, DPRK officials were adamant that an impartial third-party investigation was completely out of the question.[54] The North Korean narrative stated that the *Pueblo* had disguised itself as an oceanographic research vessel, surreptitiously intruded into DPRK territorial waters, and attempted to hide its true identity when initially hailed, responding that it was a hydrographic survey ship.[55] Because the ship was instead engaged in intelligence activities, the provisions of the 1958 Geneva Convention regarding foreign warships in the territorial sea did not apply.[56] When challenged, the North Koreans charged that the *Pueblo* had opened fire and attempted to escape, prompting the intercepting vessels to return fire in self-defense.[57] Accordingly, DPRK officials maintained, because the *Pueblo* had entered the 12-nm territorial sea without permission and had engaged in intelligence collection, its crew would be treated as criminals and dealt with according to North Korean law.

Major General Pak insisted at the outset of the negotiations that if the United States wanted to resolve the matter expeditiously, it would have to admit that it had engaged in espionage and had violated DPRK territorial waters and the Armistice Agreement.[58] Beginning with the sixth Senior Military Armistice Commission (MAC) Members Meeting on February 14, 1968, and over the next ten months, Pak asserted that the matter could be resolved only if the United States fulfilled three conditions: first, acknowledge that the *Pueblo* had illegally intruded into DPRK territorial waters; second, apologize for the acts of espionage and hostile acts committed by the *Pueblo*; and third, extend assurances that U.S. ships would not intrude into DPRK territorial waters in the future.[59] He informed Rear Admiral Smith at the seventh Senior MAC Members Meeting on February 16 that release of the ship was not open to discussion, claiming there was no precedent for return of "equipment used in espionage."[60]

The DPRK also charged that the deliberate deployment of an armed U.S. spy ship into its territorial waters was a direct violation of the Armistice Agreement.[61] The *Pueblo*'s intrusion and the subsequent U.S. force buildup on the Korean Peninsula and its adjacent waters had been part of a premeditated plan to provoke a war.[62] North Korean forces therefore had simply exercised their right of self-defense.

The DPRK appeared to rely on article II.A of the Armistice Agreement to support its position.[63] Paragraph 12 of the agreement requires a complete cessation of hostilities in Korea; paragraph 15 requires naval forces to respect the waters contiguous to the Demilitarized Zone and the land areas of Korea controlled by the opposing sides. The United States countered by asserting that the *Pueblo* had not engaged in hostilities or threatened DPRK naval units. Commander Bucher had never uncovered the ship's guns. The United States also argued that paragraph 15 did not extend beyond 12 nm from the coast.[64]

Throughout the negotiations, the United States staunchly maintained that the *Pueblo* had been illegally seized in international waters, more than 15 nm from the nearest North Korean territory. Nonetheless, American negotiators insisted that the issue be referred to an impartial fact-finding body and that the United States would be willing to express regret if the independent (or subsequent U.S.) investigation determined that the *Pueblo* had in fact inadvertently entered DPRK territorial waters.[65] Major General Pak rejected these entreaties and reiterated earlier demands for an acknowledgement, apology, and assurances.

At the sixteenth Senior MAC Members Meeting on May 8, 1968 (and again at the twenty-second meeting, on September 30, 1968), Pak delivered a draft document of apology and assurances that would satisfy North Korean demands. The draft required the United States to acknowledge the validity of the crew's confessions and the documentary evidence provided by the DPRK indicating that the *Pueblo* had been conducting espionage and had been seized in territorial waters in self-defense; shoulder full responsibility and solemnly apologize for the "grave acts of espionage" committed; give firm assurances that no U.S. ships would intrude into

DPRK territorial waters in the future; and request that the crew members be treated leniently.[66]

Realizing that the issue would not be resolved without an apology, American officials began to develop an "overwrite" plan. The scheme called for Maj. Gen. Gilbert Woodward, now head of the American negotiating team, to sign an otherwise unsatisfactory DPRK receipt for the return of the crew in a way that would allow American authorities to disavow any apology yet permit the North Koreans to argue the Americans had accepted their version of the facts. Woodward would sign the receipt by writing across it in his own handwriting a simple statement that he had received the crew. DPRK authorities would be made aware of the plan in advance through a "back channel" involving an Australian in Tokyo with good North Korean connections. The DPRK could afterward claim that the United States had signed its receipt, but the United States could declare that it had signed only what Major General Woodward had written. Both sides would understand the ambiguity.

With the Christmas holidays fast approaching and no agreement in sight, Woodward was instructed to inform his counterpart that the United States would soon have a new president and new secretaries of state and defense. If the *Pueblo* matter was not settled by January 20, 1969, the new Richard M. Nixon administration might decide on other measures to solve the impasse.[67] It appears that the veiled threat of having to deal with the new Republican administration had its desired effect. At the twenty-sixth Senior MAC Members Meeting the two sides reached agreement in principle.[68] Major General Woodward would sign the DPRK document presented on May 8 but would make the following statement before doing so:

> The position of the United States Government with regard to the *Pueblo*, as consistently expressed in the negotiations at Panmunjom and in public, has been that the ship was not engaged in illegal activity, that there is no convincing evidence that the ship at any time intruded into the territorial waters claimed by North Korea, and that we could not apologize for actions which we did not

believe took place. The signed documents were prepared by the North Koreans and were at variance with the above position, but my signature will not and cannot alter the facts. I will sign the document to free the crew and only to free the crew.[69]

The final agreement was signed on December 23, 1968, and the officers and men of the *Pueblo* were returned to American custody that same day.

– – – – • – – – –

Immediately following their release, Commander Bucher and several members of the crew held a press conference at which they denied entering DPRK territorial waters and described the beatings and abuse they had suffered during captivity.

Following their return to U.S. control, the crew members were debriefed by the NSA and the Naval Security Group (NAVSECGRU) to determine what classified information and equipment had been captured by North Korea. A joint intelligence team—composed of representatives of the CIA, DIA, and the intelligence offices of the Army, Navy, and Air Force—assessed the impact on intelligence operations of the loss of classified messages received by the *Pueblo* and now assumed to be compromised. After the debriefings, in January 1969, the Navy convened a court of inquiry to investigate all of the circumstances surrounding the seizure and loss of the *Pueblo*. Additionally, congressional hearings were held in March and April 1969 to inquire into the capture and internment of the ship and its crew.

On January 20, 1969, CINCPACFLT convened the court of inquiry at the Naval Amphibious Base Coronado, California. This court was tasked with determining culpability. It adjourned on March 13, 1969, and issued its findings on May 5. In general, the court investigated four basic issues: Was the mission assigned to the *Pueblo* well planned? Was the ship properly prepared for the mission? Was the mission executed according to Navy protocols? Was the conduct of the ship's crew during detention satisfactory?[70]

In his review of the court's findings, the convening authority, Admiral Hyland, determined, with regard to the first issue, that stationing an AGER off the coast of North Korea, even in international waters, without adequate force protection was a mistake. Admiral Hyland, however, considered it inappropriate to hold a single individual responsible for the failure because a false sense of security that sprang from the international law of freedom of the seas prevailed throughout all echelons of command. The mission plan should have provided for the contingency that had occurred, but all levels in the planning process had underestimated the risk.

Regarding the second issue, Admiral Hyland determined that the planning, training, and preparation for the mission had been less than optimal. The two most serious deficiencies noted by the court were the failure to verify the ship's ability to destroy classified material rapidly, and a lack of intelligence support. Facilities, organization, and procedures on board the ship had been inadequate to destroy classified material rapidly. Furthermore, in general, the NAVSECGRU detachment had not been well trained.

The third issue concerned whether Commander Bucher had been justified in allowing DPRK forces to board his ship, capture his crew, and seize sensitive material without offering any resistance. The ship had not been "equipped to fight a prolonged battle at sea" but still had some power to defend itself. Admiral Hyland concluded, "Bucher should have offered more spirited resistance." Moreover, the admiral determined, Bucher had been negligent in failing to complete the emergency destruction of classified material, which had then fallen into North Korean hands. All classified documents on board could have been destroyed in the available time had the effort been properly organized, in the admiral's opinion. Weighted bags should have been filled and jettisoned, which would have posed minimal exposure to North Korean gunfire topside.

Finally, with regard to the conduct of the crew during detention, the convening authority concurred with the court's opinions that the crew had attempted to minimize compromise of classified information. The convening authority also had agreed that adherence to the Navy Code of Conduct and resistance to interrogation varied according to individual willpower and threshold of pain, and that crew discipline and morale was maintained during detention.

The court recommended and Admiral Hyland concurred that Commander Bucher and Lt. Stephen R. Harris, officer in charge of the "research" detachment, be tried by general court-martial. It also recommended disciplinary action against Lt. Edward Murphy (the executive officer), Rear Admiral Johnson, and Capt. Everett P. Gladding (who had been director, Naval Security Group Pacific). On May 6, 1969, the Secretary of the Navy, however, announced his decision that no further disciplinary action would be taken against any of the personnel involved in the *Pueblo* incident. The officers and crew had "suffered enough."[71]

— — — — • — — — —

Meanwhile, as the court of inquiry deliberated, President Johnson established a committee consisting of George Ball, a career diplomat, and three retired military officers. It was to review the necessity and design of *Pueblo*-like missions, and the conduct of the operation.[72] The objective was not to fix blame but derive lessons in order to ensure more secure and effective missions in the future. The administration subsequently directed the committee to provide only an oral, not written, report to the president.

The committee determined that at the time there had been a valid basis for approving the *Pueblo*'s mission. The committee further found that there had been no indicators that might have warned mission planners that the *Pueblo* would be seized. The facts conclusively showed, it found, that the *Pueblo* had never intruded into DPRK territorial waters. The United States had a strategic interest in exercising high seas freedoms, including intelligence collection by surface ships, outside of the territorial waters of unfriendly nations. The committee also believed that using surface combatants for this purpose would be less effective or pose even greater risks than using AGERs.

Nonetheless, the committee advised the president that intelligence collection in areas where mutual tolerance, such as that between the United States and the USSR, did not exist had to be more carefully tailored to local conditions. The attack required the United States to reexamine the assumption that all nations would respect freedom of the seas and not violate the integrity of a U.S. naval vessel on the oceans. The committee recommended specifically that AGERs not be used near North Korea without protection. The necessary safeguards included increasing the armament and installing adequate onboard destruction devices on the AGERs, and stationing a surface combatant a few miles farther off the coast to deter aggression.

The committee also suggested changes to several operational matters. First, the commanding officer had to be given clear instructions on the use of force in self-defense. In the case of the *Pueblo*, the rules of engagement provided to Commander Bucher had been ambiguous and self-contradictory. They had been unclear as to whether the ship was to act like a warship on a military mission or as an unarmed naval vessel engaged in hydrographic research. Given this ambiguity, it had been difficult for the mission commander to determine when to employ force in self-defense. Second, during such operations, response forces should have been placed on alert with preplanned procedures for reaction.

Finally, the committee determined that it had been a mistake to maintain the covert character of the operation. This approach had undermined protection of the crew, the vessel, and intelligence procedures. Given the publicity surrounding the successful attack on the *Pueblo*, American officials expected adversaries to be watchful for AGER operations off their coasts. (Indeed, this analysis was prescient, since closed societies often view foreign intelligence collection on the high seas as provocative and a security threat.) Thus, the committee concluded, future surface intelligence collection missions would not be prejudiced by confusion over their character.

– – – – • – – – –

On February 18, 1969, the chair of the House Armed Services Committee (HASC) established a special subcommittee under Representative Otis G. Pike to conduct an inquiry into all matters arising from the capture and internment of the USS *Pueblo* and its crew. On July 1, the subcommittee completed its report.[73]

The HASC subcommittee focused on six specific areas: intelligence reconnaissance activities, capability and availability of support forces, risk assessment, communications, command and control, and the Code of Conduct. In its report the subcommittee found, in summary, "serious deficiencies in the organizational and administrative military command structure of both the Department of the Navy and the Department of Defense." The inquiry's scope had been expanded on April 22 to encompass the loss of a Navy EC-121 aircraft that had been shot down by the DPRK on the fifteenth over the Sea of Japan while conducting reconnaissance in international airspace.

Although the subcommittee agreed that U.S. reconnaissance provided decision makers with important national security information, it was unconvinced that the scale and magnitude of American efforts were completely justified. With regard to the *Pueblo* mission in particular, the HASC subcommittee concluded that it should not have been initiated until the crew was properly trained. For example, Lieutenant Harris knew that his linguists were not fully qualified, a deficiency that may have contributed to the absence of early warning of the intended DPRK response. The subcommittee also found a general failure by the defense intelligence community to provide essential and available information to those potentially in need of it in a timely manner.

Representative Pike discovered that the Navy had no contingency plans to aid the ship or rescue the crew during an emergency. For example, the Fifth Air Force in Japan could have supported the mission but no one on the CNFJ staff had the "faintest idea" what forces might be available during an emergency. The subcommittee was particularly disturbed by the failure of the chain of command to alert any of the numerous U.S. air bases in Japan and the USS *Enterprise* to launch aircraft to assist the *Pueblo*.

The subcommittee also faulted the risk assessment, which had assumed North Korea would observe the international law of the sea. With the exception of the NSA, responsible authorities had ignored or discounted evidence that the DPRK was becoming more sensitive toward the presence of foreign ships in its claimed territorial sea. The NSA analysts' urging that more robust protection measures be considered had never even reached senior commanders. The subcommittee concluded on this point that the risks of the *Pueblo* mission were not appropriately categorized because CNFJ had failed to observe the JCS risk criteria and because there was no requirement to assess the need for possible emergency support. The JCS, in turn, failed to ensure that its own risk criteria had been properly considered and applied. Accordingly, the HASC subcommittee recommended a reworking of risk assessment for reconnaissance missions.

As for communications, the subcommittee found that the advantages of speedy, elaborate, and highly sophisticated communications equipment had been offset by the indecision and inefficiency throughout the chain of command that had greeted the *Pueblo*'s messages. In particular, the benefit of the rapid transmission of the two Pinnacle messages had been "dissipated by human inefficiency." Unacceptable delays in delivering these messages to the responsible operational commanders had effectively precluded assistance within the compressed time frame of the situation. The subcommittee also criticized the command-and-control response during the incident, having found the decision-making infrastructure responsible for surface reconnaissance missions unresponsive to emergency situations. It therefore recommended that the JCS review its entire military reconnaissance program to ensure lines of command and control were clear and unmistakable.

The subcommittee concluded, overall, that the damage to the United States caused by the *Pueblo* incident was "incalculable" in terms of American credibility, diplomacy, and the perception of the United States as a reliable military ally. The incident caused a "serious compromise" of U.S. intelligence capabilities—one that could have been prevented by better planning.

— — — — ● — — — —

The ad hoc team formed, as mentioned above, to assess the impact of the *Pueblo*'s seizure on intelligence operations and programs considered the loss of the large cache of operation intelligence (OPINTEL) "broadcast" messages that had been received by the ship and was still on board at the time of capture. The team reviewed between seven and eight thousand messages, which contained a wide spectrum of information concerning communications intelligence-collection requirements and capabilities in East Asia.[74]

use of maritime platforms equipped with passive ELINT capabilities was suspended and ultimately stopped. By the end of 1970 all of the Navy's *Liberty*-type, *Victory*-type, and AGER ships had been decommissioned.

The AGER SIGINT program had come to an end. Despite its failings, however, today's Navy continues to rely on ships to conduct surveillance and other intelligence-gathering missions in support of joint forces. The U.S. Navy's Special Mission Program now operates twenty-two special-mission ships (SMSs) for a number of Department of Defense (DoD) and other U.S. government missions. Their specialized services include oceanographic and hydrographic surveys, underwater surveillance, missile tracking, acoustic surveys, ballistic missile monitoring, and underwater and special warfare support. Nine ships are chartered to support submarine and special warfare operations. All the others—the five oceanographic survey vessels, five ocean surveillance vessels, two missile-range instrumentation ships, and one navigation-test support ship—are government owned. SMSs are operated by civilian crews who work for private companies under contract to the Military Sealift Command (MSC).

Of the nine submarine and special warfare support ships, three are assigned to the Naval Special Warfare Command. The other six support the Navy's requirement to escort submarines entering and leaving ports. Oceanographic survey ships provide the Pentagon with information on the marine environment. These ships use multibeam, wide-angle, precision sonar systems to conduct acoustic, biological, physical, and geophysical surveys of broad sections of the ocean floor. Ocean-surveillance ships provide direct support to the Navy, using both passive and active low-frequency sonar arrays to detect and track undersea threats. Missile-range instrumentation ships monitor domestic missile launches to improve the efficiency and accuracy of U.S. missiles; they also track foreign missile and weapons tests. The MSC's navigation-test support ship assists with submarine weapons- and navigation-system testing for the Navy's Strategic Systems Programs Office. Finally, a sea-based X-band radar platform—a semisubmersible, self-propelled vessel known as SBX-1—is part of the U.S. ballistic-missile defense system, which tracks, discriminates, and assesses ballistic missiles.

Like the AGERs of the past, these ships have faced harassment and interference, particularly by China in the South China Sea and East China Sea. The United States continues to rely on the age-old presumption that other states will respect freedoms of navigation and other lawful international uses of the oceans, both on the high seas and within exclusive economic zones (EEZs). The SMSs are sovereign immune vessels, owned or operated by the U.S. government and solely on governmental, noncommercial service; they are legally inviolable and beyond the jurisdiction of any foreign government. The doctrine of sovereign immunity may be tested as these ships operate in foreign coastal waters. So far, however, no SMS has been stopped and boarded by foreign forces on the high seas or in an EEZ.

"DRAWING A LINE AGAINST ILLEGAL ACTIONS"

The SS *Mayaguez* Incident (1975)

The 1975 seizure of the SS *Mayaguez* by Khmer Rouge forces and the subsequent U.S. raid to free the ship and its crew may be called America's last battle of the Vietnam War.[1] The Khmer Rouge, which had just seized power in Cambodia, hijacked the American ship in the Gulf of Thailand on April 12. The United States responded over the next three days with an air and sea assault to free the ship and crew. The catastrophe that afflicted Cambodia, the tragic seizure of the American ship, and the final U.S. engagement in Indochina all emerged from the end of the war in neighboring Vietnam.

The Paris Peace Accords, signed by the United States, North and South Vietnam, and the Vietcong on January 17, 1973, brought a temporary end to hostilities in Vietnam.[2] Pursuant to the agreement, an indefinite cease-fire took effect on January 27, 1973. The United States agreed to discontinue military involvement in South Vietnam and to withdraw its forces from the country. The parties also agreed to repatriate prisoners of war. North and South Vietnam agreed to the future peaceful reunification of the country. The South Vietnamese government was to remain in place pending free elections under international supervision. North Vietnam agreed to respect the Provisional Military Demarcation Line at the seventeenth parallel, which had been drawn at the 1954 Geneva Conference.

As soon as the last U.S. combat forces departed South Vietnam on March 29, 1973, North Vietnam violated the cease-fire and resumed the war against the South. By late April 1975 North Vietnamese forces had captured Phuoc Long City, Quang Tri, Hue, and Da Nang and were closing in on Saigon. On April 29, President Gerald Ford ordered the immediate evacuation of all remaining American civilian personnel from South Vietnam. Over the next eighteen hours a thousand American and seven thousand South Vietnamese civilians were airlifted to safety on board the USS *Midway* (CV 41). The next day, the North Vietnamese army entered Saigon and captured the presidential palace. This action officially ended the Vietnam War and humiliated the United States. Accepting the surrender of South Vietnam from General Duong Van Minh later in the day, Colonel Bui Tin remarked, "You have nothing to fear; between Vietnamese there are no victors and no vanquished. Only the Americans have been defeated. If you are patriots, consider this a moment of joy. The war for our country is over."[3]

Just two weeks earlier, the United States had suffered a similar although lesser-known foreign policy defeat at the hands of the communist Khmer Rouge in Cambodia.[4] The kingdom of Cambodia had achieved independence from France in 1954. In March 1970, Lieutenant General Lon Nol, the prime minister, orchestrated a successful coup d'état against the head of state, Prince Norodom Sihanouk, principally over the latter's acquiescence to North Vietnamese army operations and forward bases in Cambodia supporting the Vietcong in South Vietnam. The army of the Republic of South Vietnam and U.S. Army forces conducted more than a dozen incursions into Cambodia during the spring and summer of 1970 to eradicate North Vietnamese strongholds there. Lon Nol established the Khmer Republic, which was supported by the United States and other Western nations. Over the next five years, the Forces Armées Nationale Khmer (FANK), with U.S. military assistance, fought the Khmer Rouge, or Communist Party of Kampuchea, for control of Cambodia.

In 1973, U.S. military aid to the FANK dried up with the signing of the Paris Peace Accords. More broadly, the enactment of the Case-Church Amendment eliminated funding for U.S. combat operations in Indochina.[5]

Lacking adequate American military support, by 1975 the FANK had relinquished control of most of Cambodia to the Khmer Rouge and occupied only Phnom Penh and a few outposts along the Mekong River that protected its supply route from South Vietnam. Khmer Rouge forces cut this critical route in February 1975, forcing the FANK to rely on aerial resupply into Pochentong Airport. By the end of March, Khmer Rouge forces had overrun the last remaining FANK outposts along the Mekong and had begun shelling Pochentong to disrupt the airlift.

On April 1, Premier (and general) Lon Nol resigned and went into exile, first in Indonesia and eventually the United States.[6] Ten days later, the 31st Marine Amphibious Unit was ordered to evacuate American personnel from the Cambodian capital. Over the course of several hours, 146 Americans and 444 Cambodian and third-country nationals were evacuated and flown to Utapao Air Base, about ninety miles southeast of Bangkok. Refusing to be evacuated, Prince Sirik Matak, a former prime minister, fled to the French embassy. In a letter to the U.S. ambassador, John Gunther Dean, on April 12, Matak explained that he could not leave "in such a cowardly fashion."[7] "I never believed for a moment that you would have this sentiment of abandoning a people," he declared, who had "chosen liberty. You have refused us your protection, and we can do nothing about it. I have only committed this mistake of believing in you, the Americans." On April 17, 1975, communist forces entered Phnom Penh and brought an end to the Cambodian civil war. The Khmer Rouge captured and executed the prince shortly after.[8] The U.S. embassy was closed, not to reopen until November 11, 1991.

Similarly, on April 30, South Vietnam collapsed. Indochina descended into chaos. Neighboring states sought to press their claims to islands under dispute in the east and west. In the east, Chinese naval forces and maritime militia seized the remaining Paracel Islands from Vietnam.[9] In the west, Cambodia commandeered a fleet of "Swift Boats" (American-model, fifteen-meter aluminum fast patrol craft, designed for riverine and coastal duty) from Lon Nol's government;[10] with them it occupied a handful of disputed islands, including Poulo Wai and Koh Tang in the Gulf of Thailand.

Cambodia was interested in securing the outlying islands especially because they might justify claims to offshore oil reserves. The Cambodian government also claimed a ninety-nautical-mile territorial sea and announced plans to "seize all foreign ships violating such limits."[11] Less than one month later, a Khmer gunboat attacked the SS *Mayaguez* off Poulo Wai Island. The seizure caught the United States by surprise and presented President Ford with the difficulty of trying to negotiate with a government that the United States did not recognize.

— — — • — — —

As the Khmer Rouge solidified power in April 1975, it began to lash out at foreign shipping in the Gulf of Thailand. On May 2, Khmer Rouge naval forces fired on and seized seven Thai fishing boats. The Korean Transportation Ministry issued a warning to avoid the waters around Poulo Wai and Koh Tang islands.[12] This warning was passed to the U.S. Department of State. Two days later, a communist Khmer gunboat attacked a South Korean ship, which evaded capture. The State Department's Operation Center received a copy of the Foreign Broadcast Information Service report on the incident on May 5.[13] On May 7, a Panamanian cargo ship en route to Thailand from Singapore was boarded in the Gulf of Thailand by Cambodian communist militia and detained for thirty-six hours.

The U.S. intelligence community tracked these events but failed to alert mariners.[14] At the time of the *Mayaguez* seizure, the United States operated a system for broadcasting hydrographic warnings and navigational safety information to American seafarers. Generally, there were two types of warnings: navigational warnings and special warnings. The Defense Mapping Agency and Hydrographic Center (DMAHC) was responsible for issuing navigational warnings; the Department of State Office of Maritime Affairs (DoS/OMA) issued special warnings. Radiotelegraph broadcasts were transmitted twice a day, at about 12:00 p.m. and 12:30 a.m.

Information on these events, however, was not passed to DMAHC or DoS/OMA.[15] Accordingly, American authorities did not broadcast any alerts concerning the conditions in the Gulf of Thailand, and so American merchant ships transiting the area received no warnings. DMAHC finally broadcast a special warning (advising mariners to "remain more than thirty-five nautical miles off the coast of Cambodia and more than twenty nautical miles off the coast of Vietnam including off-lying islands"), but only some nineteen hours after the initial report of the attack on the *Mayaguez* was received in Washington, D.C.[16]

– – – – • – – – –

On May 7, 1975, just one week after the fall of Saigon, the SS *Mayaguez* departed Hong Kong en route to Sattahip, Thailand, carrying a cargo of U.S. military and commercial goods.[17] The unarmed, U.S.-registered merchant ship had a crew of thirty-nine mariners.[18] Built in 1944, the vessel had been converted in 1960 into a containership, with a capacity of 382 containers belowdecks and ninety-four on deck. On May 12, five days out of Hong Kong, the *Mayaguez* was transiting through the Gulf of Thailand about sixty nautical miles off the Cambodian mainland and just seven from Poulo Wai Island.[19] The ship was in the busy international shipping lane along the most direct route between Hong Kong and Thailand.[20]

At about 1410, a Khmer gunboat flying a red flag, one of the Swift Boats the Khmer Rouge had inherited from the FANK, intercepted the ship. Ten minutes later this first boat to encounter the U.S. ship fired fifteen to twenty shots without warning from its .50-caliber machine gun into the *Mayaguez*'s side and across its bow. The American ship increased to maneuvering speed when a rocket-propelled grenade (RPG) exploded in the water and a geyser erupted; the crew went below to escape the danger. The *Mayaguez* could not outrun the Swift Boat. When it reached the containership, at about 1435, seven heavily armed Khmer soldiers leapt on board and took control.[21]

Capt. Charles Miller, master of the *Mayaguez*, immediately transmitted a "mayday" call. John Neal of Delta Exploration Company, in Jakarta, Indonesia, received at 1530 local a transmission stating that a merchant vessel had been fired upon and boarded by Cambodian armed forces. No casualties had been suffered, and the crew members did not feel in imminent danger.[22] The ship was being towed to an unknown Cambodian port.[23] Neal notified the U.S. embassy in Jakarta, which in turn sent a series of six messages to various offices in Washington reporting the incident.[24] The U.S. Defense Attaché Office in Singapore notified Commander, U.S. Seventh Fleet, which in turn notified U.S. Pacific Command (PACOM).[25]

The capture of the *Mayaguez* set off what was to be the last U.S. military engagement of the Vietnam War and the only combat between U.S. ground forces and the Khmer Rouge. Fearing an embarrassing repeat of the *Pueblo* incident, American authorities reacted swiftly with a number of diplomatic and military initiatives to compel the release of the vessel and its crew. The inherent complexity of the situation, however, was compounded by the lack of specific intelligence on the location of the crew. On May 12, after consulting with the National Security Council, President Gerald Ford demanded the immediate release of the vessel. The White House issued a statement: "We have been informed that a Cambodian naval vessel has seized an American merchant ship on the high seas and forced it to the port of Kampong Som [also known as Sihanoukville]. The President has met with the NSC. He considers this seizure an act of piracy. He has instructed [the] State Department to demand the immediate release of the ship."[26]

The president warned Cambodia that failure to release the ship and crew would bring "the most serious consequences." Following its broadcast, the Department of State attempted to deliver a message to Cambodian authorities through the head of the People's Republic of China (PRC) liaison office in Washington, demanding the immediate release of the *Mayaguez* and its crew. The telegram set forth the American legal narrative: "Naval forces controlled by the Cambodian authorities have seized an American merchant vessel, the SS *Mayaguez* . . . in the Gulf of Thailand. . . . This is an act of piracy. The vessel was in international waters and represented no danger to the authorities in Cambodia or anybody else."[27] Huang Chen, PRC ambassador to the United States, refused to accept the message.[28] The next day, the American liaison office in Beijing delivered to the Cambodian embassy in China and to the PRC Foreign Ministry (for forwarding) the demand for release of the vessel and its crew. Refusing to forward the message to the Cambodian government, the Foreign Ministry returned the telegram via routine mail.[29]

The White House, like the State Department, called the seizure an "act of piracy."[30] Under the international law of the sea, however, maritime piracy consists of "illegal acts of violence, detention or any act of depredation, committed for *private ends* by the crew or the passengers of a *private ship*."[31] The Khmer forces represented a government, so they had not seized the ship for "private ends." Furthermore, Cambodian naval forces operated on board public vessels, rather than those of private individuals. The crew of a warship commits an act of piracy only if it mutinies and takes control of its own ship. Accordingly, it was legally incorrect to label the attack an act of piracy.[32] At the time of the seizure, Cambodia claimed a twelve-nautical-mile territorial sea, although the United States recognized only a three-mile limit.[33] The merchant ship allegedly had been attacked and seized seven to eight miles off the Cambodian-claimed island of Poulo Wai. In fact, the U.S. ship actually may have been as close as three nautical miles from the island.[34] In any event, Washington claimed that the *Mayaguez* had been boarded and detained on the high seas in violation of international law.

If the capture was not piracy, per se, it was certainly unlawful on several levels. The seizure violated the freedom of the high seas recognized in the law of the sea. Unless otherwise provided for in a treaty, a ship on the high seas is subject only to the jurisdiction of the state whose flag it flies.[35] A warship that encounters a foreign-flagged merchant ship on the high seas may not board it without reasonable grounds for suspecting that the ship is engaged in one of a handful of crimes of universal jurisdiction, such as maritime piracy or slave trafficking. The *Mayaguez* was not engaged in either. Even if the ship had transited in the territorial sea of Poulo Wai Island, it would have been entitled to the right of innocent passage.

After learning that the *Mayaguez* had been captured, the National Military Command Center directed PACOM to launch reconnaissance aircraft from Thailand to attempt to locate the ship. After more than three hours, a U.S. P-3 Orion maritime patrol aircraft out of Utapao conducted the first search. To reinforce this effort, the guided-missile destroyer USS *Henry*

B. Wilson (DDG 7), the frigate USS *Harold E. Holt* (FF 1074), the stores ship USS *Vega* (AF 59), and the aircraft carrier USS *Coral Sea* (CV 43) were directed to converge on a point off Kampong Som, Cambodia's main port.[36] The carrier *Midway* was sent at twenty-five knots toward Cambodia and alerted to expect action. Ships in Subic Bay, including the carrier USS *Hancock* (CV 19), also headed for Thailand. Marines from Okinawa and the Philippines were ordered to Utapao to stage for an airborne assault. Meanwhile, the administration sought to find the ship and prevent the transfer of the crew to the mainland or the arrival of Cambodian reinforcements.[37] The United States also began to plan to retake the ship and rescue the crew.[38] Mainland targets would be attacked in support of the assault.

In the early morning hours of May 13, U.S. maritime patrol aircraft continued to track the *Mayaguez* near Poulo Wai. At about 0815, a P-3 Orion positively identified the ship a mile from Koh Tang Island. The ship rested at anchor in one hundred feet of water.[39] Koh Tang is a small island, less than three square miles, thirty miles from the Cambodian mainland. The crew had been taken off the ship and onto a Thai fishing vessel and Khmer boat. The Thai fishermen gave food and water to the crew. The Cambodians interrogated them, wanting to know the *Mayaguez*'s cargo and mission. The ship in fact carried 274 containers, 77 of them destined for Thailand, 96 for Singapore, and 101 empty. The cargo included food, beverages, clothing, parcel post, paint, chemicals, industrial raw materials, and consumer products—no weapons or ammunition.

Meanwhile, Khmer Rouge forces continued their attacks on vessels in the shipping lane of the Gulf of Thailand. That same day, they pursued a Panamanian freighter and detained it for two hours.[40] A Cambodian gunboat fired four salvoes at the Swedish cargo ship *Hirado* some 75 nm southwest of Poulo Panjang Island, near where the *Mayaguez* had been taken. The 13,000-ton *Hirado* made evasive maneuvers and avoided capture.[41] The Swedish East Asia Shipping Company ordered all of its vessels to stay at least 50 nm from the Cambodian coast.

As the night of May 13 arrived, Khmer militia forced several crew members and the master back to the *Mayaguez* to open several locked rooms. As they did, tactical aircraft from Utapao flew overhead and dropped flares; the Khmer soldiers, fearing an attack from the air, drove everyone back to the boats. U.S. Air Force aircraft, including F-4E Phantoms, F-111As, AC-130H gunships, and Navy A-7D Corsairs, flew overhead throughout the day. Just before 1600, American pilots saw smoke coming from the stack of the *Mayaguez*; the ship appeared to be preparing to get under way. Two Corsairs strafed across its bow as a warning to remain in place, and the smoke ceased. Numerous small boats milled around the *Mayaguez*, making it hard for the airmen to determine exactly what was happening. Two of the boats headed toward Koh Tang Island, one reportedly with "a lot of people on board" and the other with Caucasians.[42] Subsequent reports indicated that the personnel on the two small boats had landed on Koh Tang.[43] These reports were incorrect, and they led American planners to assume wrongly that the *Mayaguez* crew had been relocated to the island.

As the day progressed, U.S. aircraft were instructed to isolate Koh Tang to prevent any boat leaving the island from reaching the Cambodian mainland.[44] Three boats were turned back with warning shots delivered by U.S. Air Force tactical aircraft, and another was sunk. A fifth boat, however, succeeded in reaching Kampong Som Harbor, despite repeated warning shots and use of riot-control agents by U.S. fighter aircraft.[45] On May 14, a Pentagon media press release stated that these attacks had begun when it appeared the Cambodians were attempting to move the crew to the mainland and after the Cambodian vessels ignored warnings.[46]

Aircraft that had engaged this vessel reported that it had been carrying what appeared to be thirty to forty Caucasians.[47] This information, however, was not transmitted clearly to American authorities in Thailand, Hawaii, or Washington, leaving officials at the Defense and State Departments to believe only a few members of the crew had been taken to the mainland and that the remainder were still on Koh Tang Island. Nonetheless, as a subsequent GAO (Government Accounting [later, Accountability] Office) report concluded, "the weight of the evidence suggested that most or all of the crew was no longer on Koh Tang."[48]

American officials were convinced, in any case, that further delay risked removal of the crew to the mainland, where they would disappear into the countryside.[49] On May 14, not having received a positive response from the Chinese or the Cambodians, the United States appealed through its representative to the United Nations to UN Secretary General Kurt Waldheim to intercede to obtain the release of the *Mayaguez* and its crew. It informed Waldheim that the United States reserved the right to take appropriate measures in self-defense under article 51 of the UN Charter, as it might find necessary to protect the lives of American citizens and property:

> The United States Government wishes to draw urgently to your attention the threat to international peace, which has been posed by the illegal and unprovoked seizure by Cambodian authorities of the U.S. merchant vessel, *Mayaguez*, in international waters. This unarmed merchant ship has a crew of about forty American citizens. As you are no doubt aware, my Government has already initiated certain steps through diplomatic channels, insisting on immediate release of the vessel and crew. We also request you to take steps within your ability to contribute to this objective. In the absence of a positive response to our appeals through diplomatic channels for early action by the Cambodian authorities, my Government reserves the right to take such measures as may be necessary to protect the lives of American citizens and property, including appropriate measures of self-defense under article 51 of the United Nations Charter.[50]

The secretary general duly communicated with the Cambodian government and urged both sides to refrain from force and work toward a peaceful settlement.[51] Cambodia did not reply immediately, however. (It would eventually reply to the secretary general on May 19, four days after the *Mayaguez* and its crew had been returned to American control.)[52] President Ford was now convinced that negotiations for release of the ship and its

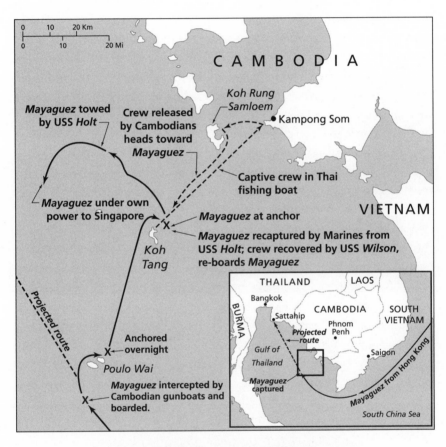

C A M B O D I A

Mayaguez towed by USS *Holt*

Crew released by Cambodians heads toward *Mayaguez*

Koh Rung
Samloem

● Kampong Som

Captive crew in Thai fishing boat

Mayaguez under own power to Singapore

X *Mayaguez* at anchor

Mayaguez recaptured by Marines from USS *Holt*; crew recovered by USS *Wilson*, re-boards *Mayaguez*

Koh Tang

Projected route

THAILAND   LAOS

Bangkok ●

BURMA

Sattahip ●

CAMBODIA

Phnom Penh ●

SOUTH VIETNAM

Saigon ●

Projected route

Gulf of Thailand

Mayaguez from Hong Kong

Anchored overnight

X

Poulo Wai

Mayaguez captured

Mayaguez intercepted by Cambodian gunboats and boarded.

X

VIETNAM

South China Sea

**MAP 3. SEIZURE OF THE SS *MAYAGUEZ*
BY CAMBODIA, APRIL 12, 1975**

crew would be unsuccessful;[53] he ordered the Marines to seize Koh Tang Island and simultaneously board and retake the SS *Mayaguez*.

The Joint Chiefs of Staff issued planning guidance to PACOM that required U.S. forces to be prepared, at first light on May 15, to secure Koh Tang Island and simultaneously board the *Mayaguez*.[54] The raid would begin with airstrikes against Kampong Som by B-52 bombers from Guam and tactical aircraft from the *Coral Sea*, while Marines stormed the *Mayaguez*. At 1645 on May 14, an "execute order" directed CINCPAC to conduct an assault by Marines, which would be embarked on USS *Holt*, to recapture the *Mayaguez* as soon as possible and steam or tow it out to sea.

The air strikes against the Kampong Som complex coincided with the rendezvous of the *Holt* with the *Mayaguez*. Aircraft from the *Coral Sea* pounded military targets and waterfront infrastructure, destroying seventeen aircraft, hangars, the runway, and several antiaircraft batteries at Ream airfield; the barracks and fuel storage facilities at the Ream naval base; and two warehouses, an oil refinery, and a railroad marshaling-yard building at the port of Kampong Som.[55] The mainland airstrikes were aimed at denying Cambodia the ability to interfere by either sea or air with the rescue operation.[56] These attacks on the mainland were carried out despite an American law that barred U.S. "combat activities" in Indochina.[57] They were justified by the administration as a prudent, limited use of force to protect the assault force and support the rescue operation.[58]

The plan also directed a Marine helicopter assault on Koh Tang. Concern for the safety of the *Mayaguez* crew precluded air strikes or naval gunfire to prepare the landing zones.[59] The Defense Intelligence Agency assessed that there were 150–200 Khmer regular troops on the island, armed with 82-mm mortars, 75-mm recoilless rifles, machine guns, and rocket-propelled-grenade launchers. Intelligence Pacific in Hawaii similarly estimated that there were between ninety and a hundred Khmer regulars on the island, reinforced by a heavy-weapons squad of ten to fifteen men. But these estimates never made it to the landing force. The DIA estimate was never communicated to the Marine planners; the Intelligence Pacific assessment did not reach the local commander at Utapao until five to six hours before the assault. There is no evidence that it was passed on to the Marines.[60] From what intelligence was available to them, the helicopter pilots expected little or no opposition; mission planners believed the island had just eighteen to forty lightly armed, irregular militia. When they landed, however, the Marines encountered a reinforced battalion of elite Khmer Rouge naval infantry.[61] So large a force was on Koh Tang because it had recently seized the island from Vietnam, and now it was prepared for a counterattack.

The first helicopters began to lift off from Utapao, which, some two hundred miles north, served as the aerial staging site. A total of sixteen Air Force HH-53 helicopters (call sign "Jolly Green") were assigned to the assault on Koh Tang, as well as a Marine assault force. The first wave comprised 175 personnel and eight helicopters. Three more helicopters carrying Marines and other personnel were to board the *Mayaguez*. Three helicopters delivered forty-eight Marines to the *Holt*, supplemented later by six personnel from the Military Sea Transportation Service (progenitor of the Military Sealift Command), six U.S. Navy explosive-ordnance disposal technicians, and a linguist. Because of the small size of the frigate's flight deck, the boarding team had to disembark from the helicopters as they hovered, only their front wheels touching the ship. Meanwhile, U.S. aircraft would saturate *Mayaguez* with riot-control agents in preparation for boarding—a Seventh Fleet idea. The forty-eight Marines approached the merchant vessel in small boats and boarded the ship without opposition. Using only hand signals because of their gas masks, they searched the ship and found it deserted.[62] The Marines then scoured the vessel for booby traps and, finding none, declared the ship secured. The boarding of *Mayaguez* went off without a hitch; the ship had been abandoned.

The landings on Koh Tang, which also began at sunrise on May 15, immediately ran into trouble. The first flight, eight helicopters in four sections, approached Koh Tang just after 0600 to offload their Marines on two landing zones (western beach and eastern beach) on the northern end of Koh Tang. The first two, CH-53s (call sign "Knife") with side numbers K 21 and K 22, met no resistance on their initial landing at the western beach. As K 21 unloaded its twenty-one Marines, however, it was hit by intense small-arms fire, RPGs, and mortars. K 21 was still on the landing zone, aided by K 22, which tried to suppress the enemy fire. Capt. Terry Ohlemeier, the pilot of K 22, later recalled that the small-arms fire from the jungle into K 21 "looked like a string of Christmas tree lights."[63] K 21 was damaged but managed to take off on one engine; it ditched in the ocean about a mile offshore. (The crew was rescued, except for one member—Staff Sgt. Elwood Rumbaugh—who was lost at sea.) Next, K 22 set down on the western beach under heavy fire to deliver its Marines but, taking heavy fire in the landing zone, aborted the landing. K 22 was hit, lost an engine, and had a ruptured fuel tank. The helicopter flew 125 miles away from Koh Tang before it made an emergency landing on the beach, where search-and-rescue helicopters recovered the crew and passengers.

Things were even worse on the eastern beach: K 23 and K 31 also received heavy small-arms fire, grenades and RPGs, while attempting to land. K 31, its fuel tanks hit, went down at the waterline. The survivors swam seaward to avoid fire from the tree line; four hours later they were rescued in the water by the *Wilson*. K 23 also suffered heavy damage and erupted in a ball of fire as it crashed on the beach. The survivors, including twenty Marines who escaped from K 31, made their way to the tree line but became isolated from the main force and would prove difficult to extricate. The four remaining helicopters in the first wave also encountered heavy fire. One was unable to reach the landing zone and deposited its Marines about one kilometer southwest of the main body.

By 0915, however, the first wave of the assault force had been inserted. Only 109 of its 180 Marines had arrived safely on the island, and twenty of those were isolated on the eastern side.[64] The remaining Marines were pinned down by heavy fire and separated into three groups.[65] At 0930 more Marines landed, bringing the strength to 131. These forces were inserted on the western beach, which was deemed less dangerous. Jolly Green 41 attempted to land and was driven back by Cambodian fire. Two helicopters, JG 42 and K 32, landed under heavy fire. They were so closely engaged that air support was risky; even strafing runs might hit American troops. Of the eight helicopters in the first wave, only one had escaped damage.[66] K 32, JG 41, and

JG 42 were so heavily damaged that they could no longer fly. Another Jolly Green, JG 13, was engaged in search-and-rescue, but was damaged trying to recover the crew and passengers of the stranded K 23. The search-and-rescue aircraft had to remain in position, absorbing punishing fire from the Cambodian forces. The helicopter was forced to abort the rescue attempt; it made an emergency landing at Rayong, Thailand, with thirty-five holes, severe rotor-blade damage, and fuel, oil, and hydraulic leaks.[67] JG 41 flew into the western beach for a fifth time and was hit in the rotor by a mortar round. The helicopter made it back but could not be returned to mission status. The landings had gone badly, and the ground forces on Koh Tang were insisting that more troops were needed, so the helicopters turned back once again toward Cambodia. This order delayed the arrival of the second wave until just after JG 41, the final helicopter of the first wave, returned.

By now mission-capable forces had dwindled to only three operational helicopters (JG 1, 12, and 43). To these were added another two CH-53s from the search-and-rescue group, K 51 and 52. That yielded a total of five helicopters to move troops to Koh Tang in the second wave. The aircraft of the second wave launched at staggered times between 0900 and 1000, carrying 127 Marines in all. En route, the pilots received word that the crew of the *Mayaguez* had been picked up by the *Wilson*.

Just one hour after the Marine assault on Koh Tang commenced, a Cambodian radio broadcast had indicated that the *Mayaguez* was going to be released.[68] Because the report did not specifically mention the crew, the assault proceeded. Washington advised Phnom Penh that offensive military operations would cease when and if the Cambodians issued an unconditional statement that guaranteed the release of the crew. "We have heard a radio broadcast that you are prepared to release the SS *Mayaguez*. We welcome this development, if true. As you know, we have seized the ship. As soon as you issue a statement that you are prepared to release the crew members you hold unconditionally and immediately, we will promptly cease military operations."[69]

At 1015, a P-3 Orion spotted a Thai fishing vessel approaching the island flying a white flag. It appeared to carry a number of Caucasians. The

Wilson investigated, and within minutes the boat, containing the entire crew of the *Mayaguez*, pulled alongside and unloaded its thirty-nine passengers.[70] The Thai fishing vessel itself and its five-man crew had been captive for five months and had been released as well. The second wave was canceled, and the helicopters turned back toward Utapao. Unbeknownst to the United States, the *Mayaguez* crew had been released one hour after the assault began. Now that the ship's crew had been recovered, the mission focused on extracting the ground forces engaged on Koh Tang. The 131 Marines and five Air Force crew members on the island were taking heavy fire. The force was separated into three enclaves: eighty-two on the western beach, twenty-nine just south of that beach, and twenty-five isolated on the eastern beach. The two beaches were separated by a narrow spit of land, only four hundred meters in width, held by Cambodian troops.

The order to cancel the second wave was remanded after forces on the ground on Koh Tang feared they would be overrun without a new covering force to extract those already on the island. Four hours after the initial assault and just before noon, the second wave began landing on the island.[71] The battle on Koh Tang Island was just getting started. The Marines were now embroiled in a firefight with Khmer Rouge armed forces. The first helicopter in the second wave, K 52, was so badly damaged that it made an emergency landing on the coast in Thailand. The four others—K 51, JG 11, JG 12, and JG 43—landed safely and disembarked one hundred more Marines.[72] They helped to consolidate the American position, although the isolated Marine platoon and five airmen remained on the eastern beach.

By midafternoon a switch in airborne forward air control from "fast movers" (attack jets) to a propeller-driven OV-10 Bronco marked a turning point in the quality of close air support. The OV-10, slower and more maneuverable, could stay "on top" more effectively and so provide more accurate and timely spotting to the AC-130 gunships that had been on station.

The effort to withdraw U.S. forces concentrated on the twenty-five Americans isolated on the eastern shore. With only two or three hours of daylight remaining, the need became urgent to evacuate the platoon. By now the main force numbered 202 Marines and could sustain a night attack, but the small force in the eastern zone was vulnerable and taking fire. At about 2:15 that afternoon, two Jolly Greens (JG 11 and 43) attempted to land at the eastern zone but failed. One of the two suffered extensive damage but made it to the *Coral Sea*. As the *Coral Sea* steamed to rendezvous with U.S. forces, the helicopters were able to utilize its deck as a floating landing strip. The carrier was significantly closer to Koh Tang than was Utapao and therefore served as a force multiplier, permitting helicopters to make more trips to and from the island. Between 1730 and 1800 the Navy, Air Force, and Marines were able to extract the platoon on the eastern shore without casualties. The *Henry B. Wilson*'s gig, call sign "Black Velvet," fired on Cambodian positions behind the eastern shore with four machine guns, the OV-10 called in F-4 and A-7 jet aircraft to attack, and the Marines on the beach kept up their fire. JG 12 and K 51 strafed Cambodian positions, while JG 11 picked up a total of twenty Marines and five crew members. The aircraft landed on the *Coral Sea*—so badly damaged that it never flew again. No Marines or aircrew were injured in the extraction.

The crew of the *Mayaguez* had returned to their ship about five o'clock and were steaming safely toward Singapore. With the ship and its crew recovered, the president suspended offensive military operations on Koh Tang. The extraction of the U.S. force there, however, would not go easily. On the eastern side of the island, K 12 was badly damaged when it searched for a lost Marine thought to be located near the wreckage of K 31. K 12 made it back to the *Coral Sea* but was then declared unflyable, leaving only three operational helicopters—JG 43, JG 44, and K 51—to evacuate the more than two hundred Marines still on Koh Tang.

The evacuation of the main force occurred in the dark. Flashlights marked the landing zone, while the Cambodians poured fire into the American position. HH-53s and the AC-130 gunship circled overhead and shot at enemy gun flashes, while Air Force F-4 Phantoms and Navy A-7 Corsairs strafed enemy positions. Successive helicopters loaded Marines from the western landing zone under fire and ferried them to ships. Most went to the *Coral Sea*, but JG 44 landed thirty-four personnel on the *Holt*, which was closer than the *Coral Sea* and so could return to the landing zone more quickly for another pickup. The *Wilson* recovered the twenty Marines and five airmen from the eastern beach, having sunk two Cambodian gunboats that had been harassing their exfiltration. The warship's two 5-inch guns fired at targets on the eastern beach, while the gig Black Velvet provided covering fire with its machine guns on the eastern beach and around toward the western zone. About this time, a U.S. Air Force cargo aircraft flew over Cambodian positions on Koh Tang and dropped a massive, 15,000-pound bomb. The blockbuster bomb, intended to shock the Cambodians into submission, wiped out an area the size of a football field.[73] Because of JG 44's shortened trip to the *Holt*, it recovered the next-to-last load of forty Marines, which left seventy-three Marines still on the island. By 2000, the last load of Marines had embarked in helicopter K-51 and left. Some 230 Marines had been evacuated. The president informed the American people of the successful rescue operation.[74]

The initial report to CINCPAC stated that all personnel had been recovered, but it was discovered later that three men were missing in action.[75] These men were never recovered, nor were their disappearances explained. Notwithstanding the successful recovery of the *Mayaguez* and its crew, the operation had been costly. Eleven Marines had been killed in action and forty-one wounded. The three missing in action were later declared dead, but their remains have never been recovered. Two Navy corpsmen were killed in action and two wounded; two airmen were killed and six wounded. The day before the assault, five Air Force crew members and eighteen passengers were killed when their CH-53 crashed due to a mechanical failure en route to Utapao. The Cambodians too suffered heavy casualties. Forty-seven Khmer Rouge soldiers died in the fighting, and fifty-five were wounded. The irony, of course, is that the Cambodians had released the *Mayaguez* and its crew just as the U.S. force was landing at Koh Tang—the entire engagement and loss of life on both sides could have been avoided.

— — — — ● — — — —

Two days after the ship was seized, the United States had officially informed the UN Security Council that the *Mayaguez* had been operating on the high seas in an international shipping lane in the Gulf of Thailand. The American representative to the United Nations sent a letter to the president of the Security Council to relay

> the grave and dangerous situation brought about by the illegal and unprovoked seizure by Cambodian authorities of a United States merchant vessel, the SS *Mayaguez*, in international waters in the Gulf of Siam.... At the time of seizure, [the ship] was en route from Hong Kong to Thailand and was some 52 nautical miles from the Cambodian coast. It was some 7 nautical miles from the Islands of Poulo Wai, which ... are claimed by both Cambodia and South Vietnam. The vessel was on the high seas, in international shipping lanes commonly used by ships calling at the various ports of Southeast Asia.[76]

After the recovery of the ship and its crew, the U.S. government instructed American diplomatic posts to emphasize that the ship had been seized in international waters.[77] The American action received widespread support from foreign governments and media. West German and British media reported sympathetically, and the ministers of the Organization of American States supported the recovery.[78] Thailand, however, did not react favorably.[79] Bangkok formally protested the use of its territory by U.S. forces during the operation.[80] The prime minister stated that unless the Marines involved were withdrawn from Utapao immediately, the good relations between the two allies would be "exposed to serious and damaging consequences." In response, the United States expressed its regrets with "regard to the temporary placement of Marines at Utapao to assist in the recovery of the *Mayaguez*."[81]

— — — — • — — — —

On June 9, 1975, Congress requested that the comptroller general of the United States (who is the head of the GAO) review the system for warning American mariners of potential political and military hazards.[82] The resulting GAO report found a number of discrepancies and criticized the State Department for not issuing a Special Warning in a timely manner.[83]

In response, the State Department and the Pentagon took steps to improve the radio broadcast warning system. DMAHC implemented procedural measures to improve broadcasts of special warnings, and DoS/OMA provided guidance on the types of situations that should be brought to its attention as possibly meriting special warnings. The procedural improvements included increasing broadcasts of each warning from twice on one day to twice a day for three days, placing the special warning at the head of each hydrographic broadcast, simultaneously transmitting the broadcast to American shipowners so that they could notify their ships and notifying the Maritime Administration (MARAD) when a special warning was issued. MARAD also established the U.S. Flag Merchant Vessel Locator Filing System, which became effective on August 8, 1975, to keep the U.S. "interagency" community abreast of the arrival, departure, and locations of U.S.-flagged merchant ships worldwide. American shipowners and operators were encouraged to retransmit special warnings to their vessels intending to transit in the critical area and to require their vessels to monitor at least one broadcast per day.

— — — — ● — — — —

Cambodia's seizure of the *Mayaguez* and its crew was of great concern to the United States because it undermined two fundamental principles— the safety of American citizens abroad and the freedom of the seas. The American response was in no small part an exercise in general deterrence to prevent such incidents in the future. A White House aide explained, "The aim was for our action to be read by North Korean president Kim Il-Sung as well as by the Cambodians."[84] The Ford administration believed that it was essential to send a clear message to friends and foes alike that the United States would not tolerate the illegal use of force against unarmed American merchant ships, or interference with its freedom of navigation on the high seas.[85] Even had the *Mayaguez* been operating within Cambodian-claimed waters, the United States maintained, it would have had a right to innocent passage.[86] Moreover, the communist Khmer Rouge government never produced evidence to support its allegations that the *Mayaguez* intentionally violated Cambodian waters to spy and "provoke incidents."

– – – – • – – – –

The United States used military force to rescue the ship and its crew. White House counsel Philip Buchen stated flatly, "We have the right of self-defense."[87] During the National Security Council meeting of May 13, President Ford agreed: "On international law, I do not think we have a problem. They [the Cambodians] have clearly violated it." Following the conclusion of the operation, the American ambassador to the UN informed the Security Council that the United States considered its actions consistent with the provisions on self-defense reflected in article 51 of the UN Charter.[88] Nonetheless, some scholars argued that the initial assault on Koh Tang may have been a legitimate exercise of self-defense but the mainland strikes were unnecessary and disproportionate once the ship and crew were recovered.[89] The administration countered that the strikes had not been punitive but rather designed to support the Marines fighting on and being extracted from Koh Tang.[90] Three ex-American T-28 Trojan fighter-bombers and six transport aircraft had been at Kampong Som airfield, and twenty-five patrol boats and four landing craft were in the vicinity and at the Ream naval base. They could have reinforced or supported the Cambodian forces engaged on the island and therefore had been legitimate targets.[91] The attacks on the mainland, the administration therefore argued, had been justifiable, constituting a prudent, defensive, and limited use of force.

– – – – • – – – –

The president's power to order the assault had arisen from article II of the Constitution. The War Powers Resolution requires the president to consult with Congress before introducing military forces into hostilities or situations in which hostilities are imminent.[92] In this instance, on May 13 the president directed his staff to contact ten House and eleven Senate members regarding military measures he had ordered to keep the *Mayaguez* and its crew from being taken to the Cambodian mainland and prevent reinforcement of Koh Tang Island.[93] That same day the chair of the House Democratic Caucus, Olin Teague (D-TX), stated, "If diplomatic efforts fail to return the ship and its crew within the next few days, I believe our military should take immediate steps to retaliate."[94] The following day, eleven House and eleven Senate members were informed that U.S. forces had sunk three Cambodian patrol boats and damaged four more as they blocked the removal of the *Mayaguez* crew to the mainland.[95] Later that day, administration officials briefed the House International Relations Committee, the Senate Foreign Relations Committee, the House Appropriations Subcommittee on the Department of Defense, and the House Committee on Armed Services. At 6:30 that evening, President Ford "personally briefed the congressional leadership on his specific orders for the recapture of the ship and crew."[96]

Despite all this interaction between the White House and Congress, the GAO saw "less than full compliance" with the statutory requirement (Title 50 of the U.S. Code, section 1542) to consult with Congress. The GAO did not, however, assert that the president failed to comply with the War Powers Resolution. Members of Congress the GAO's researchers had contacted on May 13 and 14 reported that the White House had simply "informed them of decisions already made," not "consulted" them more broadly. The complaint, however, may be invalid, as the powers of commander in chief are vested in the president. The personal briefing by the president had not occurred until ninety minutes after the order had been given for the assault on Koh Tang Island. Nonetheless, the Senate Foreign Relations Committee unanimously passed, on May 14, 1975, a resolution that supported the president's diplomatic efforts to resolve the issue peacefully and to secure the release of the ship.[97]

The War Powers Resolution also requires that the president submit a report to the Speaker of the House and the president pro tempore of the Senate within forty-eight hours of the introduction of U.S. military forces into hostilities. The report is to lay out the circumstances, the constitutional and legislative authority of the commander in chief to act, and the estimated scope and duration of the hostilities.[98] President Ford delivered written reports to the House and Senate on May 15, as required, with four hours to spare.[99]

— — — — • — — — —

Whatever the legal justifications presented by the United States to support its military intervention, the political rationale was in fact a matter of saving face.[100] The United States had already suffered two humiliating setbacks, the "loss" of Cambodia and South Vietnam in the spring of 1975. The administration believed that by seizing the *Mayaguez* the Cambodians were deliberately trying to test American will and further embarrass Washington.[101]

Although the rescue operation was a success, the casualties offered numerous lessons for the future. First, the services were unaccustomed to working together, and the resulting mishmash of units, doctrines, and capabilities created gaps in execution. These problems would become even more evident in the 1980s, and they would lead to the Goldwater-Nichols Act.[102] Second, President Ford and Secretary of State Henry Kissinger wanted immediate action, and that required a force to be thrown together from the assets that were closest to Cambodia. Vice Adm. George P. Steele (who had commanded the Seventh Fleet at the time) later suggested that the "short fuse" did not permit adequate time to plan the mission with piecemeal forces:[103] "There were too many cooks by far in this broth. Had the Seventh Fleet and its Marines been instructed to recover the *Mayaguez* and her crew, as simple as that, there probably would have been no loss of life, and the *Mayaguez* and her crew would have been recovered successfully, one or two days later." Third, modern communications tempted those in Washington to try to fix problems with a "ten thousand mile screwdriver." When the top level in the chain of command reaches down to the tactical level, decision making by the on-scene commander is disrupted. These mistakes were to be repeated in the Desert One Iranian hostage-rescue operation in 1980.

Had the Cambodians managed to remove the crew to the mainland, rescue would have been much more difficult. The United States would have had to consider such options as a *Pueblo*-like diplomatic solution. But the lengthy *Pueblo* negotiations had been humiliating. Thus, the operation accomplished two goals other than the purely military one. First, it avoided another embarrassing, lengthy negotiation. Second, in the process the United States showed resolve, even in the context of its declining influence in Southeast Asia.

At the conclusion of the crisis, public statements by administration officials reassured friends and allies of the United States that it would remain engaged in the Asia-Pacific region. On May 24, 1975, President Ford appeared on television and emphasized that the military response "should be a firm assurance that the United States is capable and has the willingness to act in emergencies, in challenges."[104] The week before, Secretary Kissinger had stated, "There are limits beyond which the United States cannot be pushed.... We believed that we had to draw a line against illegal actions and secondly, against situations where the United States might be forced into humiliating discussions about the ransom of innocent merchant seamen for a very extended period of time ... [to] make clear that the United States is prepared to defend these interests, and that it can get public support and congressional support for these actions."[105]

The ship's master would later recall that the Cambodians' fear of airstrikes and the prompt action of U.S. forces were the primary reasons for the quick release of the ship and its crew.[106] These sentiments were echoed by Secretary of Defense James Schlesinger on May 26, 1975: "American action must be firm when necessary and when important issues of principle are involved ... in all likelihood the U.S. commitments to Northeast Asia, to Korea as well as to Japan, will be perceived as something no one should challenge."[107] In short, it was clear to everyone, from the president down, that this was a test of American willpower, that it "called for quick, firm and decisive action" that would reaffirm American commitment to protecting the nation's ships and people.[108]

CROSSING THE "LINE OF DEATH"

Gulf of Sidra (1981–89)

In 1959 Libya joined a growing number of states that sought to maximize sovereignty in their coastal waters by establishing a twelve-nautical-mile (nm) territorial sea.[1] At the time, the United States argued for the traditional maximum breadth of the territorial sea, three nautical miles. American opposition to a 12-nm territorial sea would eventually fade with the adoption of the United Nations Convention on the Law of the Sea (UNCLOS) in 1982, which established complementary regimes for transit passage through international straits.[2] In October 1973, however, Libya declared the entire Gulf of Sirte (Sidra) as internal waters. A *note verbale* (a diplomatic note that refers to the originating state in the third person) circulated by the Libyan foreign ministry to the United Nations on October 19 announced that the Gulf of Sidra constituted the internal waters of Libya. The unlawful claim was delimited by a three-hundred-plus-mile "closing line" (which Libyans called the "Line of Death") connecting the cities of Benghazi and Misurata along the latitude of 32° 30′ north. The area was declared to be under its complete sovereignty and jurisdiction.[3] The decree required public and private foreign ships to obtain prior permission from Libyan authorities before entering the area.

Libya claimed it had exercised sovereignty over the Gulf of Sidra "through history and without dispute." Given the gulf's geographic location,

Libya argued, it was necessary to exercise complete control of it "to ensure the security and safety of the state." The United States rejected Libya's position as a violation of international law and protested it diplomatically in 1974 and 1979.[4] The initial American note suggested the Libyan claim was inconsistent with the international standard for internal waters, which requires longstanding, open, and effective exercise of authority over the area, the continuous exercise of such authority, and the acquiescence of foreign nations.[5] The United States complained that the Libyan action was a unilateral "attempt to appropriate a large area of the high seas," an attempt that encroached on the long-standing principle of freedom of the seas.

The United States renewed its opposition to the claim in 1985 after Libya published a notice to mariners (NOTMAR) that purported to restrict "innocent passage" in the Gulf of Sidra. An American note to the member states of the United Nations rejected Libya's claim "as an unlawful interference with the freedoms of navigation and overflight and related high seas freedoms."[6] The following year, the Department of State (DoS) published a reference aid on U.S. foreign relations explaining the American legal position:

> By custom, nations may lay historic claim to those bays and gulfs over which they have exhibited such a degree of open, notorious, continuous, and unchallenged control for an extended period of time as to preclude traditional high seas freedoms within such waters. Those waters . . . are treated as if they were part of the nation's land mass, and the navigation of foreign vessels is generally subject to complete control by the nation. . . . Since Libya cannot make a valid historic waters claim and meets no other international law criteria for enclosing the Gulf of Sidra, it may validly claim a 12-nautical-mile territorial sea measured from the normal low-water line along its coast.[7]

The U.S. position tracks with the findings of a 1962 study prepared by the UN Secretariat that found three factors to consider in determining whether a state has acquired a historic title to a maritime area. "These factors are: (1) the exercise of authority over the area by the State claiming the historic right; (2) the continuity of this exercise of authority; (3) the attitude of foreign States [i.e., absence of opposition by these States]."[8]

Australia, France, Germany, Norway, Spain, and the Soviet Union also protested Libya's claim as inconsistent with international law.[9] Thus, while international law allows states to enclose limited areas of the high seas as "historic waters," the test for doing so is notoriously difficult. In this case, Libya did not assert its claim until 1973 and the United States and other nations diplomatically protested it as unlawful. Therefore, Libya cannot be said to have a valid historic title to the Gulf of Sidra.

Beginning in 1981, U.S. naval forces conducted a series of operations designed to assert freedom of navigation (FON), to challenge Libya's excessive claims in the Gulf of Sidra, and to reinforce American diplomatic protests. Operational transits were conducted in 1981–84, 1986, 1989, 1997–98, 2000, and 2013.[10] On three of those occasions, Libya reacted unlawfully by threatening U.S. forces. These acts of aggression impelled U.S. aircraft and warships to respond in self-defense.

— — — — • — — — —

On September 1, 1969, Colonel Muammar Qaddafi led a successful coup d'état against King Idris, who was in Turkey for medical treatment. The monarchy was abolished and replaced by the Libyan Revolutionary Command Council (LRCC). Three years later, U.S.-Libyan relations sank when Libya declared a restricted area within a 100-nm radius of Tripoli and claimed the right to control access to it by foreign ships and aircraft. The United States protested the declaration in early 1973, arguing that international law and custom forbade "restricting freedom of airspace over the high seas."[11] The United States advised Libya that it would continue to "adhere to international aviation practices"; declared to the UN Security Council that Libya's "restricted area" was not in accord with the Convention on International Civil Aviation;[12] and sent reconnaissance aircraft into the restricted area to demonstrate that it did not accept the new controls.

The initial missions were flown without incident. On March 21, 1973, however, two Libyan Mirage fighters intercepted an unarmed U.S. C-130 transport approximately 82 nm off Libya and attempted to shoot it down.[13] The American plane evaded the Libyan jets by flying into a cloud bank and safely returned to its base in Athens, Greece.[14] Secretary of State William Rogers summoned the Libyan chargé d'affaires, Muharram Ben-Musa, and protested the unprovoked attack. The U.S. government passed a similar message to the Libyan Ministry of Foreign Affairs, stating that it "protests in the strongest possible terms this provocative and irresponsible act by units of the Libyan Arab Republic Air Force. Such an attack is in clear violation of international law and could have resulted in the loss of American lives and property."[15] Washington warned that it would hold Libya "fully accountable for any future actions which may threaten United States aircraft transiting international air space" and requested "an immediate investigation of the circumstances surrounding this incident."

After discussions on the issue, national security adviser Henry Kissinger counseled President Richard M. Nixon on the interagency consensus for resuming the reconnaissance operations off Libya. Kissinger emphasized to the president that the Libyan attack had been clearly illegal.[16] If the United States did not meet the attack with an appropriate response, he argued, Libya's illegal claims would be reinforced. More important, Kissinger predicted that further delays in resuming flights, notwithstanding the risks, only invited similar challenges elsewhere and even bolder challenges by Libya. There were indeed risks, downsides to action. Arabs likely would exploit any incidents as proof of American collusion with Israel. Libya might retaliate against U.S. forces or, worse yet, retaliate against American civilians (of which there were some three thousand) or industrial interests in the country (such as oil companies). In due course, the Department of Defense (DoD) was directed to recommend to the president options for responding to the attempt to shoot down the C-130.

Four such options were developed and presented to Dr. Kissinger. The first was a "diplomatic protest only." Under this scenario, the United States would reiterate that it did not recognize the Libyan claim and regarded the attack on the C-130 as an illegal and unwarranted act that undermined bilateral relations.[17] Option two involved the use of high-performance combat aircraft, with intrinsic self-defense capabilities, to challenge Libya's excessive claim. This option was attractive to the administration because it would replace the vulnerable, unarmed aircraft employed before with others capable of countering any aggressive reaction. There was some concern, however, that use of combat aircraft lacked the "desired parallelism" with the earlier mission.

Option three was similar, except that the United States would send a non-reconnaissance-equipped C-130 into the area, this time escorted by combat aircraft. Option four was and remains classified. The Department of Defense and the Joint Staff ultimately determined the best course of action was for aircraft carrier–based fighter escorts to accompany an unarmed reconnaissance aircraft replicating the mission of March 21. In this case, however, the reconnaissance aircraft would proceed point to point without any orbits en route and carry a reduced crew.[18] The closest approach to the Libyan coast would be 75 nm. The plan would provide some degree of protection to the reconnaissance aircraft. More broadly, DoD officials believed that this response would reassert the right of the United States to operate in international airspace and show that it would not sit idly by while Libya (or any other nation) declared unilateral, illegal "restricted areas" in international waters and airspace. The United States intended to collect intelligence data not only in the Mediterranean Sea but in the Persian Gulf as well; a decisive stand here would aid collection everywhere. Finally, such a response would prevent Qaddafi "from claiming that this is the way to deal with the United States." Kissinger recommended that the president approve the plan, for execution on April 17.

In Libya, however, Harold G. Josif, chargé d'affaires at the U.S. embassy, questioned the wisdom and timing of resuming reconnaissance flights over the Mediterranean. He asked Secretary Rogers and Assistant Secretary of State for African Affairs David D. Newsom to intervene and get the operation delayed. The chargé's position should not have come as a surprise to DoD planners, whose State counterparts often seek to delay or cancel FON operations. The State Department and embassy officials profess acceptance of the need to assert navigational rights and freedoms, but invariably there is never a "right time" to do so. In this instance, the chargé d'affaires argued, diplomacy should be allowed to proceed before the United States asserted its rights in a more tangible fashion.[19] Nevertheless, the reconnaissance flight was conducted on April 17 without incident.

– – – – • – – – –

Over the next several years Libya refrained from interference with routine U.S. reconnaissance flights within its claimed restricted area. Libyan aircraft rose to intercept and investigate U.S. missions, but they simply monitored the overflights from within Libya's 12-nm territorial sea. Nevertheless, Libyan government officials continued to denounce the reconnaissance operations publicly as "provocative incursions" into "national" airspace and "territorial" waters.

The U.S. Sixth Fleet also had conducted open-ocean missile exercises (OOMEs) in the Gulf of Sidra—the most suitable part of the Mediterranean for them.[20] Between July 1977 and April 1979, Sixth Fleet warships conducted five exercises of various types in international waters in the Gulf of Sidra, some of them south of the "line of death."[21] OOMEs, specifically, were conducted in September 1978 and July 1979. On July 29, aircraft from the carrier USS *America* (CV 66) flew in international airspace over the Libyan-claimed "internal waters" of the Gulf of Sidra.[22] Libya protested.[23] In contrast, flight operations and surface-ship transits in February 1979 and January 1980, respectively, generated no Libyan reaction.

Things changed in mid-1980; Qaddafi became more sensitive to U.S. military operations off the coast.[24] In September, Libyan fighters fired missiles at a U.S. EC-135 reconnaissance plane flying a sensitive mission near but north of the "line of death." The missiles missed their intended target. The American crew did not see the fighter jet or the missiles, but they intercepted radio communications between the two Libyan pilots indicating what had happened.[25]

Despite this evidence, Jimmy Carter's administration chose not to protest the incident. The American embassy in Tehran had been seized on November 4, 1979, with more than fifty American hostages, and President

Carter had suspended operations in the Libyan restricted area in the hope of dampening anti-American sentiment.[26] Despite these good intentions, a mob of two thousand Libyans burned the U.S. embassy in Tripoli on December 2, 1979. William Eagleton Jr., the chargé d'affaires, was recalled on February 8, 1980.[27] The embassy officially closed on May 2.[28]

The following month, in response to Libyan diplomatic protests, the State and Defense Departments requested that no U.S. exercises be conducted south of the "line of death."[29] Consequently, during the June and September 1980 OOMEs the United States canceled planned operations south of latitude 32° 30' N. These cancelations may have been perceived in Tripoli as tacit acquiescence to Libya's illegal claims. Furthermore, the cancelations contradicted FON policy guidance that the United States should exercise its right to freedom of navigation against illegal claims "to the extent practicable," and should avoid actions that could be interpretted as acquiescence in such illegal claims.

The incoming Ronald Reagan administration took a firmer approach toward Libya. The scope and frequency of FON operations increased significantly. In May 1981, the administration expelled all Libyan diplomats from the United States. The Libyan People's Bureau in Washington was shuttered on May 6.[30] On June 1, President Reagan approved a large-scale naval exercise in the Gulf of Sidra, involving two carrier battle groups.[31] An interagency intelligence assessment concluded that Libya would perceive the exercise as a "conspiracy directed against it";[32] there was, the study warned, a real possibility of a hostile tactical reaction by Libyan aircraft. Analysts believed a large number of Libyan interceptors and warships would approach U.S. forces, at least to monitor the exercise. Even if Libyan pilots were not cleared to attack, there was a risk of hostilities due to miscalculation.

American analysts expected Western European governments to criticize the American exercise as provocative—the importance of freedom of navigation and overflight in the oceans being ignored by European governments. Allies in Europe would find the operation lacking strategic or political purpose. Likewise, the Soviet Union was certain to exploit the situation to fashion a closer military relationship with Libya.

Nevertheless, on August 12 and 14, 1981, a NOTMAR and a notice to airmen (NOTAM) were broadcast from Madrid announcing the U.S. exercise, with dates and location.[33] On August 18, the USS *Nimitz* (CVN 68) and USS *Forrestal* (CV 59) aircraft-carrier strike groups, a total of sixteen warships, commenced the FON operation. Libyan MiG-25 Foxbat interceptors immediately sortied in response. The Foxbats were met and turned away by F-4J Phantoms off the *Forrestal* and F-14 Tomcats from the *Nimitz*. That day, Libya launched a total of thirty-five pairs of Su-22 Fitter, MiG-23 Flogger, and F-1 Mirage fighters and fighter-bombers in an effort to locate the U.S. carriers. These sorties were turned away without incident by aircraft from the *Forrestal* and the *Nimitz*.[34]

The Libyan response intensified the following day. Two F-14s—call signs "Fast Eagle 102" and "Fast Eagle 107"—were flying an orbit pattern on their combat air patrol (CAP) station off the Libyan coast.[35] Near the end of their patrol, the F-14s detected two Libyan Su-22 Fitters approaching, climbing to 20,000 feet and accelerating to 540 knots. As the Tomcats closed in on the two Fitters, it became apparent that the Libyan jets were being effectively directed from the ground—every time the F-14s maneuvered, the Su-22s would regain their positions. The American pilots were unable to achieve an advantage. The lead Fitter fired a missile at Fast Eagle 102, a thousand feet in front and five hundred feet above, but missed. The American pilots immediately, and consistent with their rules of engagement (ROE), declared the Su-22s "hostile" and engaged them with AIM-9L Sidewinder missiles. Both Fitters were hit, and both Libyan pilots ejected (only one was recovered at sea). Fast Eagles 102 and 107 returned safely to the *Nimitz*. One hour later, two MiG-25s approached the carriers but were intercepted by F-14s and turned away. The exercise ended later that day without further incident. The dogfight between the American and Libyan aircraft was the first combat for the F-14 employing the Sidewinder missile.[36]

The United States immediately protested the attack and warned Libya that any repetition would be resisted with force. Libya responded that its aircraft had been on routine reconnaissance duties over Libyan "territorial waters and airspace" when they had been unlawfully engaged by the U.S.

aircraft. Tripoli accused Washington of aggression and "a provocative terror-ist act" that would create turmoil and destabilize the region.[37] Libya faulted the United States for violation of its sovereignty and warned that it would take all necessary measures to defend its "territorial waters and air space."[38]

The U.S. intelligence community warned that Libya would oppose with force any American incursion south of the "line of death." Operational planning should take into account the likelihood of a Libyan reaction.[39] This concern was confirmed the following month during an interview with Colonel Qaddafi. Asked by the television journalist Chris Wallace what he would do if U.S. warships returned to the Gulf of Sidra, Qaddafi answered, "[We] will defend our country till the last drop of our blood and the last man and woman."[40] Nonetheless—and perhaps surprisingly, given Qaddafi's brazen response and the importance of the FON program for the Reagan administration—no U.S. warship or military aircraft entered the restricted area after the August incident.[41]

— — — — —•— — — —

Beginning in 1982, the White House imposed greater scrutiny on the FON approval process, owing to concern for Libyan and moderate Arab reaction. For example, in June 1982 DoD proposed a naval exercise in the Gulf of Sidra for that August.[42] The State Department opposed the plan, assessing that it would cause difficulty for moderate Arab governments.[43] A coordinated intelligence community assessment concluded that Qaddafi would react with force. Indeed, the mercurial Libyan leader pledged to go to war if U.S. forces did not stay out of the Gulf of Sidra.[44] Reactions from other states were also expected to be unfavorable and regional tension would be heightened.[45]

An interagency group met on June 29, 1982, to discuss the August exercise and prepare a policy-options paper for consideration by the Senior Interagency Group (SIG) in mid-July. The meeting focused on three sets of issues. First, should the United States conduct a FON exercise in August, when four carrier battle groups would be in the Mediterranean? If not, the next feasible window would be in January 1983. Second, should the challenge to Libya be a full missile exercise or some lesser demonstration, such as a simple transit of the area? Third, what would be the objectives for the operation, and what would the cost-benefit calculus look like?[46]

Ultimately, as the Joint Chiefs of Staff representative realized, the decision was political and would be made in the White House. But if an OOME were approved at all, the JCS and DoD both preferred a full missile demonstration. The DoD representative did not agree with the intelligence assessment that regional and European reactions would be unduly negative. In fact, DoD believed, regional reactions should not even be a factor. The need to show continuity and firmness toward Libya was more important.

Predictably, the State Department country-desk officer argued that because of regional tensions, the exercise should be postponed until January. The DoS policy planners present at the meeting agreed that an exercise should occur but at the later date. The State legal adviser recommended informal discussions with key congressional leaders prior to the exercise. The NSC representative was noncommittal but believed planning for the August exercise should proceed; regional tensions were a negative factor, but the NSC was optimistic that they would subside by August. In any event, the NSC staff agreed that the operation would be an important demonstration of consistency and resolve.

Conditions had changed since the 1981 operation. Israel invaded Lebanon on June 6, 1982. The SIG feared the Arabs might see the FON operation as part of a concerted effort with Israel. Even U.S. Arab allies were concerned over the precedent set by the shooting down of Libyan jets during the 1981 exercise. These states were now uneasy about further U.S. operations that might exacerbate regional instability. They also wanted to be informed before any new operation was undertaken to counter Libya's maritime claims. Nevertheless, going ahead with an August exercise would maintain pressure on Qaddafi as he began his year as chairman of the Organization of African Unity. Proponents of an August exercise believed the Arab world regarded Libya as a distinct issue from Lebanon and that many Arabs rejected Qaddafi anyway.

Libya had expressed a willingness to submit its Gulf of Sidra closure line to the International Court of Justice (ICJ) for adjudication. Arab states might question the wisdom of a new military challenge without having first explored that offer. Reaction by regional and Arab states was expected to be largely negative if the United States acted precipitously. New FON exercises also could open the door to a greater Soviet presence in Libya. In the context of the expectation that Qaddafi would attack any U.S. exercise in the Gulf, the SIG noted that Libya had improved its capabilities to resist American forces, including dispersal of its aircraft. Qaddafi's repeated threats to target American warships in the Gulf of Sidra raised the issue of prior notice and consultations with Congress under the War Powers Resolution. At the very least, some members of the SIG thought, it was prudent to consult with Congress before the operation.

Since Qaddafi might carry out his threats, ROE and response options would be needed. The group agreed that peacetime ROE would be used. These ROE were (and are) based on the inherent right of self-defense, and they present U.S. commanders with an escalatory "ladder." A commander facing a potential for hostile action is first to try to control the situation without force—by, for example, warning the potential adversary. Next, defensive measures could be employed, using the minimum force necessary. These measures might focus first on individual perpetrators, such as a jet firing a missile, and only gradually engage the entire Libyan force, if necessary. Ultimately, however, force could be used against all Libyan forces if it became evident that other means would not dissuade them from hostile action against U.S. forces.

If large-scale or repeated Libyan attacks were carried out against U.S. forces, response options could include strikes against Libyan ships and aircraft that had not yet attacked, and even land-based targets, such as airfields, naval bases, and command-and-control sites. The Central Intelligence Agency (CIA) representative believed, however, that strikes against targets ashore could attract international condemnation and even open up the possibility of Soviet advisers participating in Libyan operations against the U.S. forces.

The SIG also debated the scope of the exercise. The JCS representative recommended a missile exercise to provide necessary training and to place the task force in a better defensive posture. A simple transit without prior notification would be more benign; it would avoid a direct confrontation with Qaddafi and might therefore limit his response. The CIA cautioned, however, that the Libyans would detect the movement and respond aggressively even to a simple transit. Any U.S. action might alarm the Libyans, who might then overreact. Even if not, Qaddafi might claim he had dissuaded the United States from repeating its missile exercises. The SIG decided that the current political situation was too unstable. The operation should go ahead, but not until January 1983.[47]

On September 8, the JCS briefed an interagency working group on its "stair-step" plan for resuming U.S. naval exercises in the Gulf of Sidra.[48] The plan envisaged a series of evolutions that would slowly escalate, beginning with limited air operations north of the "line of death" and gradually moving south, to more extensive air and naval activity, and finally an OOME. Department of State and NSC participants were more concerned with process than with the merits of the plan, and they focused on the need for close interagency supervision. The DoS insisted that regional events be carefully considered within the interagency forum as the planned exercises approached. The NSC would have to approve advancing to the sixth step of the plan—operations south of the "line of death."

One month later, Secretary of Defense Caspar Weinberger nonetheless endorsed the "stair-step" plan and forwarded it to the White House for approval. National Security Adviser William Clark sent the plan to Secretary of State George Shultz and requested that the interagency working group on Libya review it and make recommendations to the SIG. Clark was concerned that the DoD approach did not make a clear distinction between sensitive exercises that required NSC consideration and more routine operations in the vicinity of Libya; he requested the working group to comment on this issue.[49] The first step had been taken in July, a notice of intent to operate in the Libyan Flight Information Region (FIR), but no actual operations had occurred. On October 20, DoD requested authority to implement the next two steps of the plan: a limited air and surface operation within the FIR but still outside Libya's claimed boundary, and air operations approaching the "line of death."[50] After the interagency working group had

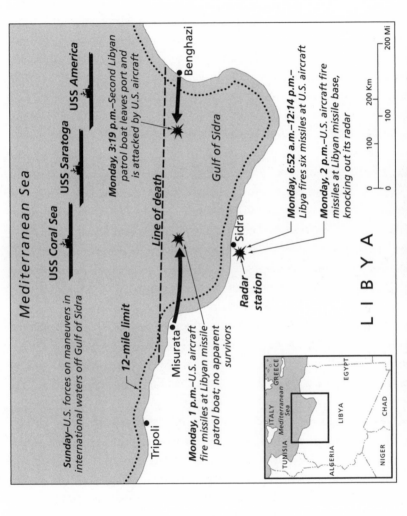

MAP 4. THE U.S. NAVY CHALLENGES LIBYA'S "LINE OF DEATH," MARCH 24, 1986

completed its review, the SIG met on November 29 to assess likely Libyan reactions.[51] The "stair-step" plan received unanimous interagency approval at the SIG. Because it increased American presence in the area gradually, rather than suddenly confronting Libya with a large-scale exercise, the plan allowed the United States to claim that the operations were entirely normal, while also helping the Pentagon gauge Libyan reactions. (See map.)

Of the first three steps of the plan that were completed, only step three generated a Libyan response. In February and August 1983, Libyan MiG-23 fighters intercepted U.S. aircraft, but there was no hostile engagement.[52] When F-14 Tomcats intercepted them, the Libyans broke off and returned to base. This reaction was consistent with American intelligence assessments that Libyan responses to aircraft in the FIR but above the closure line would involve only interceptions for identification purposes.

The intelligence community believed, however, that Qaddafi would respond with force to any penetration of the "line of death" by U.S. ships or military aircraft. Even ships above the line might be attacked if the Libyans perceived they were operating in concert with aircraft penetrating the line.[53] Accordingly, the interagency review had recommended that Congress be notified and consulted before steps four to eight were undertaken. These notifications would emphasize the universal rejection of the Libyan claim and explain the worldwide U.S. FON program and the overall American strategy to protect the freedom of the seas. These consultations would occur whether or not they were required under the War Powers Resolution; that question would be addressed later, based on the threat assessment. Due to the high likelihood of hostilities in steps six to eight, advance notice to Belgium, Egypt, Italy, Morocco, and Tunisia would be provided between one and two days before the FIR authorities were informed. Regional states, however, would not be notified of U.S. operations above the "line of death."

All steps of the plan were conducted using peacetime ROE, by which force could be used against Libyan units if they used force first or if U.S. forces noted specific indications that force was about to be employed against them. In such cases, U.S. forces could respond in self-defense against the Libyan elements directly involved. If a generalized and large-scale Libyan attack occurred, U.S. forces were authorized to broaden their response, although the president retained authority to conduct strikes in Libyan territory.

Flight operations within the Tripoli FIR but north of the line continued without incident through 1985.[54] Despite apparent support for operations farther south, however, none were approved until 1986.[55] The four-year delay may serve as emblematic of postponed FON operations generally—there are always reasons, raised by country desks and regional experts, not to conduct a FON exercise.[56]

– – – – • – – – –

On January 7, 1986, President Reagan ordered all Americans out of Libya and broke off all remaining ties with the Qaddafi regime. The following day, the State Department released a detailed report on Qaddafi's incitement of terrorism, a trail of meddling and violence that extended from the streets of Philadelphia and Cairo to the beaches of Grenada and New Caledonia. One week later, on January 13, a U.S. Navy surveillance aircraft was "buzzed" by two Libyan MiG-25 fighters in international airspace north of the "line of death." In response to the provocation, President Reagan ordered a second carrier battle group to the Mediterranean Sea. He also directed the JCS to begin planning for military operations against Libya. Later that year, evidence surfaced that the Soviet Union was providing advanced weapons to the Libyans. The JCS already had begun planning for a FON operation to be carried out in early January 1986. Intelligence assessments indicated Libya's SA-5 complex would be operational soon but would be able to track and target only one aircraft at a time. The system was not integrated into Libya's air-defense network, and the radar had not yet been calibrated.[57] Libyan warships and submarines had been staged along the coast in position to respond to any perceived threat from U.S. forces.

The Libyan navy had thirty-one missile craft and six submarines, and within twelve hours Qaddafi could send to sea about a dozen missile ships and three submarines.[58] American analysts estimated that in a twenty-four-hour period Libya could send up some 125 missile-armed fighter jets, including the MiG-23 (Flogger-G and older models), MiG-25s, and

French-built Mirages. No forceful response by Libya was anticipated, however, so long as American penetration of the "line of death" was relatively "shallow." The likelihood of hostilities increased if U.S. ships remained in the Gulf of Sidra or approached the Libyan coast. It was difficult to assess possible reactions, but American officials anticipated the Libyans would fire on aircraft that appeared intent on flying near the coast.

Operation Attain Document began at the end of January 1986. On January 23, the United States broadcast a NOTAM through the International Civil Aviation Organization (ICAO) to alert international aviators that the United States would conduct aircraft-carrier flight operations in the Tripoli FIR between January 24 and 31. On January 24, President Reagan ordered the USS *Saratoga* (CV 60) and USS *Coral Sea* (CV 43) strike groups to begin flight operations north of 32° 30′. The administration announced that the operation was "routine," conducted to show American resolve to continue to operate in international waters and airspace.[59] Libyan reaction was surprisingly muted. There were a few interceptions of U.S. aircraft inside the FIR, as Libyan jets avoided American fighters as they concentrated on their own reconnaissance and defensive patrols.[60] Nonetheless, in a television interview in Tripoli on January 29, Qaddafi warned that while U.S. maneuvers outside Libyan "territorial waters" were of no concern, any within the Gulf of Sidra would constitute an "unjustified ... attack against the soil and sanctity of Libyan territory" and would lead to war.[61]

Phase two of Attain Document occurred between February 10 and 15. Libyan reaction was similarly subdued. Libyan fighters made several dozen nonprovocative flights north of the Gulf of Sidra in response to U.S. flight operations in the Tripoli FIR. Libyan warships at sea did not approach Sixth Fleet ships north of the "line of death."[62] A NOTAM published through ICAO on March 19 notified the air-traffic control center in Tripoli that U.S. naval forces would be conducting nonprovocative and routine aerial maneuvers in the Tripoli FIR.[63] The American exercise was not, it was stated, designed to provoke a Libyan attack.

Already, however, there was a glimpse of impending conflict. Qaddafi continued to threaten to attack any U.S. warship or aircraft that penetrated the "line of death."[64] The United States replied that its forces would shoot back. Supplemental ROE for the U.S. task force delegated to its commander the authority to judge whether U.S. forces were under attack, or were confronted with a series of attacks. If a series of attacks, U.S. forces could engage all units that constituted immediate threats. This meant U.S. forces could then attack Libyan units that had committed hostile acts, as well as strike the air and naval bases from which those Libyan forces operated. The positioning of a weapon in an apparent attempt to fire it constituted hostile intent. The United States also authorized entry into the territorial seas, internal waters, or national airspace of Libya for self-defense or search and rescue.[65]

By March 22, all U.S. forces—three aircraft carriers, five cruisers, six frigates, twelve destroyers, a fast combat support ship, a replenishment oiler, 250 aircraft, and 27,000 personnel—had converged on the Gulf of Sidra to conduct phase three of Attain Document. The operation began on March 23. Aircraft from the *Saratoga*, the *Coral Sea*, and the *America* crossed the "line of death." The next morning, the cruiser USS *Ticonderoga* (CG 47) and the destroyers USS *Scott* (DDG 995) and USS *Caron* (DD 970) crossed 32° 30′ north latitude and entered the Gulf of Sidra. Two hours later, a Libyan missile battery near Sirte fired two SA-5 Gammon surface-to-air missiles at F-14s "flying CAP" to protect the U.S. warships. More missiles were fired at U.S. aircraft from the Libyan battery later in the day. All the missiles missed their targets.[66]

In a letter to the president of the UN Security Council, Qaddafi condemned the American maneuvers as dangerous and provocative and vowed that his nation would use all means to defend itself.[67] The commander in chief of the Libyan air force sent a message to the Sixth Fleet commander, Adm. Frank Kelso, warning that unless the aggressive acts were stopped, Libya would "destroy the carriers." Libya was confident it had the political and military support of the world states.[68] Admiral Kelso was not intimidated.

That afternoon, a Libyan Combattante II–type patrol craft, armed with antiship missiles, sortied from Misurata and approached the U.S. warships in the gulf. Consistent with the ROE, two A-6E Intruder attack aircraft from the USS *America* sank it with a salvo of Harpoon missiles, the first use of the Harpoon in combat.[69] Shortly thereafter, the Libyan missile site at Sirte activated its target-acquisition radars, whereupon it was quickly destroyed by two A-7E Corsairs off the USS *Saratoga*.[70] A Libyan Nanuchka-type patrol craft then entered the gulf and was attacked with Rockeye cluster bombs by more Intruders off the *Saratoga*. The patrol boat was damaged in the attack but managed to limp back to the port of Benghazi.[71]

Washington issued a statement that U.S. ships and aircraft had been conducting a peaceful FON exercise in international waters and airspace in the gulf when they were fired on by Libyan armed forces. The purpose of the exercise was to make the legal point that, beyond the internationally recognized twelve-mile limit, states may not claim exclusive rights to international waters and airspace. Administration officials warned Libya that in view of the numerous missile attacks and threat indications of further attacks, the United States would consider all "approaching Libyan forces to have hostile intent." American forces reserved the right to take additional measures in self-defense. The following day, A-6 Intruders off the *Saratoga* and the *Coral Sea* attacked another Nanuchka II–type patrol boat with Rockeye and Harpoon missiles as it entered the gulf and sank it. A second Nanuchka II was subsequently attacked and damaged; it returned to port.[72]

The White House denied Libyan claims that the naval maneuvers were designed to provoke a response or to humiliate Qaddafi, asserting instead that they demonstrated that the United States would not permit other states to dictate where its warships and military aircraft could go.[73] Notwithstanding Qaddafi's promise of a "brave confrontation" with the Americans, phase three of Attain Document ended on March 27, 1986, following two days of unchallenged operations in the gulf.[74]

President Reagan warned the Libyan dictator that he would be held fully accountable if he carried out terrorist attacks against American targets in retaliation for Libya's losses in the confrontations in the Gulf of Sidra.[75] The president praised the operation as upholding the fundamental principle of freedom of the seas, an important element of economic prosperity and military security for the Free World. Not all nations agreed with Reagan's assessment.

Libya argued that the United States had violated its sovereignty, having entered Libyan "territorial waters" and bombed Libyan territory. Iran agreed with Libya, claiming that the United States did not adhere to the right of innocent passage by engaging in military exercises and weapons practice and threatening the use of force, all in the Libyan territorial sea. Similarly, Syria argued that the issue had nothing to do with freedom of navigation or legal disagreement over the scope of Libyan sovereignty in the Gulf of Sidra. Instead, the United States was out to eliminate the Libyan regime. Syria suggested that the Security Council had a duty to stand up to this aggression. The Syrian representative called on the council to compel U.S. forces to withdraw from the gulf and evacuate its bases in the Mediterranean Sea.

The United States countered that the underlying cause of the conflict had been Libya's illegal claims to a vast area of the high seas. Libya had promised, and then carried out, attacks on U.S. warships and aircraft exercising their right to navigate in and fly over the area. By entering the Gulf of Sidra, the United States had defended freedom of navigation, which was an essential element of the global trading system and strategic security. Furthermore, U.S. forces routinely conducted such operations throughout the world. In this case, the United States had even provided prior notice through ICAO in compliance with international practice. Yet Libya had without provocation launched missiles against U.S. warships and aircraft in and over international waters. Consequently, the United States viewed its response to the attack as measured, appropriately calibrated to the circumstances, and in conformity with the right of self-defense enshrined in the UN Charter. The United States asked the Security Council to affirm the "grave challenge" to high seas freedoms and condemn Libya's resort to the use of force as a violation of international norms.

The United Kingdom and France supported the United States. The British representative endorsed the principle of freedom of navigation in international waters. The United Kingdom also "deplored any unjustified threat to or action against navigation." France similarly rejected Libya's historical claim to the Gulf of Sidra as unjustified, lacking "historical foundation," and entirely at odds with UNCLOS. The French representative further stated that France hoped to safeguard peacefully the long-standing norms of freedom of navigation in international spaces.

– – – – • – – – –

Relations between the United States and Libya continued to deteriorate. In 1988, the United States became aware that Libya was building a chemical weapons facility in Ain er Rabta, about eighty-five kilometers south of Tripoli. The intelligence community reported that Qaddafi had originally tried to produce chemical weapons in Tripoli. Research and production had been moved to the Rabta plant after U.S. strikes in Tripoli in April 1986 in retaliation for a terrorist bombing attack on a Berlin discotheque, which had been linked to Libya and in which an American soldier had been killed.[76] The Rabta facility had been covertly constructed with the assistance of German engineering companies. Given its large size and its characteristics, American officials believed the installation would produce tons of deadly chemical agents. The facility was well protected, having been built into the side of a mountain. The large production area in the center of the facility featured a high-capacity ventilation system on the roof, suggesting it could handle very toxic materials. Large storage tanks were located at one end of the facility, and precursors for the production of mustard gas and nerve agents were present. Libya had used chemical weapons in a border conflict with Chad and might have provided chemical weapons to Somalia. The proliferation threat loomed, as Libya might pass these chemical weapons to terrorist organizations. The enigmatic Libyan leader denied there were any chemical weapons at Rabta, which he said produced pharmaceuticals.

Once again, the U.S. Navy was at the tip of the spear. As a deterrent, the USS *John F. Kennedy* (CV 67) strike group was deployed to the western Mediterranean Sea to conduct FON operations. On January 4, 1989, four U.S. F-14 Tomcats were flying with an E-2C Hawkeye in international airspace near the island of Crete, about 130 miles north of Libya. Around noon, the E-2C detected the departure of four Libyan MiG-23 Floggers from a military airfield at Al Bumba, near Tobruk. Two of the

F-14s vectored toward the first two MiGs. As a warning signal, one that had been successfully employed in the past, the U.S. aircraft locked their AWG-9 radars onto the Libyan jets. These radars have a very long range and were designed to guide AIM-54 Phoenix or AIM-120 AMRAAM air-to-air missiles. Uncharacteristically, the MiGs did not respond. The Tomcats then performed a series of five defensive maneuvers, changing speed, altitude, and direction, to determine the intent of the Libyan pilots. The Libyan jets, armed with AA-7 Apex missiles, responded aggressively, turning in on the F-14s as if to maintain firing solutions. When the MiGs were within thirteen miles, the lead F-14 fired two AIM-7 Sparrow missiles at them. Both missed, and neither MiG turned away. The F-14s split up, and both Floggers turned onto the wingman, allowing the lead F-14 to maneuver behind them. As the MiGs approached to within four miles of the U.S. aircraft, the F-14 wingman engaged one of them with another Sparrow missile, destroying it. The lead F-14 then engaged and hit the second MiG with an AIM-9 Sidewinder. The two Libyan pilots ejected from their damaged aircraft but were lost at sea.[77]

Libya blamed the United States for shooting down two "unarmed" reconnaissance aircraft. The engagement, it charged, had been tantamount to an act of "American terrorism," and Libya threatened to "meet challenge with challenge."[78] Video and photographs taken by the U.S. aircraft, however, clearly showed that the Libyan MiGs had been armed with Apex air-to-air missiles and had demonstrated hostile intent.[79] The United States informed the UN Security Council of its actions. The president did not, however, deliver a War Powers Resolution report on the incident to Congress.[80]

The United States was adamant that Libyan MiGs had "aggressively challenged" routine American overflight operations well beyond the territorial sea. The U.S. aircraft had acted consistently with internationally accepted principles of self-defense. The Libyan aircraft had closed rapidly, the American pilots had repeatedly taken evasive action, but the Libyans had ignored these signals and continued to close. Since the Libyan MiGs were armed with missiles, the American pilots had viewed their aggressive approach as a demonstration of hostile intent.

The U.S. position on self-defense is based on the understanding that the UN Charter, as reflected in article 51, reflects the "customary norm"—a practice or view long and widely accepted—that all states have an inherent right of individual and collective self-defense.[81] This right predates the adoption of the UN Charter and applies to all sovereign states. American self-defense doctrine is set forth in an ROE publication of the Joint Chiefs of Staff.[82] It asserts the inherent legal right and obligation of commanders to use force in self-defense in response to hostile acts or demonstrations of hostile intent. A "hostile act" is defined as "an attack or use of force against the United States, U.S. forces, or other designated persons or property." "Hostile intent" is the "threat or imminent use of force against the United States, U.S. forces, or other designated persons or property."

Force used in self-defense must be necessary and proportional. "Necessity exists when a hostile act occurs or when a force demonstrates hostile intent."[83] "Proportionality" means that the force used in self-defense should be sufficient to respond decisively. The nature, duration, and scope of force should not exceed what is reasonably required to counter the attack or threat of attack.[84] The United States takes the position that the inherent right of self-defense includes the right of a nation to protect itself from imminent attack. Anticipatory self-defense allows the use of armed force if an attack is "imminent and no reasonable choice of peaceful means is available" to deter or prevent the attack.[85] A determination of whether an attack is imminent is based on an "assessment of all facts and circumstances known at the time."

The Security Council debated the incident further. A group of developing states joined by Yugoslavia drafted a resolution for the Security Council and submitted it on January 11, 1989. The draft resolution "deplored" the American shootdown of Libyan aircraft. It called on the United States to suspend its military operations off the Libyan coast and pushed both parties to refrain from the use of force. The resolution was not adopted, as three permanent members of the Security Council voted against it. In all, the draft resolution received nine affirmative votes and four against (Canada, France, the United Kingdom, and the United States); there were two abstentions (Brazil and Finland). France called the resolution problematic because it cast doubt on, at least implicitly, the principle of freedom of navigation in international waters and airspace. The United Kingdom took a similar position. It rejected the resolution because of the importance of "upholding the freedom of ships and aircraft to operate in international waters and airspace and their inherent right of self-defense." Canada accepted the American explanation and rejected the resolution's "one-sided treatment" of the issues. Finland, though abstaining, believed that the resolution was "out of proportion with the incident."

Between 1981 and 1989, the U.S. Navy conducted over thirty FON operations and exercises in or near the Gulf of Sidra. The most recent operational challenge to the "line of death" occurred without incident in 2015.[86] These operations were designed to demonstrate American resolve to preserve traditional navigational rights and freedoms guaranteed to all nations, despite threats.

President Reagan promoted the protection of maritime rights as an essential ingredient of the safety and security of maritime commerce, as well as the global mobility of America's armed forces. In 1987, he declared, "Freedom of navigation is not an empty cliché of international law. It is essential to the health and safety of America and the health of the [NATO] alliance."[87] Recognizing that the United States could not afford to give in to unlawful maritime claims and needed to exercise its navigational rights and freedoms in accordance with international law, the president reinvigorated the FON program to demonstrate that the nation would not acquiesce to illegal claims.

"CHOKE POINT OF FREEDOM"
The Persian Gulf (1980–88)

On September 22, 1980, Iraqi air and ground forces invaded Iran along a four-hundred-mile front. Despite initial successes, the Iraqi offensive soon bogged down. By November, both armies were on the defensive, waging a World War I–style trench campaign, with intermittent artillery barrages. On September 28, the United Nations Security Council called on the belligerents "to refrain immediately from any further use of force and to settle their dispute by peaceful means," to no effect.[1] Two weeks later, Iraq established a "prohibited war zone" in the Persian Gulf north of 29° 30′ north latitude.[2] The following year, Iran launched a counteroffensive to break the stalemate. At sea, Iran responded to the Iraqi invasion by declaring a "war area" embracing most of its coastal waters. Ostensibly to ensure safe passage of ships in the Persian Gulf, an Iranian Notice to Mariners (NOTMAR) instructed vessels transiting through the Strait of Hormuz to "pass twelve miles south of Abu Musa Island, twelve miles south of Sirri Island, south of Cable Bank Light and twelve miles south west of Farsi Island."[3] The NOTMAR also denied access to Iraqi ports and stated that Iran could not be held responsible for vessels that ignored the notice.[4]

The United States believed that the war would be destructive not only to Iran and Iraq but the entire region as well. When the conflict began, Iraq was exporting about 3 million barrels of crude oil per day, mostly to Western

Europe, Japan, and Brazil. The Reagan administration sought to maintain U.S. neutrality in the war to prevent drawing in the Soviet Union, which was suspected of coveting a warm-water port on the Gulf. The United States also wanted to keep the war from threatening Gulf oil supplies for the West. American neutrality contributed to the military stalemate between the belligerents and preserved the possibility of developing a future relationship with Iran while minimizing openings for the expansion of Soviet influence in the region.[5] Nonetheless, the United States was openly committed to keeping open the Strait of Hormuz, one of the world's primary maritime choke points for energy.[6]

By June 1982, Iraqi forces were in full retreat; Iranian forces recaptured most of the territory lost during the initial stages of the war. Having gained the upper hand, in July 1982 Iran rejected a United Nations call for a cease-fire.[7] To apply greater pressure, Iraq established a "Naval Total Exclusion Zone" around Kharg Island the following month within which, Iraq warned, its forces would attack all vessels.[8] Any oil tanker docking at Kharg Island, regardless of nationality, would be a target of the Iraqi air force.[9]

As the war progressed, the naval war zones established by both sides became, in effect, "free-fire zones." Iraqi and Iranian forces indiscriminately attacked neutral shipping in violation of the law of naval warfare. The law of neutrality regulates belligerent activities with respect to neutral shipping. Generally, neutral merchant ships engaged in legitimate, neutral commerce can be visited and searched by belligerents, but not captured or destroyed. They can be targeted only if they acquire "enemy character," which they do if they take a direct part in the hostilities or act as naval or military auxiliaries to a belligerent's armed forces. Similarly, neutral merchant ships may be treated as enemies if they operate directly under enemy control, orders, charter, employment, or direction, or if they resist attempts to establish their identity by visit and search. Neutral ships also lose their protected status and may be captured as prizes if they carry contraband supplies to a belligerent. For the most part, the ships attacked by Iran and Iraq clearly complied with their neutral duties and so had legal immunity from attack.[10]

Iraq normally used Exocet antiship cruise missiles to attack suspect ships within the Iranian-declared exclusion zone, which extended out beyond Farsi Island in the middle of the Gulf and included the coastlines of Kuwait and Iraq. Iraq targeted oil tankers without positively identifying the ships—a violation of the law of naval warfare.[11] Iran, on the other hand, focused on attacking ships engaged in trade with Saudi Arabia and Kuwait, as both of these countries were providing financial and logistical aid to Iraq.[12] The Security Council condemned attacks against nonbelligerent shipping en route to or from Kuwait and Saudi Arabia.[13] The Security Council also reaffirmed the right of freedom of navigation in international waters and sea lanes for ships of all nations that were not belligerents.[14]

American defense officials were equally concerned not only about the conventional threat to U.S. warships posed by Iraqi and Iranian naval and air forces but also terrorist and paramilitary threats. On October 23, 1983, 241 American service members were killed by a suicide truck-bomber who drove into a building serving as the barracks for the 1st Battalion, 8th Marines in Beirut, Lebanon. As a result of the attack, the United States implemented "defensive bubbles" around its forces in the Middle East, including ships and aircraft. The United States issued a Notice to Airmen (NOTAM) and a NOTMAR on January 20 and 21, 1984, respectively, warning ships and aircraft at altitudes less than two thousand feet above ground level to avoid approaching U.S. naval forces closer than five nautical miles without first identifying themselves. The notices referred to U.S. forces operating in international waters in the Persian Gulf, in transit passage in the Strait of Hormuz, or in innocent passage in foreign territorial seas. Foreign ships and aircraft closing within five nautical miles without making contact or whose intentions were unclear could be "held at risk by U.S. defensive measures."[15] Consistent with American freedom of navigation policy, the notices advised that the measures would be "implemented in a manner that does not impede the freedom of navigation of any vessel or state."[16] One month after the NOTAM and NOTMAR were released, President Reagan signed National Security Decision Directive 114, which set forth U.S. policy toward the Iran-Iraq War. The policy further clarified American resolve to maintain freedom of navigation in the Gulf.[17]

— — — — • — — — —

Although both sides had attacked shipping in the Persian Gulf since the beginning of the war, the Tanker War, as this subconflict became known, entered a new level of violence in 1984 when Iraq attacked the Iranian oil terminal at Kharg Island and nearby oil tankers. Between September 1980 and July 1984, the belligerents between them attacked 112 vessels in the Persian Gulf; between June 1984 and December 1987, the number more than tripled, to 375.[18] These attacks were designed to intimidate tanker crews and owners and impose on them unacceptable costs and dangers.[19] Iran repeatedly warned it would close the Strait of Hormuz to international shipping if Iraq succeeded in interdicting its oil exports.[20]

Growing concern over escalation of the conflict prompted President Reagan to direct the United States to improve its posture and its readiness to respond to developments in the war. First, a political-military mission was sent to consult with key Gulf states, including Saudi Arabia, Oman, and Bahrain, as well as appropriate traditional allies, including France and the United Kingdom. The mission reviewed possible escalation scenarios and "indications and warning" and tried to coordinate contingency planning. In particular, in the event of an escalation the United States sought military access to Gulf airfield and seaport facilities, from which U.S. operations could be effectively supported and where U.S. forces would be close to the scene.[21]

The secretary of defense (SecDef) and the director of the Central Intelligence Agency (CIA) were also directed to improve the intelligence assets and amplify collection in the region.[22] The SecDef was also to develop measures to build deterrence and reduce the vulnerability of Americans and U.S. facilities. The Pentagon was ordered to respond in a "timely, effective, and forceful manner" to any sudden attack on U.S. interests in the region.[23] In particular, the Department of Defense (DoD) had to determine whether it would be more advantageous to deploy additional warships to the Persian Gulf or to send land-based tactical air forces, perhaps to Diego Garcia in the Indian Ocean. The president tasked SecDef to enhance the antiterrorist posture of U.S. military forces in the Gulf, given the growing threat of Iranian-sponsored terrorism. The DoD and CIA explored new combined counterterrorism and training measures with regional allies. Finally, the secretary of state, in coordination with the SecDef and director of the CIA, was directed to develop a plan of action to avert an Iraqi collapse.[24]

On the international front, the Security Council continued in vain to call for a cease-fire and to express its discontent over attacks on neutral shipping.[25] The heads of the international shipping community called on the United Nations to protest the indiscriminate attacks on freedom of navigation in international waters and to ensure the safe transit of neutral merchant ships.[26] The shipping industry condemned the attacks as constituting a "direct contradiction of the rule of international law."[27]

Determined to protect the free flow of oil through, and open access to, the Strait of Hormuz, the United States reiterated the importance of freedom of navigation.[28] The United States also warned that it would exercise self-defense and assist other countries in collective self-defense and that any expansion of the Iran-Iraq War to the Arab Gulf states would be a major threat to American interests.[29] Notwithstanding, Iranian attacks on nonbelligerent ships (regardless of flag) continued. In 1986 and 1987, they intensified on ships bound for Saudi Arabia and Kuwaiti, to counter Saudi and Kuwaiti support for Iraq.[30]

— — — — ◆ — — — —

As Iraq stabilized its front along the land boundary with the help of aid from Arab states, the war degenerated once again into a grinding slog. To compensate for a lack of progress on the ground, Iran stepped up indiscriminate attacks on commercial shipping in the Persian Gulf. By September 1986, Tehran reached the peak of its effort against Kuwaiti-flagged vessels and tankers bound for Kuwait. For example, twenty-eight of thirty-one Iranian attacks on commercial shipping in September were directed against Kuwait-bound ships.[31] In response, Kuwait requested assistance from the United States, the Soviet Union, and the United Kingdom to protect its merchant ships. The Soviet Union responded first, agreeing to charter several Soviet tankers to Kuwait. In May 1987, the United States reached an agreement with Kuwait to "reflag" eleven Kuwaiti oil tankers as U.S. vessels in order to facilitate their protection by the U.S. Navy.[32] The United Kingdom reflagged four ships.[33] Iran condemned these reflaggings as foreign intervention and threatened to close the Strait of Hormuz to international shipping. Tehran stepped up speedboat hit-and-run attacks against international shipping and sowed mines throughout the Persian Gulf.[34]

The right of self-defense in international law is both individual and collective. Although the United States could instead have entered into a collective defense arrangement with Kuwait to protect its ships, the administration opted for reflagging as a more public and tangible expression of its commitment to the Kuwaiti monarchy. Reflagging also upstaged the offer by the USSR (Union of Soviet Socialist Republics) to lease tankers, while forestalling domestic opposition to an open-ended commitment to protect Kuwaiti ships. Iran's presumed unwillingness to attack U.S. vessels seemed to make the U.S. flag a greater deterrent than collective self-defense.[35]

— — — — • — — — —

On May 12, 1987, President Reagan reaffirmed U.S. neutrality in the war but reemphasized his resolve to assist friends and allies in collective self-defense. The president also restated America's commitment to keep the Strait of Hormuz open to international shipping and preserve freedom of navigation in international waters.[36] Five days later, the guided-missile frigate USS *Stark* (FFG 31), on routine patrol in the Persian Gulf, was suddenly attacked by an Iraqi F-1 Mirage fighter. The Mirage fired two Exocet antiship cruise missiles, which struck the hull and superstructure of the ship. Thirty-seven sailors were killed, and the frigate was severely damaged. The rules of engagement (ROE) in effect at the time allowed American commanders to defend themselves if attacked or imminently threatened by attack, but the *Stark* never fired a shot or employed any type of countermeasure.[37] It was in international waters, about eighty-five miles northeast of Bahrain, well beyond the Iraqi- and Iranian-declared war zones.

Worried that the attack might unravel relations with the United States, which had been improving, Iraqi president Saddam Hussein immediately apologized for the incident. He claimed the attack had been inadvertent, a case of mistaken identity.[38] President Reagan accepted the apology and repeated American policy to defend "friends in the Gulf" and keep open the Strait of Hormuz.[39] The president warned that he would not permit Iran to dictate how the vital Persian Gulf sea lanes would be used.[40] He also pledged the United States would block Soviet efforts to dominate the region.[41]

> Freedom of navigation is not an empty cliché of international law. It is essential to the health and safety of America and the strength of our alliance. . . . [T]he United States and its allies maintain a presence in the Gulf to assist in the free movement of petroleum, to reassure those of our friends and allies in the region of our commitment to their peace and welfare, [and] to ensure that freedom of navigation and other principles of international accord are respected and observed. . . . Until peace is restored and there's no longer a risk to shipping in the region, particularly shipping under American protection, we must maintain an adequate presence to deter and, if necessary, to defend ourselves against any accidental . . . or . . . intentional attack.[42]

In light of the attack on the *Stark* and increased terrorism in the region, the United States issued revised warnings to mariners and airmen. American warships in the Persian Gulf, Strait of Hormuz, Gulf of Oman, and the northern Arabian Sea were to implement new defensive precautions. Ships and aircraft approaching U.S. naval vessels were to identify themselves, state their intentions, and maintain radio contact with them. If requested, all ships and aircraft were to remain well clear of American vessels; any that failed to comply and operated in a "threatening manner" would place themselves at risk of "defensive measures."[43] Any "illumination" of U.S. warships by fire-control radar would be "viewed with suspicion" and might result in the immediate use of force in self-defense.[44] At the same time, Washington reassured seafarers and aviators that the heightened defensive posture would not "unduly interfere with the freedom of navigation and overflight."[45]

Another U.S. special warning advised American merchant mariners to exercise "extreme caution" in the Persian Gulf, the Strait of Hormuz, and the Gulf of Oman, where Iran and Iraq were engaged in war at sea. Mariners were warned away from Iranian and Iraqi ports and coastal waters and the declared war zones.[46]

Iranian naval forces were threatening merchant ships as far as four hundred kilometers from the Strait of Hormuz. They stopped foreign ships for visit and search for contraband, and sometimes diverted them to Iranian ports.[47] The special warning further noted that Iraq, for its part, had indicated it would attack all vessels found in its declared zone in the northern Gulf, as well as oil tankers calling at Iran's Kharg Island terminal.[48] In general, American mariners were advised to exercise caution throughout the Gulf, since moored and floating mines had been encountered—especially in the Mina Al Ahmadi and Mina' ash Shuaiba Channels near Kuwait and in the sea lanes south and west of Farsi Island.[49]

– – — – • – — – —

After seven years of fighting, the Security Council finally, under Chapter VII of the UN Charter, demanded Iran and Iraq observe an immediate cease-fire as a first step toward a negotiated settlement.[50] Article VII concerns Security Council action with respect to threats to the peace or breaches of international security. Invoking Chapter VII often conveys authority for "all necessary means," including the use of force, as recognized in article 42 of the Charter.[51] In its resolution, however, the Security Council cited only articles 39 and 40 of Chapter VII, which call upon the parties to comply. Two days later, the U.S. Navy began convoying U.S.-flagged tankers through the Gulf, as part of Operation Earnest Will. Belgium, France, Italy, the Netherlands, and the United Kingdom followed suit.[52] The first American escort included three guided-missile-equipped warships—the destroyer USS *Kidd* (DDG 993), the cruiser USS *Fox* (CG

33), and the frigate USS *Crommellin* (FFG 37); the convoy comprised the reflagged supertanker M/V (motor vessel) *Bridgeton* and the liquefied-natural-gas (LNG) tanker M/V *Gas Prince*. The administration justified the escort operation as a demonstration of American resolve to keep the shipping lanes open in the Gulf.[53]

On July 24, the M/V *Bridgeton* hit a mine eighteen miles west of Farsi Island. The crew was not injured, and the ship suffered only minor damage—a twenty-nine-foot hole in the hull and damage to an oil tank.[54] Although American authorities initially did not suggest who had laid the mine, the general consensus was that Iranian naval forces operating from a base on Farsi Island had done so. The Islamic Revolutionary Guard Corps (IRGC) routinely used the facility to conduct high-speed small-boat attacks on international shipping. As expected, Tehran disavowed any responsibility, instead blaming Iraq for the attack. Nonetheless, several days later additional mines were found in the vicinity of where the *Bridgeton* had been damaged.[55]

The U.S. intelligence community knew Iran had a stockpile of about a thousand (mostly Soviet-made) M-08 contact naval mines. Yet at the time of the first convoy the United States did not have a substantial mine-countermeasures (MCM) capability in the Gulf. The *Bridgeton* incident prompted the Joint Staff to deploy eight RH-53D Sea Stallions from Helicopter Mine Countermeasures Squadron 14 (HM-14) and six ocean minesweepers, or MSOs. The minesweepers USS *Enhance* (MSO 437), USS *Conquest* (MSO 488), USS *Esteem* (MSO 438), USS *Inflict* (MSO 456), USS *Fearless* (MSO 442), and USS *Illusive* (MSO 448) deployed to the Gulf. The helicopter assault ship USS *Guadalcanal* (LPH 7) was also deployed, to support the HM-14 detachment.[56]

NATO allies—France, Germany, Italy, and the United Kingdom—initially rejected a U.S. request to assist in mine clearing.[57] Their positions changed when the M/V *Texaco Caribbean*, a Panamanian-flagged supertanker, struck a mine in the Gulf of Oman as it was entering the United Arab Emirates port of Fujaira on August 11.[58] This incident was the first reported mine attack outside the Gulf since the start of the war, and European states viewed it as a major escalation. Ten days later, Iran finally acknowledged that it had laid mines in the Persian Gulf, purportedly to protect its coastal installations, but denied any involvement in the mining of the *Texaco Caribbean*.[59] Nonetheless, over the next several weeks, Belgium, France, Italy, the Netherlands, and the United Kingdom deployed warships and MCM ships to protect their merchant vessels operating in the Gulf. During the course of the escort operations, U.S. and allied MCM assets cleared hundreds of mines from the Persian Gulf, including the convoy shipping lanes and the "Q-routes" into and out of commercial ports.[60]

Iran's indiscriminate mining violated international law. Tehran is not a party to the 1907 Convention Relative to the Laying of Automatic Submarine Contact Mines (Hague VIII), but the terms of the treaty reflect customary international law and are therefore binding on all nations.[61] Article 1 prohibits the laying of "unanchored automatic contact mines" unless they "become harmless one hour . . . after the person who laid them ceases to control them." Unanchored Iranian mines remained active for "days if not weeks."[62] Likewise, Iran's practice of laying mines off the coasts and ports of nonbelligerent states with the sole purpose of disrupting commercial shipping, and on the high seas in established shipping lanes without providing notice to the international shipping community, violated articles 2 and 3 of the convention, as well as the judgment of the International Court of Justice in the *Corfu Channel* and *Nicaragua* cases.[63] Similarly, Iran's mining in neutral waters violated article 2 of the 1907 Convention Concerning the Rights and Duties of Neutral Powers in Naval War (Hague XIII).[64]

Fourteen months after the reflagging operation commenced, on September 26, 1988, the United States changed how it protected its ships in the Gulf, from "tight" escort to an "accompany" regime.[65] Under the new approach, American merchant ships were no longer directly escorted. Instead, American warships patrolled the area more broadly, positioned to intervene if U.S.-flagged vessels were threatened. The administration cautioned Iran that the adjustment did not represent a walking back of its commitment to freedom of navigation in the Gulf.[66] The last Earnest Will convoy was conducted in December 1988. Over the seventeen-month operation, the U.S. Navy successfully escorted 259 ships.[67]

— — — — • — — —

At this point, the United States had some twenty-six warships in the Gulf.[68] In addition to MCM assets, the United States employed Special Operations Forces (SOF) in support of its convoy escort mission. Throughout the conflict, the IRGC had used small boats—mostly "Boghammers" (converted commercial boats, so called for their Swedish manufacturer) and Boston Whaler–type craft armed with 107-mm rockets, rocket-propelled grenades, and machine guns—to harass international shipping and lay mines along the five-hundred-mile sea lane from the Gulf of Oman to Kuwait. To counter this threat, the 160th Special Operations Aviation Regiment (SOAR), Navy SEALs, and Navy Special Boat Units (SBUs) embarked in the command ship USS *La Salle* (AGF 3), the guided-missile frigates USS *Jarrett* (FFG 33) and USS *Klakring* (FFG 42), and on board two mobile sea bases (MSBs *Hercules* and *Wimbrown* VII). These expeditionary forces were to prevent mining and hit-and-run attacks on commercial shipping by Iranian small boats.[69] The SOF campaign against Iran's asymmetric naval attacks was called Operation Prime Chance.

The MSBs were converted oil-platform construction barges repurposed for amphibious warfare. Each had two SBU detachments, Mark (Mk) III patrol boats, a SEAL platoon, and an explosive ordnance demolition (EOD) detachment. They also served as "lily pads" for helicopters—the 160th SOAR's MH-6 command-and-control, AH-6 Little Bird attack, and MH-60 Black Hawk rescue aircraft. U.S. Air Force air controllers directed them. The MSBs also each carried a reinforced Marine platoon for security. The platoon was outfitted with heavy machine guns, grenade launchers, antiaircraft guns, mortars, and Stinger antiaircraft missiles.[70] The Mk IIIs conducted twenty-four-hour presence patrols, collected intelligence, and escorted U.S. commercial ships, while the Little Birds flew search-and-destroy missions at night and acted as a quick-reaction force.[71]

The MSBs became operational in October 1987 and were positioned in the northern Gulf near Farsi Island. Every few days they would move to new locations to complicate Iranian targeting. With the conclusion of Operation Earnest Will in December 1988, MSB *Wimbrown* VII returned to Bahrain and was restored to civilian use. MSB *Hercules* remained on station until June 1989.

— — — — • — — — —

On September 19, 1987, American intelligence assets detected the *Iran Ajr* getting under way from its home port. The ship was a former Japanese landing craft, built in 1978, that Iran had converted to lay mines. The USS *Jarrett*, with two SOF AH-6 helicopters embarked, was ordered to monitor the ship's movements. Two days later, *Jarrett's* AH-6s observed the *Iran Ajr* laying mines near U.S. forces in international waters fifty miles northeast of Bahrain. The Reagan administration viewed the act as hostile, posing a direct threat to U.S. warships and endangering U.S.-flagged tankers in the vicinity.[72] Accordingly, American helicopters requested permission under the ROE then in force to attack the ship; they were authorized to employ all necessary force, in self-defense, to stop the *Iran Ajr* from laying more mines.[73] The helicopters fired rockets and machine guns, disabling the vessel and preventing the release of more mines.[74] The next morning, SEALs boarded the ship and found three dead Iranian crew members, ten mines on the deck, and six more in the water.[75] Nautical charts and the logbook revealed the locations of other Iranian minefields. The following April, when the USS *Samuel B. Roberts* (FFG 58) struck a mine, Navy EOD found that the serial numbers of unexploded mines nearby the U.S. warship matched those of the mines previously discovered on the deck of the *Iran Ajr*. Similar mines were discovered throughout the Gulf.

The other twenty-eight crew members had abandoned the ship and escaped in lifeboats during the helicopter attack. All but two were recovered and taken to nearby U.S. warships for medical treatment. The twenty-six survivors, as well as the bodies of the three sailors killed in the attack, were repatriated to Iran via Oman, with the assistance of the International Committee of the Red Cross. The SEALs scuttled the *Iran Ajr* in deep water off Bahrain on September 26. Tehran admitted the *Iran Ajr* had been carrying sea mines but claimed they were not being laid at the time the ship was boarded. But the *Iran Ajr* had been caught red-handed, illegally laying contact mines, and the bilateral political and military equation between the United States and Iran was immediately affected. Secretary of Defense Caspar Weinberger later remarked that the American seizure of the *Iran Ajr* diminished Iran's credibility throughout the world and enhanced support for the U.S. patrols in the Gulf.[76]

President Reagan explained to Congress that the military response against the *Iran Ajr* had been an exercise of the right of self-defense under article 51 of the UN Charter.[77] The president emphasized that sowing contact mines on the high seas, especially without notice and along sea lanes with restricted navigation channels, is unlawful. Iran's conduct was a "serious threat to world public order" and threatened the safety of international maritime commerce. Furthermore, after the *Bridgeton* incident in July President Reagan warned Iran that the United States would take necessary action to defend its vessels. Now the United States had no alternative to military action if it was to preserve deterrence and credibility.

That same day, President Reagan stated that the United States continued to have a vital interest in thwarting Iranian designs in the region.[78] He thus set forth a three-part policy. First, the United States would bring greater international pressure to bear to produce a negotiated end to the war and stop it from spilling over to other countries and international shipping. Second, the United States would steadfastly help its friends and support the nonbelligerent nations of the Gulf in collective self-defense against Iranian threats. Third, the United States hoped to pursue greater cooperation with the states of the Gulf Cooperation Council (GCC) and other friendly states to protect freedom of navigation. Reagan stated, "We will defend ourselves as necessary. . . . We have made these points known repeatedly to Iran" through public statements and bilateral diplomacy.[79]

— — — — ● — — — —

The next phase of American involvement arose from the attack on the motor vessel *Sea Isle City*; Operation Nimble Archer was the U.S. response. On October 8, 1987, despite repeated warnings to Iran regarding its aggressive behavior, several small Iranian ships fired at three U.S. helicopters from the MSB *Hercules* on routine patrol over international waters in the Persian Gulf.

As the administration later stated, the unprovoked attack posed an "immediate and direct" threat to the helicopters and their crewmen.[80] Accordingly, consistent with the ROE, the helicopters replied in self-defense with machine guns and rockets. One of the three boats was sunk. U.S. patrol boats in the area recovered six Iranian crewmen from the water; two later died on board the USS *Raleigh* (LPD 1).[81] The survivors were subsequently repatriated to Iran. The Iranian boats were found to have been operating from derelict oil platforms that had been converted into small naval bases.

A week later, on October 16, the M/V *Sea Isle City* was struck by an Iranian Silkworm missile while at anchor five miles off the port of Shuaiba, Kuwait. The ship was a reflagged American tanker. The attack, which was the seventh Iranian antiship cruise-missile strike of 1987, had been launched from the Al Faw Peninsula, which Iranian forces had seized from Iraq in February 1986. Iran occupied three formerly Iraqi missile sites on the peninsula, and also operated a cruise missile staging facility on Iranian territory near the peninsula—that was known from evidence that included satellite and aerial reconnaissance imaging of the Al Faw area, where there were four missile sites. The United States also produced a statement by an independent expert, dated March 27, 1997, that the ship had been struck by a widely available Chinese-manufactured cruise missile, the HY-2, known as the Silkworm. Furthermore, two Kuwaiti military officers, stationed on Kuwaiti islands at the time, had witnessed the launch of six antiship cruise missiles from Iranian-controlled portions of the Al Faw Peninsula.

When one of them struck the ship, the explosion permanently blinded the master, an American citizen. Seventeen other crew members were injured.[82] The following day, President Reagan addressed the nation, reiterating the importance of keeping the shipping lanes open and calling freedom of navigation, especially in the Persian Gulf, a "cardinal principle of our policy," a vital interest. "Any risk to U.S. naval presence or to U.S.-flagged commercial ships operating in the Gulf," he pledged, "will be dealt with appropriately."[83] Iran again denied any responsibility for the attack—yet the Al Faw Peninsula, from where the missiles had been launched, though part of Iraq, was occupied by Iranian armed forces.[84]

The United States believed the *Sea Isle City* attack, the mining, and the small-boat attacks, when viewed as a single campaign, crossed a threshold of aggression that demanded a greater reaction. On October 19, the United States launched Operation Praying Mantis. First, U.S. forces struck two derelict Iranian offshore complexes. The complexes—Reshadat and Resalat—were being used by the IRGC navy and regular Iranian navy as surveillance platforms and logistics facilities. The complex consisted of three drilling and production platforms (R-3, R-4, and R-7) linked to a total of twenty-seven oil wells. The crude oil produced by the R-3 platform was carried by submarine pipeline to the R-4 platform, combined with R-4 oil, and then sent by pipeline to the R-7 platform, where there were production facilities and living quarters for the platform and a submarine pipeline connection to the Resalat complex. The Resalat complex consisted of three linked drilling and production platforms, referred to collectively as R-1. Gas and water were separated from the crude oil produced by these platforms and sent by underwater pipeline to Lavan Island. None of these platforms were producing oil at the time of the American strikes, having been damaged by Iraqi attacks in October 1986, July 1987, and August 1987.[85]

Now Iranian helicopters used the complexes to stage attacks on international shipping.[86] The Reshadat R-7 platform was armed, had radar and other surveillance equipment, and served as a command-and-control hub.[87] The U.S. response began when the guided-missile frigate USS *Thach* (FFG 43) approached R-7, warned the occupants of the impending attack, and allowed them to evacuate. Twenty minutes later, gunfire from the destroyers USS *Hoel* (DDG 13), USS *Leftwich* (DD 984), USS *Young* (DD 973), and USS *Kidd* "lit up" the R-7 platform. Following the bombardment, Navy SEALs boarded and searched the Reshadat complex, planted explosives, and destroyed it.[88]

The American task force then attacked the Reshadat R-4 platform. Once again, the occupants were offered an opportunity to abandon the structure before the naval bombardment commenced. Again, SEALs boarded and searched the platform and destroyed it, along with the radar and communications equipment that had been used to target shipping.[89] The president later called the U.S. operation a "restrained and measured" action taken in accordance with the inherent right of self-defense pursuant to article 51 of the Charter.[90]

— — — — • — — — —

On April 14, 1988, northeast of Qatar, lookouts on board the guided-missile frigate USS *Samuel B. Roberts* (FFG 58) spotted three mines approximately seven hundred yards away. The ship was en route to Bahrain following an oil tanker escort mission. The *Roberts* attempted to back out of the minefield but struck a submerged mine. The explosion tore a twenty-one-foot hole in the hull and broke the keel, nearly breaking the ship in half; ten sailors were injured.[91] Ships came to assist, only to find five additional mines nearby.

After close examination, Navy officials determined that the mines in the water near the *Roberts* were identical to the M-08 contact mines captured on board the *Iran Ajr* the previous September—the same markings, same type and series.[92] These mines had no accumulation of barnacles or marine growth, which meant they had been recently sowed. The administration concluded beyond a doubt that Iran had recently laid the mines to damage or sink American or other neutral ships.

In response, President Reagan authorized attacks on Iranian naval forces in the Gulf, as a continuation of Operation Praying Mantis, which now became the Navy's largest surface naval engagement since World War II. The operation involved two more oil platforms that were being used by the IRGC much as it had the Reshadat and Resalat structures: the Sassan and Sirri platforms. Over a third of all Iranian attacks on nonbelligerent shipping occurred within fifty nautical miles of one or the other of those installations.[93]

The United States pointed to Iran's recent resumption of mining in international waterways and the mine strike on the USS *Samuel B. Roberts* to justify the new assault. Despite continued warnings, Iran had persisted in attacks on American merchant ships and warships.[94] The administration called the new phase of Praying Mantis a "measured response to Iran's unlawful use of force," as Iran had demonstrated a complete disregard for the law of naval warfare. The operation was designed to deter Iran and degrade its capabilities to continue attacks on international shipping. The United

States continued to insist that its authority was the inherent right of self-defense under article 51 of the UN Charter. Consistent with article 51, the United States notified in advance the president of the UN Security Council.

U.S. naval forces formed three "surface action groups" (SAGs). The destroyers USS *Merrill* (DD 976) and USS *Lynde McCormick* (DDG 8) and the amphibious ship USS *Trenton* (LPD 14) formed SAG Bravo. The *Trenton* carried a Marine expeditionary unit (MEU, a composite force in the Marine Air-Ground Task Force, or MAGTF, organization). SAG Bravo would attack the Sassan oil platform. SAG Charlie, comprising the missile cruiser USS *Wainwright* (CG 28) and the frigates USS *Simpson* (FFG 56) and USS *Bagley* (FF 1069), with an embarked SEAL team, would hit the Sirri platform. The frigate USS *Jack Williams* (FFG 24) and the destroyers USS *O'Brien* (DD 975) and USS *Joseph Strauss* (DDG 16) formed SAG Delta, which was to patrol near the Strait of Hormuz. Combat air patrols would be flown from the USS *Enterprise* (CVN 65), which was on station in the Gulf of Oman. Additional support would be provided by American land-based Airborne Warning and Control System (AWACS) aircraft from Saudi Arabia and by tanker aircraft. To keep the response proportional, U.S. forces were instructed to avoid civilian casualties, minimize collateral damage, and limit adverse environmental impacts.[95]

On April 18, 1988, SAG Bravo warned the Iranians on the Sassan platform of the imminent attack. About thirty of the occupants abandoned the platform, but others stayed behind to man a 23-mm cannon, with which they engaged the SAG. The USS *Merrill* immediately silenced the cannon. UH-1 Iroquois ("Huey") and CH-46 Sea Knight helicopters airlifted Marines to the oil platforms, where they collected intelligence and later planted demolition charges that destroyed the structures. SAG Charlie attacked the Sirri platform in similar fashion, destroying that complex as well.[96]

Several hours later, the Iranian missile patrol boat *Joshan* (P 225) approached SAG Charlie in a threatening manner. After ignoring three warnings from the *Wainwright*, the Iranian warship fired a Harpoon antiship missile at the U.S. cruiser. The missile barely missed. SAG Charlie engaged the *Joshan* in self-defense with SM-1 and Harpoon missiles, crippling it;

gunfire from the *Wainwright* and the *Simpson* sank it. The *Wainwright* and *Simpson* also used extended-range Standard surface-to-air missiles to turn back a flight of elderly Iranian F-4 Phantoms bearing down on the SAG.

Meanwhile, IRGC small boats and a helicopter went after the British-flagged tanker M/V *York Marine* and the U.S.-flagged commercial tugboat *Willi Tide* near the Saleh and Mubarek oil fields in the southern Gulf.[97] An A-6 Intruder attack aircraft from the *Enterprise* that had been circling overhead sank a Boghammer patrol boat and damaged several others. To avenge the morning's actions against the two oil platforms, Iran sent the frigates *Sahand* (F 74) and *Sabalan* (F 73)—both received from the United States during the shah era—to attack nearby platforms owned by the United Arab Emirates. An A-6E Intruder from the *Enterprise* intercepted the *Sahand*. The *Sahand* launched surface-to-air missiles, to which the U.S. jet responded with two Harpoon missiles and four laser-guided bombs. The two Harpoons and two laser-guided bombs struck the Iranian ship. The guided-missile destroyer USS *Joseph Strauss* arrived shortly thereafter and fired another Harpoon missile into the *Sahand*, sinking it. Meanwhile, U.S. aircraft badly damaged the *Sabalan*, which limped back to port.[98]

Operation Praying Mantis proved a turning point in the Tanker War. Three Iranian command-and-control platforms were destroyed. Six Iranian vessels were sunk and the *Sabalan* heavily damaged. The United States lost one AH-1 Cobra attack helicopter from the *Wainwright*, and its two-man crew. Iranian attacks on nonbelligerent shipping fell dramatically. Iran also ceased mining operations and stopped its challenges to U.S. naval transits in the Gulf.[99] As it had done throughout the campaign, the administration continued to warn Iran that the United States remained ready to protect its ships and vital interests from unprovoked attacks.[100] Four months later Iran accepted UN Security Council resolution 598, and a cease-fire went into effect.

— — — — • — — — —

The conflict was not over, however. The next major event proved horrific—the downing of a civilian airliner. Given the indiscriminate attacks by Iran and Iraq and the hair-trigger defense posture they induced, it is surprising that such a tragedy had not occurred earlier in the war. As a result of the USS *Stark* incident, the United States had clarified its ROE in the Gulf. Once a ship detects an air or missile attack, it has just moments to take action to avoid being hit. The ROE revision emphasized that warship commanding officers had the authority, and indeed the duty, to defend their ships proactively. That is, the revision stressed, U.S. units did not have to be shot at before they could respond in self-defense. Waiting to act after the first shot might be too late. American commanding officers had a specific and ineluctable responsibility to protect their units and personnel. In September 1987, the United States issued a NOTMAR advising mariners of all nations of the stricter defense posture of its forces. In addition, a NOTAM advised nations operating aircraft in the Persian Gulf that U.S. Navy ships would be taking additional precautions. If queried by U.S. forces, aircraft should be prepared to identify themselves on specific frequencies and to state their intentions. Failure to respond to American queries or threatening behavior could put aircraft at risk.

American intelligence, meanwhile, concluded that Iran had recently improved its ability to attack U.S. warships. Iranian F-4s and F-14s had been reconfigured and were now armed with air-to-surface missiles, with which they meant to carry out suicide assaults. Specific warnings were disseminated to U.S. forces of a high likelihood of attack over the weekend of the Fourth of July. Iran had moved its F-14s from Bushehr to the joint military-civilian airfield at Bandar Abbas. On July 2, the cruiser USS *Halsey* (CG 23) had warned off a potentially threatening F-14 from Bandar Abbas.

The next day, the frigate USS *Elmer Montgomery* (FF 1082), in the western approaches to the Strait of Hormuz, observed a flotilla of thirteen IRGC small boats challenge a Pakistani merchant vessel. The cruiser USS *Vincennes* (CG 49), ordered to support the *Montgomery*, launched its embarked SH-60 LAMPS Mk III Seahawk helicopter to investigate. The Iranian small boats attacked the SH-60 helicopter. The *Montgomery* and the *Vincennes* closed in, determined that the Iranian craft were demonstrating hostile intent, requested permission to engage them, and received it. As the surface action was taking place, an Iranian A300B2–200 Airbus, Iran Air flight 655, took off from Bandar Abbas en route to Dubai on a flight path that took it directly over the U.S. warships. At the same time, the Combat Information Center (CIC) on board the *Vincennes* was tracking an Iranian P-3 maritime patrol aircraft some sixty nautical miles to the northwest. The P-3 was in a position to furnish targeting data to an attacking aircraft. The ingredients for a tragic mistake quickly materialized.

The *Vincennes* CIC was initially unable to detect radar emissions from the Airbus but did read an "identification, friend or foe" (IFF) "squawk"—a Mode III squawk, an identifying four-digit code assigned by an air controller, either military or civil. The contact was designated "unidentified assumed hostile," as the ROE directed for all tracks originating from Iran. Subsequently, CIC detected a Mode II IFF squawk, used only by military aircraft; the contact's designation was changed to "F-14." The Airbus was not, in fact, squawking Mode II.[101] However, it was gradually increasing speed, heading directly toward the *Montgomery* and the *Vincennes*, and not answering repeated challenges by the *Vincennes* over both military and international emergency frequencies. On board the *Vincennes*, the tactical information coordinator, an officer, erroneously informed the captain that the contact was closing on the ship and decreasing in altitude—an attack profile.

Meanwhile, in Bahrain, Rear Adm. Harold Bernsen, commander of the Middle East Force, had provided a supplemental ROE that instructed commanding officers to warn away potentially hostile contacts. If the contact persisted and commanding officers believed an attack was imminent, they had authority to use force in self-defense. This authority derived from the inherent right and responsibility to act in self-defense: "We do not want, nor intend, to absorb a first attack."[102] Accordingly, the captain of the *Vincennes* decided that the contact was demonstrating hostile intent. Given this threat profile and the ROE, the commanding officer requested and obtained permission to engage the contact. Shortly thereafter, the *Vincennes* launched SM-2 missiles at the Airbus. The missiles hit their mark, and all 290 passengers and crew on board perished.

An investigation convened by the commander in chief of U.S. Central Command reported on July 3, 1988, supporting the decision of the captain. The order to fire had been correct given "the facts which he had available to him" and the compressed time in which he had to make a decision.[103] The chairman of the Joint Chiefs of Staff concurred.[104] Similarly, in reporting the shootdown to Congress, President Reagan expressed deep regret for the tragic loss of life but agreed that the commanding officer of the *Vincennes* was not culpable. The Airbus had been "shot down by the *Vincennes*" as the ship was "firing in self defense at what it believed to be a hostile Iranian military aircraft."[105]

Nonetheless, on May 17, 1989, Iran initiated proceedings against the United States at the International Court of Justice (ICJ). In its pleadings, Iran requested that the ICJ declare the shooting down of the Airbus a violation of the Chicago Convention on Civil Aviation and of the Montreal Convention on the Suppression of Unlawful Acts against Civil Aircraft.[106] Iran sought compensation for the destruction of the Airbus and the taking of 290 lives.[107] No judgment was ever issued in the case. On February 22, 1996, American and Iranian officials notified the court that their governments had agreed to a settlement that resolved all of the connected disputes.[108] The proceedings were duly discontinued by mutual consent of the parties and removed from the ICJ case list.[109] The United States expressed "deep regret over the loss of life" and agreed to pay Iran $131.8 million in damages, $61.8 million of which was designated for the heirs and legatees of the 248 victims who had been Iranians.[110] But the U.S. government never apologized or acknowledged any wrongdoing.

— — — — • — — — —

On November 2, 1992, Iran instituted further proceedings against the United States at the International Court of Justice, this time over the destruction of the three offshore oil complexes during Operations Nimble Archer and Praying Mantis. Iran contended that the U.S. attacks constituted a fundamental breach of the 1955 bilateral U.S.-Iranian treaty of commerce, as well as of general principles of international law.[111] The United States raised a preliminary objection as to whether the ICJ had jurisdiction over the matter, but the court agreed with Iran that it could hear Tehran's claims concerning the 1955 treaty.[112] During the merits phase of the case, the United States filed a counterclaim concerning Iran's actions in the Persian Gulf during 1987–88.

The United States presented evidence that Iran had attacked U.S.-flagged and American-owned vessels and warships. Iran objected to this "counter-memorial," but the ICJ ruled that it would consider the American claims.

On March 3, 2003, Iran requested that the court declare the United States in breach of its obligations to Iran under article X of the 1955 treaty for having destroyed Iranian oil platforms on October 19, 1987, and April 18, 1988. Iran wanted the ICJ to rule that the United States bore responsibility for the attacks and owed Iran "full reparation." Two days later, the United States countered that it had not breached its obligations to Iran under the treaty and that Iran's claims should be dismissed. At a later hearing, on March 7, Iran requested that the court dismiss the U.S. counterclaim. The United States in turn claimed that Iran's indiscriminate use of mines and missiles and its other attacks on American forces had been breaches of the 1955 treaty and that therefore it was Iran that owed reparations.

The court held that to establish that it had been exercising self-defense by attacking the Iranian platforms, the United States now had to demonstrate that Iran had been responsible for the attacks on merchant shipping and that those attacks qualified as an "armed attack" in terms of customary international law of armed conflict and article 51 of the United Nations Charter. The court determined there was insufficient evidence to support the American claim that Iran had been responsible for the attack on the *Sea Isle City*. Moreover, the court found that the *Texaco Caribbean* had not been flying the U.S. flag and so the mine strike could not be equated to an attack on the United States. The court was also unconvinced by evidence presented by the United States concerning attacks on U.S. helicopters by Iranian gunboats and from the Reshadat oil platform. Finally, the court determined that there was no evidence that the minelaying carried out by the *Iran Ajr* had been aimed specifically at the United States. No concrete evidence suggested the mine that damaged the *Bridgeton* had been laid with the "specific intention of harming that ship" or other American vessels. Accordingly, the court concluded, the incidents cited did not "constitute an armed attack on the United States" under international law and therefore did not authorize the United States to use force in self-defense. Similarly, the court found that the evidence presented of Iran's responsibility for the mining of the USS *Samuel B. Roberts* was inconclusive, albeit highly suggestive. Similarly, there was insufficient evidence to hold that Operation Praying Mantis against the Sirri and Sassan platforms had been in response to an armed attack on the United States by Iran. For these reasons, the court held, by a vote of fourteen to two, that U.S. military operations against Iranian oil platforms on October 19, 1987, and April 18, 1988, could not be justified as measures to protect the "essential security interests of the United States" under the 1955 treaty. Nonetheless, the court declined to agree with Iran that the U.S. attacks had been violations of the treaty. Similarly, by a vote of fifteen to one, the court rejected the American counterclaim that Iran had breached its obligations under the 1955 treaty.

The court's technical legalism and the moral equivalency with which it regarded the parties threatened to make it irrelevant. Like the *Corfu Channel* and *Nicaragua* decisions before it, the *Oil Platforms* case illustrates the nature of the ICJ's jurisprudence on matters of aggression and self-defense, as well as the disparate legal standards used by the ICJ governing the use of force between developed, powerful states and developing, weak ones.[113] The decision reinforced the court's penchant to soft-pedal persistent but low-level aggression by weaker states while repudiating legitimate self-defense by stronger nations. This holding has profound implications for developed states, as it appears to license asymmetric attacks against them and then repudiate any response in self-defense.

— — — — • — — —

The war ended on August 20, 1988, with little to show by either side except tremendous suffering, loss of life, and ruined economies. However, U.S. actions in the Persian Gulf had effectively demonstrated American resolve to protect navigational freedoms and neutral rights against the illegal acts of belligerents engaged in unrestrained armed conflict. Very little had changed in U.S. policy since the very first war the nation had fought as an independent country, in 1798–1800.

Operation Earnest Will, the largest convoy operation since World War II, concluded a month later, on September 26, 1988. The escort mission had achieved American strategic goals in the Persian Gulf. Kuwaiti shipping was protected. Soviet presence in the Gulf was held in check. American prestige with its Arab partners was preserved. Iranian aggression was curtailed, and without either vertical or horizontal escalation of the conflict.

Nevertheless, it was apparent that, however effective they were in preventing direct attacks on U.S.-flagged vessels, American warships could not stop Iran from laying mines or harassing American shipping through maritime terrorism. Rear Admiral Bernsen had been obliged to request SOF assets for these roles. Operation Prime Chance leveraged critical SOF skills, notably night operations, to counter Iran's small-boat tactics and minelaying.

Notwithstanding the decision of the ICJ in the *Oil Platforms* case, U.S. offensive operations in response to the missile attack on the *Sea Isle City* and the mining of the USS *Samuel B. Roberts* were necessary and proportional to the threats to U.S. national security and therefore consistent with the right of self-defense under the UN Charter and customary international law.[114] The ICJ got that case wrong. More important, since Operations Nimble Archer and Praying Mantis, Iran has not used a missile or mines against U.S.-flagged vessels.

Iran's decision to forego further challenges to U.S. naval power in the Persian Gulf and halt attacks on U.S.-flagged shipping illustrates the country's typical characteristic of de-escalation when confronted with a determined, superior force.[115] This lesson risks being lost in recent American operations in the Gulf. For instance, in 2015 and 2016, the U.S. Navy reported fifty-eight "unsafe and unprofessional" interactions with Iranian vessels.[116] As recently as January 8, 2017, four IRGC patrol boats threatened and harassed the guided-missile destroyer USS *Mahan* (DDG 72) as it passed through the Strait of Hormuz. One of the boats, its main gun manned, approached the U.S. warship at high speed and passed within nine hundred yards. The IRGC boats broke off only after the *Mahan* fired three warning shots with a .50-caliber machine gun. Then, in July, the USS *Thunderbolt* (PC 12) fired warning shots at an Iranian boat that approached to within 150 yards of the American warship. Such incidents suggest it may be only a matter of time before the United States conducts a new campaign akin to Operation Praying Mantis.

"UNIFORM INTERPRETATION OF INNOCENT PASSAGE"

The Black Sea Bumping Incident (1988)

The 1988 Black Sea bumping incident involving the United States and the Soviet Union is a vivid example of how the U.S. Freedom of Navigation (FON) program has helped preserve navigational rights and freedoms for all seafaring nations. The FON operation yielded an important bilateral agreement that enhances the safety of navigation and overflight and reinforces the rule of law at sea. A fundamental tenet of that body of international law is that all ships, including warships, enjoy the right of innocent passage through the territorial seas of coastal states.

At the time of the incident, Soviet domestic law and regulations recognized the right of innocent passage for warships in the territorial sea but purported to restrict them to certain unilaterally designated sea lanes. Article 13 of the 1982 Law of the Union of Soviet Socialist Republics on the State Frontier of the USSR provided, in part, that "foreign warships and underwater vehicles shall enjoy the right of innocent passage through the territorial waters (territorial sea) of the USSR in accordance with the procedure to be established by the Council of Ministers of the USSR."[1] In April 1983, the Council of Ministers approved the Rules for Navigation and Sojourn of Foreign Warships in the Territorial Waters and Internal Waters and Ports of the USSR. Article 12.1 specified that foreign warships enjoyed the right of innocent passage through Soviet territorial waters for the purpose of crossing them, without entering internal waters or ports. However, it permitted passage only within certain routes ordinarily used for international navigation.[2] Foreign warships were not entitled to innocent passage in any other parts of the Soviet territorial sea, including the Black Sea, without prior approval.

The United States challenged the Soviet position, both diplomatically and operationally, arguing that it had no basis in international law. The dispute arising from the Black Sea bumping incident was to be peacefully resolved the following year in a series of bilateral discussions. The talks culminated in 1989 in Wyoming, where the parties signed the Jackson Hole Agreement.[3] The agreement contains an attachment, the Uniform Interpretation of Rules of International Law Governing Innocent Passage, which states that "all ships, including warships, regardless of cargo, armament or means of propulsion, enjoy the right of innocent passage through the territorial sea in accordance with international law, for which neither prior notification nor authorization is required."[4] The two superpowers signed a separate agreement designed to avoid dangerous activities when their armed forces were operating in close proximity.[5]

– – – – • – – –

The 1958 Geneva Convention on the Territorial Sea and the Contiguous Zone provides that all ships "enjoy the right of innocent passage through the territorial sea."[6] In turn, "passage is innocent so long as it is not prejudicial to the peace, good order or security of the coastal State."[7] Furthermore, innocent passage shall take place in conformity with the additional articles in the 1958 treaty and with other rules of international law.[8] The 1958 convention prohibits coastal states from hampering innocent passage through the territorial sea;[9] however, it allows a coastal state to "take the necessary steps in its territorial sea to prevent passage which is not innocent."[10] In this regard, it is unclear what steps may be considered "necessary." In addition, the convention requires foreign ships exercising the right of innocent passage to "comply with the laws and regulations enacted by the coastal

State in conformity with these articles and other rules of international law and, in particular, with such laws and regulations relating to transport and navigation."[11] Once again, the scope of coastal-state competence is vague. If a foreign warship does not do so and "disregards any request for compliance which is made to it, the coastal state may require the warship to leave the territorial sea."[12] Exactly how that is to be done, however, is unclear. States have the right to order the ship to leave the territorial sea, although warships would be immune from arrest or seizure.

At the First United Nations Conference on the Law of the Sea in 1958, the Russians were inconsistent on the issue of navigational rights. The Soviet delegate expressed concern that "certain states" had violated the principle of freedom of the high seas by "taking over large areas for naval and air force maneuvers."[13] In particular, the Russians complained, the United States had used vast areas in the Sea of Japan, Korean Straits, northwest Pacific, Yellow Sea, and Caribbean Sea for naval exercises that excluded other users of the sea.[14] Likewise, in 1957, Moscow had complained, the United Kingdom had "taken over" parts of the English Channel along international shipping routes for submarine exercises.[15] Yet the USSR pushed for an interpretation of the principle of freedom of navigation that permitted coastal states to prohibit exercises and maneuvers in areas of the "high seas near foreign shores and on international shipping routes."[16]

Upon ratification of the 1958 treaty in 1960, the Soviet Union entered a reservation to article 23 on the right of innocent passage of warships in the territorial sea. The USSR asserted that a coastal state had "the right to establish procedures for the authorization of the passage of foreign warships through its territorial waters."[17] That same year, Moscow adopted a new domestic law and implementing regulation that limited the passage of foreign warships in the Soviet territorial sea unless prior consent was obtained. The new statute established an authorization procedure that foreign warships were to use.[18] Implementing regulations required foreign warships to request permission through diplomatic channels thirty days before entering the Soviet territorial sea.[19] This new requirement was a dramatic change in Soviet policy. Prior to World War II, Soviet laws and regulations had always recognized the unimpeded right of innocent passage of foreign warships through the territorial sea.[20]

During the Cold War the U.S. Navy conducted maritime operations in the Black Sea, in order to "show the flag" and exercise its navigational rights and freedoms. For example, from January 10 to 13, 1966, the cruiser USS *Yarnell* (CG 17) and destroyer USS *Forrest Royal* (DD 872) operated in the Black Sea to exercise freedom of the seas and collect intelligence. Soviet warships and aircraft monitored the American ships from the time they entered the Black Sea until they exited the Bosporus.[21] A month later, on February 9, 1966, the destroyer USS *Corry* (DD 817) entered the Black Sea to show the flag and was overflown by Soviet Air Force surveillance aircraft.[22] Similarly, on December 9, 1968, the USS *Dyess* (DD/DDR 880) and USS *Turner* (DD/DDR 834), both radar picket destroyers, conducted a three-day presence operation in the Black Sea off the coasts of Turkey and the Soviet Union. Soviet vessels shadowed them; Moscow called their maneuvers a "provocative sortie."[23]

– – – – • – – – –

The Black Sea was not the only place where American and Soviet ships and aircraft had close encounters. During the second week of May 1967, Soviet warships operating close to the aircraft carrier USS *Hornet* (CV 12) in the Sea of Japan collided with the destroyer USS *Walker* (DD 517), which had maneuvered to stop the Soviet ships from disrupting the carrier's flight operations.[24] Two weeks later, on May 25, 1968, a Soviet Tu-16 Badger bomber made several close passes of the aircraft carrier USS *Essex* (CV 9) and then crashed into the Norwegian Sea, killing the entire crew.[25] These incidents are illustrative of more than a decade of unsafe incidents initiated by the Soviet Union against U.S. ships and air-craft, including intentional shouldering (bumping) of surface ships, close passes by low-flying aircraft, simulated surface and air attacks, and other threatening maneuvers. In an effort to lower the temperature between their forces, the Americans and Soviets negotiated the Incidents at Sea (INCSEA) Agreement.

The INCSEA negotiations began in earnest in 1971, the first round in Moscow. The parties met in Washington, D.C., in early 1972 for the second and final round. On May 25, 1972, Secretary of the Navy John Warner and Soviet admiral Sergei Gorshkov signed the agreement, which immediately entered into force. (In 1973, the parties added a protocol that extended INCSEA's prohibition on simulated attacks to commercial ships.)[26] The agreement proved practical and durable. Later that year, more than 150 American and Soviet ships deployed to the eastern Mediterranean in support of their respective allies during the Yom Kippur War. Although tensions between the two superpowers were elevated, no serious incidents occurred between them, thanks in part to INCSEA. The Russian Federation took up the agreement when the Soviet Union dissolved; with few exceptions, both sides have generally lived up to their obligations for more than forty years. The INCSEA Agreement has achieved its intended purpose of significantly reducing incidents involving unsafe and unprofessional conduct when American and Russian forces operate in close proximity on the high seas.

While Washington and Moscow were immersed in INCSEA discussions, the member states of the International Maritime Organization (IMO) were negotiating the International Regulations for Preventing Collisions at Sea (COLREGS). The IMO adopted these new "rules of the road" on October 20, 1972, some five months after the INCSEA negotiations ended.[27] COLREGS did not enter into force until 1977, but in the meantime the two superpowers were obliged by article 18 of the Vienna Convention on the Law of Treaties to refrain from acts that would defeat their "object and purpose."[28] (This provision ensures that states respect treaties that they have signed but are not yet in force.) Furthermore, article II of INCSEA specifically requires ship commanding officers to observe strictly the letter and spirit of COLREGS.

INCSEA's specific requirements include:

• When operating in close proximity, ships shall remain well clear to avoid risk of collision.

- When operating in the vicinity of a formation, ships shall avoid maneuvering in a manner that would hinder the evolutions of the formation.
- Ship formations shall not conduct maneuvers in internationally recognized traffic-separation schemes.
- Ships engaged in surveillance shall stay at a distance that avoids the risk of collision and shall avoid executing maneuvers that embarrass or endanger the ship under surveillance.
- When operating in sight of one another, ships shall use signals prescribed in COLREGS, the International Code of Signals (ICS), or other mutually agreed signals.
- Ships shall not simulate attacks, launch any object in the direction of a passing ship, or illuminate the navigation bridge of a passing ship.
- When conducting operations with submerged submarines, exercising ships shall show the appropriate signals prescribed by the ICS.
- When approaching ships engaged in launching or recovering aircraft and replenishment under way, ships shall take appropriate measures not to hinder maneuvers of such ships and shall remain well clear.[29]

The INCSEA Agreement also calls on aircraft to be cautious in approaching other aircraft and ships of the other party, in particular ships launching or recovering aircraft.[30] The agreement also prohibits simulated attacks against aircraft or ships, aerobatics over ships, and the dropping of objects that may be a hazard to a ship or to navigation.[31] Finally, the agreement requires notices to mariners and airmen in advance of any activity on the high seas that might be dangerous to navigation or flight.[32] (The International Maritime Organization and the International Civil Aviation Organization also require such notices.)[33]

Notwithstanding, U.S. freedom of navigation operations in the Black Sea continued unabated, closely monitored (and at times harassed) by Soviet naval and air forces. For example, on August 1, 1979, the destroyer USS

Caron (DD 970) and guided-missile destroyer USS *Farragut* (DDG 37) entered the Black Sea on a presence mission. The Soviet Union sent a number of military aircraft, including supersonic Tu-22M Backfire strike bombers, to track and monitor them. According to Pentagon officials, Soviet aircraft staged more than thirty simulated missile attacks against U.S. warships.[34]

– – – – • – – – –

The U.S. freedom of navigation patrols began in 1979, just as a diplomatic engagement of a different sort was winding down. The Third UN Conference on the Law of the Sea had begun in 1973, and by 1977 the bulk of the treaty had been codified in the Informal Composite Negotiating Text, the basis of what would be the United Nations Convention on the Law of the Sea (UNCLOS).[35] The Soviet Union was even more dependent upon freedom of navigation than the United States, as it lacked convenient access to the high seas from its major fleet concentrations at Murmansk on the Arctic Ocean, Sevastopol on the Black Sea, and Vladivostok on the Sea of Japan. While not above scoring diplomatic points with developing countries at the expense of the United States, Russia was a member of the "Group of Five" major maritime powers that championed freedom of the seas. The new treaty resolved a long-standing debate over whether coastal states may require foreign warships to notify them as a condition of innocent passage in their territorial sea.[36] With the agreement, the shape of coastal state rights and responsibilities in the territorial sea, particularly concerning innocent passage by foreign warships, became even more firmly established in the canon of oceans law.

During the negotiations, some states attempted (but failed) to assemble a majority in favor of prior notification or authorization in article 21, which authorizes the coastal state to adopt laws and regulations relating to innocent passage through the territorial sea.[37] Most countries, including the United States, the Soviet Union, and the other major maritime powers, opposed such conditions on innocent passage. Faced with insuperable opposition from the world's largest navies and most powerful states, the proponents of prior notice or consent did not push their proposal on article 21 to a vote.[38] Shortly before

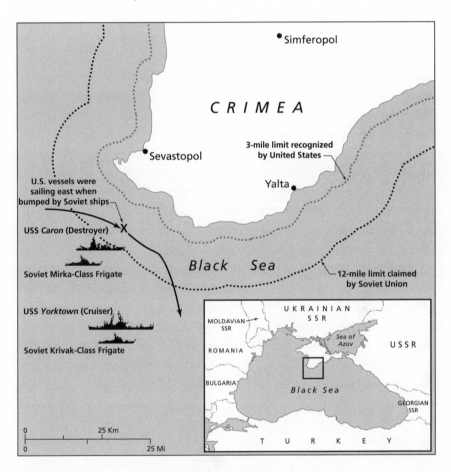

Simferopol

CRIMEA

3-mile limit recognized
by United States

Sevastopol

Yalta

U.S. vessels were
sailing east when
bumped by Soviet ships

USS *Caron* (Destroyer)

Soviet Mirka-Class Frigate

Black   Sea

12-mile limit claimed
by Soviet Union

USS *Yorktown* (Cruiser)

Soviet Krivak-Class Frigate

UKRAINIAN
SSR

MOLDAVIAN
SSR

Sea of
Azov

USSR

ROMANIA

BULGARIA

Black Sea

GEORGIAN
SSR

TURKEY

0   25 Km
0   25 Mi

MAP 5. BLACK SEA BUMPING INCIDENT, FEBRUARY 12, 1988

the conclusion of the negotiations, the conference's president, Ambassador Tommy Koh, confirmed the matter on the record: "The Convention is quite clear on this point. Warships do, like other ships, have a right of innocent passage through the territorial sea, and there is no need for warships to acquire the prior consent or even notification of the coastal State."[39]

Concurrently, in November 1982, the Supreme Soviet (the USSR's legislature) adopted the Law of the Union of Soviet Socialist Republics on the State Frontier of the USSR, which repealed the 1960 law on the state boundary.[40] Article 5 of the new law established a twelve-nautical-mile territorial sea, consistent with article 3 of UNCLOS. Article 13 recognized the right of innocent passage for foreign warships, "in accordance with the procedures to be established by the Council of Ministers of the USSR."[41] The USSR Council of Ministers (the senior executive and administrative organ of the Soviet government) adopted on April 28 implementing regulations that reversed the consent regime of the 1960 rules.[42] For the most part, the 1983 rules reflected the balance of interests expressed in UNCLOS.[43] One provision, however, proved to be problematic.

Article 13 provided, in part, that "the innocent passage of foreign warships through the territorial waters of the USSR for the purpose of traversing the territorial waters ... without entering internal waters and ports" was limited to five designated routes in the Baltic Sea, the Sea of Okhotsk, and the Sea of Japan.[44] Soviet officials interpreted these provisions as restricting innocent passage to these routes.[45] That made innocent passage by foreign warships along most of the Soviet Union's expansive coastline subject to prior approval—a position inimical to America's interests in freedom of navigation and to the global mobility of its armed forces. Neither UNCLOS nor customary international law recognizes the right of a coastal state to limit innocent passage of foreign warships to particular routes unless for safety.[46] Accordingly, the United States began to challenge the new rules under the FON program.

On February 18, 1984, Soviet aircraft harassed the destroyer USS *David R. Ray* (DD 971) in the Black Sea near Novorossiysk. A helicopter taking photographs came to within thirty feet of the ship's deck. Other Soviet aircraft fired cannon rounds into the destroyer's wake.[47] The *David R. Ray*, as it happened, and the Soviets surely would have known, was the Navy's primary test platform for the Rolling Airframe Missile (RAM) System, an autonomous fire-and-forget, inner-layer air-defense capability. INCSEA applies only on the high seas, but American defense officials viewed this incident near the coast as a violation of the "spirit" of the agreement.[48]

- - - - • - - - -

Two years later, on March 10, 1986, the cruiser USS *Yorktown* (CG 48) and destroyer USS *Caron* entered the Black Sea.[49] The Soviet frigate *Ladnyi* (801) immediately shadowed them. Three days later, at 11:11 a.m., the American warships entered the Soviet territorial sea, steaming westward along the southern Crimean Peninsula. They approached within six miles of the coast.[50] The *Ladnyi* informed the *Yorktown* and *Caron* that they had violated Soviet territorial waters and ordered them to depart immediately. Soviet Border Guard vessels and aircraft were dispatched to the scene, while Black Sea air and naval forces were placed on combat readiness.[51] (The Border Guard belonged to the Committee of State Security—Komitet Gosudarstvennoy Bezopasnosti, or KGB—not the Soviet navy.) The Americans acknowledged the warning but maintained course and speed until they left the territorial sea two hours and twenty-one minutes later.[52]

The Soviet government diplomatically protested the transit as "provocative" and warned the United States against "serious consequences," for which Washington would bear responsibility.[53] Admiral V. N. Chernavin, commander in chief of the Soviet navy, suggested that the American warships "might have been attacked had they remained longer in Soviet waters."[54] The Soviet Ministry of Foreign Affairs (MFA) held two press conferences "to emphasize its displeasure" and convey to the United States "the gravity of the situation." The MFA stressed that where the U.S. "violation" had occurred there were "no traditional seaways."[55] Admiral Chernavin elaborated on this point, claiming that innocent passage of foreign warships in the territorial sea was permitted only in "specially authorized coastal areas" designated by the government of the USSR; there being no such areas in the

Black Sea, the U.S. transit was unlawful.[56] Admiral Chernavin and the MFA were, of course, referring to the 1983 Rules for Navigation and Sojourn of Foreign Warships in the Territorial Waters (Territorial Sea) and Internal Waters and Ports of the USSR, which was precisely what the *Caron* and *Yorktown* had been sent to challenge.

Defense analyst William Arkin criticized the American operation as a potentially unlawful exercise in intelligence collection: "If the radio shack[s] on the U.S. warships were listening to anything from the coastal State not directly aimed at them, if the officers on the bridge were scanning the land, or if . . . any other activity not having a direct bearing on passage" was involved, the passage was not innocent.[57] The U.S. Navy replied that it was sensitive to the prohibition against intelligence collection in the territorial sea and had not violated it.[58] In any case, the Soviet government never accused the U.S. warships of collecting intelligence during the transit, despite the fact that both American vessels were equipped to do so.

The *Caron*, in particular, was renowned for its intelligence-collection experience, having conducted forty-three surveillance operations off the coasts of numerous nations, including three in the Black Sea over the previous decade.[59] American naval authorities admitted that the *Caron* carried extra electronic sensors and listening devices during the Black Sea operations. Still, they insisted that both the *Yorktown* and *Caron* were simply exercising their rights in the Soviet territorial sea in accord with international law. The ships were not permitted to engage in "any act aimed at collecting information to the prejudice of the defense or security of the coastal State."[60] The White House added that the operation was "routine and not intended to be provocative or defiant," as alleged by the Soviet government.[61] A subsequent statement by the State Department similarly emphasized that the purpose of the FON program "was to uphold the exercise and preservation of navigation and overflight rights and freedoms around the world."[62]

— — — • — — —

Despite the 1986 warning that violation of Soviet laws regarding the USSR's territorial sea could have "serious consequences," another Black

Sea FON operation was planned for February 1988. Ironically, the two ships chosen were the *Yorktown* and *Caron*, the same vessels that had conducted the 1986 challenge. They entered the Black Sea on February 10. Immediately, three Soviet naval vessels—the Krivak-class frigate *Bezzavetnyi*, Mirka-class frigate *SKR 6*, and an intelligence ship—shadowed the U.S. warships. Two days later, the *Caron* and *Yorktown* intentionally crossed into the Soviet territorial sea near Sevastopol. Within minutes, a flotilla of eighteen Soviet naval and Border Guard vessels positioned to surround the U.S. warships.

The *Caron* was informed by the *Bezzavetnyi* that the Soviet ships had orders to prevent violation of territorial waters."[63] The *Caron* gave the boilerplate reply that it was "engaged in innocent passage consistent with international law" and continued on its course.[64] Soviet ships shadowed and monitored the *Caron*'s movements until it approached within 10.5 nm of the Soviet coast, when a Mirka frigate bearing the hull number 824 intentionally glided into or bumped the *Caron*'s port side.[65] The U.S. warship carried on, leaving Soviet territorial waters about two hours later without further incident. The *Caron*'s closest point of approach to the Crimean Peninsula was 7.5 nm; its side suffered minimal damage, and no one was injured.

Meanwhile, the *Bezzavetnyi* contacted the *Yorktown* and ordered it to leave Soviet territorial waters or be collided with.[66] The *Yorktown*, 10.6 nm off the coast of Crimea, acknowledged the transmission but continued steadily on. Shortly thereafter, the Krivak frigate intentionally shouldered the American warship.[67] The *Yorktown* sustained minor damage to its port side and two Harpoon surface-to-surface missile canisters.[68] Approximately ten minutes later the Krivak frigate once again contacted the *Yorktown*: "We will strike you as before if you do not clear our waters."[69] This time the *Yorktown* did not acknowledge the transmission; it exited Soviet territorial waters an hour and a half later without further incident.

Although damage to the American and Soviet warships was minimal and neither side suffered injuries, the episode produced a flurry of diplomatic démarches.[70] The Soviet Union delivered a protest to the American ambassador, Jack Maddock, and laid blame squarely on the *Caron* and *York-town*. The protest stated that they "did not react to signals given by a Soviet Border Guard ship in advance to warn them of their approaching the state border of the U.S.S.R. and did not make suggested changes in their course. . . . [A] considerable distance inside Soviet territorial waters, the American naval ships executed dangerous maneuvering, which led to a collision with Soviet naval ships. . . . Responsibility for the provocation . . . lies entirely and fully on the American side."[71]

The Soviet Ministry of Defense issued a similar complaint, blaming the U.S. warships for not reacting to "warning signals of Soviet Border Guard ships" and for "dangerously maneuvering in Soviet waters."[72] The Soviet Union based its protest on four major arguments. First, Moscow argued, the FON operation had been conducted for political purposes, to undermine recent glimmers of improvement in bilateral relations.[73] Given that goal, the transit had not been innocent. Second, unlike the Black Sea affair of 1986, Soviet officials claimed that the American warships were collecting intelligence, in violation of UNCLOS.[74] Third, the Soviet Union charged, the American transit had been in violation of the 1982 Soviet law and 1983 Soviet rules, it having occurred outside of designated routes.[75] Finally, the passage was not innocent, because it had been "navigationally unnecessary"—that is, the U.S. warships could have remained on the high seas.[76] The United States, lacking a specific navigational purpose for the transit, had not been entitled to innocent passage.

Under Secretary of State for Political Affairs Michael Armacost delivered Washington's own protest to Soviet ambassador Yuri V. Dubinin. It insisted that when the incident occurred the U.S. warships had been in innocent passage in the Soviet territorial sea. Secretary of State George Shultz later stated that the FON program was supported by the "President and his Cabinet." He explained that because the United States had a complex and sensitive political relationship with the USSR, the deliberate entry into Soviet waters had been subjected to "particularly rigorous scrutiny," both prior to and during the transit. "But we cannot exempt the Soviets from the [FON] program," he insisted, as "to do so would accede to their illegal maritime claims."[77] Secretary of Defense Frank C. Carlucci echoed Shultz's position in testimony before the Senate Armed Services Committee, stating that the freedom of navigation operation was not a test of Soviet territorial waters but rather an exercise of the right of innocent passage.

> Under international law . . . [the Soviet Union] had no right to attempt to impede our ships or to use force. Force is only warranted when there is a threat, and these ships were clearly engaged in innocent passage. Our view is that unless you exercise the right of freedom of navigation, inevitably you lose it. You can always find reasons for not doing it at some particular point in time, but if we start backing off we will eventually lose some of the rights that are absolutely essential for our freedom of navigation.[78]

The U.S. protest underscored that the Soviet ships had warned that they had been "authorized to strike," a clear indication that the collisions were deliberate.[79] In addition, American officials vehemently denied that the *Caron* and *Yorktown* had been collecting intelligence in the territorial sea of the Soviet Union.[80] More important, the United States argued once again, there was no basis in customary international law or UNCLOS to limit the innocent passage of warships to predesignated routes as claimed by the Soviet Union.

At the same time, American officials recognized the right of the Soviet Union to adopt laws and regulations as provided in UNCLOS article 21.[81] They acknowledged that the Soviet Union could impose sea-lane restrictions based on safety considerations, as provided in article 22: "The coastal State may, where necessary having regard to the safety of navigation, require foreign ships exercising the right of innocent passage through its territorial sea to use such sea lanes and traffic separation schemes as it may designate or prescribe for the regulation of the passage of ships."[82]

State Department officials, however, emphasized that the 1982 law and 1983 rules violated international law, by purporting to prohibit innocent passage.[83] Assistant Secretary of Defense for International Security Affairs

Richard Armitage added that whether or not the transits had been necessary for navigation, they had been "innocent" within the meaning of UNCLOS so long as they were not prejudicial to the peace, good order, or security of the USSR.[84]

— — — — ● — — — —

Following the diplomatic exchanges after the Black Sea FON operation of 1986, American and Soviet military officials agreed to begin a series of exchanges outside the scope of the annual INCSEA review to improve military-to-military relations and reduce potentially dangerous activities.[85] The 1988 incident reinvigorated these discussions, as both sides sought to reach a mutual understanding on innocent passage and avoid further incidents that might lead to conflict.[86] In July 1988, the chairman of the Joint Chiefs of Staff, Adm. William Crowe, and his Soviet counterpart, Marshal Sergei Akhromeyev, chief of the General Staff, announced that the United States and the USSR would implement a new regime to avoid provocations when their armed forces operated in close proximity to each other. They established a joint military-to-military working group, separate from the existing INCSEA structure. Less than a year later, Admiral Crowe and the new chief of the General Staff, Colonel General Mikhail Moiseyev, signed the Dangerous Military Activities (DMA) Agreement.[87] Each party agreed to take measures to prevent dangerous military activities arising from entry into the territory of the other, unintentionally or by force majeure. The agreement also regulated the use of lasers in a manner that could harm the other side's military personnel or equipment; hampering of the other party in a designated area; or interference with command-and-control networks.[88] The militaries also agreed to take steps to resolve quickly by peaceful means any incidents.[89]

The DMA stipulates that the armed forces of each party "shall exercise great caution and prudence" when operating near the territory of the other.[90] Specific communications and protocols are laid down for units entering territorial waters accidentally or involuntarily.[91] The DMA Agreement also regulates the use of lasers.[92] If armed forces of one side believe that the other is using lasers dangerously, they can immediately request that it desist. The side using the laser is then obliged to investigate the circumstances and, if in fact it could harm persons or equipment of the other side, cease its use.[93]

The DMA authorizes "special caution areas," to be designated mutually by the parties.[94] Communications channels and protocols were to be established as set forth in annex I of the agreement, aside from other measures agreed upon to prevent dangerous activities and resolve incidents.

Article VI focuses on interference with command and control. If one side detects activity that could harm its network or damage equipment, it "may inform the . . . other Party if they believe that the interference is being caused by such personnel and equipment of the armed forces of that Party." Article VI places a specific and positive obligation on forces to act quickly to stop the interference" once it is demonstrated that "the interference with the command and control networks is being caused by their activities."

Much like INCSEA, the DMA established a Joint Military Commission to ensure compliance with the agreement and consider ways to improve bilateral coordination.[95] The DMA, however, does not abrogate or otherwise affect the other agreements, such as INCSEA, or the respective rights of freedom of navigation or self-defense.[96] The text underscores that the United States will continue to conduct freedom of navigation operations. Accordingly, when the agreement was concluded there remained a need to settle the legal contours of the right of innocent passage.

– – – – • – – – –

Consultations over innocent passage went forward accordingly, and it became evident to both sides that a "uniform," or shared, interpretation would benefit the bilateral relationship.[97] The discussions were facilitated by consensus that part II of UNCLOS, on the territorial sea, reflected international law and state practice and consequently were used as the point of departure. The discussions ultimately led to the signing, by Secretary of State James Baker and Soviet foreign minister Eduard Shevardnadze, of the Jackson Hole Agreement in September 1989.[98] A "Joint Statement" confirmed that both states accepted UNCLOS as an important part of international law and state practice. This point was reiterated in the annexed "Uniform Interpretation," that "the relevant rules of international law governing innocent passage of ships in the territorial sea are stated in . . . [UNCLOS], particularly in Part II, Section 3 [concerning innocent passage]."[99] The Joint Statement further expressed the sense of both superpowers that all states should harmonize their internal laws, regulations and practices with UNCLOS.[100]

The United States met its goals in the negotiations. In the end, the Soviet Union agreed completely with the U.S. position that "all ships, including warships, regardless of cargo, armament or means of propulsion, enjoy the right of innocent passage through the territorial sea."[101] Furthermore, it acknowledged that coastal states may not require either prior notification or authorization for such transits.[102] The Uniform Interpretation also stated that article 19(2) of UNCLOS contained an "exhaustive list" of activities that render passage not innocent, such as collection of intelligence or launching aircraft. The agreement concluded that a ship passing through the territorial sea is in innocent passage so long as it does not engage in any of the prohibited activities that are set forth in article 19(2). The subsection of the article states:[103]

(a) Any threat or use of force against the sovereignty, territorial integrity or political independence of the coastal State, or in any other manner in violation of the principles of international law embodied in the Charter of the United Nations

(b) Any exercise or practice with weapons of any kind

(c) Any act aimed at collecting information to the prejudice of the defense or security of the coastal State

(d) Any act of propaganda aimed at affecting the defense or security of the coastal State

(e) The launching, landing or taking on board of any aircraft

(f) The launching, landing or taking on board of any military device

(g) The loading or unloading of any commodity, currency or person contrary to the customs, fiscal, immigration or sanitary laws and regulations of the coastal State

(h) Any act of willful and serious pollution contrary to this Convention

(i) Any fishing activities

(j) The carrying out of research or survey activities

(k) Any act aimed at interfering with any systems of communication or any other facilities or installations of the coastal State

(l) Any other activity not having a direct bearing on passage.

The Uniform Interpretation also recognized the authority under part II of UNCLOS of a coastal state to adopt laws and regulations affecting innocent passage.[104] "These include rules requiring ships exercising the right of innocent passage . . . to use such sea lanes and traffic separation schemes as it may prescribe where needed to protect safety of navigation."[105] This provision recognized Russia's legal competence to establish sea lanes in the territorial sea. Nevertheless, in keeping with the American position regarding the Black Sea, the agreement made clear that along those areas of the coast where no such sea lanes or traffic-separation schemes exist, ships still enjoy the right of innocent passage.[106] Coastal states' laws and regulations "may not have the practical effect of denying or impairing" the right of innocent passage of foreign-flagged ships.[107] This text mirrors article 24 of UNCLOS, which forbids coastal states from hampering innocent passage of a foreign ship through their territorial sea, except in certain cases involving crimes committed on board a merchant ship. In particular, coastal state laws may not impose requirements on foreign ships having the "practical effect of denying or impairing" the right of innocent passage.

To avoid a repeat of the Black Sea bumping incident, the Uniform Interpretation states that if a coastal state questions the "innocence" of a particular transit it "shall inform the ship of the reason why" and provide the vessel with an opportunity to "clarify its intentions or correct its conduct in a reasonably short period of time."[108] The Uniform Interpretation also authorizes the coastal state to require a warship to leave the territorial sea if it violates local laws or regulations or its activities render the passage not innocent.[109] This text tracks with part II of UNCLOS, which states "in such case the warship shall do so [leave territorial waters] immediately."[110] Paragraph 8 of the U.S.A.-USSR agreement calls on the parties to refrain from threats or the use of force and instead use diplomacy to resolve disagreements.

Five days after the Jackson Hole Agreement was signed, the Department of State notified all American diplomatic posts that the Soviet Union's 1983 rules had been brought into conformity with UNCLOS. At the same time, the U.S. government assured the USSR that American warships would no longer exercise the right of innocent passage under the FON program in the Soviet territorial sea, with the caveat that "warships of both countries retained the right to conduct innocent passage incidental to normal navigation in the territorial sea" and that the United States "would continue to conduct routine operations in the Black Sea."[111]

– – – – • – – – –

In combination, INCSEA, the DMA, and the Jackson Hole Agreement succeeded in reducing naval incidents between the United States and the Soviet Union.[112] Moreover, the Soviet Union's reversal of its position on prior notice as a condition of innocent passage shows the effectiveness of the FON program and the Black Sea presence operations. Building on the success of INCSEA, the DMA enhanced safety of navigation and overflight. For the next forty years, it all but eliminated unsafe and unprofessional aerobatics and ship handling when American and Soviet (later Russian) naval forces encountered one another at sea or in the air.

Similarly, the Jackson Hole Agreement resulted in a number of immediate benefits that are still relevant. Even though the agreement was only a bilateral arrangement, it represented the shared view of the world's two preeminent naval powers and thus significantly contributed to the development of the law governing innocent passage that is accepted globally. First, it asserted the unrestricted right of innocent passage for warships. Second, it encouraged compliance with the navigational regimes set forth in

UNCLOS. Finally, it affirmed the value of negotiation to resolve maritime disputes. Today the agreement represents a model that should be applied in disagreements over navigational rights and freedoms in the South China Sea and East China Sea.

– – – – • – – – –

Despite these Cold War successes and improvement in U.S.-Russian relations following the breakup of the Soviet Union in 1991, in recent years there has been a resurgence of unprofessional and unsafe encounters between Russian and American naval ships and aircraft. Tensions have risen especially since Russia intervened in the Ukraine and annexed the Crimean Peninsula in March 2014. These aggressive practices undermine relations between the two greatest nuclear powers and could produce a serious miscalculation with devastating consequences.

In April 2014, a Russian Su-24 Fencer attack aircraft made twelve low-level passes near the guided-missile destroyer USS *Donald Cook* (DDG 75) at an altitude of about five hundred feet. The *Donald Cook* was on station in the Black Sea to reassure allies after Russia invaded the Crimea that March. The *Cook* made several unsuccessful attempts to contact the Russian jet by radio. American defense officials labeled the close encounter as "provocative and unprofessional," inconsistent with the bilateral protocols between the two armed forces.[113] The Russian foreign minister, Sergei Lavrov, accused the United States of violating the 1936 Montreux Convention by allowing the *Cook* to remain in the Black Sea more than twenty-one days. (That convention provides that "vessels of war belonging to non–Black Sea Powers shall not remain in the Black Sea more than twenty-one days, whatever be the object of their presence there.")[114] A similar incident occurred in June 2015, when an Su-24 buzzed the guided-missile destroyer USS *Ross* (DDG 71) in international waters about twenty-five miles south of the Crimea Peninsula. A video of the incident taken by the *Ross*'s crew shows the Russian jet flying about five hundred meters off the starboard side at an altitude of about six hundred feet. Russia did not deny that the incident occurred and later even claimed that it had forced the *Ross* to alter course away from

Russian territorial waters. U.S. Navy officials denied the latter, stating the American warship had stayed on course and proceeded on its mission.[115]

On April 11, 2016, two Russian Fencers buzzed the *Donald Cook* some twenty times in international waters in the Baltic Sea.[116] At the time the U.S. warship was conducting deck-landing drills with a Polish helicopter. One Fencer made several close, low passes—one within thirty feet—of the destroyer in simulated attacks. As a safety precaution, the *Cook*'s commanding officer suspended flight operations until the Russian aircraft left the area. The next day, two Ka-27 naval antisubmarine-warfare helicopters approached the *Cook*, took photographs, and ran a simulated surface ship attack profile. The Russian helicopters came in so low that they created wakes in the water.[117] U.S. European Command expressed concern about the unsafe maneuvers and warned that aggressive overflight could result in a miscalculation or accident causing serious injury or death.[118] The incidents were protested through diplomatic channels, and the U.S. Navy raised them at the annual INCSEA talks.[119]

In two separate incidents in April 2016, Russian fighter aircraft maneuvered erratically near American reconnaissance aircraft on patrol in international airspace over the Baltic Sea. In the first encounter, an Su-27 Flanker barrel-rolled over a Rivet Joint RC-135—that is, the Russian fighter came within twenty-five feet of the U.S. plane, then rolled upside down over it to the other side, risking the lives of both crews.[120] In a second incident, on April 14, a Russian Flanker aggressively approached another RC-135 to within fifty feet of the aircraft's left wingtip before, once again, flying a barrel roll over it. The United States protested, but the Kremlin denied that the incident had occurred, insisting that the Flanker had "performed strictly in accordance with the international regulations on the use of airspace."[121]

Several months later, in September 2016, a Russian Su-27 came within ten feet of a U.S. Navy P-8 maritime patrol aircraft on a routine patrol in international airspace, this time over the Black Sea, some forty miles south of the Crimea Peninsula. The Russians later claimed it did so because the Navy airplane was flying with its transponder turned off. The transponder would ordinarily automatically transmit identifying data when interrogated by radio. American officials did not clarify whether the P-8 had been operating its transponder, simply pointing out that there is no legal requirement for military aircraft to keep their transponders on. The ICAO Rules of the Air require civilian aircraft to carry transponders for safety of navigation;[122] military aircraft, however, are exempted from these rules by the Convention on International Civil Aviation.[123] American officials expressed concern at the unsafe maneuver, that it could have resulted in a "miscalculation or accident."[124]

Similarly, on February 10, 2017, the USS *Porter* (DDG 78) was harassed, again in the Black Sea, by a Russian Il-38 antisubmarine maritime patrol aircraft and three Su-24 Fencers. The four Russian aircraft buzzed the *Porter*, which was in international waters following an exercise with Romania. Russia denied it, but the United States had photographic evidence that the Russian aircraft had acted unsafely and unprofessionally. Gen. Joe Dunford, chairman of the Joint Chiefs of Staff, was already scheduled to meet with his counterpart, General Valeriy Gerasimov, chief of the Russian General Staff, in Baku, Azerbaijan, on February 16. As called for by the INCSEA and DMA agreements, the two sides discussed how to implement clear tactical military-to-military communication to avoid an incident.[125]

On May 9, 2017, a Russian Su-27 fighter armed with six missiles flew within twenty feet of an American P-8A reconnaissance aircraft in the Black Sea.[126] The two aircraft flew wingtip to wingtip twenty feet apart for several minutes. The incident occurred just one day before Lavrov visited Washington. Despite the close approach, the U.S. military described the encounter as "safe and professional." Four days later an armed Russian fighter flew within forty feet of another P-8A about thirty miles from Russia and a hundred miles from the strategic naval base in Crimea.[127] As the United States and Russia confront one another in Europe, Syria, and elsewhere, risky interceptions at sea are becoming commonplace.

The return to Cold War antics not only draws into question Russia's stature as a responsible state but raises concerns that it seeks to alter the rules-based legal order that has governed the world's oceans for hundreds of years. Russia's defiance of international law and its disturbing pattern of unprofessional behavior undermine the rule of law and liberal order of the oceans. If left unchecked, it will erode the balance of interests that was crafted during the nine-year negotiations that led to the adoption of UNCLOS. Accordingly, it is imperative for the United States, as the preeminent world maritime power, to counter the Russian threat by continuing to exercise its rights and freedoms in the world's oceans. The U.S. naval operations of the 1980s in the Black Sea had short-term costs in terms of diplomatic fallout, yet they were necessary to preserve the United States' enduring and non-negotiable rights at sea. Likewise, the challenges posed by Russia today can be addressed through resolute exercise of navigational rights.

"FREEDOM OF NAVIGATION WITH CHINESE CHARACTERISTICS"

(2001–Present)

A s a continental power, China fears it is vulnerable to coastal blockade. Its land boundaries are shared by fourteen states, yet China
has outstanding disputes with only three: India, Bhutan, and North
Korea. Among these, only the boundary dispute with India is volatile.
Having secured such relatively stable land borders, China has in recent
years focused on consolidating what it views as more permeable maritime
borders. As China's power grew in the 1990s, Beijing began to assert broad
expansive and unlawful claims over the East China Sea and South China
Sea. China's strategy is driven by its geographic position—hemmed in on
the Asian continent by the long island chain that stretches from Russia's
Kamchatka Peninsula through Japan and the Ryukyu Islands, Taiwan, and
the Philippines. The islands are seen as a natural geographical obstacle
blocking China's access to the open ocean.

This chapter offers two case studies illustrating China's efforts to
establish its maritime claims. First, Chinese fighter jets intercepted a U.S.
EP-3 maritime surveillance aircraft in 2001, igniting a dispute over the
legal regime that applies to military aircraft flying in international airspace

adjacent to the coastline. China now routinely interferes with American ships and aircraft in the East China Sea and South China Sea.[1] Second, the chapter explores China's campaign to eject U.S. military survey ships from the East China Sea, Yellow Sea, and South China Sea, in a bid to alter the legal regime that applies to foreign warships operating offshore and outside of territorial seas. These maritime confrontations often have occurred in China's 200-nm exclusive economic zone (EEZ). In great measure, China's interference with American warships and military aircraft arises from its expansive notion of its legal competence to regulate foreign military activities in its EEZ.

— — — — • — — — —

The EEZ was devised by the architects of the United Nations Convention on the Law of the Sea (UNCLOS) for the sole purpose of granting coastal states control over the living and nonliving resources adjacent to their coasts.[2] Coastal states enjoy "sovereign rights" in the EEZ for the purpose of "exploring, exploiting, conserving and managing" these natural resources; those rights include jurisdiction over most offshore installations and structures, marine scientific research (MSR), and limited jurisdiction concerning the protection and preservation of the marine environment.[3] Coastal states also exercise authority in the EEZ over such related activities as production of energy from the water, currents, and winds.[4]

Importantly, however, coastal states exercise "sovereign rights" in the EEZ, not "sovereignty."[5] The broader and more comprehensive right of "sovereignty" exists only in the 12-nm territorial sea.[6] Unlike the territorial sea, in the EEZ foreign states enjoy freedoms of navigation and overflight as if on the high seas, and other internationally lawful uses of the seas related to those freedoms, such as operating ships and aircraft and the laying of submarine cables and pipelines. These "other internationally lawful uses of the seas" capture a broad range of military activities, including but not limited to intelligence collection; sensitive reconnaissance operations (SRO); intelligence, surveillance, and reconnaissance (ISR) operations; military marine data collection; and naval oceanographic surveys.[7]

– – – – • – – – –

In the early 2000s, U.S. military aircraft conducted about two hundred SRO flights off the Chinese coast every year.[8] Chinese fighter aircraft intercepted about one-third of these flights, and most of these interceptions were conducted in a professional and safe manner. Nonetheless, at a May 2000 meeting of the Military Maritime Consultative Agreement (MMCA), People's Liberation Army Navy (PLA Navy) officers warned their American counterparts that SRO "flights were coming too close to the Chinese coast and that might cause trouble."[9] American officers dismissed the warning because the missions were conducted in international airspace. U.S. officials reiterated that the "United States had no intention of modifying its surveillance flights."[10]

But in December of that year, interceptions of U.S. aircraft by Chinese pilots based at Lingshui Air Base on Hainan Island became more aggressive.[11] Between December 2000 and April 2001, the PLA Air Force (PLAAF) intercepted forty-four SRO flights off the coast of China. The interceptions reflected a pattern of increasingly unsafe behavior by PLAAF pilots, endangering the safety of both the Chinese and the American aircraft.[12] Alarmed, Washington lodged protests with Beijing in December 2000 and January 2001, complaining that China's interceptions departed from the rules governing flights in international airspace.[13]

On the morning of April 1, 2001, an American EP-3E Aries II electronic surveillance plane was conducting a routine mission in international airspace approximately eighty miles south-southeast of Hainan Island. The EP-3, a four-engine turboprop aircraft, has a normal complement of seventeen enlisted personnel and seven officers and a range of about three thousand nautical miles. At about 0915, two PLAAF F-8 fighters based at Lingshui aggressively intercepted the U.S. aircraft.[14] After making two close approaches—as close as between three and five feet—the pilot of one of the F-8s lost control of his aircraft as he passed under the EP-3's left wing.[15] The tail of his aircraft hit the EP-3's left outboard propeller, which cut the F-8 in half. The Chinese pilot ejected over the South China Sea.[16] China refused American offers to assist in search and rescue, and he was ultimately presumed dead.[17]

The U.S. aircraft, which suffered extensive damage to its nose cone and the number-one propeller and lost its wing flaps and airspeed indicator, went into a steep nosedive.[18] After regaining control, the pilot, Lt. Shane Osborn, USN, broadcast a Mayday over the international air-distress frequency and made an emergency landing at the PLAAF base at Lingshui.[19] There, PLA soldiers detained the crew.[20] Astonishingly, none of its twenty-four members were injured. For almost two weeks American officials sought to obtain the release of the aircrew and the damaged aircraft.[21] After negotiations, the crew was finally released on April 12, 2001, and the aircraft was retrieved by a transport aircraft and returned to the United States—in pieces—on July 4, 2001.[22]

The incident raised a number of legal issues, including the right of "distress entry" for military aircraft, the "sovereign immunity" of state-owned aircraft in international airspace, the right to conduct sensitive reconnaissance in international airspace over the EEZ, and protocols for the safe interception of foreign aircraft in international airspace. ("Sovereign immunity" of state aircraft, or warships, refers to immunity from the exercise of enforcement jurisdiction—that is, from arrest, attachment, or execution—in any foreign state.[23] State-owned warships and military aircraft on foreign soil are not subject to boarding by foreign authorities unless specifically invited on board.)[24]

President George W. Bush and Secretary of Defense Donald H. Rumsfeld stated that the U.S. aircraft had been flying an overt surveillance mission in international airspace.[25] The EP-3 had been "on auto pilot and . . . did not deviate from a straight and level path" until the tail of the Chinese fighter struck it.[26] Secretary Rumsfeld released a video taken on January 24, 2001, that depicted a Chinese fighter "buzzing" an American EP-3.[27] The video showed the jet, visibly unstable, approaching and attempting to hold position within a few feet of the slower American airplane. Rumsfeld commented that fighter aircraft "are not designed to fly at such low speeds."[28]

China claimed the U.S. aircraft had caused the April 1 accident when it had suddenly veered to the left, ramming the tail of the F-8.[29] The American side should "bear full responsibility for the incident."[30] The surviving Chinese pilot stated that the two F-8s had been flying about 1,300 feet from the

EP-3 at about the same speed when the U.S. aircraft suddenly swerved and rammed Lieutenant Commander Wang Wei's airplane.[31] Wang had been unable to avoid it, and the resulting collision with the EP-3's far-left propeller destroyed the F-8's vertical stabilizer, at which point it broke in half and crashed into the sea.[32] Wang was already known by the United States as a reckless fighter pilot, however; photographs from previous encounters with EP-3s showed he had flown as close as ten feet.[33]

The commander of the U.S. Pacific Command, Adm. Dennis Blair, USN, countered that "big airplanes" like the EP-3 "fly straight and level on their path" and smaller fighter aircraft "zip around them." In any case, faster and more maneuverable aircraft are obligated to stay clear of slower aircraft. "It's pretty obvious who bumped into who."[34] Admiral Blair warned Chinese authorities to "respect the integrity of the aircraft and the well-being of the crew in accordance with international guidelines" and demanded the immediate return of the airplane and its crew.[35] President Bush reiterated this message on April 4.[36]

In Beijing, hours after the collision the American ambassador to China, Adm. Joseph Prueher (USN, Ret.) met with the assistant foreign minister, Zhou Wenzhong. Prueher stated that the United States was "sorry" that the Chinese had lost an aircraft and pilot but made it clear that the EP-3 had been sovereign U.S. property and not subject to boarding or seizure. Although the ambassador was assured that the crew was "safe," he received no indication that access to them would be granted.[37] The following day Zhou and Prueher met again, and this time Zhou demanded that the United States accept full responsibility for the incident and apologize "to the Chinese people."[38]

The American defense attaché to China, Brig. Gen. Neal Sealock, USA, was allowed to meet the aircrew on April 3, but was informed that they would not be released until China had finished an investigation. The following day, the president of China, Jiang Zemin, declared that the United States should bear "full responsibility" for the collision and insisted that Washington apologize and immediately cease surveillance flights off the Chinese coast.[39] A statement issued by the Foreign Ministry that same day reported that the accident had occurred over China's EEZ and called SRO flights a threat to the nation's security.[40] The Bush administration dismissed any prospect of issuing an apology and demanded the prompt release of the crew and airplane.[41] Unhappy with this tough stance, President Jiang repeated on April 4 that the United States should "bear full responsibility for the incident and apologize."[42] Later that day, the foreign minister, Tang Jiaxuan, summoned Ambassador Prueher and delivered a clear message: "If the United States recognized its mistake and apologized, China would allow the crew to leave."[43]

– – – – • – – – –

In an effort to appease China, Secretary of State Colin Powell publicly expressed "regret" for the loss of the Chinese pilot.[44] Later that evening, the secretary followed up with a personal letter to the Chinese vice president, Qian Quchen, again expressing "regret" for the incident but also demanding the immediate release of the crew.[45] But some Chinese officials continued to demand that the United States take full responsibility for the collision and formally apologize. China conditioned access to the aircrew on greater "cooperation" by the United States.

Ambassador Prueher, a former Navy pilot, described the Chinese version of events as "physically impossible."[46] Aviation experts agreed that the EP-3 was a "big and cumbersome plane that the far more nimble Chinese jets should have been able to avoid."[47] In fact, "aviation protocol demands that the quicker plane take steps to avoid the larger, slower, aircraft."[48] As crew members later stated, "the F-8 made two passes within three to five feet of the EP-3 before colliding on the third pass."[49] American officials cited international interception procedures that emphasize the safety of both aircraft at all times in support of their assertion that China's "violation of the 'due regard' standard" was provocative and dangerous and "most probably" the cause of the crash.[50]

President Bush issued a statement on April 5 once again expressing "regret" for the loss of the Chinese pilot and his plane.[51] At the same time, however, he warned that a prolonged impasse would damage long-term U.S.-Chinese relations. The president also suggested a joint investigation

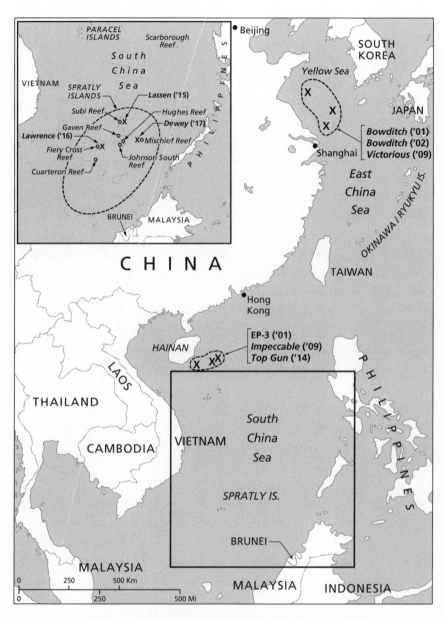

**MAP 6. CHINESE SOUTH/EAST CHINA SEA
CHALLENGES, 2001–2015**

into the incident. Meanwhile, Ambassador Prueher worked behind the scenes with Zhou Wenzhong on a five-step plan to resolve the matter. First, a portion of Powell's letter of regret to Qian would be published in the Chinese media. Second, Ambassador Prueher would issue an official public statement that America was "very sorry" for the loss of the pilot and for entering Chinese airspace without authority. Third, the aircrew would be released. Fourth, both sides would meet in Beijing to discuss ways to prevent future accidents. Fifth, the aircraft would be returned.[52]

Brigadier General Sealock and Ted Gong, a U.S. embassy consular official, met with eight crew members on April 7 and with the entire crew on the ninth and tenth.[53] On April 11, the entire crew was released, the U.S. government having stated, as arranged, that it was "very sorry" for the loss of the pilot and for the heavily damaged EP-3's entry into Chinese airspace and landing on Hainan Island without prior authorization.[54] The crew left China early the next day.

In late April, China announced that it had completed its investigation of the incident and that it would allow American inspectors to examine the damaged aircraft. On the twenty-ninth an assessment team from Okinawa flew to Hainan; it completed its inspection on May 4. The plane could have been repaired and flown out, but Beijing refused to allow that.[55] Instead, the aircraft had to be disassembled, which was done by engineers from the manufacturer, Lockheed Martin, in June. On July 4, the aircraft was loaded in sections onto a Russian-made Il-76 transport plane and returned to the United States.[56]

The MMCA took up the matter in meetings on April 18–19, 2001, and in September, where it explored several legal issues. What is the scope of the right of distress entry for military aircraft into internal waters or national airspace of a coastal state? What is the "sovereign immune" status of military aircraft that land in foreign states in distress? Are surveillance and reconnaissance lawful in international airspace? Finally, what rules govern the interception of foreign military aircraft in international airspace? These ensuing questions unfolded against the backdrop of a broader one on the legal status of the airspace above the EEZ generally.

– – – – • – – – –

The U.S. aircraft suffered catastrophic damage to two engines and its fuselage and lost its nose cone.[57] Bits of metal pierced the EP-3's fuselage, and the resulting airflow noise made it so difficult to hear that the aircrew did not know whether Lingshui had received their distress signal. It is, according to American officials, "standard procedure for a damaged plane to land at the nearest airport after issuing a mayday call."[58] Chinese authorities later denied receiving any radio communications, but when the aircraft landed, armed PLA troops were ready and on hand to greet it.[59] The Chinese were expecting them.

China justified boarding the aircraft and detaining its crew because China's territorial airspace had been violated, entered without authorization.[60] The 1944 Chicago Convention on Civil Aviation recognizes a right of "distress entry" for civil aircraft.[61] The provision does not apply, however, to "state aircraft," which it prohibits from flying over or landing in the territory of another state without prior authorization.[62] The U.S. aircraft was in extremis, however, and had no alternative but to land on Hainan Island. Therefore, its entry into Chinese national airspace for an emergency landing was fully compliant with international law, which protects seafarers and aviators in distress.[63] China did not prevent the landing or divert the aircraft as it approached, so consent for the landing could have been inferred.[64]

Experience and precedent—that is, state practice—support the U.S. position. In February 1974, for example, a Soviet ice-reconnaissance aircraft ran low on fuel off the North American coast and made an emergency landing at Gambell Airport, owned by the state of Alaska. The crew was allowed to remain overnight, was made comfortable, and supplied with space heaters and food. The next day the aircraft was refueled (with fuel flown in by an Air Force C-130) and departed without incident.[65]

A similar incident occurred in March 1994, when a Russian surveillance plane monitoring a NATO antisubmarine-warfare exercise in the North Atlantic ran low on fuel. The aircraft was forced to make an emergency landing at the U.S. air base at Thule, Greenland. The crew was fed, and the aircraft was refueled and allowed to depart that same day, without any delay. These incidents reflect the ancient custom of mariners, adopted by aviators, to render assistance to fellow voyagers in distress. Operations at sea and in the air are inherently dangerous, and the common practice of mariners and aviators has become an established legal norm.[66]

— — — — • — — — —

On April 10, 2001, satellite imagery detected seven trucks parked by the EP-3, as the Chinese had violated the sovereign immune legal status of the aircraft and were removing sensitive hi-tech equipment. The following day, Rear Adm. Craig R. Quigley, deputy assistant secretary of defense for public affairs, reiterated that the EP-3 was sovereign American property and that the United States wanted it back.[67] In fact, however, China had stripped the aircraft of its gear and disassembled the fuselage in violation of U.S. sovereign immunity. The seminal case on point on sovereign immunity is *The Schooner* Exchange *v. McFaddon*, decided by the Supreme Court in 1812.[68] The case stems from a legal dispute surrounding the schooner *Exchange*, which was owned by John M'Faddon and William Greetham. The ship got under way from Baltimore in 1809 and during its voyage was seized pursuant to standing orders from Napoleon Bonaparte. The vessel was refitted as a warship and commissioned into the French navy, renamed *Balou*. The *Balou* subsequently was compelled to enter the port of Philadelphia due to storm damage, whereupon M'Faddon and Greetham brought action for the arrest and recovery of their ship. The Supreme Court, however, ruled that the United States could not seize the French warship, even though it had been unjustly taken from M'Faddon and Greetham. Once the vessel had been converted into a French-flagged naval vessel, it was inviolable.

— — — — • — — — —

A third legal issue that arose in the EP-3 case concerns the legality of sensitive reconnaissance flights in international airspace above the EEZ. In April 2001, American officials steadfastly maintained that the EP-3 had been exercising the freedoms of navigation and overflight guaranteed in articles 58 and 87 of UNCLOS and by customary international legal rights that apply equally over the EEZ.[69] A coastal state cannot presume to regulate military activities in its EEZ, unless they have a tangible impact on its resource-related rights. Articles 56 and 58 of UNCLOS, in fact, require states to act in the EEZ with "due regard" for the rights and duties of other states.

Another close encounter occurred on August 19, 2014, when a Shenyang J-11 fighter conducted a dangerous intercept of a U.S. Navy P-8 patrol aircraft on routine surveillance 135 miles east of Hainan Island.[70] Ten days later, China responded to Washington's protest with a warning to stop its SRO flights near Chinese territory. Beijing dismissed the démarche, claiming that U.S. surveillance activities undermined China's security interests and could lead to "undesirable incidents." Similarly, on September 15, 2015, two Chinese JH-7 fighters unsafely intercepted an American RC-135 surveillance aircraft in international airspace over the Yellow Sea about eighty miles off the Shandong Peninsula. One of them crossed about five hundred feet in front of the U.S. aircraft.

China's pattern of misbehavior continued throughout 2016 and 2017. On May 17, 2016, two PLA Air Force Shenyang J-11s made an unsafe interception of an American EP-3, coming within fifty feet. The EP-3, which was patrolling over the South China Sea in international airspace, was forced to change altitude to avoid a collision. China denied that its aircraft operated unsafely.[71] Less than a month later, a Chinese Chengdu J-10 fighter, intercepting a U.S. Air Force RC-135, flew within fifty feet of it at high speed.[72] On February 8, 2017, a PLAAF Shaanxi KJ-200 airborne early warning and control aircraft intercepted a U.S. Navy P-3C in international airspace near Scarborough Shoal, approaching within a thousand feet.[73] Thus, despite nearly two decades of military-to-military engagement and strategic dialogue, there remains a wide gap between the United States and China on the right to conduct military activities in and over the EEZ. Although the overwhelming majority of PLA intercepts of American SRO flights since 2001 have been professional and nonconfrontational, these dangerous incidents demonstrate that U.S.-Chinese encounters at sea could result in a mishap.

Some observers suggest that China may be reevaluating its position as it continues to develop a more robust blue-water naval capability of its own. In recent years, PLA warships and aircraft have conducted ISR operations in the EEZs of the United States, Vietnam, the Philippines, Japan, and other countries without notice to or the consent of the affected states.[74] Since 2012, Chinese naval units have overtly operated in the American EEZ around Guam and the Hawaiian Islands, including during the 2012 and 2014 Rim of the Pacific (RIMPAC) exercises. For example, in July 2014 a PLA Navy Type 815, Dongidao-class intelligence collector (AGI) was observed in the American EEZ collecting intelligence on the USS *Ronald Reagan* strike group during the 2014 Rim of the Pacific exercise off the coast of Hawaii.[75] Similarly, China also sent a warship into Australia's EEZ to spy on the Talisman Sabre exercise in 2017.

These PLA Navy operations undercut China's decades-old position that foreign military operations and intelligence collection in its EEZ are unlawful. Notwithstanding its own naval maneuvers close to foreign shores, China continues to warn the United States to stop its SRO flights near Chinese territory. This inconsistency is especially worrisome in that it demonstrates that China does not accept the universal application of international law, does not see it as applying to itself as it does to other states—an essential ingredient of the rule of law.

— — — — • — — — —

This chapter now turns from China's challenge to U.S. overflights offshore to its interception of U.S. naval surface ships. Chinese misbehavior occurs not only in the airspace above the sea but on the surface as well, harassing U.S. military survey vessels and warships. China targets U.S. "special mission ships" (SMSs) operated by the Navy's Military Sealift Command (MSC). The Special Mission Program operates twenty-four ships that provide specialized services, including military oceanographic and hydrographic surveys, underwater surveillance, missile tracking, acoustic surveys, submarine and special-warfare support, and precision sonar to map the ocean floor.[76] Ocean surveillance ships use both passive and active low-frequency sonar arrays to detect and track undersea contacts.[77] SMSs are unarmed, except for small arms for force protection. The vessels are operated by civilian mariners who work for private companies under contract to MSC.

The PLA Navy perceives the six oceanographic survey ships and five ocean surveillance ships as the most threatening of the SMS. Accordingly, these intelligence ships have been on the receiving end of Chinese threats and harassment. On March 23, 2001, for example, the survey ship USNS *Bowditch* (T-AGS 62—an unarmed, white-hulled, *Pathfinder*-class hydrographic survey ship) was conducting a routine oceanographic military survey in China's claimed EEZ in the Yellow Sea when it encountered a Chinese Jianheu III–class frigate.[78] The frigate came within a hundred yards of the *Bowditch* and ordered it to leave the area or "suffer the consequences."[79] The *Bowditch* departed but returned to the same spot a few days later to complete its mission, this time with an escorting destroyer. The American embassy in Beijing protested that the Chinese ship's conduct had been unlawful.[80] China replied that U.S. military surveys in its EEZ pose a threat and require China's consent.[81] Similarly, on September 26, 2002, during a hydrographic survey in the Yellow Sea some 60 nm off the coast of China, the *Bowditch* was "buzzed" by PLA patrol aircraft. The aircraft flew within a few hundred yards of the ship and threatened unspecified action if it did not leave. China protested the intrusion into its EEZ, arguing that the U.S. survey ship had illegally engaged in monitoring and reconnaissance without permission.[82] Eight months later, in May 2003, Chinese fishing vessels harassed the USNS *Bowditch* again while it was carrying out an oceanographic survey in China's claimed EEZ.[83] One vessel intentionally bumped the *Bowditch*, causing minor damage.

On March 4, 2009, USNS *Victorious* (T-AGOS 19) on a surveillance mission in the Yellow Sea was illuminated with a high-intensity spotlight by a China Fisheries Law Enforcement Command (FLEC) patrol vessel 120 nm off the Chinese coast. The following day a Y-12 maritime surveillance aircraft made twelve fly-bys at an altitude of about four hundred feet and a range of five hundred yards.[84] On May 5, 2009, two Chinese fishing vessels approached within thirty meters of *Victorious*, forcing it to make evasive maneuvers to avoid a collision. The *Victorious* requested the assistance of a nearby PLA Navy vessel (WAGOR 17). The two fishing boats departed when WAGOR 17 arrived and illuminated one of them.[85]

On March 5, 2009, a PLA Navy frigate crossed the bow of the USNS *Impeccable* (T-AGOS 23) without warning at a range of about a hundred yards. This incident was followed by eleven fly-bys of a Y-12 at an altitude of six hundred feet and a range from a hundred to three hundred feet.[86] Two days later, a PLA intelligence-collection ship challenged the *Impeccable* over bridge-to-bridge radio, asserting that it was operating illegally and was to depart or "suffer the consequences."[87] On March 8, 2009, five Chinese ships—a PLA Navy intelligence ship, a FLEC patrol vessel, a State Oceanic Administration patrol vessel, and two small cargo ships—surrounded and harassed the *Impeccable* in the South China Sea about seventy-five miles southeast of Hainan Island. The two cargo ships, which operated in conjunction with the three government vessels, approached within twenty-five meters, forcing the *Impeccable* to stop to avoid a collision.[88] The *Impeccable* departed the area and returned the next day, escorted by the guided-missile destroyer USS *Chung-Hoon* (DDG 93). The White House declared that these ships would continue to operate in international waters and that the United States expected China to observe international law.[89]

On July 3, 2013, USNS *Impeccable* was again challenged, this time in the East China Sea by a China Maritime Surveillance (CMS) patrol vessel a hundred nautical miles off the Chinese coast. The CMS vessel instructed the *Impeccable* to discontinue its surveillance, warned that it was operating illegally in "Chinese waters," and demanded that it seek permission from Chinese authorities before continuing.[90] On December 15, 2016, a Chinese warship unlawfully seized a U.S. Navy unmanned underwater vehicle (UUV) that was being recovered by the USNS *Bowditch* in the South China Sea about fifty nautical miles northwest of Subic Bay. A Dalang III–class submarine-rescue ship (ASR 510) launched a small boat and retrieved the UUV.[91] The crew of the *Bowditch* immediately contacted the ASR via bridge-to-bridge radio, informed the Chinese that the UUV was U.S. property, and requested that the drone be returned immediately. The Chinese acknowledged the

U.S. transmission yet otherwise ignored the request. The following day, the U.S. government demanded that the drone, a U.S. sovereign immune vessel, be returned immediately and that China "comply with all of its obligations under international law." China responded that the drone had been retrieved to prevent it from becoming a hazard to navigation.[92] The drone was returned to American control on December 20.[93] This seizure, albeit temporary, of a "sovereign immune vessel" legally operating in international waters demonstrates China's willingness to disrupt freedom of navigation on the high seas, despite repeated assertions that it will not interfere with freedom of navigation in the South China Sea, where the UUV incident occurred.

– – – – • – – – –

Chinese defense officials have repeatedly stated that freedom of navigation in the South China Sea is not at risk, and that the United States "should stop playing up the issue."[94] These assurances are pointless because China interprets freedom of navigation as applying only to civilian or commercial ships.[95] It argues that naval vessels enjoy freedom of navigation on the high seas but that in the EEZ they have only a more limited right of "peaceful navigation"—a term not found in international law. Specifically, China maintains, U.S. warships may not engage in military activities in its EEZ and must accommodate its security interests.[96]

These positions are at variance with UNCLOS. Ships of all nations may navigate in, fly over, and make other internationally lawful uses of the sea within the EEZ. The term "ship" embraces both civilian vessels and warships. UNCLOS defines the latter as vessels "belonging to the armed forces of a State bearing the external marks distinguishing such ships of its nationality, under the command of an officer duly commissioned by the government of the State and whose name appears in the appropriate service list or its equivalent, and manned by a crew which is under regular armed forces discipline."[97]

– – – – • – – – –

China asserts that American military marine data collection, including all military surveying, SRO, and ISR, in its EEZ is akin to marine scientific research and therefore subject to Chinese control. This position, however, has no foundation in international law; it contradicts state practice and the plain language of UNCLOS.[98] UNCLOS does not define MSR, nor does it define "surveys" or other forms of marine data collection. Nonetheless, UNCLOS describes MSR as scientific activity "for the benefit of all mankind."[99] MSR includes physical oceanography, marine chemistry and biology, scientific ocean drilling and coring, geological and geophysical research, and other activities with scientific purposes and producing results normally made available to the general public and the scientific community. MSR has elsewhere been defined as "those activities undertaken in the ocean and coastal waters to expand scientific knowledge of the marine environment and its processes."[100]

Hydrographic surveys, on the other hand, collect data for navigational charts and safety of navigation.[101] The United Nations defines hydrographic surveys as "the science of measuring and depicting those parameters necessary to describe the precise nature and configuration of the sea-bed and coastal strip, its geographical relationship to the land-mass, and the characteristics and dynamics of the sea."[102] Hydrographers are concerned with water depth, the configuration of the natural bottom, the directions and forces of currents, the heights and times of tides and water stages, and hazards to navigation. Thus, hydrographic surveys are not the same as MSR: they collect and analyze different types of data and for fundamentally different purposes.[103] Neither is military marine data collection MSR, as it collects data for military, not scientific, purposes. Military operations rely on oceanographic, marine geological, geophysical, chemical, biological, and acoustic data. The results are not released to the public or the scientific community unless it is collected on the high seas beyond the EEZ.[104] Such data are not "for the benefit of all mankind" but rather for the exclusive, usually secret, use of naval forces.

The distinction between MSR and other types of marine data collection is also reflected in UNCLOS. For example, "research or survey activities" are impermissible during innocent passage in the territorial sea.[105] Article 40 prohibits ships in transit passage from conducting "any research or survey activities without the prior authorization of the states bordering straits."The same restrictions apply to ships engaged in archipelagic sea-lanes passage or in innocent passage of archipelagic waters.[106] More important, article 56 limits coastal states' jurisdiction in the EEZ to MSR; article 56 does not address surveys, article 87 refers only to "scientific research," and part XIII applies only to MSR.

Coastal states have jurisdiction over marine scientific research in the EEZ and may regulate it and surveys in the territorial sea, archipelagic waters, international straits, and archipelagic sea lanes. Yet they do not have jurisdiction over hydrographic surveys and ISR in the EEZ. These last two activities are protected high seas freedoms that constitute "other internationally lawful uses of the sea" set forth in article 87 of UNCLOS, and therefore may be exercised at will in foreign EEZs.

The distinctions embedded in UNCLOS reflect centuries of state practice. The U.S. Navy has been working to understand the sea environment for more than 185 years, since the Department of Charts and Instruments was first established in 1830. Today the Naval Meteorology and Oceanography Command and the Military Sealift Command still have that mission—to provide information to help naval and joint forces operate more safely, securely, and effectively and make decisions faster than adversaries can. Only in the past thirty years has the legality of these operations been challenged, and then only by a handful of states. The law is very clear: the authority of coastal states over MSR in the EEZ does not extend to other forms of marine data collection, including the Navy's oceanographic surveys and ISR.

– – – – • – – – –

China's EEZ law is inconsistent with UNCLOS in stating that China exercises "jurisdiction in relation to . . . protection and conservation of [the] maritime environment."[107] The law authorizes Chinese authorities "to take necessary measures for preventing, eliminating and controlling pollution to [the] marine environment and protecting and conserving the marine environment" of the EEZ.[108] China has suggested that these domestic laws, coupled with the environmental provisions in UNCLOS, have the effect of expanding its authority to include jurisdiction over foreign military activities in its EEZ that could harm the marine environment.

In the 2007 U.S.-Chinese MMCA meeting China charged that American ships' sonars were harming marine mammals and disrupting fish stocks in China's EEZ. China argued that it could regulate such matters.[109] Coincidentally, that same year a U.S. district court in Southern California ruled against the U.S. Navy in a lawsuit that challenged the use of midfrequency active sonar, claiming that it harmed marine mammals. The following year, however, the Supreme Court overturned the lower court opinion and ruled in favor of the Navy. The Supreme Court held that adequate sonar training for U.S. naval forces was essential to national security.[110]

China may not impose or enforce its domestic environmental laws on sovereign immune vessels and aircraft operating in its EEZ. State aircraft and government ships are exempt from the environmental provisions of UNCLOS; article 236 states that "provisions . . . regarding the protection and preservation of the marine environment do not apply to any warship, naval auxiliary, other vessels or aircraft owned or operated by a State." The only requirement is that these warships and aircraft "act in a manner consistent, so far as is reasonable and practicable," with UNCLOS.[111] Thus, foreign sovereign immune vessels and aircraft have no legal obligation to comply with domestic environmental regulations in the EEZ.[112]

— — — — • — — — —

China's audacious "dashed-line" claim has set the stage for further conflict over freedom of the seas. In 2009, China stated in a *note verbale* that it had "indisputable sovereignty over the islands in the South China Sea and adjacent waters, and enjoys sovereign rights and jurisdiction over the relevant waters as well as the seabed and subsoil thereof."[113] China was responding to technical submissions by the Philippines and Vietnam to the Commission on the Limits of the Continental Shelf jointly requesting exclusive rights to resources on their extended continental shelves. What became known as the "dashed-line" claim (in reference to a Chinese map setting off its expansive claim with a prominent dashed line) has become the focal point for issues of security and freedom of navigation in East Asia. The *note verbale* uses two key terms to describe China's rights in the oceans near the coast—"adjacent waters" and "relevant waters." Neither term is found in UNCLOS nor has any meaning in international law. Despite numerous calls by states throughout the world for "clarification," Beijing has wielded the ambiguity to intimidate other claimants and cow its neighbors.

Since China's dashed-line claim overlaps the Philippine EEZ, Manila submitted the matter to a tribunal under annex VII of UNCLOS. The arbitration panel ruled against China in July 2016, upending China's theory of "historic" maritime rights to the waters of the South China Sea.[114] The tribunal clarified the scope of China's claims that would be legally permissible. The tribunal ruled that China's history of navigation and fishing in the Spratly Islands, on which it had based its claims, had been merely an exercise of high seas freedoms.[115] China, in fact, had relinquished its right to fish freely in its neighbors' EEZs when it acquired exclusive rights in its own EEZ.[116] The tribunal also held that UNCLOS had established a comprehensive system of coastal zones that supersedes any incompatible earlier rights or agreements.[117] In this case, the sovereign rights of the Philippines over the resources in its EEZ and on its continental shelf displace any Chinese "historic rights" to them.[118]

The tribunal also examined which features in the Spratly Islands (i.e, islets and reefs, some not always visible above the surface of the water), merited their own EEZs or continental shelves. It found that none did. All were either "rocks" (Scarborough Shoal, Gaven Reef [North], McKennan Reef, Johnson Reef, Cuarteron Reef, and Fiery Cross Reef) entitled to a 12-nm territorial sea and associated contiguous zone, or merely "low-tide elevations" (LTEs), neither subject to appropriation or ownership nor entitled to territorial seas.[119] Subi Reef, Gaven Reef (South), and Hughes Reef were identified as LTEs.[120] These findings are significant for the United States and other users of the South China Sea, since military forces are limited to innocent passage in the territorial sea. There is no right of overflight of the territorial sea, and submarines in innocent passage must travel on the surface and show their flags.[121]

Article 13 of UNCLOS establishes that in most cases LTEs do not have their own territorial sea.[122] LTEs are not subject to national appropriation because they are merely features, either in midocean and under no state's sovereignty or on the continental shelf of a coastal state and under that state's resource rights and jurisdiction. The tribunal found some of these outcroppings, such as Mischief Reef and Second Thomas Shoal, to be solely within the Philippine EEZ

Mischief Reef and Second Thomas Shoal are special cases in military terms. Both are LTEs in the Philippine EEZ. The tribunal found that Mischief Reef is indeed within the EEZ of the Philippines, outside any possible claim by China, but not entitled to a territorial sea or other maritime zone.[123] In 1999, the Philippines grounded the warship BRP *Sierra Madre* on Second Thomas Shoal, just twenty-one nautical miles from Mischief Reef.[124] The dilapidated vessel has eight Philippine Marines serving on board in rotational shifts to maintain a physical presence at the shoal. The Chinese coast guard has maintained a continuous patrol around it since 2013 and in March 2014 even intercepted supply ships on their way to relieve the Marines on the vessel.[125]

China has built port facilities and an airstrip at Mischief Reef, constituting a civil-military base that may be designed to demonstrate that the feature is habitable. The tribunal, however, was unconvinced, noting that by definition the original feature is submerged at high tide, an LTE. Furthermore, as the Philippines argued, a military presence on a feature, supported from the outside, does not make it another type of feature. For example, a rock with troops stationed on it does not become a full-fledged island, defined as capable of sustaining human habitation or an economic life of its own.[126] In any case, Vietnam and Malaysia both station troops on LTEs they occupy in the Spratly Islands yet do not claim them as islands.

— — — — ● — — — —

Since 2015, the number of freedom of navigation (FON) operations in the South China Sea has grown. In an effort to avoid tension with China, the Obama administration strained to articulate its FON policy in language that was marked by confusion and inconsistency, and the operations it finally ordered, in its last year, may have left the United States in a somewhat worse legal position than had they not been conducted.[127] For example, in October 2015 the destroyer USS *Lassen* (DDG 82) passed inside twelve nautical miles of five maritime features in the Spratly Islands—Subi Reef, Northeast Cay, Southwest Cay, South Reef, and Sandy Cay—which are claimed by, variously, China, Taiwan, Vietnam, and the Philippines. A PLA Navy destroyer and frigate shadowed the *Lassen*, but neither Chinese warship maneuvered aggressively or unprofessionally. China, however, protested the transit and warned it would take "all necessary measures" to defend its "sovereignty" in the South China Sea.[128]

The tactical operation was executed flawlessly, but poor messaging by the Obama administration squandered its legal impact. The operation leaked to the press beforehand, in effect giving China prior notice that a U.S. warship would be challenging its claims in the South China Sea. Prior notice is not only counterintuitive in terms of force protection but also runs afoul of American oceans policy that advance notification not be given of exercises of internationally recognized navigational rights and freedoms.[129] The leak of information in advance of the operation risked fortifying China's claim that it is entitled to receive notification of warship transits, thereby undermining the American legal position. The leak also compromised the security of the mission and increased operational risk.

Moreover, Navy officials characterized the *Lassen* transit as "innocent passage."[130] One Pentagon official confirmed that the destroyer had turned off its fire-control radars during the transit.[131] Transit in innocent passage near Mischief Reef, in particular, raised concerns. Mischief Reef is an LTE in midocean, more than twelve nautical miles from the mainland or any island, and so is not entitled to a territorial sea for several reasons.[132] First, the feature is not under the sovereignty of any state. Mid-ocean low-tide elevations cannot be appropriated, so China's vast port and airfield complex on the feature is without legal effect. The feature lies 135 nm from Palawan Island and therefore is part of the Philippine continental shelf. The Philippines enjoys exclusive sovereign rights and jurisdiction over the feature, including all of its living and nonliving resources. China has expanded the LTE into a massive artificial island by adding about 1,400 acres of crushed coral and gravel siphoned from the seabed. Regardless of the size of the artificial island, however, no maritime zones accrue to it.[133]

Second, even if Mischief Reef were a naturally formed island, it still would not be entitled to a territorial sea until legal title to it was determined. Title may be negotiated, arbitrated, or adjudicated through litigation. But mere assertion of a claim is insufficient to generate lawful title. (If a new state suddenly stepped forward to claim the feature—Britain, perhaps, based on colonial presence—would it be entitled to the presumption of a territorial sea?) Even Antarctica, an entire continent, does not automatically generate a territorial sea. A territorial sea is a function of state sovereignty, and until sovereignty is lawfully obtained, no territorial sea exists.

Third, no state, including China, has established baselines around Mischief Reef in accordance with article 3 of UNCLOS. A territorial sea is measured from "baselines"; without baselines, there can be no territorial sea. What is the policy rationale? Baselines place the international community on notice that the coastal state has a reasonable and lawful departure point from which to measure the breadth of the territorial sea.

As a feature on the Philippine continental shelf, Mischief Reef is not only incapable of ever generating a territorial sea but devoid of national airspace. Aircraft of all nations may freely overfly Mischief Reef, just as warships and commercial ships may transit as close to the shoreline as is safe and practical. By indicating that the *Lassen* transited in "innocent passage," American officials implicitly recognized the LTE as a "rock," which may be entitled to 12-nm territorial seas.

In any case, maritime zones may be established only by the state exercising sovereignty over the land at issue. But sovereignty over the features of the South China Sea is not settled, and until it is, no nation may purport to establish maritime zones. Ironically, China has neither established baselines around the two features nor claimed a territorial sea around them.

The *Lassen* operation was roundly criticized for playing into China's hands; a muddy legal rationale diluted the strategic message. After the operation, the chair of the Senate Armed Services Committee, Senator John McCain, expressed dismay at the Obama administration's confusion and indecision.[134] He declared that the United States must assert its rights to "fly, sail, and operate wherever international law allows. And the South China Sea must be no exception."[135] McCain argued that future FON operations "should not be sporadic spectacles to behold, but ordinary and consistent demonstrations" of American resolve.[136] Two weeks later, American defense officials committed a similar blunder when they attempted to describe the flight path of a pair of Guam-based B-52 strategic bombers patrolling over the South China Sea on November 8–9, 2015. A Pentagon spokesman stated the planes had not come within 12 nm of Subi Reef but had remained in international airspace.[137] A few days earlier, however, another DoD official had reported that the bombers *had* come within 12 nm of the reef and that Chinese ground controllers had warned them to "get away from our islands."[138] American officials missed the opportunity to explain that Subi Reef is an LTE, with no potential to generate national airspace, and that the bombers could overfly it without notice to or the consent of China or any other state. (The Obama administration later explained that because Subi Reef may lie within twelve nautical miles of Sandy Cay, a rock, it may acquire a territorial sea as well. This legal stretch assumes that the same state owns both Sandy Cay and Subi Reef and has established baselines around them from which to declare a territorial sea.)[139] The White House grasped at straws to clean up its initial mistaken message.

China protested a similar mission on December 10, 2015, in which a B-52 came within two nautical miles of Cuarteron Reef.[140] DoD officials later admitted that the aircraft had in fact done so, inadvertently and as the result of bad weather.[141] Cuarteron Reef is a "rock" and would be entitled to a 12-nm territorial sea and national airspace if China had sovereignty over it. But China has not demonstrated a lawful claim. Calling the close approach "unintentional" was, again, tacit recognition of Chinese sovereignty over the reef.

The United States stepped up its FON operations in the South China Sea in 2016, conducting three. There had been only seven in the South China

Sea between 2011 and 2015.[142] That increase is significant and encouraging, but all of the 2016 evolutions suffered from the same fallacy—they challenged claims that do not legally exist and so risked the effect of implicitly recognizing Chinese sovereignty over the disputed features in question. American forces should be exercising high seas freedoms any time they pass near a disputed feature. This is exactly what the Trump administration did during its first freedom of navigation operation.

On May 24, 2017, the guided-missile destroyer USS *Dewey* (DDG 105) transited within twelve nautical miles of Mischief Reef. China made "stern representations" to the United States, and later the Foreign Ministry announced that the guided-missile frigates *Liuzhou* and *Luzhouto* had sortied to the area and "expelled" the *Dewey*. The operation may prove the most significant FON operation in the South China Sea yet, as it challenged China's apparent claim of a territorial sea around Mischief Reef and in doing so questioned China's sovereignty over the land feature altogether.

The Pentagon said the U.S. warship did a simple military exercise while close to the artificial island, a "man overboard" drill.[143] Such drills may not be conducted in innocent passage; the *Dewey* was instead exercising high seas freedoms near Mischief Reef. That it did so broadly repudiates China's claims of sovereignty over the feature and the surrounding waters. Unlike the *Lassen* operation, which appeared to be a challenge to some theoretical or "phantom" territorial sea, the *Dewey* transit properly reflected the high seas immediately surrounding Mischief Reef. The *Dewey* transit also reflected the findings of the 2016 tribunal, which found that China's claims were inconsistent with UNCLOS article 300 regarding good faith and abuse of rights.[144] Since Mischief Reef is an LTE and therefore not entitled to a territorial sea, ships and aircraft may exercise high seas freedoms in waters surrounding it.[145] China's attempts to diminish the freedom of navigation were incompatible with UNCLOS.

The United States should continue to conduct freedom of navigation operations in the South China Sea, exercising to the fullest its rights in international law. Legally, this arbitration award means that high seas freedoms apply throughout the entire South China Sea. No feature in the

Spratly Islands currently has a territorial sea—none. UNCLOS article 3 allows a state to "establish" a territorial sea, but one does not exist automatically. Neither China nor any other state has established a territorial sea around any feature in the Spratly Islands. States must formally establish baselines in order to do so. Whether or not American ships or aircraft stay beyond twelve nautical miles of any these features is legally immaterial— none of them have territorial seas.

Since the United States does not recognize any country's sovereignty over any of the features occupied or claimed by China, it is under no legal obligation to observe any territorial seas, even were China to establish them. No country recognizes China's sovereignty over any Spratly feature, and without sovereignty there can be no territorial sea. The United States should not recognize any nation's claim to sovereignty over the Spratly Islands until such a determination is negotiated among the claimants or adjudicated by an international court or tribunal.

CONCLUSION
Ensuring Freedom of Navigation

The jurist Hugo Grotius wrote more than four hundred years ago that the right to traverse the oceans was given to all peoples by nature; no nation may interfere with the exercise of this right.[1] The concept of freedom of the seas was inherited from the Dutch by the British, and passed on to the Americans as an expression of the freedom of all states to trade and use the global commons without hindrance. Following the Second World War, the United States renewed its focus on freedom of the seas, recognizing that unimpeded access to the world's oceans has always been essential to its prosperity, stability, and security. This book chronicles some significant episodes in the struggle to claim freedom of the seas, and concludes on a cautionary note. Twenty years ago, Ambassador John D. Negroponte observed, "The freedom of the seas was not given to mankind. It was won—won through scholarly and legal debate and in naval engagement."[2]

By the 1970s a handful of recalcitrant coastal states persisted in unilateral measures to diminish freedom of navigation and overflight at sea, either by interfering with foreign ships and aircraft exercising their rights or extending their national jurisdiction beyond lawful limits.[3] These policies, singly and in combination, pose a serious challenge to customary high seas freedoms, as well as to U.S. interests in protecting commercial and military navigation, overflight, and other internationally lawful uses of the sea. President Jimmy Carter sought options to ensure freedom of navigation in the event that the UN Conference on the Law of the Sea, which had begun in 1973, failed to conclude a treaty acceptable to the United States. On February 1, 1979, the National Security Council recommended a two-pronged approach—diplomatic protests of unlawful claims and operational assertions by U.S. naval ships and aircraft.

> The U.S. should protest claims of other States that are inconsistent with international law and U.S. policy, with particular reference to extended territorial sea claims as well as the regime therein; assertions of jurisdiction over navigation, overflight, and related matters on the high seas beyond the territorial sea; assertions of archipelago status; and assertions of certain baseline and historic bay/water claims. . . . The U.S. should exercise its rights in the face of the illegal claims . . . to the extent practicable and should avoid actions which may be viewed as acquiescence in such illegal claims.[4]

The NSC also recommended that the United States should promote freedom of navigation and overflight, at least for purposes of transit, through international straits. Accordingly, on March 20, 1979, national security Adviser Zbigniew Brzezinski tasked an interagency Law of the Sea Contingency Planning Group on Navigation to develop a policy to protect navigation, overflight, and related national security interests in the oceans.[5]

Three years later, in July 1982, President Ronald Reagan announced that the United States would not sign the United Nations Convention on the Law of the Sea (UNCLOS)[6] because its provisions on deep seabed mining were contrary to the interests and principles of industrialized nations and would not help attain the aspirations of developing countries.[7] (These issues were resolved in a 1994 implementing agreement that addressed Reagan's concerns.) Nonetheless, the president stated that the United States accepted and would adhere to the "balance of interests" relating to traditional uses of the oceans, such as navigation and overflight. While objecting to the 1982 framework for seabed mining in Part XI, the president pledged "to promote and protect the oceans interests of the

United States in a manner consistent" with what he described as "fair and balanced" rules reflected in UNCLOS.

The Reagan statement on oceans policy recognized the rights of other states in the waters off their coasts, which are reflected in UNCLOS, so long as these states recognized U.S. rights and freedoms. The president's decision still resonates and offers a way forward for all states confronted by persistent violators of UNCLOS. In this regard, President Reagan's policy is important to reproduce in its entirety because it contains a caveat that has been lost on recent U.S. administrations. Reagan stated: "[T]he United States is prepared to accept and act in accordance with the balance of interests relating to traditional uses of the oceans—such as navigation and overflight. *In this respect, the United States will recognize the rights of other states in the waters off their coasts, as reflected in [UNCLOS], so long as the rights and freedoms of the United States and others are recognized by such coastal states* [emphasis added].[8]

This policy states that the United States would withhold recognition of other countries' maritime rights if they did not recognize U.S. rights and freedoms at sea. In international law, this approach is referred to as imposing "legal countermeasures" against a state violating international law. Countermeasures may be imposed by the injured state in order to induce compliance on the part of the violating state. The United States and other nations should implement lawful countermeasures against states that violate the rules reflected in UNCLOS by withholding recognition of their maritime rights and freedom of navigation until such time as the violator complies with the law of the sea. Reagan's policy has stood the test of time and remains in effect today. The policy reflects a classic quid pro quo and the entire basis of positive law: the United States agrees to respect other states' maritime claims only if they respect U.S. claims—including the right and freedom of navigation and overflight. The United States should act true to its 1983 Oceans Policy of observing and respecting foreign maritime claims only to the extent that other coastal states respect U.S. rights at sea.

Today, China has become a serial violator of U.S. rights to freedom of navigation and overflight. In particular, since China does not respect UNCLOS rules governing the innocent passage of warships in its territorial sea or high seas freedom of navigation of warships and the overflight of military aircraft in its EEZ, the United States should withhold observation of those rights from Chinese military ships and aircraft until such time as China conforms its policy to the law. The United States still affords Chinese vessels full rights to operate freely on the oceans, including transit through the U.S. territorial seas in innocent passage and the exercise of high seas freedoms in the U.S. EEZ without restriction.

In September 2015, for example, a flotilla of five Chinese navy warships transited through the Bering Sea north of the Aleutian Islands, and then headed south to sail in innocent passage between two of the Aleutian Islands.[9] A Pentagon spokesperson stated that the operation was completely lawful and done in accordance with UNCLOS.[10] Similarly, Chinese warships have conducted military activities, including intelligence collection, in the U.S. 200-nm EEZ near Guam and Hawaii. In the aftermath of a 2015 Chinese maritime intelligence operation near Hawaii, a U.S. Pacific Fleet spokesperson stated, "[I]t is a fundamental right of all nations for military ships and aircraft to operate in international waters and airspace in accordance with well-established international law."[11] China routinely conducts military activities in the EEZs of Japan, India, and Australia as well.

The United States should invoke countermeasures against China (or any state for that matter when it does not comply with the rules reflected in UNCLOS) by withholding recognition of navigational rights and freedoms enjoyed by the violators until such time as they desist in their illegal behavior. Such lawful countermeasures in international law serve an instrumental function to produce compliance by the violator.[12]

Countermeasures flow from the customary international law of state responsibility, as reflected in the International Law Commission's Articles on State Responsibility.[13] States bear responsibility for acts that are attributable to them under international law and that constitute a breach of an international obligation under either treaty law or customary law.[14] The injured state may invoke countermeasures against the responsible state to induce compliance. Countermeasures must be proportionate, not affect the rights of third states, and not involve the violation of preemptory norms, such as basic standards of human rights. The Reagan policy was never renounced yet in practice it has fallen into desuetude. Reagan's caveat is an important but unutilized tool of international law available to all states, and is especially pertinent for the United States, Japan, India, and Australia.

President Reagan also emphasized that the United States would continue the U.S. Freedom of Navigation (FON) program to challenge unlawful maritime claims. Reagan's proclamation and the FON program have served as the linchpin of U.S. oceans policy for four decades. Successive U.S. presidents, with varying enthusiasm, have implemented policies and conducted naval operations to preserve freedom of the seas.

Chapter 11 presents some of the more egregious cases of Chinese interference with freedom of navigation. The aggressive interception of U.S. surface ships and military aircraft is complemented by low-level coercion by Chinese Coast Guard vessels and Chinese fishing vessels. These ships now operate in tandem as a maritime militia to routinely bully and intimidate foreign mariners—particularly those on the vessels of rival claimants in the Yellow Sea, East China Sea, and South China Sea. Chinese military aircraft engage in unsafe and unprofessional air and maritime behavior in violation of the International Rules of the Air.[15] At the same time, Chinese Coast Guard vessels and associated maritime militia violate the International Maritime Organization rules on preventing collisions at sea.[16] China supplements its high-end armed forces with maritime law enforcement ships operating in conjunction with a fleet of (nominally civilian) fishing vessels.[17] China's maritime militia, composed mainly of fishing vessels, also does not comply with Food and Agricultural Organization (FAO) guidelines for the handling of commercial fishing vessels and illegal, unregulated, and unreported (IUU) fishing.

In 2009, China had circulated a UN diplomatic note claiming "indisputable sovereignty" over the islands and "adjacent waters" of the South China Sea, a body of water 1.4 times as large as the Mediterranean Sea and nearly fifteen times larger than the Persian Gulf. In 2013, in response to China's sweeping maritime claims over the South China Sea, the Philippines brought an arbitration case under Annex VII of UNCLOS, which was administered at the Permanent Court of Arbitration in The Hague. China embarked on a massive land reclamation program to expand disputed features and construct artificial islands and airstrips in the Spratly Islands.[18] Between December 2013 and June 2015, for example, China had reclaimed more than three thousand acres of land on seven of its eight outposts in the Spratly Islands. Three of these facilities—Mischief Reef, Fiery Cross Reef, and Subi Reef—now feature long runways and hangars, each capable of accommodating twenty-four military aircraft. The militarization of the small, contested islands in the South China Sea suggests China intends to solidify its control of surrounding sea lanes.

The arbitration concluded in July 2016, with the tribunal issuing an award that rejected China's expansive maritime claims. The tribunal decision struck down China's dashed-line claim, rejecting in toto Beijing's vast and illegal declarations of sovereignty over some 90 percent of the South China Sea. The arbitration decision found that UNCLOS contains a comprehensive system of maritime zones.[19] If there were any preexisting or earlier rights or agreements concerning historic rights to the waters, they were superseded by UNCLOS if they were incompatible.[20] Similarly, the legal regimes of the continental shelf and the EEZ are incompatible with another state enjoying historic rights to the same resource.[21] This finding simply reflects a longstanding norm in international law, as set forth in the Vienna Convention on the Law of Treaties, in which the later-in-time legal authority prevails over earlier laws or treaties.[22]

The tribunal's decision should be referenced in bilateral and multilateral diplomatic venues and channels, military engagement, and communications with China. By pressing the importance of the Arbitration Award as a key foundation of a rules-based international order, states magnify its normative force, much as repeated references to specific indicia of liberty and freedom, such as competitive elections and a free press in the 1990 Copenhagen Document of the Helsinki Process transformed the Soviet bloc.

The tribunal also determined the legal status of the features in the South China Sea. This determination was essential to whether an entitlement exists to a maritime zone of sovereignty (territorial sea), or other zones of sovereign rights and jurisdiction (EEZ and continental shelf). The navigational regime applicable to foreign warships and military aircraft depends on the relevant zone. Furthermore, such maritime entitlement arises only once a state demonstrates lawful title or ownership over the island feature, which China in this case has failed to do.[23]

The tribunal determined there are only three types of features in the Spratly Islands, each with distinct legal and political consequences that affect freedom of navigation and overflight: submerged features, low-tide elevations, and rocks. Submerged features are always underwater. As part of the seabed or continental shelf, they are incapable of appropriation by any state, and are never a basis for a maritime zone, such as a territorial sea or national airspace. Low-tide elevations (LTEs) are underwater at high tide, but above water at low tide.[24] Such features also are incapable of appropriation by any state, as they are part of the seabed. Low-tide elevations normally do not generate a maritime zone unless they are situated within the territorial sea of an island or mainland. Rocks are (island) features above water at high tide and may generate a territorial sea of up to 12 nm. The territorial sea is under the sovereignty of the coastal state, and sovereignty extends to the airspace above the territorial sea, on the surface of the water and in the water column, and on the seabed. Foreign warships may exercise innocent passage in the territorial sea. There is no right of overflight, and submarines that operate in innocent passage must travel on the surface and show their flag.[25]

China has transformed seven features into artificial islands—four rocks (Cuarteron Reef, Fiery Cross Reef, Johnson Reef, and Gaven Reef North) and three LTEs (Hughes Reef, Subi Reef, and Mischief Reef).[26] LTEs are not entitled to a territorial sea and are not subject to appropriation or territorial title by any state. As a subset of islands that cannot sustain human habitation or an economic life of their own, rocks are not entitled to an EEZ.[27]

The tribunal decision promotes freedom of navigation and overflight in three major ways. First, it invalidates the idea that the numerous submerged features and LTEs in the South China Sea have any entitlement to generate a territorial sea or territorial airspace. About half of the features occupied by China are LTEs that are not entitled to a territorial sea, and about half are rocks that may be entitled to a territorial sea so long as valid title can be established. Regardless of which state has lawful title to the rocks in the South China Sea, those small island features generate at most a territorial sea. They are not entitled to an EEZ.

Second, the Arbitration Award provides greater fidelity to the test in UNCLOS article 121(3) concerning what types of features may generate an EEZ and a continental shelf. Islands that can sustain human habitation or an economic life of their own are entitled to a territorial sea, as well as an EEZ of up to 200 nm and a continental shelf, which might extend even beyond 200 nm. The tribunal determined that no feature in the region is an island that can sustain human habitation or economic life of its own, regardless of which state has lawful title to it. This finding greatly diminishes the value of the features to the claimants and restricts the possible area over which claimants may exercise sovereign rights and jurisdiction. China, in particular, has suffered a setback since it is the only claimant trying to use the features as a staging area to project power. Furthermore, China has stated that military activities in its EEZ require its permission, but because there are no natural land features capable of sustaining human habitation in the Spratly Islands, there are no EEZs generated by the features. Thus, the decision undermines China's efforts to intimidate its neighbors or harass U.S. naval patrols.

Third, the tribunal condemned a range of Chinese activities that encroached on the Philippines' rights over its own EEZ and continental shelf. In particular, China either acquiesced to, or more likely encouraged or even orchestrated, the interference of Philippine fishing vessels lawfully fishing in the Philippine EEZ. China also appeared to have directed its own fishing vessels to poach in the Philippine EEZ—a violation of Parts V and VII of UNCLOS as well as regulations of the UN Food and Agricultural Organization. Flag states have a legal duty to take measures to ensure fishing vessels that fly their flag are not conducting illegal, unreported, or unregulated fishing.[28]

China's construction and militarization of artificial islands in the South China Sea is an ominous sign of further challenges to freedom of navigation in Southeast Asia. Beijing's apparent efforts to control the sea lanes of the South China Sea have dismayed its neighbors and other states that rely on the waterway that is used to carry more than $5 trillion in maritime commerce annually. Left unchecked, China's efforts will destabilize the region politically and undermine the legitimacy of UNCLOS as the constitution for the world's oceans. These political-military developments have reinvigorated the U.S. FON program. In 2016, three FON operations were conducted in the South China Sea,[29] the USS *John C. Stennis* Carrier Strike Group (CSG) conducted presence operations in the South China Sea, and U.S. Air Force A-10 Thunderbolts operating out of the Philippines flew maritime patrols near Scarborough Shoal.[30] Although the FON operations during the Obama administration were fraught with miscues and inconsistent messaging, the Trump administration has moved in the right direction.[31]

Less than a month after President Trump took office, ships from CSG 1, including the USS *Carl Vinson* (CVN 70) and its embarked carrier air wing (CVW 2), and the USS *Wayne E. Meyer* (DDG 108) began routine operations in the South China Sea. As expected, China criticized the deployment: "China always respects the freedom of navigation and overflight all countries enjoy under international law. But we are consistently opposed to relevant countries threatening and damaging the sovereignty and security of littoral countries under the flag of freedom of navigation and overflight. We hope relevant countries can do more to safeguard regional peace and stability."[32] This statement reaffirmed Chinese admiral Sun Jianguo's statement in July 2016 that although China supports the concept of freedom of navigation, in Beijing's view it only applies to commercial ships and not warships and military aircraft. Warships are inherently threatening, he suggested, and therefore they are not entitled to freedom of navigation.[33] The Trump administration nonetheless conducted a FON operation within six nautical miles of Mischief Reef on May 24, 2017. During the operation, the USS *Dewey* (DDG 105) conducted a "man overboard" drill, so the transit was made under the legal regime of high seas freedom of navigation, rather than more restrictive innocent passage.[34] Unlike earlier FON operations, which appeared to respect a putative territorial sea around LTEs in the region, the *Dewey* operation was signaling that the United States would no longer entertain the fiction that such mid-ocean features could generate a territorial sea. This position reflected the holding in the arbitration decision that LTEs are not entitled to a territorial sea of their own. Two weeks later, two U.S. B-1B bombers operating out of Guam conducted an interoperability exercise in the South China Sea with the USS *Sterett* (DDG 104).[35]

China is not the only culprit. In recent years, Iran and Russia have also increased interference with U.S. freedom of navigation. In one ominous incident, Iran captured two U.S. Navy boats and their crews and held them for one day. On January 12, 2016, two U.S. Navy riverine command boats were intercepted in the Persian Gulf as they made their way from Kuwait to Bahrain. The boats inadvertently transited within 1.5 nm of Iran's Farsi Island. Because they were in the territorial sea and not threatening or using force or trying to undermine the sovereignty, territorial integrity, or political independence of Iran, the boats were in innocent passage in accordance with article 19 of UNCLOS.

Unexpectedly, one of the boats suffered an engine casualty and stopped dead in the water.[36] As the vessel proceeded to make repairs, Iranian Revolutionary Guard Corps Navy craft surrounded both boats with weapons uncovered. The U.S. boats and their crews were ordered at gunpoint to make for Farsi Island, where they were held overnight. After a flurry of diplomatic exchanges, the crews and boats were released, although Iran still has not been held accountable for its violation of the U.S. right of innocent passage in the territorial sea.

Russia also violates U.S. freedom of navigation and overflight with impunity. On June 21, 2017, an armed Russian Su-27 fighter jet approached within five feet of a U.S. Air Force RC-135 aircraft flying in international airspace over the Baltic Sea.[37] This type of unsafe and provocative approach to U.S. aircraft by Russian fighters has become all too commonplace, with more than thirty incidents just in the month of June 2017. These episodes endanger air navigation and risk another deadly encounter similar to the tragic 2001 Chinese interception of a U.S. EP-3 aircraft, which is discussed in Chapter 11.

The United States must conduct routine air and naval patrols and forward presence in all of the world's oceans or risk diminishing navigational rights and freedoms in years to come. These rights and freedoms underpin the rules-based legal order, but they are not self-enforcing. Left unused, navigational rights and freedoms atrophy over time. Their preservation requires determined U.S. leadership and continual American naval presence, and if needed application of military power to safeguard them. Consequently, U.S. air and naval forces should operate freely and persistently from the Northern Pacific Ocean to the South Atlantic, and from the Western Pacific Ocean to the Eastern Mediterranean Sea.

Just as the assertions of freedom of navigation and overflight in the Gulf of Sidra in 1981 and 1989 and the Black Sea bumping incident in 1988 elevated tension to preserve an open order of the oceans, FON operations in the South China Sea will generate blowback from Beijing that worsens bilateral relationships, at least temporarily. Accepting such costs and weathering Chinese criticism are essential if the United States is to preserve the rule of law that is essential for maintaining sea lines of communication that connect the United States to its friends and allies throughout the world.

FON operations generate international public goods, and sharing the burden of these operations' costs should be more evenly leveled among allies and strategic partners. Japan, India, and Australia, for example, have large, advanced, and capable maritime forces well positioned to conduct their own navigational assertions. So far, these states have passed the buck to the United States. Yet passing the buck has decreasing utility as China, Russia, and Iran grow more powerful. Combined operations done either independently or in conjunction with the United States remove the optic that freedom of the seas is a peculiar American prerogative and reiterate that it should concern the international community. Furthermore, state practice by several states or many states reinforces customary international law more powerfully than state practice by a single state—even if the single state is the United States.

Threats to freedom of navigation and overflight are in no small part a symptom of the uneven and lackadaisical approach states have taken to freedom of the seas. Contemporary challenges provide an opportunity to reconsider past assumptions that freedom of the seas is a cost-free public good that will persevere on the strength of its own logic and without more robust and unified action among the world's major democracies.

Countries have been reticent to speak plainly and honestly about China's unlawful claims. To refocus the problem, we should change the way we describe and challenge maritime claims that lack a basis in international law. Such claims often are described as "excessive" maritime claims because they exceed the limits or rules of the law of the sea reflected in UNCLOS.[38] The term "excessive," however, is a euphemism that is unnecessarily ambiguous and equivocating, and it suggests that the line between "reasonable" and "excessive" is quite blurred. In reality, although there are some legally complex issues of good faith disagreement in the international law of the sea, freedom of navigation is not one of them. The standards for the limits on lawful maritime claims and the extent of navigational rights and freedoms generally are rather forthright and simple.

Fortifying and shaping the law of the sea is a strategic imperative for the United States. The role of international law in the oceans is important because they from a single, coherent, interconnected geography, subject to a single set of norms, rules, laws, and institutions. The challenges now unfolding in the South China Sea, the Baltic Sea, the Persian Gulf, and elsewhere form an inflection point in the international law of the sea. To strengthen its hand, the United States should join UNCLOS and champion the navigational rights and freedoms reflected in it. The rule of law in the oceans has been a source of security, prosperity, and stability for the United States and the world. If states fail to take seriously freedom of navigation and overflight, the liberal order of the oceans will unwind. In Asia, this would mean China would establish hegemony. Likewise, Russia and Iran stand on the cusp of dominating their regions. The deteriorating maritime order will profoundly undermine the security of the United States and its allies and strategic partners, and with it, global stability.

NOTES

Introduction

1. From the Greek Ὠκεανὸς, or *okeanos* (Oceanus).
2. See, e.g., Alberico Gentili, *II De Iure Belli Libri Tres*, trans. John C. Rolfe (Oxford, UK: Clarendon, 1933 [1612]), 24; and Theodor Meron, "Common Rights of Mankind in Gentili, Grotius and Suarez," *American Journal of International Law* 85 (1991): 113–14.
3. John Norton Moore, *Navigational Freedom: The Most Critical Common Heritage*, International Law Studies 93 (Newport, R.I.: Naval War College, 2017), 259.

Chapter 1. "Millions for Defense—Not a Cent for Tribute"

1. Thomas Paterson et al., *American Foreign Relations: A History*, vol. 1, *To 1920* (Belmont, Calif.: Wadsworth, 2009), 5.
2. James Livesey, *Making Democracy in the French Revolution*, Harvard Historical Study 140 (Cambridge, Mass.: Harvard University Press, 2001), 18–19.
3. Jefferson to George Rogers Clark, December 25, 1780, in Thomas Jefferson, *The Papers of Thomas Jefferson*, vol. 4, *October 1787 to February 1781*, ed. Julian P. Boyd (Princeton, N.J.: Princeton University Press, 1951) [hereafter Boyd, *Papers of Jefferson*], 233.
4. Samuel Flagg Bemis, *A Diplomatic History of the United States*, 4th ed. (New York: Henry Holt, 1955), 875.
5. Treaty of Amity and Commerce between the United States and France, February 6, 1778 [hereafter Treaty of Amity and Commerce], in *Treaties and Other International Acts of the United States of America*, ed. Hunter Miller (Washington, D.C.: Government Printing Office [hereafter GPO], 1931) [hereafter UST], 2:3–35, *U.S. Statutes at Large* [hereafter Stat.], 8:12–31; and UST, 2:36–44, Stat., 8:6–11.
6. Richard Buel Jr., *In Irons: Britain's Naval Supremacy and the American Revolutionary Economy* (New Haven, Conn.: Yale University Press, 1998), 37.

7. Worthington Chauncey Ford, ed., *Journals of the Continental Congress 1774–1779* (Washington, D.C.: GPO, 1905), 5:576–90; Plan of Treaties as Adopted (with Instructions), 17 September 1776, in John Adams, *Papers of John Adams*, vol. 4, *February–August 1776*, ed. Robert J. Taylor (Cambridge, Mass.: Harvard University Press, 1979), 290–302.

8. Samuel Flagg Bemis, *The Diplomacy of the American Revolution: The Foundations of American Diplomacy, 1775–1823* (New York: D. Appleton-Century, 1935), 46.

9. Ford, *Journals of the Continental Congress*, 5:768–78.

10. Treaty of Amity and Commerce, in UST, 2:3–35, and Stat., 8:12–31. See also Act Separate and Secret, February 6, 1778, Stat., 17:795–96.

11. Treaty of Alliance, UST, 2:36–44, Stat., 8:6–11.

12. Benjamin Franklin to M. le Comte de Vergennes, March 16, 1783, in Benjamin Franklin, *The Papers of Benjamin Franklin*, vol. 39, *January 21 through May 15, 1783*, ed. Ellen R. Cohn (New Haven, Conn.: Yale University Press, 2008), 343–44.

13. Paterson et al., *American Foreign Relations*, 1:20.

14. Ford, *Journals of the Continental Congress*, 24:393–94.

15. John Adams to Robert R. Livingston, July 14, 1783, in John Adams, *Papers of John Adams* (Boston: Massachusetts Historical Society, 2017), vol. 15, https://www.masshist.org/publications/.

16. Declaration of His Danish Majesty Regarding the Neutrality of the Baltic Sea, communicated to the Courts of the Belligerent Powers, May 8, 1780, in *The Armed Neutralities of 1780 and 1800*, ed. James Brown Scott (Oxford, UK: Oxford University Press for the Carnegie Endowment for International Peace, 1918), 273–74.

17. M. Lambert, Councillor of State and of the Council Royal of Finance and Commerce, Comptroller General of Finance [of France] to M. Jefferson, Minister Plenipotentiary for the United States of America at the Court of Versailles, December 29, 1787, in *American State Papers: Foreign Relations 1789–1797* (Washington, D.C.: Gales and Seaton, 1833), Documents, Legislative and Executive of the Congress of the United States, Senate, 1st Congress, 3rd Session Foreign Relations [hereafter *American State Papers: Foreign Relations*], 1:115–16.

18. Gouverneur Morris to Monsieur Chambonas, Paris, July 9, 1792, in ibid., 1:332–34.

19. Georges Lefebvre, *The French Revolution from Its Origins to 1793*, trans. Elizabeth Moss Evanson (New York: Columbia University Press, 1962), 206–26.

20. William Edward Hartpole Lecky, *A History of England in the Eighteenth Century* (New York: D. Appleton, 1887), 5:599–601.

21. Jared Sparks, *The Writings of George Washington* (1923; repr. San Bernardino, Calif.: Ulan, 2012), 533.

22. Gardner W. Allen, *Our Naval War with France* (Boston: Houghton Mifflin, 1909), 5.

23. *American State Papers: Foreign Relations*, 1:140.

24. John Bassett Moore, *A Digest of International Law* (Washington, D.C.: GPO, 1906), 5:591–92.

25. Proclamation of Neutrality, April 22, 1793, in George Washington, *Writings of George Washington*, ed. John C. Fitzpatrick (Washington, D.C.: GPO, 1931–44), 32:430–31.

26. An Act to Provide a Naval Armament, March 27, 1794, Stat., 1:350–51.

27. Moore, *Digest of International Law*, 5:592–94.

28. Treaty of Amity, Commerce and Navigation, between His Britannic Majesty; and The United States of America, November 19, 1794, Stat., 8:116.

29. Larry Sechrest, "Privately Funded and Built U.S. Warships in the Quasi-War, 1797–1801," *Independent Review* 12 (Summer 2007): 103.

30. John J. Currier, *History of Newburyport, Massachusetts* (Newburyport, Massachusetts, 1906), 239–41.

31. Alexander DeConde, *The Quasi-War: The Politics and Diplomacy of the Undeclared War with France, 1797–1801* (New York: Scribner, 1966), 9.

32. Samuel Eliot Morison, *The Maritime History of Massachusetts, 1783–1860* (Boston: Houghton Mifflin, 1941; repr. 1979), 168.

33. Moore, *Digest of International Law*, 5:595.

34. Neutrality Act, June 5, 1794, Stat., 1:381. See also David P. Currie, *The Constitution in Congress: The Federalist Period, 1789–1801*, 2nd ed. (Chicago: University of Chicago Press, 1997), 181–82.

35. Moore, *Digest of International Law*, 5:598–99.

36. Treaty of Amity and Commerce between the United States of America and His Most Christian Majesty, February 6, 1778 [hereafter Treaty between America and His Most Christian Majesty], Art. XII, Stat., 8:12–14.

37. An Act for Registering and Clearing Vessels, Regulating the Coasting Trade, and for other purposes, September 1, 1789, Stat., 1:55.

38. Moore, *Digest of International Law*, 5:599.

39. Report of the Secretary of State respecting the depredations committed on the commerce of the United States since the 1st of October, 1796, *American State Papers: Foreign Relations*, 5th Congress, 1st Session, 2:28–29.

40. President John Adams, Special Message to the Senate and the House, May 16, 1797, *American State Papers: Foreign Relations*, 5th Congress, 1st Session, 1:40–42.

41. Address of the Senate to John Adams, President of the United States, May 23, 1797, *American State Papers: Foreign Relations*, 5th Congress, 1st Session, 1:42.

42. Address of the House of Representatives to John Adams, President of the United States, June 2, 1797, ibid., 43.

43. An Act to prevent citizens of the United States from Privateering against nations in amity with, or against citizens of the United States, June 14, 1797, Stat., 1:520.

44. An Act Providing a Naval Armament, July 1, 1797, Stat., 1:523–25.

45. President John Adams, May 31, 1797, *American State Papers: Foreign Relations*, 2:19.

46. Allen, *Our Naval War with France*, 24.

47. Law Relative to Vessels Laden with English Merchandise, of the 29th Nivôse, 6th year, January 18, 1796, *American State Papers: Foreign Relations*, 2:182–83.

48. Greg H. Williams, *The French Assault on American Shipping, 1793–1813: A History and Comprehensive Record of Merchant Marine Losses* (Jefferson, N.C.: McFarland, 2009), 272–73.

49. *American State Papers: Foreign Relations* (1832), 1:748.

50. John Adams, Message to the Senate and House Regarding Reports of the Envoys to France, March 19, 1798, *American State Papers: Foreign Relations*, 5th Congress, 2nd Session, 2:152.

51. Adams to Congress, *American State Papers: Foreign Relations* (1832), 2:199.

52. Alexander DeConde, *The Quasi-War: The Politics and Diplomacy of the Undeclared War with France, 1797–1801* (New York: Scribner, 1966), 74.

53. An Act to provide an additional Armament for the further protection of the trade of the United States, and for other purposes, April 17, 1798, Stat., 1:552.

54. An Act to Establish an Executive Department, to be Denominated the Department of the Navy, April 30, 1798, Stat., 1:553–54.

55. An Act supplementary to the act providing for the further defence of the ports and harbors of the United States, May 3, 1798, Stat., 1:554–55.

56. An Act to authorize the President of the United States to cause to be purchased, or built, a number of small vessels to be equipped as gallies [*sic*], or otherwise, May 4, 1798, Stat., 1:556.

57. An Act more effectually to protect the Commerce and Coasts of the United States, May 28, 1798, Stat., 1:561.

58. An Act to Suspend the Commercial Intercourse between the United States and France, and the Dependencies Thereof, June 13, 1798, Stat., 1:565.

59. An Act to amend the act, intitled [*sic*] an act providing a Naval Armament, and the Act Intitled [*sic*] An Act to authorize the President of the United States to cause to be purchased or built, a number of small vessels, to be equipped as Gallies [*sic*] or otherwise, June 22, 1798, Stat. 1: 569.

60. An Act to authorize the defence of the Merchant Vessels of the United States against French depredations, June 25, 1798, Stat., 1:572.

61. Jean Edward Smith, *John Marshall: Definer of a Nation* (New York: Holt, 1996), 236.

62. Position of Commanding General of the Army, with the Rank of Lieutenant General, Established by the Act Creating the Provisional Army, May 28, 1798, Stat., 1:558.

63. An Act to Authorize the Defense of the Merchant Vessels of the United States against French Depredations, June 25, 1798, Stat., 1:572, sec. 1.

64. Ibid., sec. 2, and An Act in addition to the act more effectually to protect the Commerce and Coasts of the United States, June 28, 1798, Stat., 1:574.

65. An Act to Authorize the Defense of the Merchant Vessels of the United States against French Depredations, June 25, 1798, Stat., 1:572, sec. 3.

66. An Act to Declare the Treaties Heretofore Concluded with France, no Longer Obligatory on the United States, July 7, 1798, Stat., 1:578.

67. An Act further to protect the Commerce of the United States, July 9, 1798, Stat., 1:578–79, sec. 1.

68. An Act for the establishing and organizing [of] a Marine Corps, July 11, 1788, Stat., 1:594–95.

69. An Act to make a further appropriation for the additional Naval armament, July 16, 1798, Stat., 1:609. See also Marshall Smelser, *The Congress Founds the Navy 1787–1798* (Bloomington: Indiana University Press, 1959), 48–59.

70. Charles Lee, "Treason," *Opinions of the Attorney-General* 1, no. 84, reprinted in *Opinions of the Attorneys General and Judgments of the Supreme Court and Court of Claims of the United States relating to the Controversy over Neutral Rights between the United States and France, 1797–1800*, ed. James Brown Scott, Carnegie Endowment for International Peace Pamphlet 25 (Washington, D.C.: Carnegie Endowment for International Peace, 1917), 1.

71. Michael V. Seitzinger, *Conducting Foreign Relations without Authority: The Logan Act* (Washington, D.C.: Congressional Research Service, February 1, 2006), 2–3.

72. James D. Richardson, ed., *A Compilation of the Messages and Papers of the Presidents, 1789–1897—Published by Authority of Congress* (Washington, D.C.: GPO, 1896–99), 1:267.

73. An Act for the punishment of certain Crimes therein specified, January 30, 1799, Stat., 1:613.

74. An Act Further to Suspend the Commercial Intercourse between the United States and France, and the Dependencies Thereof, February 9, 1799, Stat., 1:613–16.

75. Little et al. v. Barrame et al. (Flying Fish), 6 U.S. (2 Cranch) 170 (1804).

76. Bas v. Tingy, 4 U.S. 37 (1800), reprinted in Scott, *Opinions of the Attorneys General*, 6–17.

77. Ibid., 10.

78. DeConde, *Quasi-War*, 206–15. The United States withdrew its support for the uprising after the conclusion of the Quasi-War (p. 300).

79. Convention between the French Republic and the United States of America, September 30, 1800, Stat., 8:178, UST, 2:457–87.

80. George Washington, Farewell Address, September 19, 1796, *American State Papers: Foreign Relations*, 4th Congress, 2nd Session, 1:34.

81. An act concerning French Citizens that have been, or may be Captured and Brought into the United States, February 28, 1799, Stat., 1:624.

82. Williams, *French Assault on American Shipping*, 3–4.

83. George C. Daughan, *If by Sea: The Forging of the American Navy—from the Revolution to the War of 1812* (New York: Basic Books, 2008), 323.

Chapter 2. "Our Country Right or Wrong"

1. Ian Toll, review of *The Shores of Tripoli: Lieutenant Putnam and the Barbary Pirates*, by James L. Haley, *New York Times*, December 10, 2010.

2. Robert C. Davis, *Christian Slaves, Muslim Masters: White Slavery in the Mediterranean, the Barbary Coast, and Italy, 1500–1800* (London: Palgrave Macmillan, 2004), 23.

3. Robert C. Davis, *Holy War and Human Bondage: Tales of Christian-Muslim Slavery in the Early-Modern Mediterranean* (Santa Barbara, Calif.: Praeger, 2009), 11.

4. England ("Britain" after 1707) signed some twelve treaties with Algiers between 1682 and 1801. See *British and Foreign State Papers*, vol. 1, *1812–1814* (London: James Ridgeway & Sons, 1841), part 1, 354–74.

5. The Paris Peace Treaty of September 30, 1783, in UST, 2:151–57.

6. Joint Commission to Negotiate a Treaty of Amity and Commerce with Great Britain, The United States in Congress Assembled, May 12, 1784, in Boyd, *Papers of Jefferson*, 7:262–65; and John Adams, *Papers of John Adams*, ed. Gregg L. Lint et al. (Cambridge, Mass.: Harvard University Press, 2012), 16:xxv–xxviii, 207–9. On June 3,

1784, Congress authorized three additional commissions to negotiate treaties with France, the Netherlands, and Sweden.

7. The commission stated, "That Treaties of Amity or of Amity and Commerce be entered into with Morocco and the regencies of Algiers, Tunis and Tripoli to continue for the same term of ten years or for a term as much longer as can be procured." Enclosure III: Instructions to the Commissioners for Negotiating Treaties of Amity and Commerce, May 7, 1784, in Boyd, *Papers of Thomas Jefferson*, 7:266–71.

8. Thomas Jefferson to Francis Eppes, December 11, 1785, in ibid., 9:91–93.

9. Edmund Jenings to John Adams, February 5, 1781, in Adams, *Papers of John Adams*, 11:110–12.

10. Office of the Press Secretary, Joint statement by the United States of America and the Kingdom of Morocco, the White House, November 22, 2013.

11. Mr. Carmichael to Thomas Jefferson, July 19, 1785, in *The Diplomatic Correspondence of the United States of America* (Washington, D.C.: Blair and Rives, 1837), 2:379.

12. Treaty of Peace and Friendship, with additional article and Ship-Signals Agreement, June 28 and July 15, 1786, in UST, 2:185–227.

13. "U.S.-Morocco Peace and Friendship Treaty, longest unbroken treaty relationship signed by the U.S.," *Morocco World News*, February 24, 2012.

14. Message of President George Washington to the Congress of the United States, communicating a report of the Secretary of State, in relation to American prisoners at Algiers, December 30, 1790, in *Naval Documents Related to the United States Wars with the Barbary Powers* (Washington, D.C.: GPO, 1939) [hereafter NDBP], 1:19.

15. Report of the Secretary of State relative to the Mediterranean Trade, communicated to the House of Representatives, December 30, 1790, and to the Senate, January 3, 1791, in ibid., 1:23.

16. Thomas Jefferson to John Jay, August 23, 1785, in Boyd, *Papers of Thomas Jefferson*, 8:426–28.

17. Richard O'Brien, Algiers, to Thomas Jefferson, U.S. Minister to Paris, France, June 8, 1786, in NDBP, 1:3.

18. Message of President George Washington ... in relation to American prisoners, in NDBP, 1:21.

19. Thomas Jefferson, U.S. Minister to Paris, France, to John Adams, U.S. Minister to London, England, July 11, 1786, in NDBP, 1:10.

20. John Adams, U.S. Minister to London, to Thomas Jefferson, U.S. Minister to Paris, France, July 31, 1786, in ibid., 1:11.

21. Philip Corrigan and Derek Sayer, *The Great Arch: English State Formation as Cultural Revolution* (Oxford, UK: Oxford University Press, 1985), 83.

22. Neutrality Proclamation, April 22, 1793, in Christine Sternberg Patrick and John C. Pinheiro, eds., *The Papers of George Washington: Presidential Series* (Charlottesville: University of Virginia Press, 2005), 12:472–74.

23. Act of March 20, 1794, Third Congress, Session I, Ch. VII, Stat., 345. See also H. Knox, Secretary of War, Construction of Frigates Under the Act of March 20, 1794, December 29, 1794, in *American State Papers: Naval Affairs* (Washington, D.C.: Gales and Seaton, 1834), Documents, Legislative and Executive of the Congress of the United States, Senate, 1st Congress, 1st Session to the 18th Congress, 2nd Session, Naval Affairs [hereafter *American State Papers: Naval Affairs*], 6.

24. Treaty of Peace and Amity, signed at Algiers, September 5, 1795, in UST, 2:275.

25. Secretary of State to David Humphreys, U.S. Minister to Madrid, Spain, March 3, 1798, in NDBP, 1:239–43.

26. Accounts of Sundry Cargoes Shipped by the United States for Algiers, February 22, 1799, in ibid., 1:302–3.

27. Richard O'Brien, U.S. Consul General, Algiers, to Secretary of State, October 14, 1798, in ibid., 1:262–63.

28. Treaty of Peace and Friendship, signed at Tripoli, November 4, 1797, in UST, 2:349.

29. Treaty of Peace and Friendship, signed at Tunis, August 28, 1797, and, with alterations, March 26, 1799, in ibid., 2:386.

30. Truce with Tunis, for six months, concluded by Joseph Étienne Famin, for Joel Barlow, U.S. Agent, Algiers, June 15, 1796, in NDBP, 1:158–59.

31. Richard O'Brien, U.S. Consul General, Algiers, to William Eaton, U.S. Consul, Tunis, October 19, 1800, in NDBP, 1:384.

32. Extract from a letter from an officer on board the *George Washington*, Captain William Bainbridge, U.S. Navy, Commanding, October 14, 1800, in ibid., 1:381.

33. Captain William Bainbridge, U.S. Navy, to Richard O'Brien, U.S. Consul General, Algiers, October 9, 1800, in ibid., 1:375.

34. *The Papers of Thomas Jefferson*, vol. 29, *1 March 1796–31 December 1797*, ed. Barbara B. Oberg (Princeton, N.J.: Princeton University Press, 2002), 375–77.

35. Joseph J. Ellis, *American Sphinx: The Character of Thomas Jefferson* (New York: Vintage Books, 1998), 241.

36. James L. Cathcart, U.S. Consul, Tripoli, to Nicholas C. Nissen, Danish Consul General, Tripoli, May 15, 1801, in NDBP, 1:453; Circular Issued by James L. Cathcart, U.S. Consul, Tripoli, May 16, 1801, in ibid., 1:454–55.

37. Samuel Smith, for Acting Secretary of the Navy, to Captain Richard Dale, U.S. Navy, or Officer Commanding the America Squadron in the Mediterranean, in ibid., 1:465.

38. Captain Richard Dale, U.S. Navy, to Captain Samuel Barron, U.S. Navy, commanding Frigate *Philadelphia*, July 4, 1801, in ibid., 1:500.

39. To Lieutenant Colonel Commandant William W. Burrows, U.S. Marine Corps, from First Lieutenant Newton Keene, U.S. Marine Corps, July 9, 1801, in ibid., 1:506.

40. Dale to Barron, July 4, 1801.

41. Captain Richard Dale, U.S. Navy, to Lieutenant Andrew Sterett, Essex, July 30, 1801, in NDBP, 1:534.

42. "Capture of the Warship *Tripoli* by U.S. Schooner *Enterprise*," November 18, 1801, *National Intelligencer & Advertiser*, in ibid., 1:538–39.

43. An Act for the protection of the Commerce and Seamen of the United States, against the Tripolitan Cruisers, February 6, 1802, Statute II, 129–30, in NDBP, 2:51–52.

44. William Eaton, U.S. Consul, Tunis, to Secretary of State, September 12, 1802, in ibid., 2:271–71.

45. Extract from journal of Midshipman Henry Wadsworth, U.S. Navy, on board *Chesapeake*, Captain Richard V. Morris, U.S. Navy, commanding,

14 March 1803, concerning references to 10 and 13 March 1803, in ibid., 2:374.

46. First Lieutenant Hooper, U.S. Marine Corps, to William Eaton, May 22, 1803, in ibid., 2:415.

47. Extract from journal of Midshipman Henry Wadsworth, U.S. Navy, on board *New York*, Captain Richard V. Morris, U.S. Navy, commanding, 2 June 1803, in ibid., 2:435–37.

48. S. Barron, Precept of the Court, April 13, 1804, in ibid., 2:528.

49. Thomas Jefferson to P. Mazzei, July 18, 1804, in Thomas Jefferson, *Memoirs, Correspondence, and Private Papers of Thomas Jefferson, Late President of the United States*, ed. Thomas Jefferson Randolph (London: Henry Colburn and Richard Bentley, 1829), 4:22.

50. Résumé, presumably prepared in Navy Department about 1806 or 1807, concerning the U.S. frigate *Constellation*, flagship of Commodore Edward Preble, May 14, 1803, to November 9, 1804, in NDBP, 3:9–11.

51. Statement of Captain William Bainbridge before the Court Enquiring into the Loss of U.S. Frigate *Philadelphia*, June 29, 1805, in ibid., 3:192.

52. Court Enquiring into the Loss of U.S. Frigate *Philadelphia*, June 29, 1805, in ibid., 3:189–94.

53. For "heeling," see Dixon Kemp, *A Manual of Yacht and Boat Sailing* (London: Horace Cox, 1878), 350.

54. Statement of Captain William Bainbridge before the Court Enquiring into the Loss of U.S. Frigate *Philadelphia*, June 29, 1805, in NDBP, 3:190.

55. Ibid.

56. Ibid., 3;194.

57. William Bainbridge to Hon. Robert Smith, Secretary of the Navy, November 1, 1803, in *American State Papers: Naval Affairs*, 122–23.

58. Concerning the Destruction of the Frigate *Philadelphia*, in NDBP, 3:433–23.

59. Lieutenant Stephen Decatur Jr., U.S. Navy, to Captain Edward Preble, U.S. Navy, February 17, 1804, in NDBP (1941), 3:414.

60. Cyrus Townsend Brady, "Decatur and the *Philadelphia*," *McClure's Magazine* 14 (1900): 62. See also Kenneth J. Hagan, "What to Rule the Waves With," *New York Times*, April 16, 1989.

61. George Davis, U.S. chargé d'affaires, Tunis, to Tobias Lear, U.S. Consul General, Algiers, March 9, 1804 in NDBP, 3:483.

62. Extract from journal kept on board the U.S. Frigate *Constitution* by Captain Edward Preble, U.S. Navy, August 4, 1804, in ibid., 4:336–38.

63. Captain Edward Preble, U.S. Navy, to George Davis, U.S. chargé d'affaires, Tunis, August 7, 1804, in ibid., 4:340.

64. Extract from "Life of Stephen Decatur," by Alexander Slidell McKenzie, U.S. Navy, August 3, 1804, in ibid., 4:347–48.

65. Purser Noadiah Morris, U.S. Navy, to unknown, in ibid., 4:353–54.

66. Extract from journal of Midshipman F. Cornelius deKrafft, U.S. Navy, in U.S. brig *Siren* of 18 guns, Master Commandant Charles Stewart, U.S. Navy, commanding, August 24, 1804, in ibid., 4:456–57.

67. Commodore Edward Preble to the Secretary of the Navy, September 18, 1804, in *American State Papers: Naval Affairs*, 133, 137.

68. Extract from journal kept by Purser John Darby, U.S. Navy, on board *John Adams*, Master Commandant Isaac Chauncey, U.S. Navy, commanding, September 4, 1804, in NDBP, 4:506.

69. Blowing up of U.S. ketch *Intrepid*, in ibid., 4:509.

70. Preble to the Secretary of the Navy, September 18, 1804, in *American State Papers: Naval Affairs*, 137.

71. Purser Noadiah Morris, in NDBP, 4:356–57.

72. Dudley W. Knox, preface to NDBP, 5:iii.

73. William Eaton, U.S. Navy Agent for the Barbary Regencies, to Sir Alexander John Ball, British Civil Commissioner and Governor of Malta, December 16, 1804, in ibid., 5:192.

74. William Eaton, U.S. Navy Agent for the Barbary Regencies, to Secretary of the Navy, February 13, 1805, in ibid., 5:348.

75. Treaty of Peace and Amity, signed at Tripoli, June 4, 1805, in UST, 2:529–56.

76. Thomas Jefferson to United States Congress to the Senate & House of Representatives of the U.S., January 13, 1806, in Thomas Jefferson, *The writings of Thomas Jefferson: being his autobiography, correspondence, reports, messages, addresses, and other writings, official and private. Published by the order of the Joint committee of Congress on*

the library, from the original manuscripts, deposited in the Department of State, ed. H. A. Washington (New York: Riker, Thorne, 1854, reprinted 2011), 54–57.

77. Ibid.

78. Frank Lambert, *The Barbary Wars: American Independence in the Atlantic World* (New York: Hill & Wang, 2005), 175.

79. Ibid.

80. Treaty of Peace and Amity, signed at Algiers, September 5, 1795, in UST, 2:275.

81. William Spencer, *Algiers in the Age of Corsairs* (Norman: University of Oklahoma Press, 1976), 139.

82. Treaty of Peace and Amity between His Britannic Majesty and the United States of America, December 24, 1814, in UST, 2:574.

83. The battle is covered in detail in Gardner W. Allen, *Our Navy and the Barbary Corsairs* (Boston: Houghton Mifflin, 1905), 282–85.

84. Stephen Decatur and William Shaler to Hon. James Monroe, Secretary of State, July 4, 1815, in *British and Foreign State Papers*, 2:1051.

85. Treaty of Peace, signed at Algiers, June 30 and July 3, 1815, in UST, 2:585.

86. Stephen Decatur to the Hon. James Monroe, Secretary of State, July 5, 1816, in *Analectic Magazine and Naval Chronicle* 7 (February 1816): 129–30.

87. Allen, *Our Navy and the Barbary Corsairs*, 289.

88. Treaty of Peace and Amity, with Article Additional and Explanatory, signed at Algiers, December 22 and 23, 1816, in UST, 2:617. See also Allen, *Our Navy and the Barbary Corsairs*, 300.

89. *Niles' Weekly Register* 10, supp. to no. 8 (April 20, 1816): 136.

Chapter 3. "Free Trade and Sailor's Rights"

1. Preface to William S. Dudley, ed., *The Naval War of 1812: A Documentary History* (Washington, D.C.: Naval Historical Center, 1985) [hereafter Dudley, *Documentary History*], 1:xiv.

2. Gordon E. Sherman, "Orders in Council and the Law of the Sea," *American Journal of International Law* 16 (July 1922): 413–15.

3. Charles Burke Elliott, "The Doctrine of Continuous Voyages," *American Journal of International Law* 1 (January–April 1907): 64.

4. Sentence of the Vice-Admiralty Court of Nassau, New Providence, in the case of the Brig *Essex*, Joseph Orne, Master, in Dudley, *Documentary History*, 1:16–20.

5. Imperial Decree of the 21st November 1806, *American State Papers, Foreign Relations 1789–1797* (Washington, D.C.: Gales and Seaton, 1833), Documents, Legislative and Executive of the Congress of the United States, Senate, 1st Congress, 3rd Session, Foreign Relations [hereafter *American State Papers: Foreign Relations*], 2:806.

6. James Madison, Message to the Senate and House of Representatives of the United States, June 1, 1812, in Dudley, *Documentary History*, 1:76.

7. Bradford Perkins, *Prologue to War: England and the United States, 1805–1812* (Berkeley: University of California Press, 1961), 72.

8. Mr. Temple Luttrell, Debate in the Commons on Mr. Temple Luttrell's Bill for the more easy and effectual Manning of the Navy, March 11, 1777, in *Parliamentary History of England from the Earliest Period to the Year 1803*, ed. W. Cobbett and J. Wright (London, 1806–1820), 19:82.

9. Roland G. Usher Jr., "Royal Navy Impressment during the American Revolution," *Mississippi Valley Historical Review* 37 (March 1951): 673.

10. N. A. M. Rodger, *The Command of the Ocean: A Naval History of Britain, 1649–1815* (New York: W. W. Norton, 2005), 608.

11. Usher, "Royal Navy Impressment," 682.

12. Mr. Temple Luttrell, Debate in the Commons, in Cobbett and Wright, *Parliamentary History*, 19:84.

13. Francis D. Cogliano, *Emperor of Liberty: Thomas Jefferson's Foreign Policy* (New Haven, Conn.: Yale University Press, 2014), 210–11.

14. Alan Taylor, *The Civil War of 1812: American Citizens, British Subjects, Irish Rebels, & Indian Allies* (New York: Vintage Books, 2011), 104–5.

15. John Quincy Adams, Reply to the Appeal of Massachusetts Federalists, in *Documents Relating to New England Federalism 1800–1815*, ed. Henry Adams (Boston: Little, Brown, 1877; repr. 1905), 178.

16. Christopher Lloyd, *A Short History of the Royal Navy: 1805–1918* (London: Methuen, 1942; repr. London: Routledge, 2016).

17. Henry Adams, *History of the United States of America during the First Administration of Thomas Jefferson* (New York: Charles Scribner's & Sons, 1889; repr. 1909), 2:423.

18. American Minister in London Rufus King to Secretary of State James Madison, July, 1803, *British and Foreign State Papers 1810–1814* (London: James Ridgeway & Sons, undated), 2:1403–1404.

19. *The Naval Chronicle for 1812: Containing a General and Biographical History of the Royal Navy* (London: 1812), s.v. Salusbury Pryce Humphreys, 28:356.

20. An Act laying an Embargo on all ships and vessels in the ports and harbors of the United States, December 22, 1807, Stat., 2:451.

21. See United States v. The Brig Eliza [1816] 7 Cranch (Supreme Court of the United States), p. 113.

22. An act to interdict the commercial intercourse between the United States and Great Britain and France, and their dependencies, March 1, 1809, Stat., 2:528.

23. Macon's Bill No. 2, May 1, 1810, Stat., 2:605.

24. From James Madison to Congress, 1 April 1812, in James Madison, *The Papers of James Madison: Presidential Series*, ed. J. C. A. Stagg et al. (Charlottesville: University Press of Virginia, 1999), 4:279–80. See also Henry Clay, *The Works of Henry Clay*, ed. Calvin Colton (New York: Barnes & Burr, 1863), 5:60.

25. From James Madison to Congress, June 1, 1812, in Madison, *Papers of James Madison*, 4:432–39.

26. Message from the President of the United States Transmitting Copies of the Instructions Given to the Ministers of the United States Appointed to Negotiate a Peace with Great Britain, October 14, 1814, *American State Papers: Foreign Relations*, 3:695–726.

27. From James Madison to Congress, June 1, 1812, in Madison, *Papers of James Madison*, 4:432–39.

28. *Journal of the Senate of the United States of America, 1789–1873* (Washington, D.C.: Government Printing Office, n.d.), for June 17, 1812. See also *Annals of Congress*, Senate, 12th Congress, 1st Session (Hostilities with Great Britain), 271–98.

29. *Journal of the Senate*, June 17, 1812.

30. Donald R. Hickey, *The War of 1812: A Forgotten Conflict*, Bicentennial ed. (Champaign: University of Illinois Press, 2012), 307.

31. Leonard F. Guttridge, *Our Country, Right or Wrong: The Life of Stephen Decatur, the U.S. Navy's Most Illustrious Commander* (New York: Forge Books, 2006), 133.

32. Tom Halstead, "The Real, Shameful Story behind 'Don't Give Up the Ship!'" *Boston Globe*, May 19, 2013.

33. Carl Benn, *The War of 1812* (Oxford, UK: Osprey, 2002), 57.

34. Treaty of Peace and Amity between His Britannic Majesty and the United States of America (Treaty of Ghent), December 24, 1814, Stat., 8:218, and UST, 2:218.

35. Mr. Monroe, Secretary of State, to the American Plenipotentiaries at Gottenburg (Germany), January 28, 1814, in *Message from the President of the United States Transmitting Copies of the Instructions Given to the Ministers Appointed to Negotiate a Peace with Great Britain* (Washington, D.C.: Roger C. Weightman, 1814), 33.

36. James A. Carr, "The Battle of New Orleans and the Treaty of Ghent," *Diplomatic History* 3 (July 1979): 273–82.

37. Zachary F. Smith, *The Battle of New Orleans including the Previous Engagements between the Americans and the British, the Indians and the Spanish which led to the Final Conflict on the 8th of January, 1815* (Louisville, Ky.: John P. Morton, 1904), 84. Contemporary sources put U.S. casualties at eleven killed and twenty-three wounded. See Daniel Walker Howe, *What Hath God Wrought: The Transformation of America, 1815–1848* (Oxford, UK: Oxford University Press, 2009), 13.

38. Howe, *What Hath God Wrought*, 13.

39. Benn, *War of 1812*, 55.

40. Adm. James D. Watkins, dedication, in Dudley, *Documentary History*, 1:iii.

Chapter 4. "All Freedom . . . Depends on Freedom of the Seas"

1. "England Declares War on Germany," *New York Times*, August 5, 1914.

2. Adm. Sydney Stewart Hall, "Submarine Warfare," in *Transactions of the Grotius Society*, vol. 5, *Problems of Peace and War, Papers Read before the Society in the Year 1919* (Cambridge, UK: Cambridge University Press for the Hugo Grotius Society, 1919), 85.

3. Woodrow Wilson, Message to Congress, 63rd Congress, 2d Session, Senate Doc. No. 566 (Washington, D.C., 1914), 3–4.

4. James W. Garner, "Some Questions of International Law in the European War: War Zones and Submarine Warfare," *American Journal of International Law* 9 (July 1915): 594–95.

5. "Submarine Raid in the Irish Sea," *The Independent*, February 8, 1915, 191.

6. German Declaration of a Naval Zone, February 4, 1915, and Announcement of the German Admiralty Declaring the Waters Around Great Britain a War Zone, February 4, 1915, both in *Papers Relating to the Foreign Relations of the United States* (FRUS), 1915, Supplement 93–94, and Garner, "Some Questions of International Law," 594.

7. William Jennings Bryan to J. W. Gerard, February 10, 1915, in FRUS, 1915, Supplement 98.

8. German Ambassador (Bernstorff) to the Secretary of State, February 15, 1915, in ibid., Supplement 104–5.

9. British Ambassador (Spring Rice) to the Secretary of State, March 1, 1915, in ibid., Supplement 127–28.

10. "Report of a formal investigation into the circumstances attending the foundering on 28th March of the British steamship *Falaba* of Liverpool, in or near latitude 51 30' N., longitude 6 36' W., whereby loss of life ensued" (London: Darling & Son 1915) [hereafter Report on the Falaba], 5.

11. Consul General at London (Skinner) to the Secretary of State, April 7, 1915, in FRUS, 1915, Supplement 359–60.

12. "Report on the *Falaba*," 5.

13. Skinner to Secretary of State, April 7, 1915.

14. "Submarine Raid Killed American; Leon Chester Thrasher, an Engineer, Lost on the *Falaba*, Admiralty Announces," *New York Times*, March 31, 1915, 1.

15. Ambassador in Germany (Gerard) to the Secretary of State, April 14, 1915, and Secretary of State to the Ambassador in Great Britain (Page), October 12, 1915, both in FRUS, 1915, Supplement 370.

16. "Sinking of *Gulflight* Arouses Washington; Officials Regard It as Most Serious War Incident Involving American Interests," *New York Times*, May 3, 1915, 1.

17. Ambassador in Germany (Gerard) to the Secretary of State, June 1, 1915, in FRUS, 1915, Supplement 431. See also "Didn't See Our Flag on the *Gulflight*, until Torpedo Was Fired, Says German Commander," *New York Times*, June 1, 1915, 1.

18. "Germany Apologizes for the *Gulflight* Attack and Offers Reparation," *New York Times*, June 5, 1915, 1.

19. Gerard to Secretary of State, June 1, 1915, Supplement 439–40; "1,300 Die as *Lusitania* Goes to Bottom; 400 Americans on Board Torpedoed Ship," *New York Tribune*, May 8, 1915, 1.

20. "Loss of the *Lusitania* Fills London with Horror and Utter Amazement," *New York Times*, May 8, 1915, 1.

21. James W. Gerard, *My Four Years in Germany: Late Ambassador to the German Imperial Court* (New York: Grosset & Dunlap, 1917), 176.

22. Secretary of State to the Ambassador in Germany (Gerard), May 13, 1915, in FRUS, 1915, Supplement 315–16.

23. Ambassador W. H. Page to the Secretary of State, August 19, 1915, in Supplement: "Diplomatic Correspondence Between the United States and Belligerent Governments Relating to Neutral Rights and Commerce," *American Journal of International Law* 10, no. 4 (October 1916): 165.

24. The German Ambassador to the Secretary of State, September 1, 1915, in ibid., 166–67.

25. The Augusta Cotton Exchange and Board of Trade to the Secretary of State, June 25, 1915, in FRUS, 1915, Supplement 191–92.

26. Secretary of State to the Ambassador in Great Britain (Page), January 2, 1915, in ibid., Supplement 198.

27. Report of the General Board to the Secretary of the Navy, November 9, 1915, in Secretary of the Navy, *Annual Reports of the Navy Department for the Fiscal Year 1915* (Washington, D.C.: GPO, 1915), 75.

28. Naval Appropriations Act, 1916 (3 March 1915), Pub. L. 271, 63d Congress, 3d Session, Stat., 38:930.

29. Ambassador Gerard to the Secretary of State, April 11, 1916, in *Papers relating to the Torpedoing of the S.S.* Sussex (Washington, D.C.: GPO, 1916), 5.

30. Secretary of State Robert Lansing to J. W. Gerard, April 18, 1916, in ibid., 9.

31. "Breaking Diplomatic Relations and War Declarations," in *International Law Studies: Documents on Neutrality with Notes 1917* (Washington, D.C.: GPO, 1918), 222–23.

32. The Secretary of State to the German Ambassador, February 3, 1917, Severance of Diplomatic Relations Between the United States and Germany, in *American Journal of International Law* 11, no. 4 (October 1917): 336–37.

33. Address on the Essentials of Permanent Peace, delivered to the United States Senate, January 22, 1917, in Woodrow Wilson, *President Wilson's Foreign Policy: Messages, Addresses, Papers*, ed. James Brown Scott (New York: Oxford University Press, 1918), 251–52.

34. German Ambassador to the Secretary of State, January 31, 1917, Memoranda, in *American Journal of International Law* 11 (October 1917): 333.

35. Rodney Carlisle, *Sovereignty at Sea: U.S. Merchant Ships and American Entry into World War I* (Gainesville: University of Florida Press, 2009), 33.

36. "Breaking Diplomatic Relations and War Declarations," 222–23.

37. Carlisle, *Sovereignty at Sea*, 83.

38. "U-boat Captain Gave *Housatonic* an Hour's Warning before Sinking: Told American Crew He Had Orders to Sink Every England-Bound Ship, but Tows Men in Boats toward Land," *New York Times*, February 5, 1917.

39. Von Arnauld was a dashing figure and the most successful submarine captain ever—credited with sinking more than 500,000 tons of shipping before he was killed during World War II. See "Nazi Naval Chief Killed in France," February 27, 1941, 7, and "German U-Boat Expert Killed in R.A.F. Raid," February 27, 1941, 1, both *Daily Boston Globe*.

40. "Austrians Sink American Ship; Submarine Puts a Bomb Aboard the Schooner *Lyman M. Law* off Sardinia," *New York Times*, February 15, 1917, 1. The initial reports suggested that the Austrians were responsible for the sinking of the *Lyman M. Law*; in fact, the culprit was later determined to be a German U-boat.

41. "Captain of Submarine Threatened *Law*'s Men," *New York Times*, February 18, 1917, 1.

42. "*Lyman Law*'s Skipper Wished for 5-Pounder: McDonough Says He Could Have Sunk U-Boat 'As Easily as Buttering a Piece of Bread,'" *New York Times*, February 19, 1917, 2.

43. This incident is not to be confused with the torpedo attack by the German *U-156* on the British troopship *Laconia* on September 12, 1942, off the coast of West Africa. That ship went down with some 2,732 crew members, passengers, soldiers, and prisoners of war.

44. "Germany Seeks an Alliance against U.S.; Asks Japan and Mexico to Join Her," *New York Times*, March 1, 1917, 1.

45. Carlisle, *Sovereignty at Sea*, 106.

46. Ibid., 120–21.

47. Address of the President of the United States delivered at a Joint Session of the Two Houses of Congress, April 2, 1917, in *American Journal of International Law* 11 (October 1917): 352. See also "President Calls for War Declaration, Stronger Navy, New Army of 500,000 Men, Full Co-operation with Germany's Foes," *New York Times*, April 2, 1917, 1.

48. Address of the President, April 2, 1917, 357.

49. "Armed American Steamship Sunk; Eleven Men Missing," *New York Times*, April 2, 1917, 1.

50. Lothar von Arnauld also stopped the small U.S. schooner *Marguerite* that same day and burned it to the waterline after evacuating the crew.

51. George W. Baer, *One Hundred Years of Sea Power: The U.S. Navy, 1890–1990* (Palo Alto, Calif.: Stanford University Press, 1993), 77–80.

52. Ibid., 80.

53. Address on the Conditions of Peace, January 8, 1918, in Wilson, *President Wilson's Foreign Policy*, 359–62.

54. "A general association of nations must be formed under specific covenants for the purpose of affording mutual guarantees of political independence and territorial integrity to great and small [states] alike." Special Representative (House) to the Secretary of State (for the President), October 29, 1918, FRUS, 1918, Supplement 1: *The World War*, 1:405–13.

55. Ibid.

56. The President to the Special Representative (House), October 30, 1918, in ibid., 1:423.

57. The Special Representative (House) to the Secretary of State (for the President), October 30, 1918, in ibid., 1:421–23.

58. Special Representative (House) to the Secretary of State (for the President), November 3, 1918, in ibid., 1:455–56.

59. Special Representative (House) to the Secretary of State (for the President), November 4, 1918, in ibid., 1:460–62.

60. The Secretary of State to the Swiss Minister (Sulzer), November 5, 1918, in ibid., 1:468–69.

61. The *Lotus* (Judgment No. 9), 1927, P.C.I.J., Series A, No. 10, at 25.

62. Article 22, International Treaty for the Limitation and Reduction of Naval Armament, signed at London, April 22, 1930, entered into force December 31, 1930, 112 League of Nations Treaty Series 65.

63. Douglas Brinkley and David R. Facy-Crowther, eds., *The Atlantic Charter* (Basingstoke, UK: Macmillan, 1994), 40–41.

64. Address by the President, September 11, 1941, in *Department of State Bulletin 116*, September 13, 1941, 5:193.

65. Sinking of the SS *Steel Seafarer* in the Red Sea, September 10, 1941, Address by the President, September 11, 1941, in ibid., 5:197–98.

66. Sinking of the SS *Sessa* Southwest of Iceland, September 9, 1941, Address by the President, September 11, 1941, in ibid., 5:199–200.

67. Address by the President, September 11, 1941, in ibid., 5:194.

68. Ibid., 196.

69. "We Have Cleared Our Decks and Taken Our Battle Stations, Navy and Total Defense Day Address," in Franklin D. Roosevelt, *Public Papers and Addresses of Franklin D. Roosevelt*, 1941 volume, *The Call to Battle Stations*, edited by Samuel I. Rosenman (New York: Harper, 1950), 438–45.

70. Samuel Eliot Morison, *History of United States Naval Operations in World War II*, vol. 1, *The Battle of the Atlantic, September 1939–May 1943* (Boston: Little, Brown, 1947; repr. 1975), 80.

71. Arming of American-Flag Ships Engaged in Foreign Commerce, Message of the President to Congress, October 9, 1941, in *Department of State Bulletin 120*, October 11, 1941, 5:257–59.

72. The Defense of America, Address by Assistant Secretary Long, November 17, 1941, *Department of State Bulletin 126*, November 22, 1941, 5:407–409.

73. German Declaration of War with the United States, December 11, 1941, *Department of State Bulletin 129*, December 13, 1941, 5:480–81. USS *Reuben James* (DD 245), escorting an eastbound Allied convoy, was destroyed near Iceland with heavy loss of life by a torpedo apparently meant for a merchant ship.

74. Elihu Lauterpacht, C. J. Greenwood, and A. G. Oppenheim, eds., *International Law Reports* (Cambridge, UK: Cambridge University Press, 2002), 120:285.

75. The Atlantic Conference Resolution of September 24, 1941, was accepted by the governments of Belgium, Czechoslovakia, Greece, Luxembourg, the Netherlands, Norway, Poland, Soviet Union, Yugoslavia, and (Free) France. See Inter-Allied Council (London), September 24, 1941, *Department of State Bulletin 118*, September 27, 1941, 5:234.

Chapter 5. "Blank Check"

1. Lyndon B. Johnson, President's Message to Congress, H. Doc. 333, 80th Congress, 2d Session, *Department of State Bulletin 51*, no. 1313 (1964): 262.

2. Vietnam Task Forces, Office of the Secretary of Defense, "United States–Vietnam Relations 1945–1967," i–iii, top secret, declassified 2011, repr. *The Pentagon Papers*, part IV.C.2.B, available at https://www.archives.gov/research/pentagon-papers.

3. Lt. Col. Delmar C. Lang, USAF, Chief, B205, National Security Agency, "Memorandum for the Record: Chronology of Events 2–5 August 1964 in the Gulf of Tonkin, October 14, 1964," secret,

declassified July 5, 2005 [hereafter Chronology of Events in the Gulf of Tonkin]. Tactical (local) times in the Gulf of Tonkin are used in this chapter. The primary-source radio messages cited are in "Zulu" (Greenwich Mean Time), which is seven hours behind local time in the gulf.

4. COMSEVENTHFLT MSG 140536Z MAR 62, in Edward J. Marolda and Oscar Fitzgerald, *The United States Navy and the Vietnam Conflict*, vol. 2, *From Military Assistance to Combat 1959–1965* (Washington, D.C.: Naval Historical Center, 1986), 393.

5. COMSEVENTHFLT MSG 070524Z JAN 64 and COMSEVENTHFLT 151741Z AUG 1963, repr. Marolda and Fitzgerald, *Military Assistance to Combat*, 394–95.

6. Robert J. Hanyok, "Skunks, Bogies, Silent Hounds, and the Flying Fish: The Gulf of Tonkin Mystery, August 1964" (National Security Agency) *Cryptologic Quarterly* 19, no. 4 / 20, no. 1 (Winter 2000/ Spring 2001): 4–6, top secret, declassified February 24, 1998.

7. Department of State, telegram to the Embassy in Vietnam, August 2, 1964, in U.S. State Dept., *Foreign Relations of the United States, 1964–1968*, vol. 1, *Vietnam 1964* (Washington, D.C.: Office of the Historian, 1992) [hereafter FRUS *Vietnam* 1964–68], 1:592.

8. Robert McNamara, with Brian VanDeMark, *In Retrospect: The Tragedy and Lessons of Vietnam* (New York: Vintage Books, 1996), 130

9. State to the Embassy in Vietnam, August 2, 1964.

10. Chairman of the Vietnam Coordinating Committee (Forrestal), memorandum to the Secretary of State, August 3, 1964, FRUS *Vietnam* 1964–68, 1:598.

11. Chronology of Events in the Gulf of Tonkin, introduction.

12. State to the Embassy in Vietnam, August 2, 1964.

13. Forrestal to the Secretary of State, FRUS *Vietnam* 1964–68, 1:601.

14. CINCPAC MSG 140203Z JUL 64, cited in Hanyok, "Gulf of Tonkin Mystery," 6.

15. Hanyok, "Gulf of Tonkin Mystery," 12.

16. Chronology of Events in the Gulf of Tonkin, 4.

17. Hanyok, "Gulf of Tonkin Mystery," 13.

18. Edwin E. Moïse, *Tonkin Gulf and the Escalation of the Vietnam War* (Chapel Hill: University of North Carolina Press, 1996), 74–75.

19. DIRNSA MSG 02094Z AUG 64, cited in Hanyok, "Gulf of Tonkin Mystery," 16.

20. COMSEVENTHFLT MSG READDRESSED FLASH 021201Z AUG 64 and CTG 72.1 MSG 020807Z AUG 64, repr. Chronology of Events in the Gulf of Tonkin, tab 13.

21. CTG [Commander, Task Group] 72.1 MSG 021200Z AUG 64, NHC archive. CTG 72.1 was embarked on board USS *Maddox* or was the ship's commanding officer.

22. CTG 72.1 MSG 020829Z AUG 64, repr. Chronology of Events in the Gulf of Tonkin, tab 15.

23. CTG 72.1 MSG 020949Z AUG 64, repr. Chronology of Events in the Gulf of Tonkin, tab 18.

24. CTG 77.5 (USS *Turner Joy*) MSG 021008Z AUG 64, repr. Chronology of Events in the Gulf of Tonkin, tab 19.

25. Moïse, *Tonkin Gulf*, 83–84.

26. CTG 77.5 MSG 021008Z AUG 64. See also COMSEVENTHFLT MSG 021201Z AUG 64 and COMSEVENTHFLT MSG 020859Z AUG 64.

27. Moïse, *Tonkin Gulf*, 84.

28. Marolda and Fitzgerald, *Military Assistance to Combat*, 419; Moïse, *Tonkin Gulf*, 85.

29. Hanyok, "Gulf of Tonkin Mystery," 17.

30. Marolda and Fitzgerald write that *T-339* was sunk based upon erroneous intercepted communications from *T-333* and *T-336*. Marolda and Fitzgerald, *Military Assistance to Combat*, 419.

31. Moïse, *Tonkin Gulf*, 85.

32. Commander, Task Unit (CTU) 72.1.2 MSG 021443Z AUG 64, repr. Chronology of Events in the Gulf of Tonkin, tab 23.

33. CINCPACFLT MSG 021226Z AUG 64, repr. Chronology of Events in the Gulf of Tonkin, tab 21.

34. U.S. Protest to North Vietnam, *Department of State Bulletin* 51, no. 1313 (1964): 258.

35. Department of State, telegram to the Embassy in Vietnam, August 3, 1964, FRUS *Vietnam* 1964–68, 1:602.

36. U.S. Protest to North Vietnam, *Department of State Bulletin* 51, no. 1313 (1964): 258.

37. State to the Embassy in Vietnam, August 3, 1964, FRUS *Vietnam* 1964–68, 1:603.

38. CINCPACFLT MSG 021104Z AUG 64, repr. FRUS *Vietnam* 1964–68, 1:598–99; State to the Embassy in Vietnam, August 2, 1964; CINCPAC MSG 041554Z AUG 64, repr. Chronology of Events in the Gulf of Tonkin, tab 58. See also Forrestal to the Secretary of State, August 3, 1964, FRUS *Vietnam* 1964–68, 1:598–99.

39. Summary Notes of the 538th Meeting of the National Security Council, Washington, D.C., August 4, 1964, 6:15–6:40 p.m., FRUS *Vietnam* 1964–68, 1:611–12.

40. Forrestal to the Secretary of State, August 3, 1964, FRUS *Vietnam* 1964–68, 1:598–99.

41. Chairman of the Joint Chiefs of Staff (Wheeler), telegram to the commander in chief, Pacific (Sharp), August 2, 1964, FRUS *Vietnam* 1964–68, 1:593.

42. Statement by President Johnson, *Department of State Bulletin* 51, no. 1313 (1964): 259. See also Edwin L. Dale, "Johnson Directs Navy to Destroy any New Raiders, 2d Destroyer and Air Cover Ordered in Gulf of Tonkin after *Maddox* Attack," dateline: August 3, *New York Times*, August 4, 1964, 1.

43. Lyndon Baines Johnson, *The Vantage Point: Perspectives of the Presidency, 1963–1969* (New York: Holt, Rinehart and Winston, 1971), 113.

44. DRV Naval Activity Reports Losses and Claims Two Enemy Aircraft Shot Down, 2242G, August 4, 1964, Chronology of Events in the Gulf of Tonkin, tab 52; Summary of SIGINT Reflections of DRV Attack in Gulf of Tonkin 2–4 August 1964, Spot Report, August 4, 1964, Chronology of Events in the Gulf of Tonkin, tab 53; DIRNSA MSG 061604Z AUG 64, Chronology of Events in the Gulf of Tonkin, tab 55.

45. Jack Raymonds, "U.S. Suspending Naval Patrol in Gulf of Tonkin for a Time," *New York Times*, August 9, 1964, 34. See also Moïse, *Tonkin Gulf*, 92–93.

46. Hanyok, "Gulf of Tonkin Mystery," 20.

47. Marolda and Fitzgerald, *Military Assistance to Combat*, 424.

48. COMUSMACV MSG 040955Z AUG 64, cited in Moïse, *Tonkin Gulf*, 97; CTU 72.1.2 MSG 031546Z AUG 64, cited in Marolda and Fitzgerald, *Military Assistance to Combat*, 424.

49. COMUSMACV MSG 031231Z AUG 64, cited in Marolda and Fitzgerald, *Military Assistance to Combat*, 424–25; Moïse, *Tonkin Gulf*, 97.

50. Moïse, *Tonkin Gulf*, 98.

51. Michael Charlton and Anthony Moncrieff, *Many Reasons Why: The American Involvement in Vietnam*, 2nd ed. (London: Hill & Wang, 1989), 108.

52. William J. Fulbright, *The Arrogance of Power* (New York: Random House, 1967), 51.

53. David Lawrence, "The Tonkin Resolution and Politics," *Washington Star*, February 26, 1968.

54. Moïse, *Tonkin Gulf*, 103.

55. Testimony of Hon. Robert S. McNamara, Secretary of Defense, *The Gulf of Tonkin: The 1964 Incidents, Hearing Before the Committee on Foreign Relations*, Senate, 90th Congress, 2d Session [hereafter McNamara testimony], February 20, 1968, 8, 14–15.

56. Moïse, *Tonkin Gulf*, 106.

57. USN 414T MSG 041115Z AUG 64, repr. Chronology of Events in the Gulf of Tonkin, tab 31.

58. USM 626J MSG 041140Z AUG 64, repr. Chronology of Events in the Gulf of Tonkin, tab 32.

59. [Redacted] MSG 041240Z AUG 64, repr. Chronology of Events in the Gulf of Tonkin, tabs 34, 35.

60. Moïse, *Tonkin Gulf*, 113.

61. Hanyok, "Gulf of Tonkin Mystery," 21.

62. Ibid., 22; Editorial Note, FRUS *Vietnam* 1964–68, 1:604. See also CTG 77.5 MSG 041336Z AUG 64, repr. Chronology of Events in the Gulf of Tonkin, tab 36.

63. CTG 72.1 MSG 062355Z AUG 64, cited in Moïse, *Tonkin Gulf*, 115.

64. Moïse, *Tonkin Gulf*, 121.

65. CTG 77.5 MSG 041400Z AUG 64, repr. Chronology of Events in the Gulf of Tonkin, tab 37.

66. CTG 77.5 MSG 041434Z AUG 64, repr. Chronology of Events in the Gulf of Tonkin, tab 38.

67. CTG 72.1 MSG 041442Z AUG 64, repr. Chronology of Events in the Gulf of Tonkin, tab 39.

68. CTG 72.1 MSG 062355Z AUG 64, cited in Moïse, *Tonkin Gulf*, 123.

69. Hanyok, "Gulf of Tonkin Mystery," 23; Moïse, *Tonkin Gulf*, 135.

70. CTG 72.1 MSG 041442Z AUG 64; CTG 72.1 MSG 041452Z AUG 64.

71. CTU 72.1 MSG 042158Z AUG 64 and CTG 77.5 MSG 041408Z AUG 64, cited in Moïse, *Tonkin Gulf*, 118–19.

72. Moïse, *Tonkin Gulf*, 135.

73. Hanyok, "Gulf of Tonkin Mystery," 24.

74. CTG 72.1 MSG 041727Z AUG 64, cited in *Executive Sessions of the Senate Foreign Relations Committee* (Historical Series), vol. 20, 90th Congress, 2d Session 1968 (Washington, D.C.: Government Printing Office, 2010), 91, 129, 143, and 282.

75. CTG 72.1 MSG 041754Z AUG 64.

76. Moïse, *Tonkin Gulf*, 107–108.

77. Hanyok, "Gulf of Tonkin Mystery," 25.

78. Ibid., 142.

79. John L. Levinson, *Alpha Strike Vietnam: Navy's Air War 1964–1973* (Novato, Calif.: Presidio, 1989), 12.

80. Ibid., 15.

81. Editorial Note, FRUS *Vietnam* 1964–16, 1:605, 606.

82. CINCPAC MSG 041607Z AUG 64, repr. Chronology of Events in the Gulf of Tonkin, tab 59.

83. CINCPAC MSG 041554Z AUG 64.

84. CINCPAC MSG 041718Z AUG 64, repr. Chronology of Events in the Gulf of Tonkin, tab 60.

85. CINCPAC MSG 041547Z AUG 64, repr. Chronology of Events in the Gulf of Tonkin, tab 57.

86. JCS MSG [DTG unavailable], Air Strike against North Vietnam, Chronology of Events in the Gulf of Tonkin, tab 56; CINCPACFLT CTG 77.6 MSG 042014Z AUG 64, Chronology of Events in the Gulf of Tonkin, tab 61. See also Hanyok, "Gulf of Tonkin Mystery," 26.

87. "The Gulf of Tonkin Incident," *Cryptolog* (February–March 1975): 10, top secret, declassified November 4, 2005.

88. JCS MSG 052303Z AUG 64, Chronology of Events in the Gulf of Tonkin, tab 68.

89. JCS MSG [DTG unavailable], ibid., tab 56; CINCPACFLT CTG 77.6 MSG 042014Z AUG 64.

90. CINCPACFLT MSG 042014Z AUG 64.

91. JCS MSG 052303Z AUG 64.

92. Adam Roberts, "The Fog of Crisis: The 1964 Gulf of Tonkin Incidents," *World Today* 26, no. 5 (May 1970): 209.

93. JCS MSG 050124Z AUG 64, Chronology of Events in the Gulf of Tonkin, tab 64.

94. CINCPAC [?] MSG 041754Z AUG 64, repr. Chronology of Events in the Gulf of Tonkin, tab 44.

95. Ibid.; CTU 77.12 MSG 042158Z AUG 64.

96. Hanyok, "Gulf of Tonkin Mystery," 25.

97. See Moïse, *Tonkin Gulf*, 179–81.

98. McNamara and VanDeMark, *In Retrospect*, 130.

99. State to the Embassy in Vietnam, August 2, 1964.

100. Marolda and Fitzgerald, *Military Assistance to Combat*, 415.

101. George Bunn, "International Law and the Use of Force in Peacetime: Do U.S. Ships Have to Take the First Hit?" *Naval War College Review* 39, no. 3 (May–June 1986): 74–75.

102. Marolda and Fitzgerald, *Military Assistance to Combat*, 443.

103. Moïse, *Tonkin Gulf*, 185.

104. Hanyok, "Gulf of Tonkin Mystery," 25.

105. *The Vietnam War: After Action Reports, Lessons Learned Documents, Battle Assessments* (Beverly Hills, Calif.: BACM Research, 2009), 49–52.

106. National Security Agency, Role of the De Soto Patrol, September 16–20, 1964, 118 (1964), https://www.nsa.gov/.

107. CTU 72.1.2 MSG 021443Z AUG 64; CTG 72.1 MSG 021200Z AUG 64.

108. "New Shooting Incident in Tonkin Gulf," *Boston Globe*, September 19, 1964, 1; Robert Young, "U.S.–N. Viet Clash at Sea," *Chicago Tribune*, September 19, 1964, 1; Max Frankel, "U.S. Destroyers Open Fire Again in Tonkin Gulf, Targets Vanish," *New York Times*, September 19, 1964, 1; Ted Sell, "Patrols in Gulf of Tonkin Began as Watch on Reds: U.S. Insists on Freedom of the Seas," *Los Angeles Times*, September 27, 1964, pages B and 23.

109. Hanyok, "Gulf of Tonkin Mystery," 45.

110. Arnold Lubasch, "Reds Driven Off: Two Torpedo Vessels Believed Sunk in Gulf of Tonkin," *New York Times*, August 5, 1964, 1.

111. Hanyok, "Gulf of Tonkin Mystery," 32.

112. McNamara and VanDeMark, *In Retrospect*, 134–35.

113. Marolda and Fitzgerald, *Military Assistance to Combat*, 440–42.

114. Hanyok, "Gulf of Tonkin Mystery," 4.

115. George Ball, *The Past Has Another Pattern: Memoirs* (New York: W. W. Norton, 1983), 379.

116. Moïse, *Tonkin Gulf*, 203–204.

117. The Senate Foreign Relations Committee would hold inconclusive hearings on the issue in 1968. In 1975, the Senate Select Committee on Intelligence reviewed the DeSoto program and OPLAN 34A.

118. Lyndon B. Johnson, President's Message to Congress, H. Doc. 333, 80th Congress, 2d Session, *Department of State Bulletin* 51, no. 1313 (1964): 261–63.

119. Statements by Secretary Rusk and Secretary McNamara, August 6, 1964, in *Department of State Bulletin* 51, no. 1313 (1964): 263–68.

120. U.S. Reaction to Events in the Gulf of Tonkin, August 1–10, FRUS *Vietnam 1964–68*, 1:589–664; McNamara testimony, February 20, 1968, 8–106.

121. Carl Marcy, Memorandum to Senator William J. Fulbright, Tonkin Incident, January 20, 1972, available at https://www.nsa.gov/.

122. *Department of State Bulletin* 52 no. 1343 (1965): 419.

123. Statement by Adlai Stevenson, U.S. Representative to the United Nations Security Council, August 24, 1964, in *Department of State Bulletin* 51, no. 1313 (1964): 272–74.

124. Ibid.

125. Ibid.

126. Chairman Khrushchev, letter to President Johnson, August 5, 1964, FRUS *Vietnam* 1964–68, 1:636–38.

127. President Johnson, letter to Chairman Khrushchev, August 7, 1964, FRUS *Vietnam* 1964–68, 1:648.

128. The date of the meeting is uncertain but was after the Gulf of Tonkin incident and before August 8, as indicated in Commander, Military Assistance Command, Vietnam (Westmoreland), telegram to the Commander in Chief, Pacific (Sharp), August 8, 1964, FRUS *Vietnam* 1964–68, 1:649–51.

129. Seymour Topping, "Hanoi Prepares People for War: Defense Minister Says U.S. May Invade," *New York Times*, July 29, 1965, 1.

130. Director of the Policy Planning Council (Rostow), memorandum to the Secretary of State, August 5, 1964, FRUS *Vietnam* 1964–68, 1:639–42.

131. Embassy in Vietnam, telegram to the Department of State, August 9, 1964, FRUS *Vietnam* 1964–68, 1:654–56.

132. U.S. State Dept., "Aggression from the North: The Record of North Vietnam's Campaign to Conquer South Vietnam" (1965), repr. *Department of State Bulletin* 52, no. 1343 (March 22, 1965): 404–27.

133. John Norton Moore, "International Law and the U.S. Role in Viet Nam: A Reply," *Yale Law Journal* 76, no. 6 (May 1967): 1053.

134. Henry A. Kissinger, *Diplomacy* (New York: Simon & Schuster, 1994), 658–59.

135. Rostow to the Secretary of State, August 5, 1964.

136. Gulf of Tonkin Resolution, Public Law 88–408, 88th Congress, H. J. Res. 1145, 78 Stat. 384, enacted August 10, 1964 (repealed 1971).

137. Louis Harris, "Americans Are 85 Pct. with Johnson on Ordering Viet-Nam Air Strikes," *Washington Post*, August 10, 1964, A4.

138. Louis Harris, "Public Solidly Behind Johnson on Vietnam," *Los Angeles Times*, August 10, 1964, 10.

139. Testimony of Under Secretary of State Nicholas Katzenbach, Hearings on National Commitments, 82, 110th Congress, Rec. 18,403, 18,409–18,410 (1964).

Chapter 6. "False Sense of Security"

1. The United States claimed a 12-nm territorial sea in 1988. Proclamation 5928 of December 27, 1988, Territorial Sea of the United States of America, 54 Fed. Reg. 777 (January 9, 1989).

2. 1958 Geneva Convention on the High Seas, 450 *United Nations Treaty Series* [hereafter UNTS], vol. 450, 82, done at Geneva, April 29, 1958, entered into force September 30, 1962, art. 2.

3. Gen. Earle G. Wheeler, Chairman, Joint Chiefs of Staff, to Admiral Sharp (CINCPAC), top secret cable, January 25, 1968, available at http://nsarchive.gwu.edu/.

4. Robert Newton, *The Capture of the USS* Pueblo *and Its Effect on SIGINT Operations* (Fort George G. Meade, Md.: Center for Cryptologic History, National Security Agency, 1992), 174–75, available at http://nsarchive.gwu.edu/.

5. U.S. State Dept., Pueblo *Crisis: Presidential Decisions and Supplementary Chronology* (Washington, D.C.: December 12, 1968) [hereafter DOS *Pueblo* Crisis Report], 10.

6. Ibid.

7. Newton, *Capture of the USS* Pueblo, 9, 11.

8. DOS *Pueblo* Crisis Report, 10.

9. Newton, *Capture of the USS* Pueblo, 29.

10. Joint Chiefs of Staff, Memorandum for the Deputy Secretary of Defense, Subject: USS PUEBLO Incident, CM-3163–68, March 29, 1968 [hereafter JCS Memo for DEPSECDEF].

11. Message, COMNAVFORJAPAN 180752Z DEC67, Operational Order [hereafter OPORD].

12. Newton, *Capture of the USS* Pueblo, 33.

13. The JRC included representatives from the four military services, the DIA, the NSA, the State Department, and the Defense Department.

14. *Inquiry into the USS* Pueblo, Report of the Special Committee on the USS *Pueblo* of the Committee on Armed Services, House of Representatives, HASC No. 91–12, 91st Congress, 1st Session, July 26, 1969 [hereafter HASC *Pueblo* Report], 1654–55.

15. JCS Memo for DEPSECDEF.

16. Director of Central Intelligence Helms, memorandum to Secretary of Defense McNamara, January 23, 1968, in U.S. Dept. of State, *Foreign Relations of the United States, 1964–1968*, vol. 29, part 1, *Korea* (Washington, D.C.: Office of the Historian, n.d.) [hereafter FRUS *Korea*], Doc. 215.

17. HASC *Pueblo* Report, 1649.

18. OPORD, paras. 1.A.(1)–(3).

19. Message, CTF NINE SIX 050512Z JAN 68, Sailing Orders, para. 6.B.

20. OPORD, para. 1.A.(3).(A)–(C).

21. Skip Schumacher, Operations Officer, "The Hi-jacking," *USS* Pueblo (AGER-2), http://www.usspueblo.org/.

22. Newton, *Capture of the USS* Pueblo, 46–47.

23. HASC *Pueblo* Report, 1658.

24. "Seoul Infiltrator Says President Was Target: 31 Specially Trained N. Koreans Were to Hit Park Chung Hee Mansion, Kill Staff," *Los Angeles Times*, January 23, 1968, 4.

25. Newton, *Capture of the USS* Pueblo, 55.

26. DOS *Pueblo* Crisis Report, 2.

27. Department of State, telegram to the U.S. Embassy in Korea, January 28, 1968, FRUS *Korea*, Doc. 234.

28. HASC *Pueblo* Report, 1666.

29. Newton, *Capture of the USS* Pueblo, 74.

30. DOS *Pueblo* Crisis Report, 4.

31. HASC *Pueblo* Report, 1668.

32. Notes on the President's Thursday Night Meeting on the Pueblo Incident, January 25, 1968, FRUS *Korea*, Doc. 226.

33. Newton, *Capture of the USS* Pueblo, 96.

34. Department of State, telegram to the U.S. Embassy in the Soviet Union, January 23, 1968, FRUS *Korea*, Doc. 212.

35. Newton, *Capture of the USS* Pueblo, 99.

36. Helms to McNamara, January 23, 1968, FRUS *Korea*, Doc. 215.

37. U.S. Embassy in the Soviet Union, telegram to the Department of State, January 27, 1968, FRUS *Korea*, Doc. 227.

38. Department of State, telegram to the U.S. Embassy in the Soviet Union, January 25, 1968, FRUS *Korea*, Doc. 224.

39. U.S. Embassy in the Soviet Union, telegram to the Department of State, January 27, 1968, FRUS *Korea*, Doc. 230.

40. U.S. Embassy in the Soviet Union, telegram to the Department of State, February 3, 1968, FRUS *Korea*, Doc. 260.

41. U.S. Embassy in the Soviet Union, telegram to the Department of State, January 27, 1968, FRUS *Korea*, Doc. 231.

42. U.S. Embassy in Korea, telegram to the Department of State, January 27, 1968, FRUS *Korea*, Doc. 232.

43. Department of State to U.S. Embassy in Korea, January 28, 1968, FRUS *Korea*, Doc. 233.

44. U.S. Embassy in Korea, telegram to the Department of State, January 24, 1968, FRUS *Korea*, Doc. 219.

45. U.S. Embassy in Korea, telegram to the Department of State, December 22, 1968, FRUS *Korea*, Doc. 330.

46. U.S. State Dept., *"Pueblo* Seizure and North Korean Intrusions"; Notes of the President's Meeting with the National Security Council, January 24, 1968, FRUS *Korea*, Doc. 218.

47. Department of State to U.S. Embassy in Korea, January 28, 1968, FRUS *Korea*, Doc. 234.

48. Department of State to U.S. Embassy in Korea, February 3, 1968, FRUS *Korea*, Doc. 262. For a contemporary source, see The "ARA Libertad" Case (Argentina v. Ghana), ITLOS Case No. 20, Provisional Measures; and James Kraska, "The 'ARA Libertad' (Argentina v. Ghana), *American Journal of International Law* 107, no. 2 (April 2013): 404–10.

49. Minutes of Meeting on Korea Crisis without the President, January 24, 1968, FRUS *Korea*, Doc. 220.

50. U.S. Embassy in Korea to State, February 2, 1968, FRUS *Korea*, Doc. 254.

51. Department of State to U.S. Embassy in Korea, February 3, 1968, FRUS *Korea*, Doc. 262.

52. U.S. Embassy in Korea, telegram to the Department of State, March 9, 1968, FRUS *Korea*, Doc. 293.

53. National Security Lunch Meeting, January 23, 1968, FRUS *Korea*, Doc. 213; U.S. Embassy in Korea to State, February 2, 1968, FRUS *Korea*, Doc. 254.

54. Rusk to Johnson, March 14, 1968, FRUS *Korea*, Doc. 297; U.S. Embassy in Korea, telegram to the Department of State, March 21, 1968, FRUS *Korea*, Doc. 299.
55. U.S. Embassy in Korea, telegram to the Department of State, April 22, 1968, FRUS *Korea*, Doc. 305.
56. Memorandum from the Director of the Korean Task Force (Berger) to Secretary of State Rusk, February 15, 1968, FRUS *Korea*, Doc. 276.
57. Ibid.
58. Berger to Rusk, February 2, 1968, FRUS *Korea*, Doc. 255.
59. Berger to Rusk, February 15, 1968, FRUS *Korea*, Doc. 276.
60. U.S. Embassy in Korea to State, February 16, 1968, FRUS *Korea*, Doc. 277.
61. U.S. Embassy in Korea to State, February 2, 1968, FRUS *Korea*, Doc. 254.
62. U.S. Embassy in Korea to State, March 28, 1968, FRUS *Korea*, Doc. 302.
63. Agreement between the Commander in Chief, United Nations Command, on the one hand, and the Supreme Commander of the Korean People's Army and the Commander of the Chinese People's volunteers, on the other hand, concerning a military armistice in Korea, with Annex, signed at Panmunjom on July 27, 1953, 4 UST 234, *Treaties and Other International Acts Series* 2782.
64. Department of State to U.S. Embassy in Korea, February 3, 1968, FRUS *Korea*, Doc. 262.
65. Department of State, telegram to U.S. Embassy in Korea, February 1, 1968 (1552Z), FRUS *Korea*, Doc. 250.
66. U.S. Embassy in Korea to State, May 8, 1968, FRUS *Korea*, Doc. 306.
67. Department of State, telegram to the U.S. Embassy in Korea, December 11, 1968, FRUS *Korea*, Doc. 325.
68. U.S. Embassy in Korea, telegram to the Department of State, December 17, 1968, FRUS *Korea*, Doc. 326.
69. State to U.S. Embassy in Korea, December 11, 1968, FRUS *Korea*, Doc. 325.
70. Court of Inquiry to Inquire into the Circumstances Relating to the Seizure of USS *Pueblo* (AGER 2), 1st Endorsement, 1, available at http://www.usspueblo.org/.

71. John H. Chafee, Secretary of the Navy, statement, May 6, 1969 [hereafter SECNAV *Pueblo* Statement], available at http://www.usspueblo.org/.
72. *Pueblo* Committee Report to President, 6th Draft, February 7, 1968, 1, available at http://nsarchive.gwu.edu.
73. HASC *Pueblo* Report.
74. "Damage Assessment of Compromise of Operational Intelligence Broadcast Messages on Board USS PUEBLO (AGER 2), National Security Agency Report," March 17, 1969, available at http://nsarchive .gwu.edu.
75. NSA *Pueblo* Report, 10.
76. SECNAV *Pueblo* Statement.
77. "The *Pueblo*," Director of Central Intelligence briefing for members of unnamed congressional defense appropriation committee, September 23, 1968, at 6, available at http://nsarchive.gwu.edu.

Chapter 7. "Drawing a Line against Illegal Actions"

1. See Ralph Wetterhahn, *The Last Battle: The Mayaguez Incident and the End of the Vietnam War* (New York: Carrol & Graf, 2001).
2. Agreement on Ending the War and Restoring Peace in Vietnam, signed in Paris and entered into force on January 17, 1973, *Treaties and Other International Acts Series* 7542, in *Treaties and Other International Acts of the United States of America*, ed. Hunter Miller (Washington, D.C.: Government Printing Office, 1931), 24:4–23.
3. Gilbert Morales, ed., *Critical Perspectives on the Vietnam War* (New York: Rosen, 2005), 125.
4. Kevin Ponniah, "Remembering the Fall of Phnom Penh," *Diplomat*, April 17, 2015.
5. Public Law 93–52, July 1, 1973, sec. 108.
6. Lon Nol died on November 17, 1985, in California. Penelope McMillan, "Ex-Cambodian President Dies in Fullerton," *Los Angeles Times*, November 18, 1985.
7. *Congressional Record*, House, 110th Congress, 1st Session (Washington, D.C.: GPO, 2007), vol. 153, part 3, February 16, 2007.
8. Ponniah, "Remembering the Fall of Phnom Penh."

9. David K. Shipler, "Saigon mil command repts Chinese Planes and Ground Troops Secured Paracels Jan 20. Lt Col Le Trung Hien says Saigon does not yet consider islands lost. Diplomats in Saigon mystified by Chinese attack. Mil action and Chinese and S Vietnamese claims to islands revd," *New York Times*, January 21, 1974, 2.

10. John Moore, ed., *Jane's Fighting Ships* 1975–76 (London: MacDonald & Jane's, 1975), 223.

11. *The Seizure of the* Mayaguez: *A Case Study of Crisis Management*, Reports of the Comptroller General of the United States, submitted to the Subcommittee on International Political and Military Affairs, Committee on International Relations, 94th Congress, 2d Session, October 4, 1976 (Washington, D.C.: GPO, 1976) [hereafter GAO Report on Crisis Management], app. VI (Status of Incident at Time of Each National Security Meeting), 111. See also Minutes of the National Security Council Meeting, May 12, 1975, U.S. State Dept., *Foreign Relations of the United States, 1969–1975*, vol. 10, *Vietnam* [hereafter FRUS *Vienam*] (Washington, D.C.: Office of the Historian, n.d.) [hereafter Minutes of National Security Council Meeting], 977–85.

12. The Khmer word for "island" is *koh. Tang* means "legend." Robert Simmons, *The Pueblo, EC-121, and Mayaguez Incidents: Some Continuities and Changes*, Occasional Papers/Reprints Series in Contemporary Asian Studies, no. 8, (20) (Baltimore: University of Maryland, School of Law, 1978) [hereafter Occasional Paper 8], 41; Wetterhahn, *Last Battle*, 28.

13. *The Seizure of the* Mayaguez: *System to Warn US Mariners of Potential Political/Military Hazards—SS* Mayaguez, *a Case Study*, Reports of the Comptroller General of the United States, submitted to the Subcommittee on International Political and Military Affairs, Committee on International Relations, 94th Congress, 2d Session, October 4, 1976 (Washington, D.C.: GPO, 1976), part IV, [hereafter GAO Report on Warning System], 11; GAO Report on Crisis Management, app. 7, 116.

14. GAO Report on Crisis Management, app. 7, 116.

15. GAO Report on Warning System, 6, 10.

16. Defense Mapping Agency and Hydrographic Center [hereafter DMAHC], Special Warning no. 45, May 12, 1975; GAO Report on Warning System, 6, 21, 25–29.
17. GAO Report on Crisis Management, app. 8, 127.
18. Subcommittee on International Political and Military Affairs of the House Committee on International Relations, 94th Congress, 2d Session, *Report of the Comptroller General of the Seizure of the* Mayaguez, Washington, D.C., 1976, 61–62, 127.
19. GAO Report on Crisis Management, 61–62.
20. *Seizure of the* Mayaguez*: Hearings before the Subcommittee on International Political and Military Affairs of the House Committee on International Relations*, 94th Congress, 1st Session, July 31 and September 12, 1975, Washington, D.C., 1975 [hereafter *Mayaguez* Hearings], part. 3, 265, 267.
21. Minutes of National Security Council Meeting, May 12, 1975, 977–85.
22. GAO Report on Crisis Management, 116.
23. Minutes of the Secretary of State's Regional Staff Meeting, May 12, 1975, Doc. 284, FRUS *Vietnam*, 974–76.
24. The National Security Agency, the White House, the Central Intelligence Agency, the Defense Intelligence Agency, and the National Military Command Center received the message. Commander in Chief, U.S. Pacific Command, Commander in Chief Pacific Command History (1975) (Camp H. M. Smith, Hawaii: Headquarters CINCPAC, Command History Branch, Office of the Joint Secretary, 1976), app. 6, The SS *Mayaguez* Incident [hereafter CINCPAC Command History], 3.
25. GAO Report on Crisis Management, 116.
26. White House, Statement of the Press Secretary, Office of the Press Secretary, Washington, D.C., May 12, 1975 [hereafter Statement of the Press Secretary, date].
27. Department of State, telegram to the Liaison Office in China, May 13, 1975, FRUS *Vietnam*, 985–86.
28. GAO Report on Crisis Management, 66; State to Liaison Office in China, May 13, 1975.
29. GAO Report on Crisis Management, 66, app. 6, 112–13.

30. Statement of the Press Secretary, May 12, 1975. See also Minutes of National Security Council Meeting, May 12, 1975, 977–85.

31. Emphasis added. See 1958 Geneva Convention on the High Seas, April 29, 1958, 450 UNTS 11 [hereafter High Seas Convention], art. 15.

32. Minutes of National Security Council Meeting, May 15, 1975, FRUS *Vietnam*, 1039–43.

33. GAO Report on Crisis Management, 72.

34. The GAO report indicates that the ship was six to seven miles south of Poulo Wai; ibid., 61; Minutes of National Security Council Meeting, May 12, 1975, 977–85.

35. High Seas Convention, arts. 6.1 and 22.1.

36. GAO Report on Crisis Management, 65, and app. 6, 112.

37. CINCPAC Command History, 23.

38. GAO Report on Crisis Management, 71. See also CINCPAC Command History, 23.

39. Statement of the Press Secretary, May 13, 1975.

40. Occasional Paper 8, 41.

41. "Swedish Ship Shot At," *Fort Scott (Kansas) Tribune*, May 17, 1975.

42. GAO Report on Crisis Management, 73.

43. During his debriefing, Captain Miller "indicated that the crew had never set foot on Koh Tang Island." GAO Report on Crisis Management, 74.

44. The Ford administration believed that it would be more difficult to extract the crew by force if it was taken to the mainland. Similarly, it was believed that extraction through negotiation would be more humiliating if the crew was on the mainland. GAO Report on Crisis Management, 65.

45. GAO Report on Crisis Management, at 74; Transcript of Telephone Conversation between President Ford and the President's Deputy Assistant for National Security Affairs (Scowcroft), May 13, 1975 (8:10 p.m.), and Transcript of Telephone Conversation between President Ford and the President's Deputy Assistant for National Security Affairs (Scowcroft), May 13, 1975 (9:50 pm), both FRUS *Vietnam*, 1000.

46. GAO Report on Crisis Management, 74. See also telephone conversations between Ford and Scowcroft, May 13, 1975, 8:10 and 9:50 p.m.;

and Minutes of National Security Council Meeting, May 13–14, 1975, FRUS *Vietnam*, 1004–19.

47. CINCPAC Command History, 17.
48. GAO Report on Crisis Management, 64, 73–75, app. 6, 114.
49. Statement of Hon. Robert S. Ingersoll, Acting Secretary of State, *Mayaguez* Hearings [hereafter Ingersoll statement], 258.
50. GAO Report on Crisis Management, 66, app. 6, 112–13.
51. *Mayaguez* Hearings, 274.
52. GAO Report on Crisis Management, 67. See also *Mayaguez* Hearings, app. 6, 322.
53. Ingersoll statement, 257–58.
54. GAO Report on Crisis Management, 88–89.
55. Ibid., 96–97.
56. Acting Assistant Secretary, International Security Affairs, Department of Defense, letter, "Department of Defense Comments on the GAO Draft Report, *The Seizure of the* Mayaguez: *A Case Study of Crisis Management*, March 16, 1976" [hereafter DoD Comments on GAO Draft Report], GAO Report on Crisis Management, app. 5, 111.
57. PL 93–52, July 1, 1973, sec. 7.
58. GAO Report on Crisis Management, 96. In retrospect, the lack of reinforcement or interference with the Koh Tang operation by mainland forces reflects the success of the mainland strikes; DoD Comments on GAO Draft Report, GAO Report on Crisis Management, 2. See also Statement of the Press Secretary, May 14, 1975: "Aircraft from the carrier 'Coral Sea' to undertake associated military operations in the area in order to protect and support the operations to regain the vessel and members of the crew."
59. GAO Report on Crisis Management, 89–91. See also CINCPAC Command History, 19, 26; and Statement of Col. Vincent Dambrauskas, Joint Chiefs of Staff, Communications-Electronics Agency, in *Mayaguez* Hearings [hereafter Dambrauskas statement], 316: "The typical assault on an island of this type would require softening up with fighter-bombers or naval gunfire."
60. GAO Report on Crisis Management, 89–91.

61. John J. Kruzel, "*Mayaguez* Incident Tested President Ford's Mettle," American Forces Press Service, January 3, 2007.
62. Ibid., 92.
63. Thomas D. Des Brisay, "Fourteen Hours at Koh Tang," in *The Vietnamese Air Force, 1951–1975: An Analysis of its Role in Combat and Fourteen Hours at Koh Tang*, USAF Southeast Asia Monograph Series, vol. 3, monographs 4 and 5 (Washington, D.C.: GPO, 1985 [1976], 83, 106.
64. GAO Report on Crisis Management, 92. See also Commander in Chief, Pacific (Gayler), message to the Joint Chiefs of Staff, May 15, 1975, FRUS *Vietnam*, 1038–39.
65. CINCPAC Command History, 26.
66. George R. Dunham and David A. Quinlan, *U.S. Marines in Vietnam: The Bitter End, 1973–1975* (Washington, D.C.: Headquarters U.S. Marine Corps, History and Museums Division, 1990), 251.
67. Des Brisay, "Fourteen Hours at Koh Tang," 121.
68. The Cambodian government "will order the *Mayaguez* to withdraw from Cambodian territorial waters and will warn it against further espionage or provocative activities. This applies to the *Mayaguez* or any other ships like the ship flying the Panama flag which we released on May 9, 1975." "Text of Cambodian Communiqué," *New York Times*, May 16, 1975, 15.
69. Text of a Message to the Cambodian Authorities from the United States Government, Office of the White House Press Secretary, May 15, 1975. See also CINCPAC Command History, 27.
70. GAO Report on Crisis Management, 65, 94. There were also five Thai fishermen on board who had been held captive by the Cambodians since March 5, 1975. Gayler, message to the Joint Chiefs of Staff, May 15, 1975, 1038–39.
71. GAO Report on Crisis Management, 90–93; CINCPAC Command History, 26.
72. Dunham and Quinlan, *Bitter End*, 253.
73. Des Brisay, "Fourteen Hours at Koh Tang," 144–45.
74. Statement by the President on the SS *Mayaguez*, Office of the White House Press Secretary, May 15, 1975. See also Gayler, message to the

Joint Chiefs of Staff, May 15, 1975, 1038–39; and GAO Report on Crisis Management, 97–98.

75. LCpl. Joseph N. Hargrove, Pvt. 1st Class Gary C. Hall, and Pvt. Danny G. Marshall were missing. The body of Lance Cpl. Ashton N. Looney, KIA, was left on the island. Dunham and Quinlan, *Bitter End*, 262–63.

76. Permanent Representative of the United States of America to the United Nations, letter to the President of the Security Council, May 14, 1975, United Nations Security Council, S/11689, May 15, 1975.

77. GAO Report on Crisis Management, 69. A Japanese Foreign Ministry spokesman stated that the *Mayaguez* was "on open waters," should not have been seized, and that Japan viewed the U.S. military response as "limited." Minutes of National Security Council Meeting, May 15, 1975, 1039–43.

78. Minutes of National Security Council Meeting, May 15, 1975, 1039–43.

79. Minutes of National Security Council Meeting, May 14, 1975, FRUS *Vietnam*, 1021–36.

80. *Mayaguez* Hearings, app. 6, 113. See also Embassy in Thailand, telegram to the Department of State, May 13, 1975, FRUS *Vietnam*, 987–88.

81. GAO Report on Crisis Management, 69. See also *Mayaguez* Hearings, app. 6, 323

82. GAO Report on Crisis Management, 1–50; Special Warning 45 was updated on June 14, 1975, to advise mariners that "hostile activities between Khmer and Vietnamese air and surface forces have been noted in the vicinity of Poulo Wai and other nearby islands." GAO Report on Warning System, 21.

83. GAO Report on Warning System, 12.

84. Wetterhahn, *Last Battle*, 38.

85. Ingersoll statement, 257–58.

86. Permanent Representative to the Security Council, May 14, 1975: "Even if, in the view of others, the ship [was] considered to be within Cambodian territorial waters, it would clearly have been engaged in innocent passage to the port of another country. Hence, its seizure was unlawful and involved a clear-cut illegal use of force."

87. Minutes of National Security Council Meeting, May 13–14, 1975, 1004–19.

88. Charter of the United Nations, signed June 26, 1945, entered into force October 24, 1945, art. 51.

89. Dambrauskas statement, 317: "[S]ome people have been very critical about the operation on the mainland, as being totally unnecessary and that it was punitive in nature." Jordan Paust, "The Seizure of the *Mayaguez*," *Yale Law Journal* 85 (1976): 774.

90. Dambrauskas statement, 317; Michael David Sandler, "Correspondence," *Yale Law Journal* 86 (1976), 206.

91. Minutes of National Security Council Meeting, May 13–14, 1975, 1004–19.

92. The statute codified at 50 U.S.C. § 1542, Nov. 7, 1973, states: "The President in every possible instance shall consult with Congress before introducing United States Armed Forces into hostilities or into situations where imminent involvement in hostilities is clearly indicated by the circumstances, and after every such introduction shall consult regularly with the Congress until United States Armed Forces are no longer engaged in hostilities or have been removed from such situations. Public Law 93–148, sec. 3, November 7, 1973, 87 Stat. 555.

93. GAO Report on Crisis Management, 70. See also Talking Points for Congressional Notification, May 13, 1975, John Marsh Files, box 122, Gerald R. Ford Presidential Library, Grand Rapids, Mich. [hereafter Ford Library], available at Gerald R. Ford Presidential Library and Museum, https://www.fordlibrarymuseum.gov: "With these objectives in mind, the President has directed that US aircraft should attempt to stop the movement of Cambodian boats between the ship or the island and the Cambodian mainland, and to prevent movement of the ship itself. Our military commanders have been directed to use the minimum force required to achieve these objectives."

94. Statement by Chairman Olin Teague, May 13, 1975, Ford Library.

95. GAO Report on Crisis Management, 70; Discussion Paper, May 14, 1975, Ford Library. Representative Teague issued a second statement on May 14, 1975, declaring that he supported the "President's action 100%." Statement by Chairman Olin Teague, May 14, 1975, Ford Library.

96. GAO Report on Crisis Management, 70.

97. Spencer Rich, "Congress Rallies behind President on Use of Force," *Washington Post*, May 15, 1975.

98. 50 U.S.C. § 1543.

99. Memorandum for Max Friedersdorf, Subject: SS Mayaguez Incident: Report to Congress War Powers Resolution, May 15, 1975, Ford Library.

100. Minutes of the Secretary of State's Regional Staff Meeting, May 12, 1975, 974–76.

101. GAO Report on Crisis Management, 99–100. See also Occasional Paper 8, 34: following the seizure of the *Mayaguez*, administration officials stated, "The seizure of the vessel might provide the test of determination in Southeast Asia ... the United States had been seeking since the collapse of ... South Vietnam and Cambodia."

102. James R. Locher III, *Victory on the Potomac: The Goldwater-Nichols Act Unifies the Pentagon*, rev. ed. (College Station: Texas A&M University Press, 2004), 30.

103. Dunham and Quinlan, *Bitter End*, 264.

104. Occasional Paper 8, 43.

105. Bernard Gwertzman, "Kissinger Calls Ship Action Proof U.S. Stands Firm," *New York Times*, May 17, 1975, 1, 59.

106. Chairman, Joint Chiefs of Staff, *After Action Report: US Military Operations SS* Mayaguez/Kaoh [*sic*] *Tang Island* (Washington, D.C., n.d.), part I, tab B, encl. 2, Mayaguez Crew Debrief.

107. Occasional Paper 8, 43–44.

108. CINCPAC Command History, 1.

Chapter 8. Crossing the "Line of Death"

1. Libyan Arab Republic, Act No. 2 of 18 February 1959 Concerning the Delimitation of Libyan Territorial Waters, art. 1.

2. United Nations Convention on the Law of the Sea, opened for signature December 10, 1982, entered into force November 16, 1994, UN Doc. A/CONF.62/122 (1982), 1833 *United Nations Treaty Series* [hereafter UNTS] 3.

3. Libyan Arab Republic Ministry of Foreign Affairs, Note Verbale, MQ/40/5/1/3325, October 11, 1973, U.N. Legislative Series: National

Legislation and Treaties Relating to the Law of the Sea, pp. 26–27, U.N. Sales No. ST/LEG/SER.B/19 (1980).

4. U.S. Defense Dept., *Maritime Claims Reference Manual*, DOD 2005.1-M (Washington, D.C.: November 5, 2014) [hereafter MCRM].

5. U.S. State Dept. [A. Rovine], *Digest of United States Practice in International Law* (Washington, D.C.: Government Printing Office for the Office of the Legal Adviser, 1974), 293.

6. Communication Transmitted to the Permanent Missions of the States Members of the United Nations at the Request of the Permanent Representative of the United States to the United Nations, UN Doc. NV/85/11, July 10, 1985, reproduced in *UN Law of the Sea Bulletin No. 6*, October 1985, 40.

7. U.S. State Dept., *Navigation Rights and the Gulf of Sidra* (Washington, D.C.: Global Innovation through Science and Technology, 1986).

8. United Nations, "Juridical Regime of Historic Waters, including Historic Bays," UN Doc. A/CN.4/143, 9 March 1962, 56, available at legal.un.org/.

9. U.S. State Dept., *United States Responses to Excessive National Maritime Claims*, Limits in the Seas, no. 112 (Washington, D.C.: Bureau of Oceans and International Environmental and Scientific Affairs, March 9, 1992), 17.

10. MCRM.

11. President's Assistant for National Security Affairs (Kissinger), memorandum to President Nixon, Subject: Escorted Reconnaissance Flight off Libya, April 12, 1973, U.S. State Dept., *Foreign Relations of the United States, 1969–1976*, vol. E-9, part 1, *Documents on North Africa, 1973–1976* (Washington, D.C.: Office of the Historian, 2014) [hereafter FRUS *North Africa*], 18-20.

12. Permanent Representative of the United States of America to the United Nations, letter addressed to the President of the Security Council, June 18, 1973, UN Doc. S/10956, June 20, 1973. See Convention on International Civil Aviation, December 7, 1944, 15 UNTS 295.

13. Kissinger to Nixon, April 12, 1973. See also Department of State, telegram 62911 to the Embassy in Libya, Subject: Libya Air Space Problem, FRUS *North Africa*, 15.

14. John Maclean, "Libyans Fire on Unarmed US Aircraft," *Chicago Tribune*, March 22, 1973.

15. Department of State, telegram 51869 to the Mission to the United Nations, Subject: LARG attack on US Plane, March 29, 1973, FRUS *North Africa*, 11–12.

16. Kissinger to Nixon, April 12, 1973, 18–20.

17. Deputy Secretary of Defense (Clements), letter to the President's Assistant for National Security Affairs (Kissinger), April 5, 1973, FRUS *North Africa*, 12–14.

18. Kissinger to Nixon, April 12, 1973, 18–20.

19. Embassy in Libya, telegram 460 to the Department of State, Subject: Policy Questions re Recon Flights Off Libya, April 11, 1973, FRUS *North Africa*, 16–18.

20. Senior Interagency Group No. 14 [hereafter SIG 14], "SIG Discussion Paper on Gulf of Sidra," July 12, 1982 [hereafter SIG Discussion Paper], CIA Freedom of Information Act Electronic Reading Room, https://www.cia.gov/library/readingroom/home/.

21. Ad Hoc Interdepartmental Group for Africa, "US Policy toward Libya," July 6, 1973, in FRUS *North Africa*, 41–67. SIG Discussion Paper.

22. Director, Joint Staff (Lt. Gen. John A. Wickham Jr.), memorandum to Assistant Secretary of Defense (International Security Affairs), April 18, 1979, encl. "Navigational Freedom and US Security Interest, 15 April 1979 to 01 November 1979" (confidential, declassified June 21, 1985), Jimmy Carter Presidential Library and Museum, https://jimmycarterlibrary.gov.

23. Ad Hoc Interdepartmental Group for Africa, "US Policy toward Libya." SIG Discussion Paper.

24. CIA, Interagency Intelligence Assessment, "Ramifications of Planned US Naval Exercise in the Gulf of Sidra, 18-20 August 1981," August 10, 1981 [hereafter Interagency Intelligence Assessment].

25. George Wilson, "Libyan Fighters Suspected of Firing on US Aircraft," *Washington Post*, September 18, 1980.

26. SIG Discussion Paper. See also "Off Tripoli's Shores," *New Republic*, September 9, 1981.

27. "Embassy of the US in Libya Is Stormed by a Crowd of 2,000," *New York Times*, December 3, 1979.

28. U.S. State Dept., *A Guide to the United States' History of Recognition, Diplomatic, and Consular Relations, by Country, since 1776: Libya* (Washington, D.C.: Office of the Historian, n.d.), [hereafter *Libya Guide*], available at https://history.state.gov/countries/libya.

29. SIG Discussion Paper.

30. U.S. State Dept., *Libya Guide*.

31. Assistant to the President for National Security Affairs, memorandum, Subject: NSC Meeting: June 1, 1981, July 10, 1981, CIA Freedom of Information Act Electronic Reading Room.

32. Interagency Intelligence Assessment.

33. Steven Ratner, "The Gulf of Sidra Incident of 1981: A Study of the Lawfulness of Peacetime Aerial Engagements," *Yale Journal of International Law* 10 (1984): 62. See also Bernard Gwertzman, "US Reports Shooting Down 2 Libya Jets That Attacked F-14's over Mediterranean," *New York Times*, August 20, 1981.

34. Dario Leone, "How Two US Navy F-14 Tomcats Shot Down Two [of] Gaddafi's Su-22 Fitters, 32 Years Ago Today," *Aviationist*, August 19, 2013.

35. Ibid. Fast Eagle 102's pilot was Cdr. Henry "Hank" Kleemann; its radar intercept officer (RIO) was Lt. Dave Venlet. The pilot of Fast Eagle 107 was Lt. Larry "Music" Muczynski, and Lt. James Anderson was RIO.

36. Gwertzman, "US Reports Shooting Down 2 Libya Jets."

37. Chargé d'Affaires A.I. [ad interim] of the Permanent Mission of the Libyan Arab Jamahiriya to the United Nations, letter to the President of the Security Council, August 20, 1981, UN Doc. S/14636.

38. Ibid. See also "Al-Gaddafi News Conference," LD220902 Tripoli, *JANA in Arabic*, 0700 August 22, 1981.

39. Memorandum for the Director of Central Intelligence, Subject: 25 February NSC Meeting on Libya, February 24, 1982, CIA Freedom of Information Act Electronic Reading Room.

40. "Colonel Muammar Qaddafi Interviewed," *The Today Show*, Radio TV Reports, Inc., March 8, 1982. See also SIG Discussion Paper.

41. SIG Discussion Paper.

42. Memorandum for the Secretary of State, Subject: Gulf of Sidra Exercise, June 21, 1982, CIA Freedom of Information Act Electronic Reading Room.

43. Central Intelligence Agency, Chief, Near East and South Asia Division, Memorandum for the Record, Subject: New Gulf of Sidra Exercise, June 25, 1982, CIA Freedom of Information Act Electronic Reading Room.

44. "Libya Warns U.S. To Stay Out of Gulf," *New York Times*, March 5, 1982, A5.

45. Memorandum for Director of Central Intelligence, Subject: Proposed Gulf of Sidra Exercise, June 28, 1982, CIA Freedom of Information Act Electronic Reading Room.

46. The intelligence community assessed that reactions to the exercise, whether large scale or lesser scale, would be the same as long as an incident occurred, and that an incident would occur if U.S. forces were detected by the Libyans. Memorandum for Director of Central Intelligence, Subject: Proposed Gulf of Sidra Operation, July 1, 1982, CIA Freedom of Information Act Electronic Reading Room.

47. Memorandum for Mr. William P. Clark, the White House, Subject: Senior Interdepartmental Group Recommendation on Gulf of Sidra Exercise, July 17, 1982, CIA Freedom of Information Act Electronic Reading Room.

48. Memorandum for Director of Central Intelligence, Subject: US Exercise, Gulf of Sidra, September 13, 1982, CIA Freedom of Information Act Electronic Reading Room.

49. Memorandum for the Honorable George P. Shultz, Subject: Operations in the Vicinity of Libya, October 8, 1982, CIA Freedom of Information Act Electronic Reading Room.

50. Memorandum for Director of Central Intelligence, Subject: Possible Exercise in Gulf of Sidra on 25 October, October 21, 1982, CIA Freedom of Information Act Electronic Reading Room.

51. SIG 14, Subject: Restricted SIG Meeting: Libya Stair Step Plan, November 23, 1982, CIA Freedom of Information Act Electronic Reading Room.

52. "Libya MIGs Are Intercepted By Jets From a U.S. Carrier," *New York Times*, August 3, 1983, A3.

53. SIG 14, Subject: Restricted SIG Meeting: Libya Stair Step Plan, November 23, 1982, CIA Freedom of Information Act Electronic Reading Room.

54. Prior to the 1986 incident, the last time the Navy had conducted air operations in the vicinity of Libya was January 27–28, 1985. Bob Woodward and George Wilson, "US Navy Planes to Begin Operations North of Libya," *Washington Post*, January 24, 1986.

55. Memorandum for the President, Subject: Libya-US: Repercussions of the President's Special Measures, January 8, 1986 [hereafter Repercussions of the President's Special Measures], CIA Freedom of Information Act Electronic Reading Room.

56. In this regard, see the problem of "country desk–itis" in James Kraska, *Maritime Power and the Law of the Sea: Expeditionary Operations in World Politics* (Oxford, UK: Oxford University Press, 2011), 388–94.

57. Talking Points for the Deputy Director for Intelligence, Subject: Potential Scope of Libyan Military Reactions, January 15, 1986; Repercussion of the President's Special Measures.

58. Libya Working Group, Talking Points for the Deputy Director for Intelligence, Subject: Potential Scope of Libyan Military Reactions, January 15, 1986, CIA Freedom of Information Act Electronic Reading Room.

59. Don Kirk, "USA Flexes Muscle at Libya," *USA Today*, January 24, 1986.

60. Libya Working Group, Talking Points for the Director of Central Intelligence, Subject: Libyan Military Reaction and Threat to US Operations, January 29, 1986, CIA Freedom of Information Act Electronic Reading Room.

61. "Al-Qadhdhafi Threatens War with US in Interview," LD292304, *Tripoli Television Service in Arabic*, January 29, 1986, CIA Freedom of Information Act Electronic Reading Room.

62. Talking Points for the Assistant Deputy Director for Intelligence, Subject: Update on Libyan Activities, February 12, 1986, CIA Freedom of Information Act Electronic Reading Room.

63. Niles Lathem, "Reagan Sends Fleet to Libya to Test Khadafy," *New York Post*, March 19, 1986.

64. George Wilson, "US Naval Forces to Cross Qaddafi's 'Line of Death' Soon," *Washington Post*, March 21, 1986.

65. U.S. State Dept., "Rules of Engagement for U.S. Military Operations in the Gulf of Sidra" (top secret, declassified January 10, 2005), GALE|CK2349695664, *U.S. Declassified Documents Online*, www.galegroup.com/.

66. Eleanor Clift and James Gerstenzang, "US Warplanes Destroy Libya Missile Site, Sink Patrol Craft: Strike after Attack by Kadafi Forces; No American Losses," *Los Angeles Times*, March 25, 1986.

67. "Chronology of US-Libya Relations," *UPI | Archives*, January 4, 1989, www.upi.com/archives/.

68. Richard Stengel, "Sailing in Harm's Way: Action and Tension behind the Scenes during 'Operation Prairie Fire,'" *Time Magazine*, April 7, 1986.

69. Statement by Principal Deputy Press Secretary Speakes on the Gulf of Sidra Incident, March 24, 1986; Letter to the Speaker of the House of Representatives and the President Pro Tempore of the Senate on the Gulf of Sidra Incident, March 26, 1986, Reagan Library.

70. The intruders used high-speed antiradiation missiles (HARMs).

71. Letter to the Speaker and the President Pro Tempore, March 26, 1986, Reagan Library.

72. Statement by Principal Deputy Press Secretary Speakes on the Gulf of Sidra Incident, March 25, 1986, Reagan Library.

73. Clift and Gerstenzang, "US Warplanes Destroy Libya Missile Site"; Rachel Flick and Niles Lathem, "Blown Out of the Water," *New York Post*, March 25, 1986.

74. Statement by Principal Deputy Press Secretary Speakes on the Gulf of Sidra Incident, March 26, 1986, Reagan Library.

75. James Gerstenzang, "US Navy Ends Maneuvers in Gulf of Sidra," *Los Angeles Times*, March 28, 1986.

76. Memorandum of Conversation, Subject: The Secretary's Meeting with Shevardnadze, January 8, 1989, in *Foreign Relations of the United States, 1981–1988*, vol. 6, *Soviet Union, October 1986–1989*, 1252–68.

77. Naval History and Heritage Command, "In 1989 Dogfight Navy Tomcats Best Libyan MiGs," *Sextant*, January 4, 2015, http://usnhistory.navylive.dodlive.mil/.

78. John Broder, "US Shoots Down 2 Libya Jets: Kadafi Vows to Seek Revenge: F-14s Fired in Self-Defense, Carlucci Says," *Los Angeles Times*, January 5, 1989.

79. Leone, "Two F-14 Tomcats." See also "Chapter VIII, Agenda Items in 1989–1992," *Repertoire of the Practice of the Security Council*, 277, www.un.org [hereafter *Repertoire of the Security Council*, 1989–92].

80. Matthew Weed, *The War Powers Resolution: Concepts and Practice*, CRS Report 7–5700 (Washington, D.C.: Congressional Research Service, April 3, 2015).

81. U.S. Navy Dept./U.S. Dept. of Homeland Security, *The Commander's Handbook on the Law of Naval Operations*, NWP 1–14M / MCWP 5–12.1 / COMDTPUB P5800.7A (Washington, D.C., June 2007), para. 4.4.3, pages 4–4, 4–5.

82. Chairman, Joint Chiefs of Staff, "Standing Rules of Engagement (SROE) / Standing Rules for the Use of Force (SRUF) for US Forces," CJCSI 3121.01B, June 13, 2005 [hereafter SROE/SRUF CJCSI 3121.01B].

83. Ibid., encl. A, para. 4(2). See also *Repertoire of the Security Council*, 1989–92, 276–77.

84. SROE/SRUF CJCSI 3121.01B, encl. A, para. 4(3). See also *Repertoire of the Security Council*, 1989–92, 276–77.

85. *Repertoire of the Security Council*, 1989–92, 276–77.

86. Office of the Under Secretary of Defense for Global Security Affairs, U.S. Department of Defense Freedom of Navigation Report for Fiscal Year 2015, April 19, 2016.

87. Richard J. Grunawalt, "Freedom of Navigation in the Post–Cold War Era," in *Navigational Rights and Freedoms in the New Law of the Sea*, ed. Donald R. Rothwell and Sam Bateman (The Hague: Martinus Nijhoff, 2000), 15.

Chapter 9. "Choke Point of Freedom"

1. United Nations Security Council Resolution [hereafter UNSCR] 479 (1980), September 28, 1980.

2. Richard Jacques, ed., *Maritime Operational Zones* (Newport, R.I.: Naval War College, 2006) [hereafter *Maritime Operational Zones*],

4–12. See also Defense Mapping Agency and Hydrographic Center [hereafter DMAHC] Special Warning no. 53, May 27, 1981, reprinted in *Maritime Operational Zones*, app. C, C-11, and Special Warning no. 72, August 7, 1987, reprinted in *Maritime Operational Zones*, app. C, C-29.

3. Notice to Mariners no. 17/59, September 22, 1980, reprinted in *Maritime Operational Zones*, app. C, C-10.

4. Ibid. The 1980 notice was revised in May 1981, to state specifically that "all transportation of cargo to Iraqi ports is prohibited"; DMAHC Special Warning no. 53.

5. Nicholas Veliotes and Jonathan Howe, "Iran-Iraq War: Analysis of Possible U.S. Shift from Position of Strict Neutrality," memorandum to Mr. Eagleburger, October 7, 1983, available at http://nsarchive.gwu.edu/.

6. Zbigniew Brzezinski, Memorandum for the President, *NSC Weekly Report 156*, October 3, 1980.

7. UNSCR 514 (1982), July 12, 1982, and UNSCR 522 (1982), October 4, 1982.

8. DMAHC Special Warning no. 62, August 16, 1982, reprinted in *Maritime Operational Zones*, app. C, C-18.

9. Ibid.

10. Louise Doswald-Beck, ed., *San Remo Manual on International Law Applicable to Armed Conflicts at Sea: Adopted in June 1994* (Geneva: International Institute of Humanitarian Law, 1995), para 67.

11. Richard Mobley, "Fighting Iran: Intelligence Support during Operation Earnest Will, 1987–88," *Studies in Intelligence* 60, no. 3 (September 2016): 3.

12. Ibid.

13. UNSCR 552 (1984), June 1, 1984.

14. Ibid.

15. USCINCCENT MSG 202222Z JAN 84, reprinted in *Maritime Operational Zones*, app. C, C-21.

16. Ibid.

17. U.S. White House, "U.S. Policy toward the Iran-Iraq War," National Security Decision Directive 114, Washington, D.C., November 26, 1983.

18. Report of the Secretary-General in Pursuance of Security Council Resolution 552 (1984), S/16877, December 31, 1984, Add. 1, January 22, 1985, Add. 2, December 31, 1985, Add. 3, December 31, 1986, Add. 4, January 22, 1987, Add. 5, December 31, 1987, and Add. 6, January 26, 1988.

19. U.S. Central Intelligence Agency, *The Tanker War: Ship Attacks in the Persian Gulf: A Reference Aid* (Washington, D.C.: Directorate of Intelligence, June 1987) [hereafter CIA Reference Aid].

20. For example, in February 1984, the Iranian ambassador to the United Nations warned that Iran would close the Strait of Hormuz to all tankers if Iraq attacked Iranian oil installations in the Gulf. J. T. Nguyen, "Iran Threatens to Close Hormuz," *United Press International Archives*, February 14, 1984.

21. U.S. White House, "Measures to Improve U.S. Posture and Readiness to Respond to Developments in the Iran-Iraq War," National Security Decision Directive 139, Washington, D.C., April 5, 1984.

22. Ibid.

23. Ibid.

24. Ibid.

25. UNSCR 582 (1986), February 24, 1986; UNSCR 588 (1986), October 8, 1986.

26. Cable to the Secretary-General from the heads of maritime organizations, November 3, 1986. See also Report of the Secretary-General, S/18480, November 26, 1986, annex 4. The cable was signed by the Baltic and International Maritime Council, International Chamber of Shipping, International Shipping Federation, Intercargo, Intertanko, International Shipowners' Association, International Maritime Industries Forum, Council of European and Japanese National Shipowners' Association, and Comité des Associations d'Armateurs des Communautés Européenes.

27. Ibid.

28. Statement by Principal Deputy Press Secretary Speakes on Attacks on Shipping in the Persian Gulf, May 12, 1986, Ronald Reagan Presidential Library and Museum, https://www.reaganlibrary.archives.gov [hereafter Reagan Library].

29. Ibid.

30. CIA Reference Aid.

31. David Crist, *Gulf of Conflict: A History of U.S.-Iranian Confrontation at Sea*, Policy Focus 95 (Washington, D.C.: Washington Institute for Near East Policy, June 2009), 2.

32. Ibid., 3. Kuwait established a front company in Delaware—Chesapeake Shipping, Inc.—"to serve as its American 'owner' for the tankers."

33. Case Concerning Oil Platforms (Iran v. U.S.), 2003 International Court of Justice [hereafter ICJ] [hereafter *Oil Platforms* case], 176.

34. Charles Wallace and Don Shannon, "Kuwait Tanker *Gas Prince* Sails with U.S. Escort," *Los Angeles Times*, August 2, 1987.

35. *Oil Platforms* case, 188.

36. Written Responses to Questions Submitted by the Kuwaiti Newspaper *Al-Qabas*, May 12, 1987, Reagan Library.

37. The *Stark* had, but did not employ, weapons systems that included SM-1 MR (medium-range) surface-to-air missiles, an Mk 75 76-mm gun with rotary magazine, a close-in weapon system (CIWS) for short-range point defense, .50-caliber guns, and Super Rapid Blooming Off Board Chaff (SRBOC). Rear Adm. U. S. Grant Sharp, USN, to Commander in Chief, U.S. Central Command, "Formal Investigation into the Circumstances Surrounding the Attack on the USS *Stark* (FFG 31) on 17 May 1987," June 12, 1987, 16–17, http://www.jag.navy.mil/library/.

38. See Richard Gross, "Iraq Apologized Monday for Its Mistaken Attack on the USS *Stark*," *United Press International Archives*, May 18, 1987.

39. President Reagan Statement on the Attack against the USS *Stark*, May 18, 1987, in "Remarks on United States Policy in the Persian Gulf, May 29, 1987," in *Public Papers of the Presidents of the United States: Ronald Reagan, 1987* (Washington, D.C.: Government Printing Office, 1989) [hereafter *Public Papers: Reagan*], 1:524–25.

40. Ibid., 1:581–82.

41. Ibid.

42. Ibid.

43. JCS/DJS MSG 2123357Z JUL 87, reprinted in *Maritime Operational Zones*, app. C, C-26–27; HYDROPAC 870/87 (62), Persian

Gulf–Strait of Hormuz–Gulf of Oman–North Arabian Sea, August 3, 1987, reprinted in *Maritime Operational Zones*, app. C, C-28.

44. JCS/DJS MSG 2123357Z JUL 87.
45. Ibid.
46. DMAHC Special Warning no. 72.
47. Ibid.
48. Ibid. The Iraqi war zone was delimited as 29° 30' N, 48° 30' E; 29° 25' N, 49° 09' E; 28° 23 N, 49° 47' E; and 28° 23' N, 51° 00' E; ibid.
49. Ibid.
50. UNSCR 598 (1987), July 20, 1987.
51. Ibid.
52. *Oil Platforms* case, 175.
53. Robert Gillette, "More Mines Found in Area of Tanker Blast," *Los Angeles Times*, July 29, 1987.
54. Alan Cowell, "A Kuwaiti Tanker under U.S. Escort Hits Mine in Gulf," *New York Times*, July 25, 1987.
55. Gillette, "More Mines Found in Area of Tanker Blast."
56. "Operation Earnest Will," *102 Minesweepers*, http://102msos.8m.net /operationernestwill.html.
57. Ibid.
58. Charles Wallace, "U.S. Tanker Hits Mine Near Gulf: Explosion Occurs Outside Previous Sea Combat Zone," *Los Angeles Times*, August 11, 1987.
59. Edward Cody, "Iran Admits It Mined Gulf but Says It Was for Defense," *Washington Post*, August 21, 1987.
60. Ibid. A "Q-route" is a traffic lane specifically cleared for entry and egress of warships and other vessels involved in clearing mines.
61. Hague Convention VIII Relative to the Laying of Automatic Submarine Contact Mines, The Hague, 18 October 1907, 36 Stat. 2332, TS no. 541, 205 Parry's TS 331. Persia signed but did not ratify the convention.
62. Margaret Wachenfeld, "Reflagging Kuwaiti Tankers: A U.S. Response in the Persian Gulf," *Duke Law Journal* 37 (1988): 197.
63. Military and Paramilitary Activities In and Against Nicaragua (Nicar. v. U.S.), 1986 ICJ 14, 112.

64. Hague Convention XIII Concerning the Rights and Duties of Neutral Powers in Naval War, The Hague, 18 October 1907, 36 Stat. 2415, *American Journal of International Law* 2 (Supp.): 202.

65. "Statement by Assistant to the President for Press Relations Fitzwater on Protection of United States-Flagged Shipping in the Persian Gulf, September 26, 1988," Reagan Library.

66. Ibid.

67. United States Special Operations Command History, 10th Anniversary, April 16, 1997, 17.

68. "Reagan Alters Persian Gulf Escort Policy," *United Press International*, September 26, 1988.

69. Dwight Zimmerman, "Operations Prime Chance and Praying Mantis: USSOCOM's First Test of Fire," *Defense Media Network*, June 27, 2013.

70. Crist, *Gulf of Conflict*, 5.

71. Ibid.

72. Letter to the Speaker of the House of Representatives and the President Pro Tempore of the Senate on the United States Air Strike in the Persian Gulf, September 24, 1987, at Gerhard Peters and John T. Woolley, *The American Presidency Project*, http://www.presidency.ucsb.edu.

73. Zimmerman, "Operations Prime Chance and Praying Mantis."

74. Molly Moore, "U.S. Helicopters Hit Iranian Navy Ship in Persian Gulf: Strike on Alleged Minelayer Follows Gunboat Attack on Tanker—U.S. Strikes Iranian Navy Ship, Alleges It Laid Mines in Gulf," *Washington Post*, September 22, 1987.

75. Richard Halloran, "26 Iranians Seized with Mine Vessel; More U.S. Shooting," *New York Times*, September 23, 1987, A14.

76. Crist, *Gulf of Conflict*, 6.

77. Zimmerman, "Operations Prime Chance and Praying Mantis."

78. Statement on United States Policy in the Persian Gulf, September 24, 1987, in *Public Papers: Reagan*, 1:1075–76.

79. Ibid.

80. Letter to the Speaker of the House of Representatives and the President Pro Tempore of the Senate on the United States Air Strike in the

Persian Gulf, October 10, 1987, in *Weekly Compilation of Presidential Documents* 23:1159.

81. Ibid.
82. John Kifner, "U.S. Flag Tanker Struck by Missile in Kuwait Waters: First Direct Raid," *New York Times*, October 17, 1987, 5.
83. Radio Address to the Nation on Foreign Policy, October 17, 1987, in *Public Papers: Reagan*, 1:1197–98.
84. *Oil Platforms* case, 184.
85. Ibid., 93.
86. Letter to the Speaker and the President Pro Tempore, October 10, 1987.
87. Ibid.
88. *Oil Platforms* case, 184.
89. Ibid.
90. Ibid.
91. Letter to the Speaker of the House of Representatives and the President Pro Tempore of the Senate on the Military Strike in the Persian Gulf, April 19, 1988, Reagan Library. See also Tim Comerford, "Operation Praying Mantis Demonstrates Same Priorities Navy Values Today," *Navy News Service*, April 17, 2013.
92. Letter to the Speaker and the President Pro Tempore, April 19, 1988.
93. Crist, *Gulf of Conflict*, 18.
94. "Statement by Assistant to the President for Press Relations Fitzwater on the United States Military Strike in the Persian Gulf, April 18, 1988," Reagan Library.
95. Zimmerman, "Operations Prime Chance and Praying Mantis"; J. B. Perkins, "Operation Praying Mantis: The Surface View," U.S. Naval Institute *Proceedings* 115/5/1,035 (May 1989).
96. Zimmerman, "Operations Prime Chance and Praying Mantis."
97. Letter to the Speaker and the President Pro Tempore, April 19, 1988.
98. Zimmerman, "Operations Prime Chance and Praying Mantis"; Perkins, "Operation Praying Mantis."
99. Zimmerman, "Operations Prime Chance and Praying Mantis." See also Crist, *Gulf of Conflict*, 9, 13.

100. "Statement by Assistant to the President for Press Relations Fitzwater on the United States Military Strike in the Persian Gulf, April 18, 1988," Reagan Library.
101. The subsequent investigation of the incident surmised that the remote-control indicator might have detected the Mode II squawk from an F-14 at Bandar Abbas airfield.
102. Commander, Middle East Forces Operations Order 4000–85, as reprinted in CJTFME MSG 232220Z MAY 88, in William S. Fogarty, letter, Subj: Formal Investigation into the Circumstances Surrounding the Downing of Iran Air Flight 655 on 3 July 1988, July 28, 1988, Exhibit 131, Defense Technical Information Center, www.dtic.mil.
103. Fogarty, Formal Investigation, 61.
104. Chairman of the Joint Chiefs of Staff, second endorsement on Fogarty, Formal Investigation, August 18, 1988.
105. Letter to the Speaker of the House of Representatives and the President Pro Tempore of the Senate on the Destruction of an Iranian Jetliner by the United States Navy over the Persian Gulf, July 4, 1988, Reagan Library.
106. Convention for the Suppression of Unlawful Acts Against the Safety of Civil Aviation (1971), 974 UNTS 177; Convention on International Civil Aviation (1944), (1994) 15 UNTS 295.
107. Aerial Incident of 3 July 1988 (Islamic Republic of Iran v. United States of America), Application Instituting Proceedings, May 17, 1989.
108. Ibid., Order of 22 February 1996, ICJ Reports 1996, 9.
109. Ibid.
110. Ibid., Settlement Agreement, February 9, 1996.
111. Treaty of Amity, Economic Relations and Consular Rights between the United States and Iran, 15 August 1955, 284 UNTS 93; *Oil Platforms* case, 166.
112. *Oil Platforms* case, 166–67. The court held that Iran's claims could be pursued at the ICJ, pursuant to Article XXI of the 1955 bilateral treaty.
113. See John Norton Moore, "Jus ad Bellum before the International Court of Justice," *Virginia Journal of International Law* 52 (2012): 916–19; James Kraska, "A Social Justice Theory of Self-Defense of

World Court Jurisprudence," *Loyola University Chicago International Law Review* 9 (2011): 33–36.

114. George K. Walker, ed., *The Tanker War, 1980–88: Law and Policy*, International Law Studies 74 (Newport, R.I.: Naval War College, 2000), 608.

115. J. Matthew McInnis, *Iran at War: Understanding Why and How Tehran Uses Military Force* (Washington, D.C.: American Enterprise Institute, December 2016), 28.

116. Dan Lamothe, "Navy Destroyer Opens Fire after 'Harassing' Behavior by Iranian Patrol Boats," *Washington Post*, January 9, 2017.

Chapter 10. "Uniform Interpretation of Innocent Passage"

1. Law of the Union of Soviet Socialist Republics on the State Frontier of the USSR (November 24, 1982) [hereafter State Frontier Law 1982], reprinted in United Nations, *The Law of the Sea: Current Developments in State Practice* (New York, 1987), 99–100.

2. Rules for Navigation and Sojourn of Foreign Warships in the Territorial Waters and Internal Waters and Ports of the USSR, ratified by the Council of Ministers Decree No. 384 of April 25, 1983, reprinted in *International Legal Materials* [hereafter ILM] (1985) [hereafter 1983 Rules], 24:1717.

3. United States of America–Union of Soviet Socialist Republics: Joint Statement with Attached Uniform Interpretation of Rules of International Law Governing Innocent Passage, signed at Jackson Hole, Wyoming, September 23, 1989, 28 ILM 1444 (1989), United Nations, *Law of the Sea Bulletin* 14 (December 1989): 12.

4. Ibid.

5. Agreement between the Government of the United States of America and the Government of the Union of Soviet Socialist Republics on the Prevention of Dangerous Military Activities, signed in Moscow, June 1, 1989, entered into force January 1, 1990 [hereafter DMA Agreement], 28 ILM 977 (1989).

6. Geneva Convention on the Territorial Sea and the Contiguous Zone, signed in Geneva, April 29, 1958, entered into force September 10,

1964, *United Nations Treaty Series* [hereafter UNTS] (2005), 516:205, art. 14(1).

7. Ibid., art. 14(4).
8. Ibid.
9. Ibid., art. 15(1).
10. Ibid., art. 16(1).
11. Ibid., art. 17.
12. Ibid., art. 23.
13. United Nations Conference on the Law of the Sea, *Official Records*, vol. 4, *Second Committee (High Seas: General Regime)* (Geneva, 24 February–27 April 1958), 10, para. 12.
14. Ibid.
15. Ibid.
16. Ibid.
17. Reservation of the USSR upon ratification of the Convention on the Territorial Sea and the Contiguous Zone, November 22, 1960. The reservation states: "Article 23 (Sub-Section D. Rule applicable to warships): The Government of the Union of Soviet Socialist Republics considers that the coastal State has the right to establish procedures for the authorization of the passage of foreign warships through its territorial waters." This reservation was consistent with Russian judge Krylow's dissenting opinion in the Corfu Channel case, that "the right to regulate passage of warships through its territorial waters appertains to the coastal State." Corfu Channel Case (UK v. Albania), Merits (Judgment of April 9) (Krylow, J., dissenting), 1949 ICJ Rep. 4, 74.
18. Statute on the Protection of the State Boundary of the U.S.S.R., adopted August 5, 1960, in S. Houston Lay, Robin Rolf Churchill, and Myron H. Nordquist, eds., *New Directions in the Law of the Sea* (New York: Oceana, 1973), 1:30, art. 16.
19. *Vedimosti SSSR* 17, no. 34 (1960), item 324, translated in *Soviet Statutes and Decisions* (1969): 6:63, as cited in William E. Butler, "Innocent Passage and the 1982 Convention: The Influence of Soviet Law and Policy," *American Journal of International Law* 81 (1987): 333.

20. The 1924 Instruction for the Navigation of Vessels in Coastal Waters within Artillery Range of Shore Batteries in Peacetime, the 1927 Statute on the Protection of the State Boundary of the U.S.S.R., the 1931 Provisional Rules for Foreign Warships Visiting USSR Waters, and the 1936 Rules for the Entrance of Vessels into Areas of Restricted Movement all recognized the right of innocent passage in the Soviet territorial sea "consistent with the prevailing customary rules of international law." Butler, "Innocent Passage and the 1982 Convention," 331–32.

21. W. W. Rostow, Memorandum for the President, "Black Sea Operations by U.S. Naval Vessels," secret, declassified November 18, 1993, ref: B07129, Lyndon B. Johnson Library, Austin, Texas.

22. Ibid.

23. Benjamin Welles, "While Keeping the Flag Flying," *New York Times*, December 15, 1968, 3E.

24. Robert Trumbull, "U.S. Skipper Views Bumpings as Error, but Criticizes Soviet," *New York Times*, May 18, 1967, 1; Richard Halloran, "Soviet Sideswipes Called Accidental by U.S. Captain: Destroyer Collisions Held Accidental near Soviet Base, Russians Laughed," *Washington Post*, May 18, 1967, A1.

25. Associated Press, "Soviet Bomber Falls after Pass near U.S. Carrier," *New York Times*, May 26, 1968, 4.

26. Agreement on the Prevention of Incidents On and Over the High Seas, U.S.-U.S.S.R., signed at Moscow, May 25, 1972, UST, 23:1168 [hereafter INCSEA]; Protocol to the Agreement on the Prevention of Incidents On and Over the High Seas, May 22, 1973, 24 UST 1063.

27. Convention on the International Regulations for Preventing Collisions at Sea, signed at London, October 20, 1972, 28 UST 3459, TIAS 8587, 1050 UNTS 16 (1977), entered into force July 15, 1977 [hereafter COLREGS].

28. Vienna Convention on the Law of Treaties, signed at Vienna, May 23, 1969, 1155 UNTS 331, entered into force January 27, 1980.

29. INCSEA, art. III.

30. Ibid., art. IV.

31. Ibid.
32. Ibid., art. VI.
33. The International Maritime Organization–International Hydrographic Organization World-Wide Navigational Warning Service and the International Civil Aviation Organization Aeronautical Information Service require notices. See International Maritime Organization World-Wide Navigational Warning Service, ann. 1 para. 4.2.1.3.12, IMO Res. A.706 (17) (November 16 1991); and Information Services, International Civil Aviation Organization, Convention on International Civil Aviation, *International Standards and Recommended Practices: Aeronautical Annex*, 13th ed. (July 2010), vol. 15, para. 5.1.1.1.(l).
34. Associated Press, "U.S. Ships Report Soviet Mock Attack," *Los Angeles Times*, August 11, 1979, A5, and "After Diplomatic Dickering, Soviets to Return U.S. Torpedo," *Washington Post*, August 11, 1979, A7.
35. UN Doc. A/CONF.62/WP.10, July 15, 1977, reprinted in United Nations Conference on the Law of the Sea, *Official Records*, vol. 3, *Sixth Session* (New York, 23 May–15 July 1977), 1–64.
36. United Nations Convention on the Law of the Sea, signed at Montego Bay, December 10, 1982, entered into force November 16, 1994, 1833 UNTS 397 [hereafter UNCLOS].
37. Ibid., art. 21.
38. Satya N. Nandan and Shabtai Rosenne, eds., *United Nations Convention on the Law of the Sea 1982: A Commentary*, vol. 2, arts. *1 to 85, Annexes I and II, Final Act, Annex II* (Dordrecht, Neth.: Martinus Nijhoff, 1993) [hereafter Virginia Commentary II], 195–99.
39. Bernard H. Oxman, "The Regime of Warships under the United Nations Convention on the Law of the Sea," *Virginia Journal of International Law* 24 (1984): 854 n159.
40. State Frontier Law 1982.
41. Ibid., art. 13.
42. 1983 Rules.
43. Union of Soviet Socialist Republics: Law on the State Boundary of the U.S.S.R., entered into force March 1, 1983, reprinted in 22 ILM 5 (September 1983), 1055–76.

44. "In the Baltic Sea: according to the traffic separation systems in the area of Kypu Peninsula (Hiiumaa Island) and in the area of the Pork-kala Lighthouse; in the Sea of Okhotsk: according to the traffic separation schemes in the areas of the Cape Aniva (Sakhalin Island) and the Fourth Kurile strait (Paramushir and Makanrushi Islands); in the Sea of Japan: according to the traffic separation system in the area in Cape Kril'on (Sakhalin Island)." 1983 Rules.

45. Butler, "Innocent Passage and the 1982 Convention," 340–43.

46. Pursuant to article 22.1 of UNCLOS, "the coastal State may, where necessary having regard to the safety of navigation, require foreign ships exercising the right of innocent passage through its territorial sea to use such sea lanes and traffic separation schemes as it may designate or prescribe for the regulation of the passage of ships."

47. Rick Atkinson, "High Seas Diplomacy Continuing: Navies Keep Superpower Diplomacy Afloat," *Washington Post*, June 8, 1984, A1.

48. Article II of INCSEA provides, in part, that "the Parties recognize that their freedom to conduct operations on the high seas is based on the principles established under recognized international law and codified in the 1958 Geneva Convention on the High Seas."

49. Richard Halloran, "2 U.S. Ships Enter Soviet Waters off Crimea to Gather Intelligence," *New York Times*, March 19, 1986, A1. For legal analysis of the U.S. operation, see William J. Aceves, "Diplomacy at Sea: U.S. Freedom of Navigation Operations in the Black Sea," *Naval War College Review* 46, no. 2 (Spring 1993): 59; and John W. Rolph, "Freedom of Navigation and the Black Sea Bumping Incident: How 'Innocent' Must Innocent Passage Be?" *Military Law Review* 135 (1992): 137.

50. Halloran, "2 U.S. Ships Enter Soviet Waters off Crimea to Gather Intelligence."

51. Butler, "Innocent Passage and the 1982 Convention," 344.

52. "Kremlin Protest on US Warships Adds to Superpower Tensions," *Times* (London), March 19, 1986, 5.

53. 2 V MID SSSR, *Izvestiia*, March 19, 1986, 4, as cited in Butler, "Innocent Passage and the 1982 Convention," 344.

54. Central Intelligence Agency, cable to the Department of State, 13 February 1988, declassified 28 November 1989, as cited in Aceves, "Diplomacy at Sea," 65.

55. Christopher Walker, "Moscow Claims US Ships Were Spying," *Times* (London), March 21, 1986, 7.

56. V. Lukashin, "*Flot proiavil vyderzhku*" (interview of Adm. V. N. Chernavin), *Izvestiia*, March 23, 1986, 3, as cited in Butler, "Innocent Passage and the 1982 Convention," 345.

57. William M. Arkin, "Spying in the Black Sea," *Bulletin of Atomic Scientists* 5 (May 1988): 5.

58. William L. Schachte Jr., "The Black Sea Challenge," U.S. Naval Institute *Proceedings* 62 (June 1988): 62.

59. Arkin, "Spying in the Black Sea."

60. UNCLOS, art. 19.2(c).

61. Ibid.

62. Ibid.

63. Associated Press, "Soviets Bump 2 U.S. Warships," *Chicago Tribune*, February 13, 1988, 1.

64. Associated Press, "U.S. Says Act Was Unprovoked, Lodges Protest with Envoy," *Los Angeles Times*, February 14, 1988, 1.

65. "Soviets Bump 2 U.S. Ships in Black Sea," *Chicago Tribune*; "U.S. Says Act Was Unprovoked," *Los Angeles Times*, 1.

66. "Soviets Bump 2 U.S. Warships," *Chicago Tribune*, 1.

67. Ibid.

68. Aceves, "Diplomacy at Sea," 251.

69. Ibid., 251–52.

70. John Cushman, "2 Soviet Warships Reportedly Bump U.S. Navy Vessels," *New York Times*, February 13, 1988.

71. Philip Taubman, "Soviet Says It Hopes 'Provocation' by U.S. at Sea Won't Hurt Talks," *New York Times*, February 14, 1988.

72. "Soviets Bump 2 U.S. Warships," *Chicago Tribune*, 1.

73. Taubman, "Soviet Says It Hopes 'Provocation' by U.S. at Sea Won't Hurt Talks."

74. Ibid.

75. Rolph, "How 'Innocent' Must Innocent Passage Be?" 145.
76. Alfred P. Rubin, "Innocent Passage in the Black Sea?" *Christian Science Monitor*, March 1, 1988, 14; Eugene J. Carroll Jr., "Black Day on the Black Sea," *Arms Control Today* 18 (May 1988): 15.
77. Aceves, "Diplomacy at Sea," 253.
78. U.S. Congress, Senate, Committee on Armed Services, Department of Defense Authorization for Appropriations for Fiscal Year 1989, Hearings (1988), 97–98.
79. Ibid.
80. Ibid., 253.
81. UNCLOS, art. 21.1(a) provides: "The coastal State may adopt laws and regulations, in conformity with the provisions of this Convention and other rules of international law, relating to innocent passage through the territorial sea, in respect of all or any of the following: (a) the safety of navigation and the regulation of maritime traffic."
82. UNCLOS, art. 22.1.
83. Aceves, "Diplomacy at Sea," 254.
84. Richard Armitage, "Asserting U.S. Rights on the Black Sea," *Arms Control Today* 18 (June 1988): 13–14.
85. Agreement on the Prevention of Incidents On and Over the High Seas, U.S.-U.S.S.R.; Protocol to the Agreement on the Prevention of Incidents On and Over the High Seas. INCSEA article IX requires the parties to meet annually to review the implementation of its terms; John H. McNeill, "Military-to-Military Arrangements for the Prevention of U.S.-Russian Conflict," *International Legal Studies* 68 (1995): f 577.
86. Ibid., 577; Aceves, "Diplomacy at Sea," 255.
87. DMA Agreement, 28 ILM 4 (July 1989), 877–95. See also Kurt Campbell, "The U.S.-Soviet Agreement on the Prevention of Dangerous Military Activities," *Security Studies* 1, no. 1 (Autumn 1991): 109–31.
88. DMA Agreement, art. II.
89. Ibid.
90. Ibid., art. III.

91. Ibid., art. III. See annex I and II for the communications channels and protocols.
92. A "laser" is defined in the DMA Agreement, art. I.7, as "any source of intense, coherent, highly directional electromagnetic radiation in the visible, infrared, or ultraviolet regions that is based on the stimulated radiation of electrons, atoms or molecules."
93. DMA Agreement, art. IV.
94. Ibid., art. I.8.
95. Ibid., art. IX.
96. Ibid., art. VIII.
97. McNeill, "Military-to-Military Arrangements," 579.
98. Union of Soviet Socialist Republics–United States: Joint Statement with attached Uniform Interpretation of Rules of International Law Governing Innocent Passage, signed at Jackson Hole, Wyoming, September 23, 1989, entered into force July 10, 1991, *Treaties and Other International Acts Series* 11448, 28 ILM 1444 (1989).
99. Ibid., para. 1.
100. Ibid.
101. Ibid., para. 2.
102. Ibid.
103. UNCLOS, art. 19(2).
104. Ibid., para. 5. The relevant UNCLOS articles are 21, 22, 23, and 25.
105. Ibid.
106. Ibid.
107. Ibid., para. 6.
108. Ibid., para. 4.
109. Ibid., para. 7.
110. UNCLOS Article 30 provides, "If any warship does not comply with the laws and regulations of the coastal State concerning passage through the territorial sea and disregards any request for compliance therewith which is made to it, the coastal State may require it to leave the territorial sea immediately."
111. Aceves, "Diplomacy at Sea," 258, citing International Law Division of the Soviet Ministry of Foreign Affairs, July 11, 1990.

112. Rick Atkinson, "High Seas Diplomacy Continuing," *Washington Post*, June 8, 1984. See also Rolph, "How 'Innocent' Must Innocent Passage Be?" 163.

113. Sam LaGrone, "Russian Fighter Buzzes U.S. Destroyer in Black Sea," *USNI News*, April 15, 2014.

114. Convention Regarding the Regime of Straits (1936), *League of Nations Treaty Series*, 173:213, art. 18(2).

115. Barbara Starr, "Russian Planes, U.S. Warship Have Close Encounter near Crimea," CNN, June 1, 2015.

116. "USS *Donald Cook* Buzzed Again by Russian Jets in Baltic," *CBS News*, April 13, 2016.

117. Sam LaGrone, "Russian Fighters Buzz USS *Donald Cook* in Baltic Sea," *USNI News*, April 25, 2016.

118. Ibid.

119. Barbara Starr, Ryan Browne, and Kevin Liptak, "U.S. Issues Formal Protest to Russia over Baltic Sea Incident," CNN, April 14, 2016.

120. Barbara Starr, "First on CNN: Russians 'Barrel Roll' over Another U.S. Air Force Plane," CNN, April 29, 2016.

121. Sophie Tatum and Barbara Starr, "Russia Denies Wrongdoing after Jet Barrel-Rolls over U.S. Aircraft," CNN, April 17, 2016.

122. International Civil Aviation Organization, "Rules of the Air: Annex 2 to the Convention on International Civil Aviation," 10th ed., July 2005, *ICAO*, www.icao.int/.

123. Article 3.1 provides that "this Convention shall be applicable only to civil aircraft, and shall not be applicable to state aircraft." Convention on International Civil Aviation, signed at Chicago, December 7, 1944, entered into force April 4, 1947, 15 UNTS 295 (1948).

124. "Russian Jet Flies within 10 Feet of US Navy Spy Plane, Defense Official Says," *Fox News World*, September 7, 2016.

125. Ivan Watson and Sebastian Shukla, "Russian Fighter Jets 'Buzz' US Warship in Black Sea, Photos Show," CNN, February 16, 2017.

126. Luis Martinez, "Russian Fighter Flies 20 Feet from US Navy Plane over Black Sea," *ABC News*, May 12, 2017.

127. Lucas Tomlinson, "Russian Jet 'Buzzes' Another US plane in Black Sea, Second Incident This Week," *Fox News*, May 13, 2017.

Chapter 11. "Freedom of Navigation with Chinese Characteristics"

1. U.S. Defense Department, *Asia-Pacific Maritime Security Strategy* (Washington, D.C., 2015), 14.
2. UNCLOS; Virginia Commentary II, 491–821.
3. UNCLOS, art. 56.
4. Ibid. See also Virginia Commentary II.
5. UNCLOS, art. 89, provides that "no State may validly purport to subject any part of the high seas to its sovereignty."
6. UNCLOS, art. 2. See also Virginia Commentary II.
7. *Official Records of the Third U.N. Conference on the Law of the Sea*, vol. 17, *Plenary Meetings*, UN Doc. A/CONF.62/WS/37 and ADD. 1 and 2 (New York: United Nations, n.d.) 243.
8. Agence France-Presse, "US Aircraft Carrier May Be Deployed in South China Sea," April 16, 2001.
9. Wu Xinbo, *Managing Crisis and Sustaining Peace between China and the United States*, Peaceworks 61 (Washington, D.C.: United States Institute of Peace, April 1, 2008) [hereafter Peaceworks 61], 15.
10. Ibid.
11. Rear Adm. Craig R. Quigley, Deputy Assistant Secretary of Defense for Public Affairs (presenter), U.S. Defense Dept. News Briefing, April 3, 2001 [hereafter Rear Admiral Quigley news briefing, April 3, 2001].
12. "U.S. Accuses China over Air Collision," CNN, April 2, 2001.
13. Shirley A. Kan, *China-U.S. Aircraft Collision Incident of April 2001: Assessments and Policy Implications*, CRS Report for Congress 14 (Washington, D.C.: Congressional Research Service, 10 October 2001) [hereafter Kan, CRS Report]; Peaceworks 61, 15; John Keefe, *Anatomy of the EP-3 Incident, April 2001* (Washington, D.C.: Center for Strategic Studies, October 26, 2001), 2.
14. Rear Admiral Quigley news briefing, April 3, 2001. See also Statement by the President on American Plane and Crew in China, April

2, 2001, National Archives and Records Administration, Washington, D.C. [hereafter POTUS statement].

15. Rear Admiral Quigley news briefing, April 3, 2001.

16. Gerry J. Gilmore, "Diplomats' Mission: 'Bring the People Home,' Bush Says," *American Forces Press Service*, April 6, 2001.

17. POTUS statement.

18. Gerry J. Gilmore, "Chinese Jet Struck Navy EP-3 Aircraft, Rumsfeld Says," *American Forces Press Service*, April 13, 2001.

19. Rear Admiral Quigley news briefing, April 3, 2001.

20. The crew comprised twenty-four personnel: twenty-two Navy, one Marine Corps, and one Air Force.

21. Co-author Raul "Pete" Pedrozo served as legal adviser on the U.S. delegation that traveled to China to negotiate the return of the U.S. aircraft.

22. Sean D. Murphy, "Aerial Incident off the Coast of China," *American Journal of International Law* 95 (July 2001): 626.

23. *Restatement of the Law Third: The Foreign Relations Law of the United States* (Philadelphia: American Law Institute, 1987), vol. 1, sec. 457, Reporter's Note 7.

24. Rear Admiral Quigley news briefing, April 3, 2001; Secretary of Defense, memorandum, April 10, 2001 [hereafter SECDEF memo, April 10, 2001].

25. "Collision with China, Bush on China: 'Different Values, Common Interests,'" *New York Times*, April 13, 2001.

26. Gilmore, "Chinese Jet Struck Navy EP-3 Aircraft."

27. Ibid.

28. Ibid.

29. "Who Caused the Crash?" *BBC News*, April 5, 2001.

30. Ibid.

31. Margaret K. Lewis, "An Analysis of State Responsibility for the Chinese-American Airplane Collision Incident," *New York University Law Review* 77 (2002): 1424; Kan, CRS Report, 18.

32. Kan, CRS Report, 18.

33. Ibid., 15, 19.

34. Ibid.

35. Ibid.
36. POTUS statement.
37. Peaceworks 61, 16.
38. Ibid.
39. Kan, CRS Report, 3. See also Peaceworks 61, 17.
40. Kan, CRS Report, 3.
41. Ibid., 3.
42. Peaceworks 61, 18.
43. Ibid.
44. Kan, CRS Report, 4. Secretary Powell did not apologize but did state, "We regret that the Chinese plane did not get down safely, and we regret the loss of the life of that Chinese pilot."
45. Peaceworks 61, 18.
46. Keefe, *Anatomy of the EP-3 Incident*.
47. Ibid.
48. "Under international air space rules, the faster more maneuverable aircraft has [the] obligation to stay out of the way of the slower aircraft." "U.S. Accuses China over Air Collision," CNN, April 2, 2001.
49. Lewis, "Analysis of State Responsibility," 1426–27.
50. SECDEF memo, April 10, 2001.
51. Ibid. See also Kan, CRS Report, 4. The following day, the president also sent to the wife of Wang Wei a letter expressing "regret" for the loss of her husband.
52. Peaceworks 61, 18–19. See also Keefe, *Anatomy of the EP-3 Incident*.
53. Kan, CRS Report, 5.
54. Ambassador Prueher, letter to Chinese Minister of Foreign Affairs Tang, April 11, 2001, reprinted as "Text of U.S. Letter to China," *ABC News*, April 10, 2001 [hereafter Ambassador Prueher letter]. The letter stated that the United States was "very sorry" for the loss suffered by "the Chinese people and to the family of pilot Wang Wei."
55. Chris Plante, "U.S. Quietly Resumes Surveillance Flights off China," CNN, May 15, 2001.
56. Paul Eckert, "Dismantled U.S. Spy Plane Flown Out of China," *ABC News*, July 3, 2001.

57. Rear Admiral Quigley news briefing, April 3, 2001; and Gerry J. Gilmore and Jim Garamone, "Landing Permission in China Requested, EP-3 Pilot Says," American Forces Press Service, April 12, 2001.

58. "Who Caused the Crash?" *BBC News.* See also SECDEF memo, April 10, 2001, attaching General Counsel of the Dept. of Defense, memorandum, "EP-3 Incident-Guidance on Legal Issues," April 6, 2001, certified as unclassified January 9, 2009.

59. Gilmore, "Chinese Jet Struck Navy EP-3 Aircraft"; SECDEF memo, April 10, 2001.

60. "Who Caused the Crash?" *BBC News.* See also Rear Admiral Quigley news briefing, April 3, 2001, and Lewis, "Analysis of State Responsibility," 1430.

61. Convention on International Civil Aviation, 15 *United Nations Treaty Series* [hereafter UNTS] 295, 61 Stat. 1180, *Treaties and Other International Acts Series* (TIAS) No. 1591, December 7, 1944, entered into force April 4, 1947, as amended 1175 UNTS 297, entered into force October 1998.

62. Ibid. Article 3(a) provides, "This Convention shall be applicable only to civil aircraft, and shall not be applicable to state aircraft." Article 3(c) requires that "no state aircraft of a contracting State shall fly over the territory of another State or land thereon without authorization by special agreement or otherwise, and in accordance with the terms thereof."

63. SECDEF memo, April 10, 2001.

64. Ibid.

65. U.S. Defense Dept., "Secretary Rumsfeld Briefs on EP-3 Collision," news transcript, April 13, 2001, 2:00 p.m. EDT.

66. Oliver J. Lissitzyn, "The Treatment of Aerial Intruders in Recent Practice and International Law," *American Journal of International Law* 47 (1953): 560.

67. Rear Adm. Craig R. Quigley, DASD PA, U.S. Defense Dept. Briefing on Return of EP-3 Crew, April 11, 2001.

68. M'Faddon v. the Exch., 16 F. Cas. 85, 88 (CCD Pa. 1811) rev'd sum nom. The Schooner Exch. v. M'Faddon, 11 U.S. 116, 3 L. Ed. 287

(1812), reprinted in *American Journal of International Law* 3 (January 1909): 227.

69. SECDEF Memo, April 10, 2001.

70. Robert Burns and Lolita C. Baldor, "Pentagon Cites 'Dangerous' Chinese Jet Intercept," Associated Press, August 22, 2014; Craig Whitlock, "Pentagon: China Tried to Block U.S. Military Jet in Dangerous Mid-Air Intercept," *Washington Post*, August 22, 2014.

71. Sam LaGrone, "China Contests Pentagon Account of 'Unsafe' Intercept of U.S. Navy Surveillance Plane by PLA Fighters," *USNI News*, May 19, 2016.

72. Reuters, "U.S. Accuses China of Dangerous, High-Speed Intercept of Spy Plane in South China Sea," June, 6, 2016.

73. Reuters, "US, China Military Planes Come Inadvertently Close Over South China Sea," February 10, 2017.

74. Office of the Secretary of Defense, *Annual Report to Congress: Military and Security Developments Involving the People's Republic of China* (Washington, D.C., 2013), 39; Raul (Pete) Pedrozo, "Preserving Navigational Rights and Freedoms: The Right to Conduct Military Activities in China's Exclusive Economic Zone," *Chinese Journal of International Law* 9 (2010): paras. 16–18.

75. Zachary Keck, "China Is Spying on RIMPAC," *Diplomat*, July 20, 2014; Office of the Secretary of Defense, *Annual Report to Congress: Military and Security Developments Involving the People's Republic of China* (Washington, D.C., 2015), 68.

76. Oceanographic survey ships (all USNS) are: *Bowditch, Bruce C. Heezen, Henson, Mary Sears, Maury*, and *Pathfinder*. "Special Mission Program," *Military Sealift Command*, http://www.msc.navy.mil.

77. Ocean surveillance ships (all USNS) are: *Able, Effective, Impeccable, Loyal*, and *Victorious*. Ibid.

78. Plante, "U.S. Quietly Resumes Surveillance Flights"; Mark Oliva, "Before EP-3, China Turned Away U.S. Research Ship in International Waters," *Stars and Stripes*, May 20, 2001; Shirley Kan, memorandum for Representative Randy Forbes, "China's Military and Security Developments," January 20, 2011, Congressional Research Service, Washington, D.C., 5.

79. See Raul Pedrozo, "Close Encounters at Sea: The USNS *Impeccable* Incident," *Naval War College Review* 63, no. 3 (Summer 2009): 101–11; also Oliva, "Before EP-3."

80. See Pedrozo, "Close Encounters at Sea."

81. Ibid.

82. Erik Eckholm, "China Complains about U.S. Surveillance Ship," *New York Times*, September 27, 2002; Kan, "China's Military and Security Developments," 6.

83. James Bussert, "China's Phantom Fleet," *Signal*, October 1, 2011.

84. "Pentagon: Chinese Ships Harassed Unarmed Navy Craft in International Waters," FoxNews.com, March 9, 2009.

85. Kevin Baron, "Navy: Surveillance ship Called On Chinese to Shake Off Fishing Boats," *Stars and Stripes*, May 6, 2009; James Kraska and Raul Pedrozo, *International Maritime Security Law*, (The Hague: Brill/Martinus Nijhoff, 2013), 311.

86. "Chinese Ships Harassed Unarmed Navy Craft in International Waters."

87. Ibid.

88. See Pedrozo, "Close Encounters at Sea."

89. "Chinese Ships Harassed Unarmed Navy Craft in International Waters."

90. Bill Gertz, "Chinese Naval Vessel Tries to Force U.S. Warship to Stop in International Waters," *Washington Free Beacon*, December 13, 2013; Pedrozo, *Military Activities in the Exclusive Economic Zone*, 522.

91. U.S. Defense Dept., "Statement by Pentagon Press Secretary Peter Cook on Incident in the South China Sea," News Release NR-448–16, December 16, 2016.

92. Christopher Bodeen, "China Says It Will Give Drone Back, But Trump Says 'Keep It,'" Associated Press, December 18, 2016.

93. Andrew Browne, "China Throws Out South China Sea Rule Book," *Wall Street Journal*, December 21, 2016.

94. Xinhua News Agency, "South China Sea Issue Should Not Be Hyped Up: Chinese Defense Minister, Ministry of National Defense, People's Republic of China," May 26, 2016.

95. China's ambassador to the Philippines, Zhao Jianhua, described Beijing's view of "freedom of navigation" as follows: "Freedom of navigation does

not mean to allow other countries to intrude into the airspace or the sea which is sovereign. . . . We say freedom of navigation must be observed in accordance with international law. No freedom of navigation for warships and airplanes." Jim Gomez, "Chinese Diplomat Outlines Limits to Freedom of Navigation," *Philippine Star*, August 12, 2015.

96. "PRC Scholar on US 'Close-In Reconnaissance' of China, PRC's Countermeasures," *Guoji Xianqu Daobao Online in Chinese*, December 20, 2013, http://fortunascorner.com/.

97. UNCLOS, art. 29.

98. See Raul Pedrozo, "Coastal State Jurisdiction over Marine Data Collection in the Exclusive Economic Zone: U.S. Views," in *Military Activities in the EEZ: A U.S.-China Dialogue on Security and International Law in the Maritime Commons*, ed. Peter Dutton, China Maritime Studies 7 (Newport, R.I.: Naval War College Press, 2010), 23–26. See also Kraska, *Maritime Power and Law of the Sea*, 221–90, and J. Ashley Roach and Robert W. Smith, *Excessive Maritime Claims*, 3rd ed. (Leiden, Neth.: Martinus Nijhoff, 2012), 413–50.

99. UNCLOS, art. 246.

100. Alfred Soons, *Marine Scientific Research and the Law of the Sea* (Deventer, Neth.: Kluwer, 1982), 124. See also J. Ashley Roach and Robert W. Smith, *United States Responses to Excessive Maritime Claims*, 2nd ed. (The Hague: Martinus Nijhoff, 1996), 425.

101. Roach and Smith, *United States Responses to Excessive Maritime Claims*, 426.

102. *Consolidated Glossary of Technical Terms Used in the United Nations Convention on the Law of the Sea* (New York: UN Office for Ocean Affairs and the Law of the Sea, 1989), definition 40, "The Law of the Sea: Baselines."

103. See Pedrozo, "Coastal State Jurisdiction over Marine Data Collection in the Exclusive Economic Zone," 28.

104. Roach and Smith, *United States Responses to Excessive Maritime Claims*, 427.

105. UNCLOS, art. 19(2)(j).

106. UNCLOS, art. 52. For archipelagic sea-lanes passage, see art. 54.

107. 1998 Chinese EEZ Law, art. 3; UNCLOS, art. 56.
108. 1998 Chinese EEZ Law, art. 3.
109. Capt. Stacy A. Pedrozo, JAGC, USN, *China's Active Defense Strategy and Its Regional Impact*, Testimony before the U.S.-China Economic and Security Review Commission, House, 112th Cong., 1st Sess., 2011.
110. Winter v. Natural Resources Defense Council, Inc., 555 U.S. 7 (2008).
111. UNCLOS, art. 236.
112. UNCLOS, arts. 95 and 96.
113. "China *note verbale*, April 13, 2009, concerning the Republic Act No. 9522: An Act to Amend Certain Provisions of Republic Act No. 3046, as Amended by Republic Act No. 5446, to Define the Archipelagic Baselines of the Philippines, and for Other Purposes, Deposited by the Republic of the Philippines with the Secretary-General, May 9, 2009," *Law of the Sea Bulletin* 70 (New York: United Nations, 2009), 58.
114. In the Matter of the South China Sea Arbitration (Phil.-China), PCA Case No. 2013–19, Award, July 12, 2016 [hereafter Arbitration Award], para. 1158.
115. Ibid., para. 270.
116. Ibid., para. 271.
117. Ibid., paras. 231, 246–47. This rationale is also consistent with article 30 of the Vienna Convention on the Law of Treaties, 1155 UNTS 331, 8 *International Legal Materials* 679, entered into force January 27, 1980. Legal authority of later date prevails over earlier authorities.
118. Arbitration Award, paras. 243, 244.
119. Ibid., para. 1203(6)(B)(3)(b). Rocks, as opposed to islands, are not entitled to EEZs.
120. Ibid., para. 1203(6)(B)(3)(c).
121. UNCLOS, Art. 19(2). Foreign states also may enjoy a right of entry into the territorial sea in cases of force majeure; NWP 1–14M, para. 2.5.2.1.
122. Arbitration Award, paras. 1203(6)(B)(3)(c), 1203(6)(B)(4).
123. Ibid., paras. 1203(7), 1025.

124. Jeff Himmelman, "A Game of Shark and Minnow," *New York Times*, October 27, 2013.

125. Gregory Poling, "Potential New Runway Presents New Headaches," *Asia Maritime Transparency Initiative*, September 15, 2015, https://amti.csis.org/.

126. David Anderson, "Islands and Rocks in the Modern Law of the Sea," in *United Nations Convention on the Law of the Sea, 1982: A Commentary*, vol. 2, *Articles 1 to 85, Annexes I and II, Final Act, Annex II*, ed. Satya N. Nandan and Myron H. Nordquist (Dordrecht, Neth.: Martinus Nijhoff, 2002), 313.

127. Raul Pedrozo and James Kraska, "Can't Anybody Play This Game? US FON Operations and Law of the Sea," *Lawfare*, November 17, 2015, https://www.lawfareblog.com/.

128. Raul Pedrozo, "Freedom of Navigation Exercises Essential to Preserve Rights," *Straits Times*, October 30, 2015.

129. Ibid.

130. Christopher Cavas, "Navy Chiefs Talk, New Details on Destroyer's Passage," *Defense News*, October 31, 2015.

131. Kristina Wong, "US Flies B-52 Bombers near Disputed Islands Claimed by China," *The Hill*, November 12, 2015.

132. UNCLOS, art. 13(2).

133. UNCLOS, art. 60[4]: "The coastal State may, where necessary, establish reasonable safety zones around such artificial islands . . . in which it may take appropriate measures to ensure the safety both of navigation and of the artificial islands. . . . 5. The breadth of the safety zones shall . . . not exceed a distance of 500 meters around them."

134. October 27, 2015, https://www.mccain.senate.gov.

135. Ibid.

136. Ibid.

137. Yeganeh Torbati and David Alexander, "U.S. Bombers Flew near China-Built Islands in South China Sea: Pentagon," Reuters, November 15, 2015.

138. Wong, "US Flies B-52 Bombers near Disputed Islands Claimed by China."

139. Secretary of Defense Ash Carter letter to Senator John McCain (R-AZ) concerning U.S. Freedom of Navigation Operations, October 27, 2015, https://news.usni.org.

140. "China Accuses US of B-52 'Provocation' over Spratly Islands," *BBC News*, December 29, 2015.

141. "US Says B-52 Bombers Didn't Intend to Fly over China's Man-Made Island," FoxNews.com, December 20, 2015.

142. Secretary of Defense Ash Carter letter to Senator John McCain (R-AZ) concerning U.S. Freedom of Navigation Operations, October 27, 2015, https://news.usni.org.

143. Jane Perlez, "U.S. Warship Sails Near Island Claimed by Beijing in South China Sea," *New York Times*, May 24, 2017.

144. Arbitration Award, para. 1017.

145. Sam LaGrone, "U.S. Warship Came within 6 Miles of Chinese Artificial Island in Toughest Challenge Yet to Beijing South China Sea Claims," *USNI News*, May 25, 2017.

Conclusion

1. Hugo Grotius, *The Freedom of the Seas*, trans. Ralph Van Deman Magoffin (New York: Oxford University Press, 1916), 24.

2. John D. Negroponte, "Who Will Protect Freedom of the Seas?" *Department of State Bulletin* 86 (October 1986): 41.

3. Bernard H. Oxman, "The Territorial Temptation: A Siren Song at Sea," *American Journal of International Law* 100 (2006): 830.

4. National Security Council Memorandum, Subj: Navigation and Overflight Policy, February 1, 1979, confidential, declassified October 31, 2013.

5. Zbigniew Brzezinski, The White House, Memorandum for the Secretary of State, the Secretary of Defense, et. al, Navigational Freedom and U.S. Security Interests, March 20, 1979.

6. UNCLOS.

7. Statement by the President, United States Oceans Policy, 19 *Weekly Compilation of Presidential Documents* 383 (March 10, 1983), available at https://www.reaganlibrary.archives.gov/.

8. Ibid.

9. Jeremy Page and Gordon Lubold, "Chinese Navy Ships Came Within 12 Nautical Miles of U.S. Coast," *Wall Street Journal*, Sept. 4, 2015.

10. Ibid.

11. Wyat Olson, "Report: China dispatching surveillance vessels off Hawaii," *Stars and Stripes*, Sept. 4, 2015.

12. Gabčíkovo-Nagymaros Project (Hungary/Slovakia), ICJ Rep. 1997, 7, 56–57, para. 87.

13. International Law Commission, Responsibility of States for Internationally Wrongful Acts, G.A. Res. 56/83 annex, U.N. Doc. A/RES 56/83 (12 Dec. 2001).

14. Articles on State Responsibility, Arts. 1–2.

15. Rules of the Air, Convention on International Civil Aviation, Annex 2 (10th ed., July 2005).

16. Convention on International Regulations for Preventing Collisions at Sea, October 20, 1972, 1050 *United Nations Treaty Series* [hereafter UNTS] 17.

17. *Military and Security Development Involving the People's Republic of China 2017*, DOD Annual Report to Congress, 8, 56.

18. *The Asia-Pacific Maritime Security Strategy: Achieving U.S. National Security Objectives in a Changing Environment*, Dept. of Defense, 2015, 15–16.

19. Arbitration Award, para. 231.

20. Ibid., para. 246–47.

21. Ibid., para. 243–244.

22. Vienna Convention on the Law of Treaties, May 23, 1969, 1155 UNTS 331, Art. 30.

23. Raul Pedrozo and James Kraska, "Can't Anybody Play This Game? US FON Operations and Law of the Sea," *Lawfare*, November 17, 2015.

24. Arbitration Award, para. 280.

25. Article 19(2), UNCLOS.

26. Arbitration Award, para. 1203(6)(B)(3)(c).

27. Ibid, para. 1203(6)(B)(3)(b).

28. Request for an Advisory Opinion, ITLOS Case No. 21, 2015, para. 741.

29. U.S. forces conducted only seven such operations in the South China Sea between 2011 and 2015.

30. Sam LaGrone, "U.S. Destroyer Passes Near Chinese Artificial Island in South China Sea Freedom of Navigation Operation," *USNI News*, May 10, 2016.

31. See, for example, our critiques of some earlier FON operations in the South China Sea, available at www.lawfareblog.com.

32. "China opposes U.S. naval patrols in South China Sea," Reuters, February 21, 2017.

33. Erik Slavin, "Chinese admiral contests freedom of navigation in South China Sea," *Stars & Stripes*, July 19, 2016.

34. Sam LaGrone, "U.S. Warship Came within 6 Miles of Chinese Artificial Island in Toughest Challenge Yet to Beijing South China Sea Claims," *USNI News*, May 25, 2017.

35. David Cenciotti, "Air Force and Navy assets train in South China Sea," *The Aviationist*, June 8, 2017.

36. Executive Assistant, Chief of Naval Operations, Memorandum for the Record, Dept. of the Navy, June 29, 2016.

37. Sam Meredith, "Pentagon admonishes Russia for 'unsafe' intercept of US spy plane over Baltic Sea," CNBC, June 21, 2017.

38. See *Limits in the Seas No: 112*: "United States Responses to Excessive National Maritime Claims," U.S. Dept. of State, March 9, 1992.

SELECTED BIBLIOGRAPHY

Adams, Henry, ed. *Documents Relating to New England Federalism 1800–1815.* Boston: Little, Brown, 1877. Reprint, 1905.

———. *History of the United States of America during the First Administration of Thomas Jefferson.* Vol. 2. New York: Charles Scribner's Sons, 1889. Reprint, 1909.

Adams, John. *Papers of John Adams.* Edited by Robert J. Taylor. Cambridge, Mass.: Harvard University Press, 1979.

———. *Papers of John Adams.* Edited by Gregg L. Lint et al. Cambridge, Mass.: Harvard University Press, 2012.

———. *Papers of John Adams.* Boston: Massachusetts Historical Society, 2017. https://www.masshist.org/publications.

Adams, John Quincy. *Memoirs of John Quincy Adams.* Edited by Charles Francis Adams. Philadelphia: J. B. Lippincott, 1874.

Allen, Gardner W. *Our Naval War with France.* Boston: Houghton Mifflin, 1909.

———. *Our Navy and the Barbary Corsairs.* Boston: Houghton Mifflin, 1905.

American State Papers: Foreign Relations 1789–1797. Vol. 1. Washington, D.C.: Gales and Seaton, 1833.

American State Papers: Naval Affairs. Vol. 1. Washington, D.C.: Gales and Seaton, 1834.

Annals of Congress. Washington, D.C.: Gales and Seaton, 1853.

Armbrister, Trevor. *A Matter of Accountability: The True Story of the* Pueblo *Affair.* Guilford, Conn.: Lyons, December 1, 2004.

Attard, David J. *The Exclusive Economic Zone in International Law.* Oxford, UK: Clarendon, 1990.

Baer, George W. *One Hundred Years of Sea Power: The U.S. Navy, 1890–1990.* Palo Alto, Calif.: Stanford University Press, 1993.

Ball, George W. *The Past Has Another Pattern: Memoirs.* New York: W. W. Norton, 1983.

Bartlett, Ruhl J. *The Record of American Diplomacy: Documents and Readings in the History of American Foreign Relations.* 2nd ed. New York: Alfred A. Knopf, 1950.

Barton, William. *A Dissertation on Freedom of Navigation and Maritime Commerce.* Philadelphia: John Conrad, 1802.

Bemis, Samuel Flagg. *The Diplomacy of the American Revolution: The Foundations of American Diplomacy, 1775–1823.* New York: D. Appleton-Century, 1935.

———. *A Diplomatic History of the United States.* 4th ed. New York: Henry Holt, 1955.

———. *Jay's Treaty: A Study in Commerce and Diplomacy*. New Haven, Conn.: Yale University Press, 1962.

Benn, Carl. *The War of 1812*. Oxford, UK: Osprey, 2002.

Bentwich, Norman. *Declaration of London, with an Introduction, Notes and Appendices*. London: Effingham Wilson, 1911.

Bolyatko, Anatoly. "Russian National Security Strategy and Its Implications for East Asian Security." In *Russian Security Policy in the Asia-Pacific Region: Two Views*. Edited by Stephen J. Blank. Carlisle, Pa.: Strategic Studies Institute, May 27, 1996.

Bradford, James C. *America, Sea Power, and the World*. Hoboken, N.J.: Wiley-Blackwell, 2016.

Brinkley, Douglas, and David R. Facy-Crowther, eds. *The Atlantic Charter*. Basingstoke, UK: Macmillan, 1994.

British and Foreign State Papers. Vol. 1, part 1, *1812–1814*. London: James Ridgeway & Sons, 1841.

British and Foreign State Papers. Vol. 2, *1815–1816*. London: James Ridgeway & Sons, 1841.

British and Foreign State Papers. Vol. 55, *1864–1865*. London: William Ridgway, 1870.

Buel, Richard, Jr. *In Irons: Britain's Naval Supremacy and the American Revolutionary Economy*. New Haven, Conn.: Yale University Press, 1998.

Bushong, William. "Sicilian Salvador Catalano: An American Naval Hero." White House Historical Association, February 23, 2016. https://www.whitehousehistory.org/sicilian-salvador-catalano.

Carlisle, Rodney. *Sovereignty at Sea: U.S. Merchant Ships and American Entry into World War I*. Gainesville: University of Florida Press, 2009.

Carr, E. H. *The Twenty Years' Crisis: An Introduction to the Study of International Relations*. New York: Perennial, 2001.

Chalmers, George. *A Collection of Treaties between Britain and Other Powers*. London: John Stockdale, Piccadilly, 1790.

Charlton, Michael, and Anthony Moncrieff. *Many Reasons Why: The American Involvement in Vietnam*. 2nd ed. London: Hill & Wang, 1989.

Clay, Henry. *The Papers of Henry Clay: Secretary of State, January 1, 1828–March 4, 1829*. Edited by Robert Seager II. Lexington: University Press of Kentucky, 2015.

———. *The Works of Henry Clay*. Edited by Calvin Colton. New York: Barnes & Burr, 1863.

Cobbett, W., and J. Wright, eds. *Parliamentary History of England from the Earliest Period to the Year 1803*. London, 1806–20.

Cogliano, Francis D. *Emperor of Liberty: Thomas Jefferson's Foreign Policy.* New Haven, Conn.: Yale University Press, 2014.

Colombos, C. John. *International Law of the Sea.* 2nd rev. ed. New York: Longmans, Green, 1950.

Consolidated Glossary of Technical Terms Used in the United Nations Convention on the Law of the Sea. New York: UN Office for Ocean Affairs and the Law of the Sea, 1989.

Cooper, Thomas. *Lectures on the Elements of Political Economy.* Columbia, S.C.: Doyle E. Sweeny at the Telescope Press, 1826. E-book made available through Rarebooksclub.com, 2012.

Corrigan, Philip, and Derek Sayer. *The Great Arch: English State Formation as Cultural Revolution.* Oxford, UK: Oxford University Press, 1985.

Creasy, Sir Edward. *Fifteen Decisive Battles of the World: From Marathon to Waterloo.* New York: Harper & Bros., 1863.

Crist, David. *Gulf of Conflict: A History of U.S.-Iranian Confrontation at Sea.* Policy Focus 95. Washington, D.C.: Washington Institute for Near East Policy, June 2009.

Currie, David P. *The Constitution in Congress: The Federalist Period, 1789–1801.* 2nd ed. Chicago: University of Chicago Press, 1997.

D'Amato, Anthony A. *The Concept of Custom in International Law.* Ithaca, N.Y.: Cornell University Press, 1971.

Daughan, George C. *1812: The Navy's War.* New York: Basic Books, 2013.

———. *If by Sea: The Forging of the American Navy—from the Revolution to the War of 1812.* New York: Basic Books, 2008.

Davis, Robert C. *Christian Slaves, Muslim Masters: White Slavery in the Mediterranean, the Barbary Coast and Italy, 1500–1800.* London: Palgrave Macmillan, 2004.

———. *Holy War and Human Bondage: Tales of Christian-Muslim Slavery in the Early-Modern Mediterranean.* Santa Barbara, Calif.: Praeger, 2009.

Dear, I. C. B., and Peter Kemp. *The Oxford Companion to Ships and the Sea.* 2nd ed. Oxford, UK: Oxford University Press, 2016.

Debrett, John. *A Collection of State Papers Relative to the War Against France.* London, 1798.

DeConde, Alexander. *The Quasi-War: The Politics and Diplomacy of the Undeclared War with France, 1797–1801.* New York: Scribner, 1966.

Department of State. Telegram to the Embassy in Vietnam, August 2, 1964. In U.S. State Dept., *Foreign Relations of the United States, 1964–1968.* Vol. 1, *Vietnam 1964.* Washington, D.C.: Office of the Historian, 1992.

The Diplomatic Correspondence of the United States of America. Vol. 2. Washington, D.C.: Blair and Rives, 1837.

Doswald-Beck, Louise, ed. *San Remo Manual on International Law Applicable to Armed Conflicts at Sea: Adopted in June 1994.* Geneva: International Institute of Humanitarian Law, 1995.

Dudley, William S., ed. *The Naval War of 1812: A Documentary History.* Washington, D.C.: Naval Historical Center, 1985.

Dunham, George R., and David A. Quinlan. *U.S. Marines in Vietnam: The Bitter End, 1973–1975.* Washington, D.C.: Headquarters U.S. Marine Corps, History and Museums Division, 1990.

Ellis, Joseph J. *American Sphinx: The Character of Thomas Jefferson.* New York: Vintage Books, 1998.

Executive Sessions of the Senate Foreign Relations Committee. Historical Series. Washington, D.C.: Government Printing Office, n.d.

Fassbender, Bardo, and Anne Peters, eds. *The Oxford Handbook of the History of International Law.* Oxford, UK: Oxford University Press, 2012.

Firth, C. H., and R. S. Rait, eds. *Acts and Ordinances of the Interregnum, 1642–1660.* London: Wyman & Sons/His Majesty's Stationery Office, 1911.

Ford, Worthington Chauncey, ed. *Journals of the Continental Congress 1774–1779.* Washington, D.C.: Government Printing Office, 1905.

Franklin, Benjamin. *The Papers of Benjamin Franklin.* Vol. 39, *January 21 through May 15, 1783.* Edited by Ellen R. Cohn. New Haven, Conn.: Yale University Press, 2008.

Fremont-Barnes, Gregory. *The Wars of the Barbary Pirates: To the Shores of Tripoli— The Rise of the US Navy and Marines.* Oxford, UK: Osprey, 2006.

Fulbright, William J. *The Arrogance of Power.* New York: Random House, 1967.

Fulton, Thomas Wemyss. *Sovereignty of the Sea.* Edinburgh, UK: William Blackwood & Sons, 1911.

Galloway, George, and Charles G. Rose. *History of the United States House of Representatives, 1789–1994.* Washington, D.C.: Government Printing Office, 1994.

George, Hereford B. *Invasion of Russia.* London: T. Fisher Unwin, 1899.

Gerard, James W. *My Four Years in Germany: Late Ambassador to the German Imperial Court.* New York: Grosset & Dunlap, 1917.

Goebel, Julius, Jr. *Antecedents and Beginnings to 1801.* History of the Supreme Court of the United States. New York: Macmillan, 1971.

Great Britain. *Parliamentary Papers.* London, 1911.

Grenfield, Jeanette. *China's Practice in the Law of the Sea.* Oxford Monographs in International Law. Oxford, UK: Oxford University Press, 1992.

Guttridge, Leonard F. *Our Country, Right or Wrong: The Life of Stephen Decatur, the U.S. Navy's Most Illustrious Commander*. New York: Forge Books, 2006.

Hackworth, Green. *Digest of International Law*. Washington, D.C.: Government Printing Office, 1943.

Hall, Adm. Sydney Stewart. "Submarine Warfare." In *Transactions of the Grotius Society*. Vol. 5, *Problems of Peace and War, Papers Read before the Society in the Year 1919*. Cambridge, UK: Cambridge University Press for the Hugo Grotius Society, 1919.

Helms, Director of Central Intelligence. Memorandum to Secretary of Defense McNamara, January 23, 1968. In U.S. Dept. of State, *Foreign Relations of the United States, 1964–1968*. Vol. 29, part 1, *Korea*. Washington, D.C.: Office of the Historian, n.d.

Hickey, Donald R. *The War of 1812: A Forgotten Conflict*. Bicentennial edition. Champaign: University of Illinois Press, 2012.

Hollick, Ann L. *U.S. Foreign Policy and the Law of the Sea*. Princeton, N.J.: Princeton University Press, 1981.

Holwitt, Joel Ira. *Execute against Japan: The U.S. Decision to Conduct Unrestricted Submarine Warfare*. College Station: Texas A&M University Press, 2009.

Howe, Daniel Walker. *What Hath God Wrought: The Transformation of America, 1815–1848*. Oxford, UK: Oxford University Press, 2009.

Hugill, Peter J. *World Trade since 1431: Geography, Technology, and Capitalism*. Baltimore: Johns Hopkins University Press, 1983.

International Law Studies: Documents on Neutrality with Notes 1917. Washington, D.C.: Government Printing Office, 1918.

Jacques, Richard, ed. *Maritime Operational Zones*. Newport, R.I.: Naval War College, 2006.

Jefferson, Thomas. *Memoirs, Correspondence, and Private Papers of Thomas Jefferson, Late President of the United States*. Edited by Thomas Jefferson Randolph. London: Henry Colburn and Richard Bentley, 1829.

———. *The Papers of Thomas Jefferson: Retirement Series*. Vol. 4, *18 June 1811 to 30 April 1812*. Edited by J. Jefferson Looney. Princeton, N.J.: Princeton University Press, 2007.

———. *The Papers of Thomas Jefferson: Retirement Series*. Vol. 5, *1 May 1812 to 10 March 1813*. Edited by J. Jefferson Looney. Princeton, N.J.: Princeton University Press, 2008.

———. *The Papers of Thomas Jefferson*. Vol. 4, *October 1787 to February 1781*. Edited by Julian P. Boyd. Princeton, N.J.: Princeton University Press, 1951.

———. *The Papers of Thomas Jefferson.* Vol. 29, *1 March 1796–31 December 1797.* Edited by Barbara B. Oberg. Princeton, N.J.: Princeton University Press, 2002.

———. *The Works of Thomas Jefferson: Correspondence and Papers.* Vol. 10, *1803–1807.* Federal edition. New York: G. P. Putnam's Sons, 1904–1905.

———. *The writings of Thomas Jefferson: being his autobiography, correspondence, reports, messages, addresses, and other writings, official and private. Published by the order of the Joint committee of Congress on the library, from the original manuscripts, deposited in the Department of State.* Edited by H. A. Washington. New York: Riker, Thorne, 1854. Reprint, 2011.

Johnson, Lyndon Baines. *The Vantage Point: Perspectives of the Presidency, 1963–1969.* New York: Holt, Rinehart and Winston, 1971.

Journal of the Senate of the United States of America, 1789–1873. Washington, D.C.: Government Printing Office, n.d.

Kaplan, Herbert H. *Russian Overseas Commerce with Great Britain during the Reign of Catherine II.* Philadelphia: American Philosophical Society, 1995.

Kemp, Dixon. *A Manual of Yacht and Boat Sailing.* London: Horace Cox, 1878.

King, Greg, and Penny Wilson. Lusitania: *Triumph, Tragedy, and the End of the Edwardian Age.* New York: St. Martin's, 2015.

Kissinger, Henry A. *Diplomacy.* New York: Simon & Schuster, 1994.

Kraska, James. *Maritime Power and the Law of the Sea: Expeditionary Operations in World Politics.* Oxford, UK: Oxford University Press, 2011.

Kraska, James, and Raul Pedrozo. *International Maritime Security Law.* The Hague: Brill/Martinus Nijhoff, 2013.

Kwiatkowska, Barbara. *The 200 Mile Exclusive Economic Zone in the New Law of the Sea.* Dordrecht, Netherlands: Martinus Nijhoff, 1989.

Lambert, Frank. *The Barbary Wars: American Independence in the Atlantic World.* New York: Hill & Wang, 2005.

Lay, S. Houston, Robin Rolf Churchill, and Myron H. Nordquist, eds. *New Directions in the Law of the Sea.* Vol. 1. New York: Oceana, 1973.

Lecky, William Edward Hartpole. *A History of England in the Eighteenth Century.* New York: D. Appleton, 1887.

Lefebvre, Georges. *The French Revolution from Its Origins to 1793.* Translated by Elizabeth Moss Evanson. New York: Columbia University Press, 1962.

———. *The French Revolution from 1793 to 1799.* New York: Columbia University Press, 1964.

Levinson, John L. *Alpha Strike Vietnam: Navy's Air War 1964–1973.* Novato, Calif.: Presidio, 1989.

Livesey, James. *Making Democracy in the French Revolution*. Harvard Historical Study 140. Cambridge, Mass.: Harvard University Press, 2001.

Lloyd, Christopher. *A Short History of the Royal Navy: 1805–1918*. London: Methuen, 1942. Reprint, London: Routledge, 2016.

Locher, James R., III. *Victory on the Potomac: The Goldwater-Nichols Act Unifies the Pentagon*. Revised edition. College Station: Texas A&M University Press, 2014.

Mackenzie, Alexander Slidell. *Life of Stephen Decatur, a Commodore in the Navy of the United States*. Boston: Little, Brown, 1846.

Mackinder, John Halford. *Britain and the British Seas*. 2nd ed. Oxford, UK: Clarendon, 1907.

Madison, James. *The Papers of James Madison*. Presidential Series. Edited by J. C. A. Stagg et al. Charlottesville: University of Virginia Press, 1999.

———. *The Papers of James Madison*. Secretary of State Series. Edited by David B. Mattern. Charlottesville: University of Virginia Press, 2005.

Mahan, Alfred Thayer. *The Influence of Sea Power upon History, 1660–1783*. London: Marston, Low, 1894. Reprint, Mineola, N.Y.: Dover, 1987.

Malone, Dumas. *Jefferson and His Time*. Vol. 5, *Jefferson the President: Second Term, 1805–1809*. Boston: Little, Brown, 1974.

Marolda, Edward J., and Oscar P. Fitzgerald. *The United States Navy and the Vietnam Conflict*. Vol. 2, *From Military Assistance to Combat 1959–1965*. Washington, D.C.: Naval Historical Center, 1986.

McDonald, Forrest. *The Presidency of Thomas Jefferson*. Lawrence: University Press of Kansas, 1976.

McDougal, Myres S., Harold D. Lasswell, and Ivan A. Valsic. *Law and Public Order in Space*. New Haven, Conn.: Yale University Press, 1963.

McInnis, J. Matthew. *Iran at War: Understanding Why and How Tehran Uses Military Force*. Washington, D.C.: American Enterprise Institute, December 2016.

McNamara, Robert, with Brian VanDeMark. *In Retrospect: The Tragedy and Lessons of Vietnam*. New York: Vintage Books, 1996.

Miller, Hunter, ed. *Treaties and Other International Acts of the United States of America*. Washington, D.C.: Government Printing Office, 1931.

Minot, George, ed. *Reports of Cases Argued and Determined in the High Court of Admiralty 1798–1808*. Boston: Little, Brown, 1853.

Moïse, Edwin E. *Tonkin Gulf and the Escalation of the Vietnam War*. Chapel Hill: University of North Carolina Press, 1996.

Moore, John, ed. *Jane's Fighting Ships 1975–76*. London: MacDonald & Jane's, 1975.

Moore, John Bassett. *A Digest of International Law*. Washington, D.C.: Government Printing Office, 1906.

———. *International Law Topics and Discussions*. Newport, R.I.: Naval War College, 1913.

Morales, Gilbert, ed. *Critical Perspectives on the Vietnam War*. New York: Rosen, 2005.

Morison, Samuel Eliot. *History of United States Naval Operations in World War II*. Vol. 1, *The Battle of the Atlantic, September 1939–May 1943*. Boston: Little, Brown, 1947. Reprinted 1975.

———. *The Maritime History of Massachusetts, 1783–1860*. Boston: Houghton Mifflin, 1941. Reprinted 1979.

———. *The Two-Ocean War: A Short History of the United States Navy in the Second World War*. Boston: Little, Brown, 1963.

Morris, Richard B. *Seven Who Shaped Our Destiny: The Founding Fathers as Revolutionaries*. New York: Harper & Row, 1973.

Nandan, Satya N., and Shabtai Rosenne, eds. *United Nations Convention on the Law of the Sea 1982: A Commentary*. Vol. 2, *Articles 1 to 85, Annexes I and II, Final Act, Annex II*. Dordrecht, Netherlands: Martinus Nijhoff, 1993.

———. *United Nations Convention on the Law of the Sea, 1982: A Commentary*. Vol. 3, *Articles 86 to 132 and Documentary Annexes*. Dordrecht, Netherlands: Martinus Nijhoff, 1995.

The Naval Chronicle for 1812: Containing a General and Biographical History of the Royal Navy. London, 1812.

Naval Documents Related to the United States Wars with the Barbary Powers. Washington, D.C.: Government Printing Office, 1939.

Newton, Robert. *The Capture of the USS* Pueblo *and Its Effect on SIGINT Operations*. Fort George G. Meade, Md.: Center for Cryptologic History, National Security Agency, 1992.

Papers Relating to the Foreign Relations of the United States. Washington, D.C.: Department of State, n.d.

Papers Relating to the Torpedoing of the S.S. Sussex. Washington, D.C.: Government Printing Office, 1916.

Paterson, Thomas, J. Garry Clifford, Shane J. Maddock, Deborah Kisatsky, and Kenneth Hagan. *American Foreign Relations: A History*. Vol. 1, *To 1920*. Belmont, Calif.: Wadsworth, 2009.

Patrick, Christine Sternberg, and John C. Pinheiro, eds. *The Papers of George Washington*. Presidential Series. Vol. 12. Charlottesville: University of Virginia Press, 2005.

Peng, Guangqian, and Yao Youzhi, eds. *The Science of Military Strategy*. Beijing: Military Science, 2005.

Perkins, Bradford. *Prologue to War: England and the United States, 1805–1812*. Berkeley: University of California Press, 1961.

Perkins, Roger, and K. J. Douglas-Morris. *Gunfire in Barbary: Admiral Lord Exmouth's battle with the Corsairs of Algiers in 1816: The story of the suppression of white Christian slavery*. Reprint, Havant, UK: K. Mason, 1982.

Piggot, Sir Francis. *Freedom of the Seas Historically Treated*. London: Oxford University Press, 1919.

Pillsbury, Michael. *The Hundred-Year Marathon: China's Secret Strategy to Replace America as the Global Superpower*. New York: St. Martin's Griffin, 2014.

Plischke, Elmer. *U.S. Department of State: A Reference History*. Westport, Conn.: Greenwood, 1999.

Potter, Pitman B. *Freedom of the Sea in History, Law and Politics*. New York: Longmans, Green, 1924.

Richardson, James D., ed., *A Compilation of the Messages and Papers of the Presidents, 1789–1897—Published by Authority of Congress*. Washington, D.C.: Government Printing Office, 1896–99.

Roach, J. Ashley, and Robert W. Smith. *Excessive Maritime Claims*. 3rd ed. Leiden, Netherlands: Martinus Nijhoff, 2012.

———. *United States Responses to Excessive Maritime Claims*. 2nd ed. The Hague: Martinus Nijhoff, 1996.

Rodger, N. A. M. *The Command of the Ocean: A Naval History of Britain, 1649–1815*. New York: W. W. Norton, 2005.

Roosevelt, Franklin D. *Public Papers and Addresses of Franklin D. Roosevelt*. 1941 volume, *The Call to Battle Stations*. Edited by Samuel I. Rosenman. New York: Harper, 1950.

Rothwell, Donald R., and Sam Bateman, eds. *Navigational Rights and Freedoms in the New Law of the Sea*. The Hague: Martinus Nijhoff, 2000.

Scheiber, Harry N., and James Kraska, eds. *Science, Technology and New Challenges to Ocean Law*. Leiden, Netherlands: Brill/Martinus Nijhoff, 2015.

Schindler, Dietrich, and Jiri Toman. *The Laws of Armed Conflicts*. Leiden, Netherlands: Martinus Nijhoff, 1988.

Scott, James Brown, ed. *The Armed Neutralities of 1780 and 1800*. Oxford, UK: Oxford University Press for the Carnegie Endowment for International Peace, 1918.

———. *Opinions of the Attorneys General and Judgments of the Supreme Court and Court of Claims of the United States relating to the Controversy over Neutral Rights between the United States and France, 1797–1800*. Carnegie Endowment for International Peace Pamphlet 25. Washington, D.C.: Carnegie Endowment for International Peace, 1917.

Seitzinger, Michael V. *Conducting Foreign Relations without Authority: The Logan Act*. Washington, D.C.: Congressional Research Service, February 1, 2006.

The Seizure of the Mayaguez: *A Case Study of Crisis Management.* Report of the Comptroller General of the United States, submitted to the Subcommittee on International Political and Military Affairs, Committee on International Relations, 94th Congress, 2d Session, October 4, 1976. Washington, D.C.: Government Printing Office, 1976.

The Seizure of the Mayaguez: *System to Warn US Mariners of Potential Political/ Military Hazards—SS* Mayaguez, *a Case Study.* Reports of the Comptroller General of the United States, submitted to the Subcommittee on International Political and Military Affairs, Committee on International Relations, 94th Congress, 2d Session, October 4, 1976. Part IV. Washington, D.C.: Government Printing Office, 1976.

Sherman, Charles Phineas. *Roman Law in the Modern World.* Boston: Boston Suburban Book, 1917.

Simmons, Robert. *The Pueblo, EC-121, and Mayaguez Incidents: Some Continuities and Changes.* Occasional Papers/Reprints Series in Contemporary Asian Studies, no. 8. Baltimore: University of Maryland, School of Law, 1978.

Smelser, Marshall. *The Congress Founds the Navy 1787–1798.* Bloomington: Indiana University Press, 1959.

———*The Democratic Republic 1801–1815.* New York: Harper & Row, 1968.

Smith, Adam. *An Inquiry into the Nature and Causes of the Wealth of Nations.* London, 1776.

Smith, Jean Edward. *John Marshall: Definer of a Nation.* New York: Holt, 1996.

Smith, Zachary F. *The Battle of New Orleans including the Previous Engagements between the Americans and the British, the Indians and the Spanish which led to the Final Conflict on the 8th of January, 1815.* Louisville, Ky.: John P. Morton, 1904.

Soons, Alfred. *Marine Scientific Research and the Law of the Sea.* Deventer, Netherlands: Kluwer, 1982.

Sparks, Jared. *The Writings of George Washington.* 1923. Reprint, San Bernardino, Calif.: Ulan, 2012.

Spencer, William. *Algiers in the Age of the Corsairs.* Norman: University of Oklahoma Press, 1976.

Stagg, J. C. A. *The War of 1812: Conflict for a Continent.* Cambridge, UK: Cambridge University Press, 2012.

Stephens, James. *War in Disguise: Frauds of Neutral Flags.* 2nd ed. Reprint, New York, 1806.

Stockton, Charles H. *The Laws and Usages of War at Sea: A Naval War Code.* Washington, D.C.: Government Printing Office, 1900.

Stone, David R. *A Military History of Russia: From Ivan the Terrible to the War in Chechnya.* Westport, Conn.: Praeger 2006.

Sullivan, William. *Historical Causes and Effects from the Fall of the Roman Empire, 476, to the Reformation, 1517.* Boston: James B. Dow, 1838.

Taylor, Alan. *The Civil War of 1812: American Citizens, British Subjects, Irish Rebels, & Indian Allies.* New York: Vintage Books, 2011.

Thomas, A. R., and James C. Duncan, eds. *Annotated Supplement to the Commander's Handbook on the Law of Naval Operations.* International Law Studies, vol. 73. Newport, R.I.: Naval War College, 1999.

Toll, Ian W. *Six Frigates: The Epic History of the Founding of the U.S. Navy.* New York: W. W. Norton, 2006.

Turner, Frederick Jackson. *The Frontier in American History.* New York: Henry Holt, 1920.

UK Ministry of Defence. *British Maritime Doctrine.* Joint Doctrine Publication 0–10. London, August 2011.

United Nations. *The Law of the Sea: Current Developments in State Practice.* New York, 1987.

U.S. Central Intelligence Agency. *The Tanker War: Ship Attacks in the Persian Gulf: A Reference Aid.* Washington, D.C.: Directorate of Intelligence, June 1987.

U.S. Defense Department. *Asia-Pacific Maritime Security Strategy.* Washington, D.C., 2015.

———. *Department of Defense Law of War Manual.* Washington, D.C.: Office of General Counsel, June 2015.

———. *Maritime Claims Reference Manual.* DOD 2005.1-M. Washington, D.C., June 2008.

U.S. National Security Agency. *Cryptologic-Cryptographic Damage Assessment, USS* PUEBLO, *AGER 2, January 23–December 23, 1968.* Washington, D.C., n.d.

U.S. Navy Department/U.S. Department of Homeland Security. *The Commander's Handbook on the Law of Naval Operations.* NWP 1–14M/MCWP 5–12.1/ COMDTPUB P5800.7A. Washington, D.C., June 2007.

U.S. State Department [A. Rovine]. *Digest of United States Practice in International Law.* Washington, D.C.: Government Printing Office for the Office of the Legal Adviser, 1974.

———. *Navigation Rights and the Gulf of Sidra.* Washington, D.C.: Global Innovation through Science and Technology, 1986.

———. Pueblo *Crisis: Presidential Decisions and Supplementary Chronology.* Washington, D.C., December 12, 1968.

———. *United States Responses to Excessive National Maritime Claims*. Limits in the Seas, no. 112. Washington, D.C.: Bureau of Oceans and International Environmental and Scientific Affairs, March 9, 1992.

The Vietnam War: After Action Reports, Lessons Learned Documents, Battle Assessments. Beverly Hills, Calif.: BACM Research, 2009.

Von Heinegg, Wolff Heintschel. *Naval Blockade*. International Law Studies, vol. 75. Newport, R.I.: Naval War College, 2000.

Washington, George. *Writings of George Washington*. Edited by John C. Fitzpatrick. Washington, D.C.: Government Printing Office, 1931–44.

Weed, Matthew. *The War Powers Resolution: Concepts and Practice*. CRS Report 7-5700. Washington, D.C.: Congressional Research Service, April 3, 2015.

Wetterhahn, Ralph. *The Last Battle: The Mayaguez Incident and the End of the Vietnam War*. New York: Carrol & Graf, 2001.

Wheaton, Henry. *History of the Law of Nations in Europe and America from the Earliest Times to the Treaty of Washington 1842*. New York: Gould, Banks, 1845.

Whiteman, Marjorie M. *Digest of International Law*. Washington, D.C.: Government Printing Office, 1963.

Williams, Greg H. *The French Assault on American Shipping, 1793–1813: A History and Comprehensive Record of Merchant Marine Losses*. Jefferson, N.C.: McFarland, 2009.

Wilson, Woodrow. *President Wilson's Foreign Policy: Messages, Addresses, Papers*. Edited by James Brown Scott. New York: Oxford University Press, 1918.

———. *President Wilson's State Papers and Addresses*. Edited by Albert Shaw. New York: Doran, 1918.

Wolf, John B. *The Barbary Coast: Algiers under the Turks 1500 to 1830*. New York: W. W. Norton, 1979.

INDEX

ABOUT THE AUTHORS

James Kraska is department chair and Howard S. Levie Chair in the Stockton Center for the Study of International Law at the U.S. Naval War College. He has taught at Harvard Law School and Duke University and retired as a commander in the U.S. Navy, where he served as oceans law and policy adviser on the Joint Staff. **Raul Pedrozo** is a visiting fellow in the Stockton Center for the Study of International Law at the U.S. Naval War College, where he was professor of international law. He retired as a captain in the U.S. Navy and served as the top legal adviser to Navy Special Warfare Command and U.S. Pacific Command.